13th IADIS International Conference Information Systems 2020

Sofia, Bulgaria
2-4 April 2020

Editors:

Miguel Baptista Nunes Pedro
Isaías
Philip Powell
Boyan Bontchev
Luís Rodrigues

ISBN: 978-1-7138-1011-7

Printed from e-media with permission by:

Curran Associates, Inc.
57 Morehouse Lane
Red Hook, NY 12571

Some format issues inherent in the e-media version may also appear in this print version.

International Association for Development of the Information Society (IADIS)
Rua Sao Sebastiao Da Pedreira
No. 100, 30, 1050-209
Lisbon, Portugal

Phone: 351 21 3151373
Fax: 351 21 3151244

secretariat@iadis.org

Additional copies of this publication are available from:

Curran Associates, Inc.
57 Morehouse Lane
Red Hook, NY 12571 USA
Phone: 845-758-0400
Fax: 845-758-2633
Email: curran@proceedings.com
Web: www.proceedings.com

13th IADIS INTERNATIONAL CONFERENCE

INFORMATION SYSTEMS 2020

PROCEEDINGS OF THE 13th IADIS INTERNATIONAL CONFERENCE

INFORMATION SYSTEMS 2020

2 - 4 APRIL, 2020

Organised by

iadis

international association for development of the information society

Co-Organised by

SOFIA UNIVERSITY
ST. KLIMENT OHRIDSKI

As a member of Crossref (a non-profit membership organization for scholarly publishing working with the purpose to make content easy to find, link, cite and assess) each published paper in this book of proceedings will be allocated a DOI (Digital Object Identifier) number for its fast and easy citation and indexation.

Edited by Miguel Baptista Nunes, Pedro Isaías, Philip Powell and Boyan Bontchev

Associate Editor: Luís Rodrigues

TABLE OF CONTENTS

SHORT PAPERS

REFLECTION PAPERS

DOCTORAL CONSORTIUM

FOREWORD

These proceedings contain the papers of the 13th IADIS International Conference Information Systems 2020, which was organised by the International Association for Development of the Information Society and co-organised by the Sofia University "St. Kliment Ohridski", 2 - 4 April 2020. Due to an unprecedented situation caused by the COVID-19 pandemic, this year the conference was hosted virtually.

The IADIS Information Systems Conference 2020 aims to provide a forum for the discussion of IS taking a socio-technological perspective. It aims to address the issues related to design, development and use of IS in organisations from a socio-technological perspective, as well as to discuss IS professional practice, research and teaching. A set of key areas has been identified. However, these do not aim at being prescriptive, or set in stone, and any innovative contributions that do not fit into these areas have also been considered.

The following main tracks have been object of paper submissions:

- IS in Practice, Technology Infrastructures and Organisational Processes
- IS Design, Development and Management Issues and Methodologies
- IS Professional Issues
- IS Research
- IS Learning and Teaching

The IADIS Information Systems Conference 2020 had 71 submissions from more than 20 countries. Each submission has been anonymously reviewed by an average of 3 independent reviewers, to ensure the final high standard of the accepted submissions. Out of the papers submitted, 15 got blind referee ratings that published them as full papers, which means that the acceptance rate was 21%. Some other submissions were published as short, reflection and doctoral papers. Extended versions of the best papers will be selected to be published in the Journal of Electronic Commerce in Organizations (JECO) journal (ISSN: 1539-2937) and also in the IADIS Journal on Computer Science and Information Systems (ISSN: 1646-3692) indexed by Emerging Sources Citation Index by Thomson Reuters.

The conference, besides the papers' and poster presentations, also includes a keynote presentation from an internationally distinguished researcher. We wish to thank Associate Professor John Dong, Director, Digital Business Focus Area, Faculty of Economics & Business, University of Groningen, The Netherlands, for accepting our invitation as keynote speaker.

As we all know, a conference requires the effort of many individuals and this year we faced a new challenge that brought us more together. We would like to thank all members of the Program Committee for their hard work in reviewing and selecting the papers that appear in the book of the proceedings. We would also like to thank all the authors who have submitted their papers to this conference. We wish to thank all members of our organizing committee.

Last but not the least, we hope that everybody enjoyed the presentations and we invite all participants for the next year edition of the IADIS International Conference on Information Systems.

Philip Powell, Dean of the Faculty of Business, Law and Politics, University of Hull, UK
Boyan Bontchev, Sofia University, Bulgaria
Conference Co-Chairs

Miguel Baptista Nunes, School of Information Management, Sun Yat-sen University, Guangzhou, China
Pedro Isaias, The University of New South Wales (UNSW – Sydney), Australia
Program Co-Chairs

April 2020

PROGRAM COMMITTEE

CONFERENCE CO-CHAIRS

Professor Philip Powell, Dean of the Faculty of Business, Law and Politics, University of Hull, UK
Boyan Bontchev, Sofia University, Bulgaria

PROGRAM CO-CHAIRS

Miguel Baptista Nunes, School of Information Management, Sun Yat-sen University, Guangzhou, China
Pedro Isaias, The University of New South Wales (UNSW – Sydney), Australia

COMMITTEE MEMBERS

Abdelkrim Meziane, Cerist, Algeria
Adam Wojtowicz, Poznan University of Economics and Business, Poland
Amelia Badica, University of Craiova, Romania
Betim Cico, Epoka University, Albania
Bulend Terzioglu, Australian Catholic University, Australia
Christos Kalloniatis, University of the Aegean, Greece
Claudia Pons, Universidad Nacional de La Plata, Argentina
Dimitar Trajanov, Ss Cyril and Methodius University, Macedonia
Dimitris Karagiannis, University of Vienna, Austria
Dimitris Kardaras, Athens University of Economics and Business, Greece
Edward Bernroider, Vienna University of Economics and Business, Austria
Eleana Asimakopoulou, University of Bedfordshire, United Kingdom
Farshad Badie, Aalborg University, Denmark
Hans-Peter Steinbacher, University of Applied Sciences, Austria
Haralambos Mouratidis, University of Brighton, United Kingdom
James Thong, HKUST Business School, Hong Kong
Jeffrey Parsons, Memorial University of Newfoundland, Canada
Jinjun Chen, Swinburne University of Technology, Australia
Josephina Antoniou, Uclan Cyprus, Cyprus
Kalinka Kaloyanova, Sofia University, Bulgaria
Kamel Rouibah, Kuwait University, Kuwait
Kamelia Stefanova, University of National and World Economy, Bulgaria
Karsten Boehm, University of Applied Sciences, Austria
Konstantinos Rantos, International Hellenic University, Greece
Kun Chang Lee, Sungkyunkwan University, Republic of Korea
Leandro Antonelli, Lifia, Universidad Nacional de La Plata, Argentina
Lilian Mitrou, University of the Aegean, Greece
Lorna Uden, Staffordshire University, United Kingdom

KEYNOTE LECTURE

LEVERAGING BIG DATA FOR COMPETITIVE ADVANTAGE: A CONFIGURATIONAL APPROACH

by Associate Professor John Dong,
Director, Digital Business Focus Area,
Faculty of Economics & Business, University of Groningen,
The Netherlands

Abstract

Big data have been widely considered as the most valuable assets for firms to achieve a competitive edge, which potentially changes the rules of the game in many industries. Despite the increased investment in big data, firms are ambivalent about it as they are finding it challenging to realize business value from big data. Gartner estimated that 60% of big data projects failed in 2016. A year later, Gartner said it was "too conservative" with 60% estimate and put the failure rate at closer to 85%. In light of the notable challenge, this keynote will guide you through a novel configurational approach to better understand why firms may succeed or fail in using big data. Drawing on the systems theory, various configurations for a big data system are examined with components of data, technologies, skills, and processes. The underlying idea is to examine how the interdependence and interactions among various components in a big data system may enable or inhibit synergistic relationships with super-additive value. Using a large-scale data set from almost 19,000 firms as an example, different configurations improving or diminishing firm performance in revenue are uncovered. These new findings inform several propositions, which jointly suggest that the success of a big data system is contingent on nuanced configurations based on compatible technologies, skills and other facilitating conditions.

FULL PAPERS

THE EUROPEAN CODE OF CONDUCT ON CLOUD SERVICES AND DATA PORTABILITY: WHAT CHANGES IN THE CLOUD ECOSYSTEM

Maro Androutsopoulou[1], John Violos[2], Dimitrios Askounis[1], Theodora Varvarigou[2], Panagiotis Kokkinakos[1] and Christos Kontzinos[1]

[1]*Decision Support Systems Laboratory, School of Electrical and Computer Engineering, National Technical University of Athens, 9, Heroon Polytechniou Str, 15773, Zografou, Greece*

[2]*Electrical and Computer Engineering, National Technical University of Athens, 9, Heroon Polytechniou Str, 15773, Zografou, Greece*

ABSTRACT

Cloud computing, IaaS Cloud Services and Data Portability are topics of great interest and largely contemplated lately not only because of the focus the academia and the research community is showing, but also of the enterprises and the ECs continuously growing interest. Even though the adoption of cloud computing by European enterprises specially is steadily growing, it has not been as big as it would have been expected due to specific barriers faced by Cloud Service Customers (CSCs) such as lack of trust, uncertainty about the applicable law, unclear compliance to existing schemes and legislation, as well as the lack of interoperability among service providers, of transparency in security aspects and of control of the data.

The work presented deliberates what effect a Code of Conduct (Code) for Data Portability and Cloud Service Switching for IaaS Cloud services would have if included in the Certification Scheme for Cloud Computing already being prepared by the EC, and if the impact will in fact be the increase of CSCs condense regarding porting and switching between IaaS cloud services, at a low cost and with minimal disruption. The economics of IaaS Cloud Services will play a significant role on how cloud computing will grow, so a review of available economic models used to forecast the economic impact of cloud computing will be presented, along with a proposal of a model that could potentially be used to forecast the economic footprint of a Code for Data Portability and Cloud Service Switching.

KEYWORDS

Code of Conduct, Cloud Infrastructure Services Providers, Data Portability, Cloud Services Switching

1. INTRODUCTION

The Regulation of the European parliament and of the council of 14 November 2018 on a framework for the free flow of non-personal data in the European Union sets the principles for the cloud switching and the transfer of non-personal data between two different Cloud Infrastructure Services Providers (CISP), or between the cloud customer on-premises facilities and a CISP. The purpose of the Regulation is to: "achieve a more competitive and integrated EU market for data storage and/or processing services and activities." (EU Regulation, 2018). To meet this goal the Regulation covers the following three issues:

- Improving the mobility of non-personal data across borders in the single market, which is limited today in many Member States by localisation restrictions or legal uncertainty in the market;
- Ensuring that the powers of competent authorities to request and receive access to data for regulatory control purposes, such as for inspection and audit, remain unaffected and
- Making it easier for professional users of data storage or other processing services to switch service providers and to port data, while not creating an excessive burden on service providers or distorting the market.

The Regulation consists of ten articles. The Article 6 which is named "porting of data" prompts Cloud stakeholders to write a self regulatory Code of Conduct (Code) at Union level that covers the guidelines on technical, legal and economical best practices for the switching of cloud providers. As consequence, the article

6 spurred the creation of the Digital Single Market (DSM) Cloud Switching and Porting Data (SWIPO) Stakeholder Working group which is responsible to develop this Code.

DSM translates the strategy of providing digital opportunities for people and business into policy actions and enhance Europes position in the digital economy (Havu, 2017). DSM provides an environment of fair competition, consumer and data protection, removing geo-blocking and copyright issues based on better access to digital goods and innovative services (Martens, 2013).

The free flow of non-personal data is vital for a competitive data economy and sets the goal that users and companies to be capable to migrate their cloud stored data on their premises or to a different cloud server providers on an easy way with seamless operations and overcome the difficulties of legal uncertainty, lack of trust and the various technical difficulties of service provides (Kouatli, 2016).

The Code covers technical and economical aspects. It constitutes a structured and standardised tool for the stakeholders to communicate and assess the various procedures that should be followed by the Cloud Service Providers (CSPs), the Cloud Service customers (CSCs) and the intermediaries. In the following paragraphs we give a comprehensive relative work (Section 2), we make a description and an analysis on the Code (section 3), we describe the impact of the Code to the CSCs and CSPs (section 4). We cast a critical view on the Code (section 5), and make a review on the models that can estimate the economic impact of the Code in the cloud market (section 6) and discuss our conclusions and future work (section 7).

2. RELATED WORK

A Code of Conduct defines how a companys or industrys employees or companies should act on a day-to-day basis (Taylor et al., 2019). It reflects the daily operations, core values and overall culture. As a result, every Code of conduct is unique to the organization or industry it represents and involves ethical principles, company values, accountability, disciplinary actions, and standard of conduct and practises.

A Code of Conduct has been drafted related to the consumer data processing by business and governments (Payne et al., 2015). This Code takes into consideration the desire of consumers for privacy and the businesses for extracted knowledge with data mining methods. It states that a good developed Code, from the one side it maintains some level of privacy and from the other side it can provide better services and improve the economy. At European Union level, Codes related to the Information Community Technology, and specifically data centers and cloud infrastructures has been prepared and drafted. The Code of Conduct for Data Centre Energy Efficiency (FPFIS, 2018) is a voluntary initiative related to the increasing energy consumption in data centres and documents best practises for energy management in order to promote the positive economic and environmental the decrease of power usage of facilities would have. An analysis of the aforementioned Code (Avgerinou et al., 2017) reveals that the average power usage effectiveness of the facilities that follow the Code is constantly improved and confirms that Codes could be effective and of great benefit for European Enterprises and citizens. Additionally, a Code of Conduct for Data Portability and Cloud Service Switching for Infrastructure as a Service (IaaS) Cloud services has been prepared and drafted by a working group of experts.

Why suddenly the need for Codes of Conduct? The answer is pretty simple. Even though the adoption of cloud computing by European enterprises specially is steadily growing, it has not been as big as it would have been expected due to specific barriers faced by Cloud Service Customers (CSCs) such as lack of trust, uncertainty about the applicable law, unclear compliance to existing schemes and legislation, as well as the lack of interoperability among service providers, of transparency in security aspects and of control of the data.

In an attempt to overcome the barriers mentioned above, the ISO/IEC 27018 (de Hert et al., 2016) standard has been published to address the the lack of trust and transparency and to improve the data protection and security challenges of cloud computing. In addition, the European General Data Protection Regulation (GDPR) (Díaz, 2016) gave control to individuals over their personal data and the data portability. on-personal data though is a topic not covered by GDPR, and even more so the non-personal data porting and switching between cloud providers or between on-premise facilities and cloud providers. The Code of Conduct presented in the following section comes, among other things, to cover that topic also.

As it has been very accurately stated in a relevant working paper (Bayrak et al., 2011) Despite the wide consensus that cloud computing is a new and disruptive general purpose technology, there does not seem to be a comparable consensus in denying what exactly cloud computing is, nor a common understanding of how it affects economic fundamentals. Additionally, a study carried out for the European Commission in 2014

(Deloitte, 2017) provides an overview of how the cloud computing industry has developed in Europe, focusing in the absence of policy measures, and of the most important barriers for its further development. The same study also provides an assessment of the likely impacts (costs and benefits) of policy measures supporting cloud computing to be implemented consistently with the free flow of data initiative recently launched by the Commission.

Deloittes study also confirms the positive impact most guess but cannot prove: a positive economical impact of cloud computing for the EU Estimates regarding the impact of cloud computing adoption to the macro-economic performance of the EU (including impact on GDP) vary. All of them, however, agree in identifying a positive impact. It is estimated that over the next five years, cloud computing could add a cumulative total revenue of EUR 449 billion to the EU28 GDP (including in the public sector). Of these, EUR 57.7 billion and EUR 103.2 billion would be net new GPD generated in the years 2016 and 2020 respectively, representing a share of 0.4 and 0.71% of total EU GDP respectively5. It is estimated that in 2013, the adoption of cloud computing contributed EUR 27.9 billion to EU GDP, making up 0.2% of total EU GDP6.

The work presented here deliberates what effect a Code of Conduct for Data Portability and Cloud Service Switching for IaaS Cloud services would have if included in the Certification Scheme for Cloud Computing already being prepared by the EC and based on a few economic models also presented here, the economic impact it might have.

3. ANALYSIS OF THE CODE OF CONDUCT

The purpose of the Code of Conduct is to increase CSCs confidence regarding porting and switching between IaaS cloud services or between on- premise facilities and IaaS cloud services, at a low cost and with minimal disruption. Additionally, the Code supports the European Union Free Flow for non personal data Regulation objectives and promotes its stated purpose to achieve a more competitive and integrated EU market for data storage and/ or processing services and activities.

Objectives of the Code (aligned with the aforementioned ECs Regulation) are:

- Reduce the number and range of the data localization restrictions
- Facilitate cross border availability of data for regulatory control purposes
- Improve the conditions under which users can:
    1. switch data storage
    2. and/ or processing service providers
    3. part their data back to their own IT systems
- Enhance trust in the security of cross border data storage and/ or processing.

Overall, the Code intends to support an open and competitive cloud marketplace, which in turn should drive continued adoption and growth of cloud computing, including multi-cloud and hybrid cloud solutions to widen possibilities in the market. Vendor lock-in is not an acceptable business practice. The main characteristics of the Code are described in the following subsections.

3.1 Purpose of the Code, Target Audience and Responsibility

The Code is a voluntary instrument, allowing a CISP to evaluate and demonstrate its adherence to the Code requirements for one or more of its Cloud Services by a third party certification or by self-assessment. It intends to provide a set of high level requirements for CISPs, adherence to which will improve a CSCs confidence in achieving an open, transparent and in a meaningful manner successful transfer request of their Infrastructure Artefacts from one cloud service to another or more or between a CISP and a on premise facility.

The target audience of the Code is any party who has an interest in provision of IaaS cloud services (CISPs, CSCs, third party system integrators). The Code does not impose any obligation on the CSC, but recommends that a CSC:

- Be aware of the exit conditions for the discontinuation of a cloud service before entering into a contract with a CISP.
- Develops a cloud service migration plan in anticipation of such an operation.

- Ensures that the source and destination cloud service(s) can meet their needs with regard to infrastructure portability and cloud service switching.

3.2 Cloud Services Model for Data Portability

There is a wide spectrum of CISPs providing a variety of different cloud services, and data portability approaches may differ between cloud services. The Code is not intended to be a one-size-ts-all response to how data portability is conducted for all cloud services or by all CISPs. There is a different Code of Conduct for the Software as a Service (SaaS) cloud services and it is possible there will also be written a Code of Conduct about the Platform as a Service (PaaS). CISPs adopting the Code identify their cloud services which are compliant.

3.3 Legal Status - Scope/ Personal Data vs non Personal Data

The Code does not replace a written agreement (CSA) and does not constitute legal advice. It applies to the transfer CSC Infrastructure Artefacts, including both personal and non personal data. Such mixed data sets, where personal and non personal data are inextricably linked, the application of GDPR should not be prejudiced.

3.4 Scope/ Policy Aspects of Portability

The transfer of Infrastructure Artefacts between a source and a target has to comply any applicable legal, organizational and policy framework. It is the responsibility of all parties to ensure applicable laws and appropriate software licensing requirements, as relates to them, are followed before, during and after the transfer. This Code does not cover policy related aspects of portability, though a CISP may provide guidance, especially with respect to licensing.

4. THE ADHERENCE OF THE CLOUD PROVIDERS AND THE IMPACT ON THE CLOUD CUSTOMERS

Declaration of adherence with the Code obligates a CISP to comply with all the Code Requirements, as explicitly described in Sections 6, 7 and 8 of the Code. The Declaration of Adherence confirms that a specific cloud service complies with the Code and a detailed description of compliance measures along with the Declaration shall be conveyed to the CSC, while the Declaration has to be incorporated into the Portability Public Register.

The CISP must promptly reassess its compliance if any change to the cloud service results in a permanent material change to the Declaration the CSC must be noticed accordingly in due time.

The Code denes the requirements and contractual specications which the CSPs should adhere. The adherence on these responsibilities provides to the CSC the confidence that the CSPs can transfer its data in an open, transparent, predictable and meaningful way. The declaration of a CSP that adheres to the

Code has the prerequisite that it complies with all the following Requirements:

4.1 Requirements

The Data Portability and Interoperability and IaaS cloud services switching involves sets of requirements:

Procedural requirements, that dene the processes that should be followed and allow CSCs to retrieve their data from CSPs, to upload their data to CSPs, or to port data between two CSPs. These are the initiation of switching and porting from the CSP when it is a porting source. The initiation of switching and porting to the CSP when it is a destination source. The declaration how the porting takes place. The CSP should advise and agree with the CSP about the terms and charges. The activation of a new CSP service when it is the porting destination. The CSP should manage the porting and switching process. The CSP should make the exit process in the source CSP after the porting process is accomplished.

Data portability, that identies the technical measures and the legal obligations that support the porting process. The source CSP take all the reasonable steps to proceed the data transfer with an easy and secure manner. From the other side, the destination CSP should provide support for the inter- operability between the

CSCs user functions, business functions and the cloud services and support for the CSC application programmatic access to the ported data. The destination CSP should facilitate the porting in an easily and securely way. These data will be in commonly used structures and machine-readable for- mats, but the CSPs are not required to transform the data in different formats. The transfer of data should follow open standards and protocols and as consequence the CSPs should support commonly used formats and packaging. If the data involves code artefacts, the CSPs should describe how they can execute the service dependencies and environment in which they will be executed. Last but not least the CSP shall provide an interface for data retrieval which can be subject for additional costs.

Scope and compatibility requirements that should be explicity defined in the Cloud Service Agreement (CSA) between the CSP and the CSC. These involve the extent of the data and the cloud service interoperability that concern the CSP switching and ensure that there will be no loss of functionality and high security. Derived data such as security records incident history are not a requirement for the CSP to be ported. But they can be ported if it is clearly agreed and described in the CSA.

Planning requirements that are included in the CSA and concerns performance, testing of APIs and pricing mechanisms. The testing of APIs concern the APIs for porting data and the APIs to access and manage the stored data. The CSA should also define the anticipated volume of data, the appropriate duration for the transfer, the transfer rate, the minimum network bandwidth, and the period the ported data will be available to the CSC. The CSA can also include an allocation of security responsibilities such as access control, authentication of users integrity and confidential through the process.

4.2 Contractual Specifications

The role of the Code is not to replace the CSA. The CSA denes the terms between the CSPs and CSCs but the contractual rights and the obligations of the Code are not diminished by the CSA. The CSA can be in writing form: in a single document, a set of documents or online terms and conditions.

Transparency should be ensured by the CSPs, which involves that the terms and conditions should be noticed to the CSCs. In addition, the CSPs should describe to the CSCs all the mechanisms that concern the porting of data, that involve the tools that they use, the available support that the CSPs o ers, descriptions of the data porting processes, how the CSPs handles the CSCs data after the exit process, a description of anyone who has access to the CSCs data through the porting process and a description in any kind of conversion, translation and transfer of the data from a third-party service.

A description of the mechanisms related to the porting of the data should be provided from the CSPs to the CSCs, which should at least involve the procedures, terms and conditions, costs and policies concerning the porting, technical, physical and organisational measures to undertake the porting. The data model, data semantics and schema should be explained for functional and no-functional data, the locations where the data going to be stored and the costs that would be charged by the CSP.

In general, the CSPs should made available to the CSCs all the information related to data portability and in case of any change to the conditions and mechanisms the CSPs should inform the CSCs timely and the CSCs would have the right to terminate the agreement.

5. A CRITICAL VIEW ON THE CODE OF CONDUCT

The Code will establish new regulations, processes and activities in the Cloud community. Even though it has not been finalized yet and some topics may change, this part of our work is to consider the weak parts of the Code. The cloud stakeholders should be aware of them and act proactively to reduce the risk of their enterprises and the EC should take them into account while forming the new certification scheme for cloud computing.

The first sections of the Code can be quite confusing, since there is not a specic section dedicated to its purpose and another one to the benefits and risks it may have, as it is customary. As a matter of fact, risks are not mentioned in the Code nor the way that could be possible handled, in case one realizes, by a CSC. Additionally, the reader, unless well informed, can be baffled by the Purpose section, the objectives subsection and the intentions paragraph.

A section that is potentially missing is one about GDPR and how the CISP and CSC are affected. Even though the topic of personal and non-personal data is mentioned, no clear guidelines are given and it is not mentioned how GDPR and the ECs Free Flow of non-personal data Regulation t/ are taken into account in the

Code Requirements or that they simply are. The internal processes of the CISP regarding GDPR are extremely important and it should be mandatory for the CISP to provide at least a minimum amount of information of how its adhering to the Code.

Another issue that is not clearly defined and explained is the Portability Public Registry and the incentive a CISP will have to register the services adhering to the Code there. It is mentioned that a CISP should register the services(s) that adhere to the Code without mentioning the data required, and only at the end of the text there is a referral that the Registry will be created by the Executive Board (Governance Section). No information is provided on what type of data a CISP will be required to provide, what data will be available to the CSC, in which infrastructure the Registry will be operating from, who is going to be responsible for the quality control of the Registry, etc. and of course why it would be on a CISPs benefit to register.

A better description of how a CSC will be able to le a complaint, anonymously, for a CISPs breach of the Code for a service that is registered for adhering the Code has to be included, as well as the specific steps that will be taken to ensure a resolution. Since the Code is no legal document there should be a way, maybe through the initial subscription to the Registry, that if a complaint is filled the CISP will have to perform certain actions, otherwise it will be deleted from the Registry and a notification will be sent and posted.

Additionally, as it is mentioned, the Code will require continuous adaptation and change. How the intervals of review or the extraordinary circumstances requiring one will be defined, who will initiate the process, how the CSCs and CISPs are to be notified, who will be responsible for checking if the Registry is updated after a new version of the Code is released, are a few of the questions that have to be taken into account before the Code becomes a part of a certification scheme.

Overall, the Code will be extremely helpful and will allow for CSCs to be more con dent when it comes to porting and switching but the EC has to fully adopt, approve and promote it in order for it to have an impact.

A collaboration with ISO will be extremely helpful if the Code was to be mentioned in certifications for CISPs. An impact analysis and a needs assessment report have to be performed (and described in the Code how and when) at certain time intervals after the Code is approved in order to secure that the necessary changes and requirements of both the CSCs and CISPs are taken into consideration in the Codes review process. The Code should provide, as an Annex, a list of links or even an actual template of a CSA that will include the adherence of a service to the Code.

Incentives will have to be provided to the CISPs in order to bent their resistance to additional requirements/ conformities they have to adhere to after all they are private companies aiming at pro t and are not interested in creating internal processes that require more resources.

6. THE ECONOMIC IMPACT OF THE CODE OF CONDUCT

Plenty of articles and books have been written about cloud computing the last two decades since the IT (systems and processes) industry transformed significantly in order to keep up with the public, but most importantly, private sector adoption of cloud computing. The recent financial crisis and recession has also contributed to the accelerating adoption of cloud computing as companies have been forced to find cost-effective IT solutions, which was supported by an IDC (2009) survey of 696 IT executives and CIOs where 51% of respondents reported that the key driver behind adopting or considering cloud computing is the need to cut costs, while another 29% report that budget issues force them to find cheaper IT solutions (Gartner, 2016). The literature on topic though, economics of IaaS cloud services, is pretty poor and limited and is presented briefly in the following paragraphs. The fact remains though that, in terms of business creation, approximately 303.000 new businesses, in particular SMEs, could be created between 2015 and 2020 through the development and deployment of cloud computing (Marston et al., 2011) .Most articles published on the topic deal with the pricing of the services and how Nashs equilibrium can be used in order for an equilibrium in the sector to be reached - no studies have been published though examining in depth based on economic models the impact of this sector to economy, so only theories can be presented.

According to Etro (Etro, 2015), through cloud computing, firms will be able to rent computing power (both hardware and software in their latest versions) and storage from a service provider and that will have a profound impact on the cost structure of all the industries using hardware and software, and therefore it will have crucial consequences on:

- Business creation and macroeconomic performance;

- Job creation in all industries and job reallocation in the ICT sector;
- Public finance accounts, through the direct impact on the public sector spending and the indirect one on the tax revenues.

Additionally, Etro in another article (Etro, 2009) is using a DSGE model to perform his calculations and show a significant medium term impact of the diffusion of cloud computing on entry of SMEs, employment and growth. Starting from conservative assumptions on the cost reduction process, the analysis of the calculations based on his model, shows that the diffusion of cloud computing will provide (in a medium term range of ve years) a positive impulse to the annual growth rate, contributing to create about a million new jobs through the development of a few hundred thousand new SMEs in the countries he was investigating. What is highlighted though, is that services maintain market power over providers even when services are highly competitive, and that one should not expect the cloud marketplace to support a large number of providers.

In the The Economics of Cloud Computing (Bayrak et al., 2011) article, a different economic perspective is presented, based on the argument that the technological categorizations used in cloud computing (Software, Platform and Infrastructure as a Service) do not correlate well to the economic impacts of cloud technologies, and the proposal made is that economists should perceive it as wholesale and retail cloud applications. Wholesale cloud applications are primarily aimed at businesses and facilitate large-scale data integration projects, rapid, low-fixed cost entry and expansion of new start-ups, as well as the outsourcing of many noncore aspects of a given firms activities. Retail cloud applications, on the other hand, are primarily aimed at consumers and the fact that they move applications and content off personal computers to various types of cloud platforms and make both consumers produced and purchased content available in increasingly device and location agnostic ways (Bayrak et al., 2011).

Even though cloud computing is understandably by now extremely important, several factors limit the adoption of cloud computing services by professional users (Deloitte, 2017) such as from professional users' prospective data access and control, data portability, and interoperability. From the providers' perspective, these are the local support, procurement rules and for both of them the data localization requirements and information security.

How will the Code of Conduct affect the cloud computing sector, and most importantly, what is its possible economic footprint? Well, according to Gartner (Gartner, 2016), globally, through 2015, more than 90% of private cloud computing deployments will be for infrastructure as a service and as it is depicted in a gure at Deloittes study (Etro, 2009) the market for private cloud is estimated at EUR 5.9 billion in 2015, and by 2020, the market value of private cloud would be worth EUR 12.06 billion across EU Member States (up to EUR 14.6 billion in the optimistic scenario and EUR 10.3 billion in the pessimistic one). Removing barriers that have been recorded for both consumers and providers of cloud computing services will only benefit this economic sector and can only have positive economic impact.

From the research performed for the purpose of this paper, we suggest that the economic theory that can be used and have usable outcomes, is to perceive and deal with it as wholesale and retail cloud applications, since both consumers and providers will be a affected by the implementation of the Code. Wholesale cloud applications are primarily aimed at businesses: how they will be able to facilitate large-scale data integration projects, rapid low-fixed cost entry and expansion of new start-ups, along with the outsourcing of many non-core aspects of a given firm's activities. Retail cloud applications are primarily aimed at consumers, who are or will move applications and content off on site computers to various types of cloud platforms and make both consumer produced and purchased content available in increasingly device and location agnostic ways (Etro, 2015) .The Code will come and set ground rules on how both of these categories will do business with an aim to remove as many obstacles as possible - both of them will be affected, so a wholesale - retail economic theory has to be applied.

7. CONCLUSION AND FUTURE WORK

The Code of Conduct aims to become the basic text that CSCs will be required to have knowledge of in order to be clear of what their contract or CSA includes regarding data portability and switching among CISPs. Additionally, the Code fills the existing gap of requirements that the CISPs should adhere to in order to prove in a very simple and straightforward way that they are in a position to achieve an open, transparent and successful transfer request of Infrastructure Artefacts to another CISP.

Even though the economic impact of cloud computing will continue to be positive, which is supported by almost all studies and articles, there is no clear picture on the specific sector of IaaS. According to the research performed for this paper, the best option is likely to follow the theory of wholesale - retail to develop an economic model that could be initially used to forecast the economic footprint of a Code for Data Portability and Cloud Service Switching that can be later be followed by a game theory application.

Concluding, let us borrow the conclusion of a very interesting article (Marston et al., 2011) \that states the famous physicist Niels Bohr once said, Prediction is very difficult, especially about the future. The fluid and uncertain environment that surrounds cloud computing be it in terms of the technology, its adoption, the industry structure or the regulatory regime that will eventually need to be in place makes such an exercise that much more difficult. Hopefully, with our work, the bases for new research initiatives regarding economic models for cloud computing and the impact the implementation of new regulations such as a Code will have has been established and new discussions and debates will open up for this specific topic.

REFERENCES

Avgerinou, M., Bertoldi, P., Castellazzi, L., 2017. Trends in Data Centre Energy Consumption under the European Code of Conduct for Data Centre Energy Efficiency. Energies 10, 1470. https://doi.org/10.3390/en10101470

Bayrak, E., Conley, J., Wilkie, S., 2011. The Economics of Cloud Computing (Vanderbilt University Department of Economics Working Paper No. 1118). Vanderbilt University Department of Economics.

De Hert, P., Papakonstantinou, V., Kamara, I., 2016. The cloud computing standard ISO/IEC 27018 through the lens of the EU legislation on data protection. Computer Law & Security Review 32, 16–30. https://doi.org/10.1016/j.clsr.2015.12.005

Deloitte, 2017. Measuring the economic impact of cloud computing in Europe [WWW Document]. Digital Single Market - European Commission. URL https://ec.europa.eu/digital-single-market/en/news/measuring-economic-impact-cloud-computing-europe (accessed 6.7.19).

Díaz, E.D., 2016. The new European Union General Regulation on Data Protection and the legal consequences for institutions. Church, Communication and Culture 1, 206–239. https://doi.org/10.1080/23753234.2016.1240912

Etro, F. 2009. The Economic Impact of Cloud Computing on Business Creation, Em- ployment and Output in Europe. An application of the Endogenous Market Struc- tures Approach to a GPT innovation. In Review of Business and Economic Litera- ture, KU Leuven, Faculty of Economics and Business, pages 179-208.

Etro, F. 2015. The Economicsof Cloud Computing. InI.ManagementAssociation (Ed.), Cloud Technology: Concepts, Methodologies, Tools, and Applications. Hershey, PA: IGI Global. https://doi.org/10.4018/978-1-4666-6539-2.ch101

Forecast Overview: Public Cloud Services, Worldwide, 2011-2016, 4Q12 Update [WWW Document], n.d. . Gartner. URL https://www.gartner.com/en/documents/2332215/forecast-overview-public-cloud-services-worldwide-2011-2 (accessed 6.7.19).

FPFIS, 2018. 2018 Best Practice Guidelines for the EU Code of Conduct on Data Centre Energy Efficiency: Version 9.1.0 [WWW Document]. EU Science Hub - European Commission. URL https://ec.europa.eu/jrc/en/publication/2018-best-practice-guidelines-eu-code-conduct-data-centre-energy-efficiency-version-910 (accessed 6.4.19).

Havu, K., 2017. THE EU DIGITAL SINGLE MARKET FROM A CONSUMER STANDPOINT: HOW DO PROMISES MEET MEANS? Contemporary Readings in Law and Social Justice 9, 146–183.

Implementing Codes of Conduct | How Businesses Manage Social Performance in Global Supply Chains | Taylor & Francis Group [WWW Document], n.d. URL https://www.taylorfrancis.com/books/9781351280723 (accessed 5.24.19).

Kouatli, I., 2016. Managing Cloud Computing Environment: Gaining Customer Trust with Security and Ethical Management. Procedia Computer Science, Promoting Business Analytics and Quantitative Management of Technology: 4th International Conference on Information Technology and Quantitative Management (ITQM 2016) 91, 412–421. https://doi.org/10.1016/j.procs.2016.07.110

Marston, S., Li, Z., Bandyopadhyay, S., Zhang, J., Ghalsasi, A., 2011. Cloud computing - The business perspective. DECISION SUPPORT SYSTEMS 51, 176–189.

Martens, B., 2013. What Does Economic Research Tell Us About Cross-Border E-Commerce in the EU Digital Single Market? (SSRN Scholarly Paper No. ID 2265305). Social Science Research Network, Rochester, NY.

Payne, D.M., Landry, B.J.L., Dean, M.D., 2015. Data Mining and Privacy: An Initial Attempt at a Comprehensive Code of Conduct for Online Business. CAIS 37, 34. https://doi.org/10.17705/1cais.03734

Regulation (EU) 2018/1807 of the European Parliament and of the Council of 14 November 2018 on a framework for the free flow of non-personal data in the European Union (Text with EEA relevance.), 2018. , OJ L.

A PATTERN META-MODEL FOR BUSINESS PROCESS IMPROVEMENT

Nesrine Missaoui[1,3] and Sonia Ayachi Ghannouchi[2, 3]

[1]*University of Sousse, Higher Institute of Computer Science and Communication Techniques of Sousse ISITCOM, 4011, Hammam Sousse, Tunisia*

[2]*University of Sousse, Higher Institute of Management of Sousse, 4000, Sousse, Tunisia*

[3]*University of Manouba, ENSI, RIADI Laboratory, 2010, Manouba, Tunisia*

ABSTRACT

Although there are many initiatives related to defining specific Business Process Improvement patterns (BPIP), we don't find any general description of such patterns. Determining the essential attributes constituting a BPIP can be very helpful in this context and will certainly contribute to describing the general structure of any improvement pattern. Thus, the purpose of this paper is to propose a meta-model, presenting a complete and global structure of an improvement pattern. The definition of the meta-model was based on a study of the different attributes defined in literature for existing meta-models, presenting not only the structure of a BPIP but also other types of patterns. The defined meta-model gives detailed information about the core attributes and types of BPIP while being based on the flexibility concept. The main benefit of this research study is presenting a complete and general meta-model for BPI patterns by defining the core attributes of a pattern as well those specific to a particular type of patterns, selected based on the context of application.

KEYWORDS

Business Process Improvement, Meta-Model, BPI Patterns, Business Process Flexibility

1. INTRODUCTION

Business process improvement (BPI) is an approach used to analyze, review and improve existing business processes by identifying inefficiencies and redesigning the process in order to reduce execution time and eliminate waste in a process. Indeed, the need for improving a business process (BP) has increased after the business process reengineering wave (Davenport, 1993) where it was adopted in many research works.

In fact, the main difference between BPR and BPI is that BPR presents revolutionary changes in a BP, while BPI focuses on the continuous improvement and the evolutionary changes of a process: it is considered as the top priorities in both academic and industry fields (Zellner, 2011) where it was defined by (Coskun et al., 2008) as "the most important and common titles in both literature and applications". This is explained by the fact that a process improvement has become an important task to achieve, and a crucial step in a process lifecycle. Organizations nowadays look at it as an ongoing issue that permits matching with the changing business environment by adapting business processes to technological, organizational and structural changes: it addresses the root causes of process deficiencies, analyses it and identifies areas of potential improvement in order to highlight the type of changes that could add value to the performance of a process.

For this, efforts to present effective methods/techniques for BPI were developed in literature where three holistic methods for process improvement were defined: Six Sigma, Lean Methodology and TQM (Total Quality Management). The first methodology is used to measure defects in a process and eliminates them for better quality of the final product. It consists of five phases, Define, Measure, Analyze, Improve and Control known as (DMAIC). On the opposite, Lean methodology aims at optimizing the process itself. It focuses on improving employee productivity rather than the product. While the main priority of TQM methodology is delivering value to the end-customer by focusing on the organization as a whole, rather than individual processes.

Among the proposed BPI techniques, a model-based and integrated process improvement (MIPI) methodology was presented by (Adesola, 2005). It is a seven steps procedural approach that guides the actions and the decisions of a process design team. Another research presented by Johannsen et al., (2017) focuses on managing knowledge within the process of improvement by proposing a BPI roadmap, supporting the systematic transformation of implicit process knowledge into explicit process knowledge during the improvement process. Despite their usefulness, some of these methods were considered as the most expensive methodologies to deploy into BPI project that could negatively affect the profitability of an organization e.g. TQM, Six Sigma (Johannsen et al., 2017).

Thus, a new solution permitting better management and improvement of a BP was introduced and adopted by several BP projects. This approach called BPM (Business Process Management) is considered as "the most powerful approach for organizations to improve their performance and satisfy their customer needs" (Forster, 2006). It provides an end-to-end process understanding, visibility and control while ensuring effective communication across an organization. BPM combines BPI, performance management and organizational change management with technology to ensure the success and sustainability of process improvements.

However, it is widely agreed in literature that the most value-adding phase in a BPM project named as the act of improving, lacks sufficient guidelines and is poorly supported especially on presenting the exact instructions to improve business processes (Dumas et al., 2013; Forster, 2006). Therefore, to better represent the act of improvement of a BP, i.e. the transformation from an as-is process model to a desired to-be process model, a new era for BPI has been discovered which is the pattern concept. This concept introduces a set of solutions used for resolving a specific problem identified from a specific context. It is widely used in different fields in information systems such as Software Development (Gamma et al., 1994), Workflow Management (Van Der Aalst et al. 2003), the automation of a BP (Aldin et al., 2012) and Business Process Configuration (Weber et al. 2008; Ayora et al., 2016).

In BPI, a pattern approach is defined as an abstract form of a recurring instance of a process modification step used in a business process improvement activity (Forster, 2006) where a number of BPI approaches were defined based on this concept (Falk et al. 2013; Bergener et al. 2015; Kim et al. 2008; Yousfi et al. 2015; Nidermann et al. 2011). Despite being identified as one of the most promising approaches addressing the actual act of improvement in a process, this concept is barely used in BPI field (Falk et al., 2013; Forster, 2006). Only few works have been inspired by this concept to actually present the act of improvement phase. Also, not all of the defined approaches present a detailed description of their proposed patterns i.e. a holistic presentation of the defined patterns (attributes and their relationship). Thus, a meta-model for BPI patterns is recommended to clearly define and specify the structure of a pattern. The use of meta-models helps in establishing consistency in the description of a pattern which facilitates their application and consequently improves the performance of a process and its flexibility.

This work is part of an ongoing research study which aims to propose an approach for BPI based on a set of improvement patterns. The goal of this paper is to define a meta-model presenting the structure of a BPI pattern. It describes the core attributes of a pattern and their interrelationship. The definition of the meta-model was first based on an analysis of the literature where we highlight the research studies proposing a meta-model for patterns along with the attributes defined in it. Then, we have been based on the flexibility concept in order to represent the structure of our meta-model.

The remainder of this paper is organized as follows: section 2 gives an overview of proposed pattern meta-models in literature. In section 3, a meta-model for BPI patterns is developed, and the interrelationships between the involved attributes are shown. Afterwards, a discussion about the derived meta-model and those identified in literature is elaborated in section 4. The conclusion in section 5 gives a summary of the presented work and deals with implications for further research.

2. PATTERN META-MODELS IN LITERATURE

As discussed above, this work focuses on defining a pattern meta-model for BPI. Thus, the literature review will concentrate on presenting the research studies where a meta-model for patterns was proposed as well as the approaches that have been proposed based on already defined meta-models. Before presenting the meta-model, it is necessary to distinguish between the terms "model" and "meta-model". A model is a simplified representation of a certain reality. It is based on modeling methods/tools which allow representing an abstraction of reality for a certain purpose. These methods are represented by a modeling language describing a (formal) notation where the elements are defined by diagrams using graphical symbols such as UML diagram, Petri Net, BPMN, etc. In contrast, a meta-model is seen as a description of another model using a modeling language. It can be defined as a model of a (modeling) language, representing an abstract syntax of all model classes of a language. To generate such meta-models, a meta-modeling process is applied. It is defined as the analysis, the development and the construction of frames, rules, constraints and models in order to model a predefined class of problems.

In fact, meta-modeling is the most desired and used concept to formalize a modeling language. It helps into using the language in a consistent way and checking for syntactic correctness of implemented rules and constraints. In the domain of BPM, many research studies use the concept of meta-modeling to represent their approach e.g. Johannsen and Fill (2017). Specifically, for BPI, several researches were inspired by the concept of meta-modeling in order to propose meta-models for patterns such as Tran et al. 2011; Falk et al. 2013 and Yousfi et al. 2015. Their proposed meta-models give an overview of the structure of a pattern by describing the different attributes used to define it and their relationships. It helps users (modelers, developers) into understanding the pattern, the way to apply it and to implement it in a specific context.

In literature, the most common descriptions of a pattern are the format proposed by Gamma et al. (1995) and that proposed by Alexander et al. (1997). They were applied in the definition of several patterns such as Business Process Patterns (Tran et al., 2011), Process Pattern (Störrle, 2001) and BPIP (Forster, 2006; Falk et al., 2013; Ayora et al., 2016; etc.). It includes the following attributes: the name of the pattern, the problem that a pattern is intended to solve, the context of applying the pattern, the solution facilitating its implementation, a pictorial representation of the pattern (image, model, architecture), the motivations that surround the use of the pattern (forces), the application of the pattern on a simplified example or a real life situation (examples) and the relationships between the defined pattern (related patterns).

Based on these elements, a number of research studies related to the definition of patterns have been defined, based on a SLR research study established in previous work (Missaoui et al., 2019). In the area of Workflow Management, Van Der Aalst et al. (2003) define a list of workflow patterns used to specify aspects related to control flows, data flows, resource assignments, etc. These patterns were defined by five attributes: Name, description, solution, related patterns and implementation. For Process Modeling domain, the work of Gschwind et al. (2008) proposes an approach of pattern application during process modeling based on the context and the consequences of applying it. The work of Cherfi et al. (2008) provides a set of quality patterns to evaluate the quality of a modeled process. The structure of the defined patterns contains the following attributes: name, problem, context, solution, related patterns and quality metrics. Tran et al. (2011) focuses on the concept of pattern reuse where they have defined an approach assuring a correct application of a given pattern and reducing modeling time. They have proposed a meta-model for process patterns where the structure is essentially presented by four attributes: name, problem, context and applied task.

In the area of BPI, a number of pattern approaches has been identified. Appleton (1997) focuses on software process improvement and provides 10 patterns for process improvement projects, described by a list of attributes such as name, context, problem, solution, related patterns, know uses, etc. Forster (2006) presents a framework defining the structure of a BPI pattern; he only describes the idea of BPIP and how to implement it without detailing its structure. Another approach proposed by Kim et al. (2008) aims at defining a set of process change patterns within BPI projects based on the structure of Workflow patterns. The defined patterns were only presented by a textual description along with a graphic representation of pattern implementation. Nidermann et al. (2011) elaborate the concept of business process optimization and propose a formalized approach for pattern optimization. The approach presents a list of optimization patterns presenting opportunities for improvement. The structure was presented in the form of an algorithm defining the specification, detection and application of the pattern. The majority of these publications simply adapt former schema of descriptions to present their patterns. As an example, the schema proposed by Gamma et al., was taken as a basis by (Störrle, 2001) to validate the proposed approach. But there are also works that emphasize the importance of describing patterns (Kim et al., 2008; Nidermann et al., 2011). However, they do not focus on presenting the structure of their patterns. Nevertheless, the work of Falk et al. (2013) is considered as "the only" research where a meta-model for BPI patterns was defined. It focuses on presenting the general structure of a BPIP by using the Design Science Research methodology (DSRM) and presenting an overview of pattern notation formats defined in literature. The meta-model includes attributes already defined in literature (name, context, problem, solution) and others related to the domain of BPI (KPI, effects).

To sum up, despite having some recognizable pattern approaches in literature aiming to improve BPs based on the concept of patterns. There are a few works dealing with presentation of attributes that determine the structure of a pattern and providing a general and a comprehensible meta-model especially for BPI patterns. Thus, the main intention of this research is to examine and present the most important attributes to describe a BPI pattern by proposing a meta-model supporting the development of patterns as well as the creation of a pattern repository. The definition of the meta-model is based on the study of the different pattern attributes presented in literature, where we focus on those determining a BPIP and especially those presented by Falk et al. (2013) to determine those considered as necessary to define our BPIP meta-model.

3. PROPOSED META-MODEL FOR BPI PATTERNS

For defining the meta-model, we were based on the attributes presented in section 2. In fact, proposing an approach of BPI must consider three general aspects: Process effectiveness for better informed decision and better execution of necessary tasks; Process efficiency for improving execution time and reducing resource reuse and Process flexibility for adapting the process to any type of change affecting its performance. The last concept has been recognized as a critical quality of an effective business process that must be able to adapt to any change in the environment (Schonenberg et al. 2008). The definition of our meta-model focuses on the concept of flexibility where we have considered that the main objective of a BPI technique is to ensure greater process flexibility by permitting the process to adapt to any type of change occurring during design-time or run-time. Indeed, to qualify a process as flexible, we have to take into account four principal requirements (needs): Variability, Adaptation, Evolution and Incompleteness/Looseness (Reichert and Weber, 2008). Each of these needs may affect each of the process perspective (behavior, organization, information, time, etc.). The first type of need defines the capacity of a process to consider different variants. These variants have either the same goal or a similar one but differ depending on the context. The second presents the capacity of a process to deal with emerging events that leads to modifying the structure of a process and its execution. These events can be triggered by the appearance of several factors. The evolution need focuses on evolutionary changes that a process can have. These changes may be permanent (valid from the moment when will be implemented) or temporary (valid for a specific period of time). It represents the ability of a process to change when the corresponding BP evolves. The evolution can be triggered by external changes and/or internal changes. The common goal of these three requirements is to ensure the flexibility of the process by taking into consideration the types of changes and their context. However, for the incompleteness need we generally focus on loosely defined models, i.e. in this type, only the objectives of the process are known in advance which results in a not fully defined process model. In this case, the design phase must be completed during the execution phase where the changes concern only one part of process definition. Based on these requirements and taking into consideration the work of (Falk et al., 2013) as well as the pattern format of (Gamma et al. 1995), we have developed our own meta-model for BPI pattern which corresponds to a graphical description of a BPI pattern highlighting its core attributes and presenting four types of BPIP: variability pattern, adaptation pattern, evolution pattern and looseness pattern. These patterns were derived from the defined requirements where we have considered that an improved and a flexible process adopt one (or more) of these patterns, by being based on the context to which it will be applied.

The meta-model, as described in Figure 1, details the structure of a BPI pattern presenting the core attributes of a pattern (context, problem, solution) and other attributes related to its definition. In the center of the model, the class presents the BPI pattern which has a name as its identifier and a set of methods (add, remove, modify, select) on which the process of pattern definition and selection will be based on. Every pattern is specified with a single problem to solve, a single solution to present and a single context to address. The context attribute is defined based on a set of drivers, facilitating the definition and the classification of patterns. The problem concerns a specific BP lifecycle phase described by its characteristics and a description of the corresponding phase. The solution presents a number of mechanisms, defining the way to apply a pattern into a set of case studies. The implementation depends on the purpose of the case study and its effect on time, cost, quality and flexibility values. The meta-model presents four types of patterns: Variability patterns, Adaptation patterns, Evolution patterns and Looseness patterns. Each type possesses its own meta-model, defined for a specific problem and a specific context where each meta-model includes the general attributes of BPIP and others specific to the defined type.

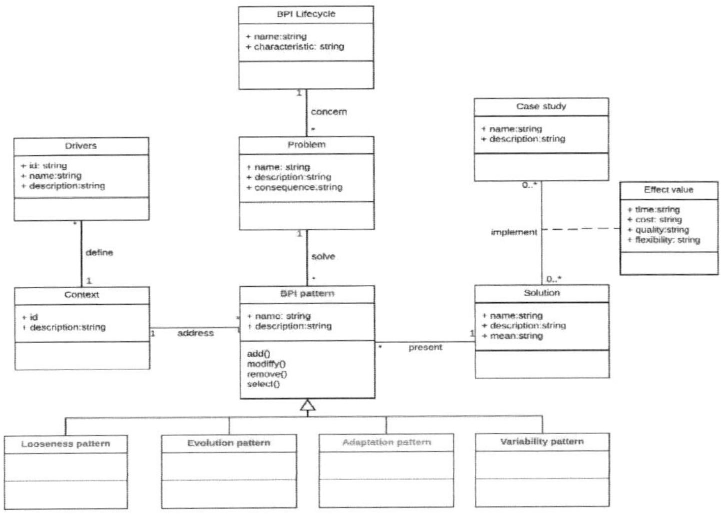

Figure 1. Meta-model for business process improvement pattern

3.1 A Meta-Model for Variability Patterns

The first type is variability pattern (see Figure 2 **left picture**) used to model and execute a variable business process. It is presented by a specific solution and concerns a specific variability objective describing the conflicts handled by a variable BP, related to a specific process family. A variable BP can have one to several variable process parts describing the object of change. These parts can be associated to different variant points defining the subject of changes which is the place where the variation occurs: variants can be removed or included from variant points by changing the flow of events, the sequence flow or the activities of the model. These changes are applied by a number of variability mechanisms that permit adding, removing, modifying or replacing a variant.

3.2 A Meta-Model for Adaptation Patterns

The second type of BPIP is the adaptation pattern. It allows a structured modification of a process schema by using a number of operations. The structure of the pattern is presented by the core attributes of BPIP and those specific to the presented pattern. As presented in Figure 2 (**right figure**), the adaptation pattern is based on a number of adaptation changes determined by the framework of application and the type of adopted changes (high level changes, small changes). These adaptations are triggered by a specific factor that can be internal or external and applied into several process parts using a number of operations. These operations can be applied at high level by adding new activities or an entire process fragment or at low-level by adding or deleting a single node.

3.3 A Meta-Model for Evolution Patterns

The evolution pattern considers the evolutionary changes that a process can have. It is triggered by a specific type of drivers defined by the context attribute. These drivers have two types: internal drivers (design errors, technical problems, and poor model quality) and external drivers. It is presented by a specific solution that is based on a number of evolution changes (see Figure 3 on the **left**) defined in a category of evolution presenting the concepts of incremental evolution, continuous evolution or revolutionary evolution. These evolutions are introduced by a set of operators determining the way to add, remove, modify one to several process artefacts. These artefacts comprise information about the structure of the process and define the element(s) on which the pattern is being applied on (role, activity, event, sub-process, etc.).

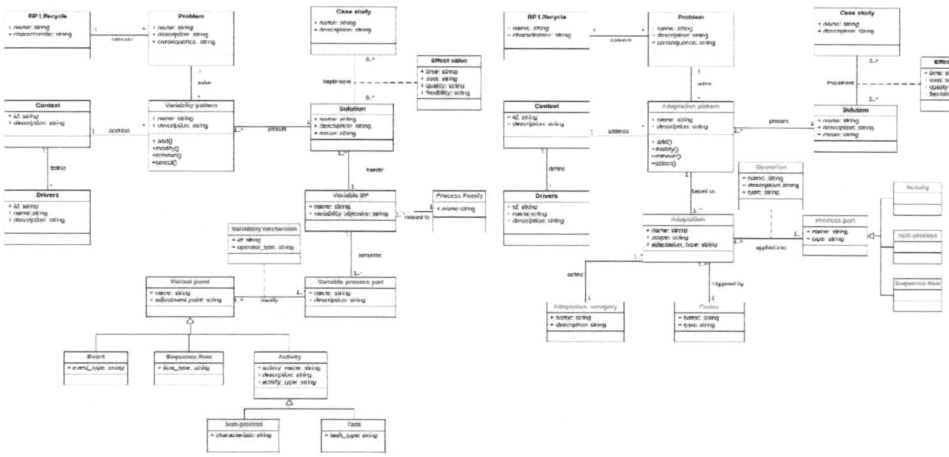

Figure 2. Meta-models for Variability pattern (left) and adaptation pattern (right)

3.4 A Meta-Model for Looseness Patterns

This type of pattern focuses on loosely specified models where only their goal is known in advance and the parameters determining the exact cause of an action are typically not known and might change during process execution. To deal with this, decisions regarding the exact specification of selected parts of the process have to be defined. These decisions can be defined, as demonstrated in Figure 3 (**on the right**), by a loosely point presenting the loosely specified parts: it can concern the control flow part in a BP or the activity part. These points are presented by a category of loosely points defining different types of looseness and expressed by a number of compliance rules determining the exact type of action to apply on the part. The definition of these rules is based on a number of constraints and a set of analysis techniques that present a number of metrics allowing to measure the degree to which these rules have been respected during the modeling of a single loosely point.

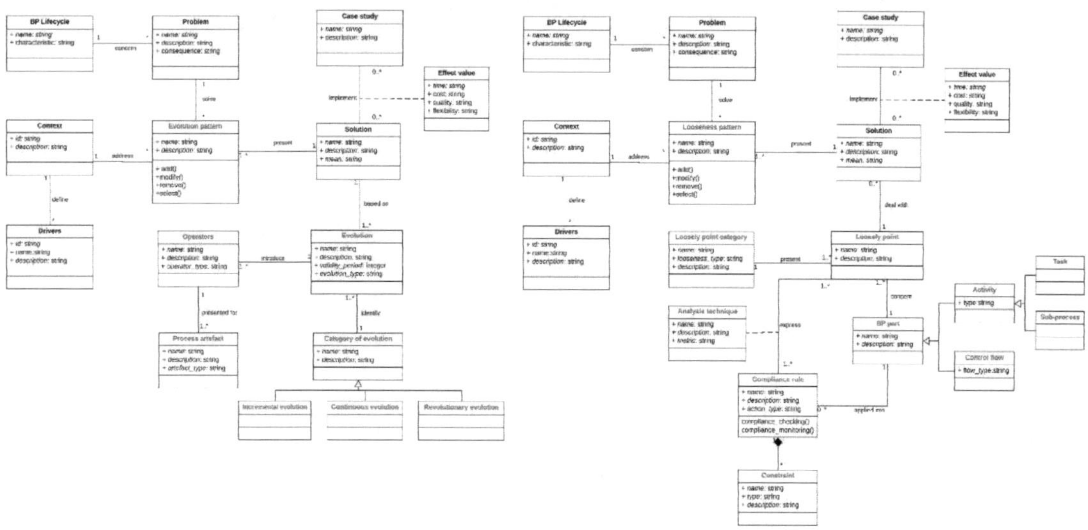

Figure 3. Meta-models for evolution (left) and looseness patterns (right)

4. DISCUSSION

This paper aims to proposing a meta-model for BPI patterns, presenting the general structure of an improvement pattern based on the flexibility concept. It includes four types: Variability, adaptation, evolution and Looseness patterns where each type has its own model. In fact, in literature, all of the defined meta-models focus only on one flexibility need where we may cite the work of (Yousfi et al., 2015) for variability needs, (Nidermann et al., 2011; Weber et al., 2008) for adaptation need.

For evolution need we have the works of (Forster, 2006; Falk et al., 2013) and Reichert and Weber, (2012) for Looseness need. This means that each of the proposed patterns can be applied only in the context in which it was defined. Among these studies, we found that only the work of (Falk et al., 2013) proposes a meta-model for BPIP while focusing on the evolution needs of a process. So overall, we can conclude that so far no work has proposed a complete meta-model for BPIP that includes all of these needs. Thus after reviewing the literature and determining its shortcomings, we defined a meta-model presenting the global structure of an improvement pattern. The proposed meta-model may serve as a reference for defining any type of BPI pattern by only determining the context to which it will be applied. Also, it can be considered as a tool for pattern selection and categorization since it provides a global overview of BPIP structure which will facilitate the process of pattern definition and use. As with every research, our work is subject to limitations. A first one concerns the completeness of the meta-model as we covered only one concept of BPI which is process flexibility. We can justify this by arguing that a flexible BP can be easily adapted to any type of change which will reduce modeling as well as execution time of a process, eliminate waste time and permit better quality of a BP. As a consequence, the proposed meta-model set intends to be complete in the sense that it allows the definition of an improvement pattern, covering all possible improvement aspects. Also, the work lacks a validation of the defined meta-model where we are in the process of implementing the defined structure on a real process describing the workflow of patient treatment within the emergency department.

5. CONCLUSION

We proposed a meta-model describing the structure of BPI patterns based on process flexibility. It presents a number of attributes considered as essential to the definition of a BPIP. Our work is, to the best of our knowledge, the only one which presents a complete structure of a BPI pattern by regrouping all BPIP types into a single meta-model that determines the core attributes of any improvement pattern as well as attributes specific to the type of the pattern. This will certainly facilitate the process of pattern selection and application. However, we cannot claim the feasibility of the meta-model, considering that no evaluation step was introduced. For this, the evaluation will take place in further research studies as we plan to define a list of BPIP based on the meta-model and demonstrate the way to apply it on real example of BP models. The definition of these patterns will essentially be based on the context attribute from which we will be able to categorize these patterns. Then, we will develop a prototype based on a pattern database that we will create and conduct experiments to study the impacts of these patterns on the BP lifecycle. This will help us in validating the feasibility of our patterns and presenting an approach for pattern definition and reuse.

REFERENCES

Adesola, S. and Baines, T., 2005. Developing and evaluating a methodology for business process improvement. *In BPM Journal*, Vol. 11, No.1, pp. 37–46.

Aldin, L., Alfaris, A. and De Cesare, S. 2012, Business process pattern automation: State of the art and research challenges. *IADIS International Conference Information Systems*. Berlin, Germany, pp. 175-185

Alexander, C., Ishikawa, S., Silverstein, M., Jacobson, M., Fiksdahl-King, I., and Angel, S., 1997. A pattern language. Towns, Buildings, Construction. *Oxford University Press*, New York.

Appleton, B., 1997. Patterns for conducting process improvement. *Conference on Pattern Languages of Program Design*.

Ayora, C., Torres, V., De la Vara, J.L. and Pelechano, V., 2016. Variability management in process families through change patterns. *In Journal of Information and Software Technology*, Vol. 74, pp. 86–104.

Bergener P, Delfmann P, Weiss B and Winkelmann, A., 2015. Detecting potential weaknesses in business processes: an exploration of semantic pattern matching in process models. *In BPM Journal*, Vol. 21, No. 1, pp. 25–54.

Cherfi, S.S, Comyn-Wattiau, I. and Akoka, J., 2008. Quality patterns for conceptual modeling. *International Conference on Conceptual Modeling-ER.*. Springer, Heidelberg, pp. 142–153.

Coskun, S., Basligil, H., and Baracli, H., 2008. A weakness determination and analysis model for business process improvement. *In BPM Journal*, Vol.14, No.2, pp. 243-261.

Davenport, T., 1993. Process Innovation-Reengineering work through Information Technology. *Harvard Business School Press*, Boston.

Dumas, M., Rosa, M.L., Mendling, J. and Reijers, H., 2013. *Fundamentals of Business Process Management*, Springer, Berlin, Heidelberg.

Falk, T., Griesberger, P. and Leist, S., 2013. Patterns as an artifact for business process improvement -insights from a case study. *International Conference on Design Science Research in Information Systems and Technology*. Helsinki, Finland, pp. 88-104.

Forster, F., 2006. The Idea Behind Business Process Improvement: Toward a Business Process Improvement Pattern Framework. *Journal of BPTrends*, pp. 1-14.

Gamma, E., Helm, R., Johnson, R. and Vlissides, J., 1994. Design Patterns: Elements of Reusable Object-Oriented Software. *Addison-Wesley Professional, Upper Saddle Riv*er, United States.

Gschwind, T., Koehler, J. and Wong, J., 2008. Applying patterns during business process modeling. *The 6th International Conference on Business Process Management*. Springer, Heidelberg, Vol. 5240, pp. 4-19.

Johannsen, F., and Fill, H.G., 2017. Meta Modeling for Business Process Improvement. *In Journal of Business & Information Systems Engineering*, Vol. 59, No. 4, pp.251-275.

Kim, D., Kim, M. and Kim, H., 2007. Dynamic business process management based on process change patterns. *International Conference on Convergence Information* Technology. Gyeongju, South Korea, pp. 1154–1161.

Missaoui N. and Ayachi Ghannouchi S., 2019. Pattern-Based Approaches for Business Process Improvement: A Literature Review. *Park J., Shen H., Sung Y., Tian H. (eds) Parallel and Distributed Computing, Applications and Technologies. PDCAT 2018. Communications in Computer and Information Science*, Springer, Singapore. Vol. 931, pp.390-400.

Nidermann, F., Radeschütz, S. and Mitschang, B., 2011. Business process optimization using formalized optimization patterns. *International conference on Business Information System.* Springer, Heidelberg, pp.123–135.

Reichert, M. and Weber, B., 2012. *Enabling flexibility in Process-Aware Information Systems: Challenges, Methods, and Technologie.* Springer, Verlag, Berlin, Heidelberg.

Rinderle-Ma, S., Reichert, M. and Weber, B., 2008. On the formal semantics of change patterns in process-aware information systems. *International conference on conceptual modeling-ER.* Springer, Heidelberg, pp. 279–293.

Schonenberg, H., Mans, R., Russell, N., Mulyar, N. and Van Der Aalst, W., 2008. *Process flexibility: a survey of contemporary approaches*: *Advances in Enterprise Engineering*. Springer-Verlag, Berlin, pp. 16-30.

Störrle, H., 2001. Describing process patterns with UML. *Europian Workshop on Software Process Technology, Software Process Technology.* Springer, Heidelberg, Vol. 2077, pp.173–181.

Tran, H.N., Coulette, B., Tran, D.T. and Vu, M.H., 2011. Automatic reuse of process patterns in process modeling. *Proceedings of the ACM Symposium on Applied Computing*TaiChung. Taiwan, NY, USA, pp. 1431–1438.

Van Der Aalst, W.M.P., Ter Hofstede, A.H.M., Kiepuszewski, B. and Barros, A.P., 2003. Workflow Patterns. I*n Journal of Distributed and Parallel Databases*, Vol. 14, No.3, pp.5-51.

Weber, B., Reichert, M. and Rinderle Ma, S., 2008. Change patterns and change support features- enhancing flexibility in process-aware information systems. *In Journal of Data & Knowledge Engineering*, Vol. 66, No.3, pp. 438– 466.

Yousfi, A., Saidi, R. and Dey, A.K., 2016. Variability patterns for business processes in BPMN. *In Journal of Information Systems and e-Business Management,* Vol.14, No.3, pp.443–467.

Zellner, G., 2011. A structured evaluation of business process improvement approaches. *In BPM Journal*, Vol. 17, No.2, pp.203–237.

KNOWING WHICH APPS MANAGERS LIKE: A MANAGER APP PORTAL ACCOMMODATING THEIR USER PREFERENCES

Jorg H. Mayer, Markus Esswein, Reiner Quick and Sanjar Sayar
Darmstadt University of Technology
Hochschulstrasse 1, 64289 Darmstadt, Germany

ABSTRACT

Nowadays, even apps for corporate management are respectable. Manager app portals complement such "run-a-business" apps with apps that make managers' business life easier. However, the right mix of apps makes the difference. Accommodating the user perspective, the objective of this article is to examine which apps disproportionately influence managers' perception of IS usefulness. Applying the Kano model and considering both "analyst-" and "consumer-type" managers, we employ findings from a manager focus group survey to discuss the strongest differentiators: (1) Offer collaboration bars and push notifications on changes to shared office documents for analyst managers. Get consumer managers "online" with news tickers. (2) Make core reports more interactive with drill downs and filters for manager self-service. (3) Take "fun and enjoyment" into account when accommodating managers' business life. (4) Consider that tablets create their own manager use case as a "first-stop information shop."

KEYWORDS

Apps for Managers, Kano Model, Information Systems (IS) Design for Use, IS Success, User-Group Preferences

1. INTRODUCTION

Mobility is still one of the most visible trends in Information Systems (IS) and companies expect mobile IS to make their workforce more efficient. Smartphones and tablets will be the first "go-to" device for more than 50% of all users (Gartner, 2018). Thanks to Apple's (Wired, 2010) million-dollar slogan "There's an app for that" and SAP's (SAP, 2019) FIORI tiles even apps for corporate management have been established. However, finance content alone is not sufficient to convince managers to go mobile. One of the managers we interviewed outlined, "I will not use an iPad just to have my financials electronically." Thus, the right mix of both "run-a-business" apps and those that make managers' business life easier are crucial to make the difference.

Understanding the *perception of IS usefulness* is particularly important in the field of management support, where strong idiosyncrasies must be considered. Managers tend to have higher expectations with respect to IS accommodating their user preferences (Volonino et al., 1995). Therefore, IS research must broaden its scope beyond pure deployment to include managers' IS use and impact perspective (Kettinger & Marchand, 2011).

We define *manager app portals* as a combination of apps that conform to a model based on a standard (Heinemann & Council, 2001). According Shneiderman's (1997) mantra "overview first, zoom and filter, then details-on-demand," app portals have to provide both a personalized "first-stop information shop" and an easy-to-use navigation for detailed information. Such portals promise managers to make fact-driven decisions faster than before—especially when they are mobile (Ostrov, 2014).

Following the task-technology fit theory, Goodhue and Thompson (1995) describe *IS success* as the degree to which IS accommodate a user's tasks. *User preferences* describe differences in the way humans use IS. Based on existing manager user group preferences, we specify "IS fit" as the way different apps (small capsulated software components (Zigurs & Buckland, 1998)) accommodate these preferences. User preferences result in requirements with respect to how IS should provide functions.

Based on Shneiderman (1997), Al-Kassab et al. (2014) examine the impact of visualization and analytics on managerial decision-making. However, an app portal accommodating managers' user perspective is currently not covered in literature. Thus, the objective of this article is to examine which *apps disproportionately influence managers' perception of IS usefulness*. We consider managers as either "analysts" (those who primarily work more interactively with IS) or "consumers" (those who primarily consume IS information).

We motivate this article in terms of closing gaps in managers' perception of IS usefulness through a manager app portal. Based on the state of the art (*literature review*), we apply the Kano model (*research model*). With findings from a manager focus group, we come up with the strongest differentiators for successfully implementing manager app portals (*results*). We then discuss our results in manager interviews and present a prototype (*synthesis*). We end with a summary and avenues for future research.

2. LITERATURE REVIEW

By conducting a *journal search*, we focused on leading IS research outcomes provided by the London School of Economics[1] (Wilcocks et al., 2008) and complemented them with journals from Human-Computer Interaction, computer science, and systems and software engineering. We added proceedings from ICIS, ECIS, AMCIS, and HICSS and accessed the journals via EBSCOhost, ScienceDirect, Google Scholar, and AIS Electronic Library. Table 1 informs about our Boolean search string.

Our *search on titles and abstracts* resulted in 461 hits, of which we found 32 to be relevant. We added user satisfaction and adoption as well as IS antecedents, determinants, and elements to our search string as they are associated with IS use (Benbasat & Nault, 1990). A final *back- and forward* search led to 90 relevant publications, 23 of which deal with directly applicable requirements. We structured them regarding the elements of IS design theories employed as follows (Walls et al., 1992): (A) User model and effects of use (Zhang et al., 2002; Benbasat & Nault, 1990); (B) Functional or non-functional user requirements (Sommerville, 2010); (C) Guidelines (March & Smith, 1995).

Table 1. Boolean search string

		OR				
AND	**Apps**	Information presentation	(Visual) navigation and dialog control	(Visual) information analysis and processing		Manager portals, workplaces, dash-boards, cockpits
	Cognitive fit	User preferences	User require-ments, attitudes, styles, pattern	Use cases, design guidelines	User satis-faction, adoption	IS antecedents, determinants, elements

(A) User Model: A rigorous app clustering from managers' perspective is missing: With 34 publications, the state of the art of IS user models is comprehensive. 13 publications deal with cognitive styles and cover techniques for *user-group analysis*. According to Witkin et al. (1977), we examined two basic working styles among managers. *Analyst managers* seek causal relationships, prefer quantitative data, and pay attention to details (Huysmans, 1970). *Consumer managers*, in turn, pay less attention to details and rely on predefined content.

The remaining 21 publications cover *effects of use* by differentiating characteristics that impact IS design (age, gender, or expertise) or identifying groups of managers and their IS usage (Powell & Jonson, 1995). Involving managers in IS design is more relevant than ever (Fteimi, 2017). *Management Support Systems* (MSS) have a five-decade tradition and represent a class of IS covering. Management Information Systems (MIS), Decision Support Systems (DSS), Executive Information Systems (EIS), and Knowledge Management Systems (KMS), and Business Intelligence (BI) for managers (Carlsson et al., 2009).

[1] This catalog incorporates not only mainstream IS journals, but also social studies. We chose the five top journals from each set, namely: MIS Quarterly, Information Systems Research, Information & Management, Journal of Management Information Systems, and Decision Support Systems, as well as European Journal of Information Systems, Information & Organization, Information Systems Journal, Journal of Organizational and End User Computing, and Journal of Information Technology.

(B) Requirements analysis can be enhanced by considering "fun & enjoyment:" Papageorgiou and De Bruyn (2010) identified monthly (financial) reporting as a key MSS capability. Associated analyses help managers to investigate details (Bergeron, 1995)., e.g. by applying *filters* or *drill downs* (Turban et al., 2013) or by creating own reports (Laudon & Laudon, 2018). *News ticker* offer an overview so that managers do not have to collect the information from various sources. Neyem et al. (2012) emphasizes collaboration which offers asynchronous communication such as *business emails* (Lee-Partridge & Snyder, 2012) and *business calendars* (Belkadi et al., 2013; Alvarado et al., 2011). Integrating an *office suite* is still uncommon in MSS (Watson & Frolick, 2006; Lee & Shim, 2006). *Direct messages* to colleagues are recognized. Herskovic et al. (2011) state that emails "at the push of a button" are important. Riemer et al. (2009) argue for shared office documents. Video conferencing offers synchronicity of face-to-face communication (Kim et al., 2018). Hess et al. (2014) include private email into the corporate environment.

Semi-business apps support managers' logistics when travelling (Kaneshige, 2011) and offer a search function. Wixom and Watson (2010) identify *web browsers* for pervasive MSS. Finally, we identified *newspaper* or *business journal readers* (Watson & Frolick, 2006) and convenience apps such as *restaurant finders or weather* (Lee & Shim, 2006). Thus, manager app portals should incorporate both constitutive apps for corporate management and complementing components, which may support managers' collaboration and new mobile business life requirements.

(C) Ready-to-use design guidelines are lacking: The publications we reviewed provide both lists of apps without a rigorous basis for their selection and attributes of single apps. Two articles consider managers' IS use situations and apps. We only found one method for clustering MSS user interface apps to examine which ones influence managers' user satisfaction. These findings focus on layouts for desktop PCs (Wu et al., 2011). We define mobile MSS as IS offering services for managers while they move from place to place, especially outside their workplace, where technology is accessible, but not necessarily embedded in the environment.

3. RESEARCH MODEL

The *Kano model* is an adequate approach to identify attractive quality attributes from a "customer" perspective (Chen et al., 2011), e.g., to differentiate between motivators that increase workspace satisfaction and hygiene factors that cause dissatisfaction when absent (Herzberg et al., 1959). The model is widely applied in several industry sectors and business objectives (Luor et al., 2015) mainly because it is appropriate to systematically accommodate managers' user preferences in a detailed manner. Compared to other methods for determining desired product attributes, e.g. preference regression or a conjoint analysis, the Kano model is less fatiguing for respondents. Thus, the Kano model enables researchers to focus systematically on managers' perception of IS usefulness. We follow a two-step approach to reach diverse results. First, we examine the user acceptance and experience. Second, we obtain data from both analyst and consumer managers of several companies.

3.1 Examine Managers' Perception of IS Usefulness

We transferred the Kano model to a model of understanding IS designs (Figure 1) and differentiate five categories of apps as follows (Matzler & Hinterhuber, 1998):

1. *Attractive apps* ("A") disproportionately influence managers' satisfaction and function as the strongest
differentiator in design. Since managers do not expect IS to include these apps, the app's implementation and offering the features increase managers' enthusiasm.
2. *One-dimensional apps* ("O") result in satisfaction when present and in dissatisfaction when absent. Their presence impacts IS performance regarding a linear (one-dimensional) relation. Considering "the more, the better", managers' user satisfaction increases while the apps improve.
3. *Must-be apps* ("M") are taken for granted. Their absence strongly dissatisfies managers. However, these basic apps do not have the power to shift managers' user satisfaction beyond a neutral state.
4. Apps that managers do not care about are assigned into the *indifferent* ("I") category.
5. For apps in the *reverse* category ("R") a high degree of achievement results in dissatisfaction. Users who like easy-to-use IS handling might perceive the presence of too many app features as reverse quality.

Figure 1 illustrates how these five categories of apps are classified by means of a Kano questionnaire containing a pair of questions for each app. The left side of Figure 1 shows both the first question determining managers' response to an app portal *with* a proposed app (functional question), and the second question concerning their response to the same portal *without* this app (dysfunctional question). Here, managers can answer as follows: (1) I *dislike* the app, meaning I will not use it. (2) *I can live with it,* meaning I do not like this app, (3) I am *neutral*. (4) *It must be that way, meaning* this app is essential and every manager should have it. (5) *I like it that way very much, meaning* it is a great and unexpected differentiator: The right side of Figure 1 demonstrates the apps' classification in one of the five Kano clusters.

Based on our state of the art, we arrived at *30 apps* for the portal design. We structured them in three groups: (1) Besides the constitutive apps of supporting managers' *corporate management* task, we complement the portal design with apps (2) for *manager collaboration,* and (3) for *mobile business life*.

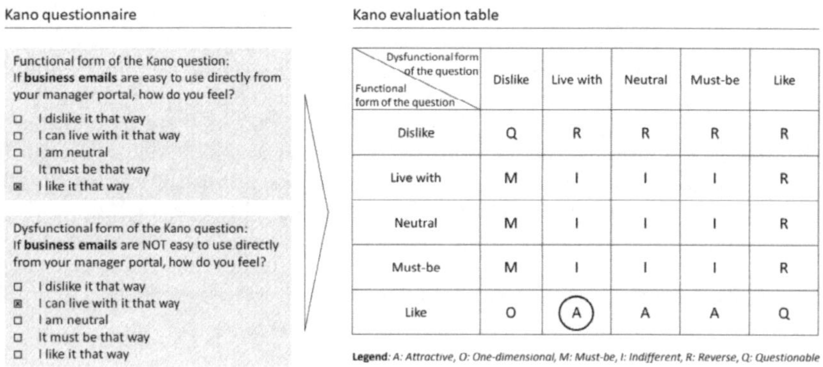

Figure 1. Kano model for IS design (Matzler & Hinterhuber, 1998)

In order to find answers to the Kano questions, our *manager focus group* consisted of 25 Level 1 and Level 2 managers from eight companies (Table 2). Since 2006, they meet regularly three times a year to discuss trends in corporate management and IS support. The participants consisted of 16 analyst and 9 consumer managers. Taking into account that managers are difficult to attract for surveys, the total number of 25 can be considered as reasonable. Kano interviews were conducted in 30-minute face-to-face interviews. We calculated Cronbach's alpha (Cronbach, 1951) to determine the reliability of our results. Due to the scheme of the Kano questionnaire, the collected data was split and analyzed in two groups (functional and dysfunctional). Smartphones and tablets, as well as analyst and consumer managers were treated separately. With alpha values above 0.7 for both manager types and tablets, the results meet standard requirements for psychometric tests (analyst managers: 0.71, consumer managers: 0.78). The scores for smartphones (0.58, 0.55) are slightly below this threshold. Based on Cronbach (1951), higher values enhance interpretability but lower values do not necessarily prevent interpretability. Therefore, we did not discard the results for smartphones.

Table 2. Sample characteristics

Position	No.	%	Sector	No.	%
Executives (L1)	11	44	Industrial	17	68
Director business dpt. (L2)	6	24	Financial services	2	8
Director BI department (L2)	8	32	Other services	6	24
Frequency of IS use	No.	%	Working style	No.	%
Permanent	2	8	Analyst	16	64
Multiple times/day	7	28	Consumer	9	36
Once every day	10	40			
2-3 times/week	6	24	Total	25	
Once a week	0	0			

3.2 Results

We analyzed the results in four ways: First, all *must-be apps* ("M") were integrated in the manager app portal. Second, for the remaining apps, we calculated a coefficient to highlight *most satisfying apps*, the Extent of Satisfaction (EoS), with $EoS = (n_A + n_O)/(n_A + n_O + n_M + n_I)$. EoS can vary on a scale from 0.00 (no impact on satisfaction) to 1.00 (strong impact). We complement must-be apps by apps in our design with an EoS of 0.30 or more (Figure 2). We screened our results for apps with a high number of reverse evaluations, because EoS scores are calculated without taking reverse results into consideration. Fourth, we propose the use of an Extent of Dissatisfaction (EoD), which considers the most dissatisfying lacks of apps through $EoD = (n_M + n_O)/(n_A + n_O + n_M + n_I)$.

Figure 3 presents a two-dimensional combination of EoS and EoD for all apps on the grid of the four Kano categories. The figure provides a classification of the apps as follows: Apps which several users consider a "must-be," a number consider attractive, and the remaining consider apps as indifferent and therefore do not receive the attention they should. They fall through the grid of the first must-be screening and get a relatively weak EoS score of around 0.3.

(1) Manager collaboration: Starting with the must-be apps on tablets and smartphones, analyst and consumer managers name *business emails* (app 1.1, numbering according to Figure 2, SC for software component) and *business calendar* (SC1.2.1). For analyst managers, *annotations* (SC 1.4.1.) are a must-be, whereas consumer managers consider them as satisfying (0.56; 0.44). *One-click collaboration* (SC.1.4.3) is the app suited to increasing analyst managers' perception of IS usefulness most. It received an exceptional score on both tablets (0.88) and smartphones (0.56), whereas consumer managers are less interested (0.33 on both devices). *Notifications on changes* (SC1.5.2, 0.81; 0.63) in *shared office documents* (SC1.5.1, 0.63, 0.53) are also very attractive for analyst managers on both tablets and smartphones. Consumer managers are rather indifferent (0.33, 0.11). Finally, analyst managers ranked an *office suite* (SC1.3) as attractive (positioned almost in the center of Figure 3, left) on tablets (0.44), and less attractive on smartphones (0.36, positioned almost all the way to the left of Figure 3, right). Regarding apps that both manager types consider satisfying, high EoS scores were given to a *news ticker* (SC1.8) on smartphones (0.69, 0.71) and tablets (0.69; 0.63). *Video calling/conferencing* (SC1.6) is attractive for both manager types on tablets and smartphones (0.60/0.56; 0.60/0.44). *Direct emails* (SC1.4.2) received a similar EoS score from analyst (0.63 on tablets and smartphones) and consumer managers (0.67 on both devices). *Private emails* (SC1.7.1) are relevant for analyst managers (0.38; 0.31). *Private apps* (SC1.7.2) are somewhat satisfying to them (0.33; 0.36). Consumer managers are indifferent (0.11). *Instant messaging* (SC1.5.4) or *other users' location* (SC1.2.3) do not play a role (0.25/0.07;0.13/ 0.0).

Strongest differentiators for manager collaboration: Offer collaboration bars and push notifications on changes to shared office documents for analyst managers. Get consumer managers "online" with news tickers.

(2) Corporate management: Analyst managers evaluated *monthly (financial) reporting* (SC2.1), *management dashboards* (SC2.2) as well as *filters* (SC2.3.1) as must-be components. Consumer managers, in turn, ranked management dashboards as a must-be on both devices. Filters are considered attractive by consumer managers on both devices (0.67; 0.56). *Drill-downs* (SC2.3.2) are evaluated by both manager types as satisfying on tablets and smartphones (analysts: 0.38 and 0.31; consumers: 0.44 on both devices). *Creating own reports* (SC2.3.3) is only satisfying to some degree for analyst managers on tablets (0.31), but not for consumer managers (0.13; 0.00). Finally, a *news ticker* (SC2.4) is very satisfying for analyst and consumer managers on tablets (0.63; 0.63) as well as on smartphones (0.69; 0.63).

Strongest differentiators for corporate management: Make core reports more interactive with drill downs and filters for manager self-service.

(3) Mobile business life: Analyst and consumer managers highlight the need for *flights and trains apps* (SC3.2.1) on tablets and smartphones as must-be apps. A *taxi app* (SC3.2.2) was evaluated as more satisfying by analyst (0.38; 0.44) than consumer managers (0.33; 0.33). The former evaluates a *web browser* (SC3.1.2) as a must-be app and a *search engine* (SC3.1.1) as satisfying (0.38; 0.38) becoming a must-be app (Figure 3). Consumer managers rated this app as satisfying to some degree (0.33; 0.33). In turn, *business journal* (SC3.4.2, 0.94; 0.63) and *newspaper readers* (SC3.4.1, 0.63; 0.44) are very attractive for analyst managers. The same rating applies to consumer managers on tablets (0.89; 0.78). Convenience apps promise further benefits.

A *weather forecast* (SC3.5.1, analyst managers: 0.63 on both devices; consumer managers: 0.56) or a *restaurant finder* (SC3.5.2, 0.50; 0.44) were evaluated by both manager types as equally attractive on both devices.

Strongest differentiators for mobile business life: Take "fun and enjoyment" into account when accommodating managers' business life.

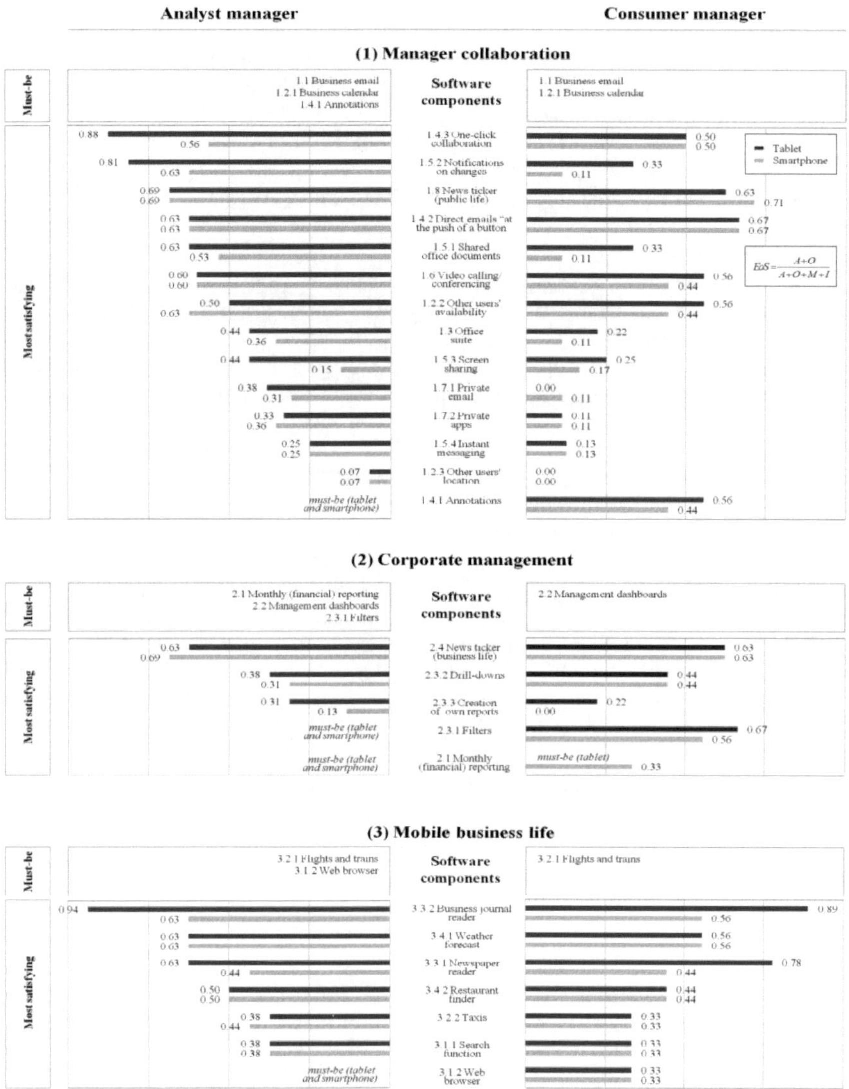

Figure 2. Results of the structured interviews

(4) Device selection: Eight apps such as video calling/conferencing or business journal readers received higher EoS scores on *tablets* than on smartphones. The reverse occurred three times for analyst managers and twice for consumer managers (e.g., news ticker for public life). Analyst managers argue that they are more satisfied with tablets than smartphones, because they can use them for sharing office documents simple ad-hoc analyses (create your own reports, SC2.3.3). Consumer managers can start using the app portal on a tablet, especially reading electronic newspapers. Some consumer managers would even use their smartphone instead of a tablet. However, from our interviews, managers do not feel comfortable with smartphones larger than 5 inches.

Strongest differentiators for device selection: Consider that tablets create their own manager use case as their "first-stop information shop."

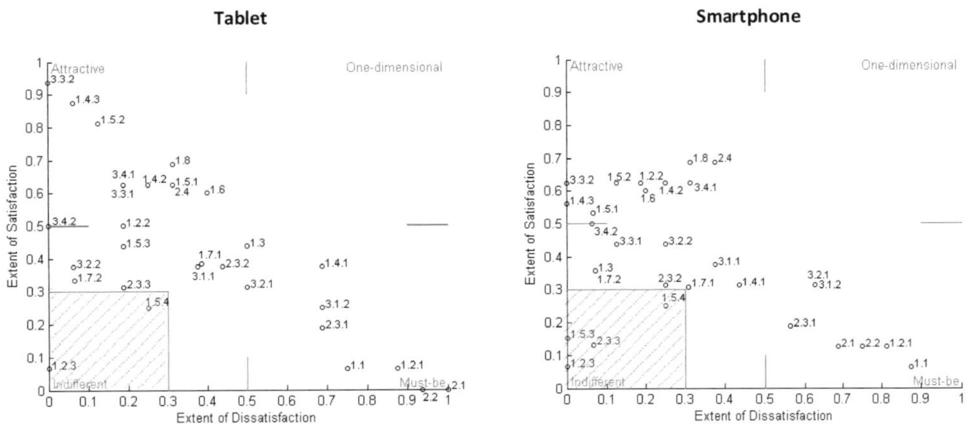

Figure 3. Representation of the results along EoS and EoD for analyst managers

4. SYNTHESIS

We discussed our results in January 2018 with two companies improving their manager IS support. Interviews were conducted with the head of management accounting (report provider) and a divisional head (recipient) of a chemical company (sales: 50 bn. EUR) and a divisional head of an automotive supplier (30 bn. EUR).

Based on the results from the Kano model (Figure 2 and 3), differences between analyst and consumer managers were clearly found. Thus, we propose the development of a *basic manager app portal* for consumer managers, which can be adapted to the more individual analyst manager. Both manager app portal designs incorporate the constitutive app cluster "corporate management" in the middle and the complementary clusters "manager collaboration" and "mobile business life" to the left and right of it (Krönke et al., 2017).

The top row covers a *news ticker*, a weather app, and search engine. There are the must-be apps like business email and calendar as well as travel apps. This extends to integrating document sharing and notifications on changes. However, the app portal designs for analyst and consumer managers have three differences: (1) Consumer managers evaluated neither screen sharing nor an office suite as must-be or attractive apps. Thus, these apps have been omitted. (2) In additional to filters and drill downs, the analyst manager app portal supports the creation of own reports. (3) The analyst manager app portal includes private apps (Figure 4).

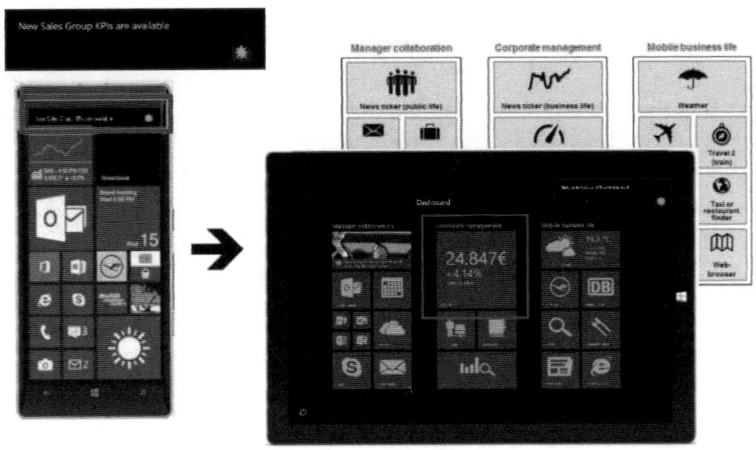

Figure 4. Analyst manager app portal on a tablet with a smartphone push functionality (Krönke et al., 2017)

Several comments by the interviewed managers highlighted efficiency when mobile, e.g., "Draw my attention to critical events and I will be happy. *I don't want to be bombarded with notifications every minute.*" The divisional head of the automotive supplier asked for a web browser: "I want to be able to check things on the internet," whereas his counterpart was less enthusiastic about restaurant finders and point-of-interest maps: "It is easier to ask the concierge."

Looking forward, remarks about *intelligent automation* were made such as filtering news relevant to the current travel destination(s) or an intelligent push of emails to the mobile device. Overall, the managers concluded that the "right" mix of apps will make the difference. Finally, all managers stated that our portal design would embrace *manager self-service*. The head of management accounting stated, "That is what is on my mind, when I think about manager self-service. However, for security reasons we will only allow choosing apps from a company pool."

5. CONCLUSION

The objective of this article was to examine which apps disproportionately influence managers' perception of IS usefulness. We propose a user-driven manager app portal design. We highlighted differences between "analyst-" and "consumer-type" managers. For *practice*, our findings can serve as a reference for both improving existing designs and future IS designs. For *research* purposes, the Kano model is an alternative starting point for investigations, not only for portal designs, but also for other kinds of IS in general.

Due to the number of apps the *Kano model* was best suited to our research. Although we introduced the Kano model to the interviewees, participants' understanding of the dysfunctional questions remains questionable. Future research should ensure that managers understand the Kano model more thoroughly, and, thus, provide more consistent answers. Hauser (1993) stated that 20-30 Kano interviews determine about 90–95% of all possible requirements. Our investigations were conducted with 25 individuals from eight different companies. Cheng et al. (2016) conducted a study with 22 participants. Our final number of interviews seems reasonable because of two reasons. Firstly, we interviewed experienced managers providing substantiated answers and secondly motivating this special kind of professionals to participate in surveys is difficult.

Another limitation is our number of *IS use factors*. Age, gender, education, IS experience, and working styles were not examined, which should be addressed in future work. Incorporating latest research on the Kano model (Madzík, 2018) might increase the quality of results further. Finally, examining the growing importance of *fun and enjoyment* when using IS is another avenue for research.

REFERENCES

Al-Kassab, J. et al., 2014. Information visualization to support management decisions. *In International Journal of Information Technology & Decision Making*, Vol. 13, No. 2, pp. 407-428.

Alvarado, B. et al., 2011. *Managing user-to-user contact with inferred presence information*. Google Patents.

Belkadi, F. et al., 2013. A situation model to support awareness in collaborative design. *In International Journal of Human-Computer Studies*, Vol. 71, No. 1, pp. 110-129.

Benbasat, I. and Nault, B.R. 1990. An Evaluation of Empirical Research in Managerial Support Systems. *In Decision Support Systems*, Vol. 6, No. 3, pp. 203-226.

Bergeron, F. et al., 1995. Determinants of EIS use: Testing a behavioral model. *In Decision Support Systems*, Vol. 14, No. 2, pp. 131-146.

Carlsson, S.A. et al., 2009. An approach for designing MSS: the design science research process and its outcomes. *Proceedings of the 4th International Conference on Design Science Research in Information Systems and Technology*. Philadelphia, USA, pp. 1-11.

Chen, L.-S. et al., 2010. C-Kano model: a novel approach for discovering attractive quality elements. *In Total Quality Management*, Vol. 21, No. 11, pp. 1189-1214

Cheng, J. et al., 2016. Using the Kano Model to Balance Delight and Frustration for an Enterprise Application. *Proceedings of the 2016 CHI Conference Extended Abstracts on Human Factors in Computing Systems*. San Jose California, USA, pp. 3021-3027.

Cronbach, L.J., 1951. Coefficient alpha and the internal structure of tests. *In Psychometrika*, Vol. 16, No. 3, pp. 297-334.

Fteimi N., 2017. A Taxonomy of IS Projects' Knowledge-sharing Mechanism. *In Communications of the Association for Information Systems*, Vol. 41 No. 26, pp. 611-638.

Gartner, 2018. Gartner Says By 2018, More Than 50 Percent of Users Will Use a Tablet or Smartphone First for All Online Activities. Available at: https://www.gartner.com/en/newsroom/press-releases/2014-12-08-gartner-says-by-2018-more-than-50-percent-of-users-will-use-a-tablet-or-smartphone-first-for-all-online-activities [Accessed: 16 Jan. 2020].

Goodhue, D.L. and Thompson, R.L., 1995. Task-technology fit and individual performance. *In MIS Quarterly*, Vol. 19, No. 2, pp. 213-236.

Hauser, J.R., 1993. How Puritan-Bennett used the house of quality. *In Sloan Management Review*, Vol. 34, Spring, pp. 61-70.

Heineman, G.T. and Councill, W.T., 2001. *Component-Based Software Engineering: Putting the Pieces Together*. Pearson Education, Addison-Wesley, UK.

Herskovic, V. et al., 2011. The iceberg effect: Behind the user interface of mobile collaborative systems. *In Journal of Universal Computer Science,* Vol. 17, No. 2, pp. 183-202.

Herzberg, F. et al.,1959. *The Motivation to Work*. John Wiley, New York.

Hess, T. et al., 2014. Digital Life as a Topic of Business and Information Systems Engineering? *In Business & Information Systems Engineering*, Vol. 6, No. 4, pp. 247-253.

Huysmans, J.H. 1970. The Effectiveness of the Cognitive-Style Constraint in Implementing Operations Research Proposals. *In Management Science*, Vol. 17, No. 1, pp. 92-104.

Kaneshige, T., 2011. 15 Best iPhone Apps for busy CEOs. Available at: https://www.networkworld.com/article/2838481/15-best-iphone-apps-for-busy-ceos.html [Accessed 16 Jan. 2020].

Kettinger, W.J. and Marchand, D.A., 2011. Information management practices (IMP) from the senior manager's perspective: An investigation of the IMP construct and its measurement. *In Information Systems Journal*, Vol. 21, No. 5, pp. 385-406.

Kim H. et al., 2018. Unpacking organizational awareness: scale development and empirical examinations in the context of distributed knowledge sharing. *In Journal of Applied Communication Research*, Vol. 47, No. 1, pp. 47-68.

Krönke, B. et al., 2017. Manager App Portal at Continental: A Content, Collaboration, and Convenience App Selection That Works. *In CONTROLLING – Zeitschrift für erfolgsorientierte Unternehmenssteuerung*, Vol. 29, No 5, pp. 36-45.

Laudon, K.C. and Laudon, J.P., 2018. *MIS: managing the digital firm*. Pearson, Harlow, UK.

Lee, C.-P., Shim, J., 2006. An empirical study on user satisfaction with mobile business applications use and hedonism. *In Journal of Information Technology Theory and Application (JITTA)*, Vol. 8, No. 3, pp. 57-74.

Lee-Partridge, J.E. and Snyder, J., 2012. Using the Layered Model to Understand Employee Selection of Information and Communication Channels for Information and Knowledge Sharing in Project Teams. *Proceedings of the Conference on Information Systems Applied Research*, San Antonio, USA, pp. 1508.

Luor, T. et al., 2015. Contribution to quality research: a literature review of Kano's model from 1998 to 2012. *In Total Quality Management & Business Excellence*, Vol. 26, No. 3-4, pp. 234-247.

Madzík, P., 2018. Increasing accuracy of the Kano model – a case study. *In Total Quality Management & Business Excellence*, Vol. 29, No. 3-4, pp. 387-409.

March, S.T., Smith, G.F., 1995. Design and Natural Science Research on Information Technology. *In Decision Support Systems*, Vol. 15, No. 4, pp. 251-266.

Matzler, K. and Hinterhuber, H.H. 1998. How to make product development projects more successful by integrating Kano's model of customer satisfaction into quality function deployment. *In Technovation*, Vol. 18, No. 1, pp. 25-38.

Neyem, A. et al., 2012. A reusable structural design for mobile collaborative applications. *In Journal of Systems and Software*, Vol. 85, No. 3, pp. 511-524.

Ostrov, P., 2014. Sales Analytics: Data Driven Forecasting for Better Quota Attainment. Available at: https://www. Aberdeen.com/cmo-essentials/sales-analytics-data-driven-forecasting-for-better-quota-attainment-2 [Accessed: 16 Jan. 2020].

Papageorgiou, E., De Bruyn, H., 2010: Creating Strategic Value Through Executive Information Systems: An Exploratory Study. *Proceedings of the 3rd European Conference on Information Management and Evaluation, Gothenburg*, Gothenburg, Sweden, pp. 380-399.

Powell, P.L. and Johnson, J., 1995. Gender and DSS Design: The Research Implications. *In Decision Support Systems*, Vol. 14, No. 1, pp. 27-58.

Riemer, K., et al., 2009. eCollaboration: On the nature and emergence of communication and collaboration technologies. *In Electronic Markets*, Vol. 19, No. 4, pp. 181-188.

SAP, 2019. Reimagine the SAP user experience with SAP FIORI. Available at: https://www.sap.com/products/fiori. html [Accessed: 8 Aug. 2019]

Shneiderman, B., 1997. A grander goal: A thousand-fold increase in human capabilities. *In Educom Review*, Vol. 32, No. 6, pp. 4-10.

Sommerville, I.: Software Engineering. Pearson, München (2010)

Turban, E. et al., 2013.: IT for management: Advancing sustainable, profitable business growth. Hoboken. NJ: Wiley (2013)

Volonino, L. et al., 1995. Using EIS to respond to dynamic business conditions. *In Decision Support Systems*. Vol. 14, No. 2, pp. 105-116.

Walls, J.G. et al., 1992. Building an Information System Design Theory for Vigilant EIS. *In Information Systems Research*, Vol. 3, No. 4, pp. 36-59.

Wang W., and Reani M., 2017. The rise of mobile computing for Group DSS: A comparative evaluation of mobile and desktop. *In International Journal of Human-Computer Studies*, Vol .104, August 2017, pp. 16-36.

Watson, H.J. and Frolick, M.N. 2006. Determining information requirements for an EIS. *In MIS Quarterly*, Vol. 17, No. 3, pp. 255-269.

Willcocks, L. et al., 2008. The Ranking of Top IS Journals: A Perspective from the London School of Economics. *In European Journal of Information Systems*, Vol. 17, No. 2, pp. 163-168.

Wired, 2010. Apple Registers Trademark for "There's an app for that". Available at: https://www.wired.com/2010/10/app-for-that [Accessed: 16 Jan. 2020].

Witkin, H.A. et al., 1977. Field-Dependent and Field-Independent Cognitive Styles and Their Educational Implications. *In Review of Educational Research*, Vol.47 No. 1, pp. 1-64.

Wixom, B.H. and Watson, H.J., 2010. The BI-Based Organization. *In International Journal of Business Intelligence Research*, Vol. 1, No. 1, pp. 13-28.

Wu, C.-S., et al., 2011. User Acceptance of Wireless Technology in Organizations: A Comparison of Alternative Models. *In Computer Standards & Interfaces*, Vol.33, No. 1, pp. 50-58.

Zhang, P. et al., 2002.: AMCIS 2002 Panels and Workshops I: HCI Research in the MIS Discipline. *In Communications of the Association for Information Systems*, 9, pp. 334-355.

Zigurs, I. and Buckland, B.K., 1998. A theory of task/technology fit and group support systems effectiveness. *In MIS Quarterly*, Vol. 22, No. 2, pp. 313-334.

INVESTIGATING THE CRITICAL DETERMINANTS OF TRUST AND THEIR IMPACT ON MOBILE PAYMENT ADOPTION

Tuan Anh Nguyen[1,2], Martin Dick[1] and Hiep Cong Pham[3]
[1]*School of Business IT and Logistics, RMIT University, Australia*
[2]*Faculty of Information Technology, National Academy of Education Management*
[3]*School of Business & Management, RMIT University, Australia*

ABSTRACT

This study proposes a model investigating the critical determinants for trust, and the impact of trust on mobile payment adoption. This research aims to address the importance of trust in m-payment adoption, and overcome the limitations of previous studies which are a lack of understanding of the determinants of trust in m-payment adoption, a lack of adopting trust as a multi-dimensional construct, and a lack of consideration of the moderating role of culture. In this research, the authors employ the Unified Theory of Acceptance and Use of Technology, Siau and Shen's framework for building consumer trust in mobile commerce, and Hofstede's cultural framework as the theoretical basis. The proposed model encompasses four types of trust including mobile payment provider trust, mobile technology trust, institution-based trust, and seller trust, which are well-defined in the related literature, and a moderating role for culture between the four types of trust and mobile payment adoption. The model of the study not only may be used to improve understanding of trust in mobile payment adoption, but also contribute to the literature of the determinants for trust in mobile payment adoption.

KEYWORDS

Mobile Payment, Mobile Payment Adoption, Mobile Payment Acceptance, Trust, Mobile Payment Use

1. INTRODUCTION

Mobile payment (m-payment) refers to financial transactions made via mobile devices (Stringfellow 2018). Simply, m-payment users can use mobile devices to pay for goods or services that they purchase online or offline. Remote m-payment is implemented from a distance, without direct interaction between buyers and sellers or the merchants' point of sale systems (POS). Common examples of remote m-payment are carrier billing, short message service (SMS) payments or using mobile phones to pay directly via applications such as Paypal. In contrast, the proximity m-payment method based on Near Field Communications (NFC) allows customers to use their mobiles phones via Apple Pay, Samsung Pay or Google Pay functions to interact with a seller's POS to pay. Mobile payment is considered as the newest means of payment in the evolution of payment methods based on the Internet and mobile devices (Kolaki 2017). Global use of m-payment is predicted to rise 28% by 2022, and surpass cash and credit cards, therefore m-payment will contribute to bringing societies towards the future of a cashless world (MerchantSavvy 2019).

Many studies have found that trust has a significant positive influence on consumers' intention to adopt m-payment (Andreev, Pliskin & Rafaeli 2012; Liu 2012). However, little attention has been paid to which factors are the critical determinants for m-payment trust (Patil et al. 2018). As well, trust is often regarded as a single construct in previous studies when trust is a complex phenomenon and a better understanding of trust dimensions in m-payment adoption can better predict adoption and potentially use patterns (Meng, Min & Li 2008). Another factor is culture which often plays a crucial role in consumer technology adoption because it may cause and explain a discrepancy in consumer behaviour in acceptance or intention to adopt a new system or technology (Choi et al. 2014). Hofstede's cultural dimensions is one of the most frequent cultural frameworks used in culture research (Eringa et al. 2015). Many studies have found a significant moderating role of Hofstede's cultural dimensions on the consumer adoption of a system or technology (Baptista & Oliveira 2015; Yoon 2009). Nonetheless, the moderating role of Hofstede cultural dimensions have not yet been examined in m-payment adoption, therefore, it is likely to be productive to address it.

Consequently, this study aims to identify the critical determinants for a multi-dimensional model of trust in relation to m-payment adoption including m-payment provider trust, technology trust, institution-based trust, and seller trust with a moderating effect of culture on each type of trust. The paper contributes to a more comprehensive understanding of trust's antecedents in m-payment adoption, and the impact of a multi-dimensional trust on m-payment adoption.

2. LITERATURE REVIEW

2.1 Previous Studies Involved in Trust in m-Payment Adoption

Trust is generally essential in any economic activity (Coyle 2013). A lack of trust has been historically found as a significant barrier to conducting any mobile commerce (m-commerce) services (Joubert & Belle 2009). As a result, trust also plays an important role in m-payment adoption, and therefore, has received the attention of researchers.

Many studies have adopted the Technology Acceptance Model (TAM) or the Unified Theory of Acceptance and Use of Technology (UTAUT) as their theoretical framework and found a significant impact of trust on intention to adopt m-payment of consumers. When researching drivers of the willingness to use m-payment in Israel, Andreev, Pliskin and Rafaeli (2012) extended TAM and included Diffusion of Innovation theory (DOI), and found a direct and significant impact of vendor trust, and a non-significant impact of mechanism trust on willingness to use m-payment. Phonthanukitithaworn, Sellitto and Fong (2015) extended TAM to test user intentions to adopt m-payment services in Thailand and found that perceived trust had a significant influence on behavioural intention. The study of Slade et al. (2015) based on UTAUT2, collected data in the UK, and revealed that trust is an important predictor for intention to adopt m-payment. Based on UTAUT and TAM, Qasim and Abu-Shanab (2016) examined the impact of network externalities including performance and effort expectancy, social influence, and trust on m-payment acceptance in Jordan. Data analysis revealed that except for effort expectancy, the important role of the other drivers was proven. Gao and Waechter (2017) integrated TAM and the Information System Success model (ISS) to argue that a lack of trust is the most significant long-term inhibitor for acceptance and success of m-payment, and examined the role of initial trust on perceived benefit and convenience which in turn influenced intention to adopt m-payment. Gao and Waechter collected data from a sample in Australia, and revealed that perceived system quality, perceived uncertainty, information quality and service quality also positively and significantly influenced initial trust, which positively impacts on intention to adopt m-payment. In China, several studies also found that trust have a significant impact on m-payment adoption (Liu 2012; Mingxing, Jing & Yafang 2014; Yan & Yang 2014; Zhou 2011).

Besides TAM and UTAUT, several studies have adopted other theories and also found the important effect of trust on m-payment acceptance such as Lu et al. (2011) using the valence framework; and Jia, Hall and Zhu (2015) utilising a multi-stage decision making model and initial trust building theory. Zhou (2014) adopted the ISS model and identified the important effect of factors including trust on online payment, system quality, and information quality on trust in m-payment, which significantly influences continuance usage of m-payment. Xin, Techatassanasoontorn and Tan (2015) collected data in New Zealand and suggested a model of antecedents of trust in m-payment. This model encompasses five groups of factors: characteristics of the mobile service provider including perceived reputation of mobile service provider and perceived opportunism of mobile service provider, characteristics of the mobile payment provider including perceived reputation of mobile payment vendor and perceived opportunism of mobile payment vendor, characteristics of mobile technology including perceived structural assurance and perceived environmental risk, a cultural variable which is uncertainty avoidance, and a personality variable which is disposition to trust.

2.2 Limitations of Existing Studies

The literature review of m-payment adoption shows that trust is highly likely to be a vital driver for m-payment adoption from an individual or consumer perspective. However, the existing research on trust in m-payment adoption has largely investigated the influence of trust on the consumer intention to adopt m-payment, while little attention has been paid to explore determining factors of m-payment trust (Patil et al. 2018). As a result, research on factors which can be employed as determinants for trust in m-payment adoption needs to be empirically investigated further.

Another limitation of existing research on m-payment trust and its adoption is the lack of investigation of moderating variables between trust and m-payment adoption. A moderating variable plays an important role in psychological or behavioural research because it can enhance or reduce the magnitude of the relationship between a predictor and an outcome (Lani 2018). Undoubtedly, the role of moderating variables should be evaluated to provide a comprehensive understanding of the impact of trust on customer intention to adopt m-payment. Culture is defined as the "collective programming of the mind which distinguishes the members of one group or category of people from those of another" (Hofstede 1993, p. 4). Many studies have been conducted to test the significant moderating impact of Hofstede's cultural dimensions on intention of consumers to adopt a new system or technology (Baptista & Oliveira 2015; Yoon 2009). However, an examination of the moderating role of culture between trust and the use of m-payment has not yet been performed. As a result, an investigation of the moderating impact of culture on the relationship between trust and consumers' m-payment adoption is necessary and significant.

Finally, trust is considered a complex concept, thus, it should be modelled as a multifaceted phenomenon (Jimenez, San-Martin & Azuela 2016; McKnight, Choudhury & Kacmar 2002; Meng, Min & Li 2008). However, most existing research on m-payment trust models trust as a single construct. Researchers have pointed out that exploring different types of trust in m-commerce can achieve a better understanding of consumer trust, which has a significant impact on understanding and predicting consumer adoption (Meng, Min & Li 2008). Accordingly, research on trust in m-payment adoption needs to distinguish the different types of trust. This is necessary to acquire a clear understanding of how each type of trust can influence m-payment adoption.

2.3 Research Aims and Questions

The main objective of this research is to investigate the critical determinants of trust, and the moderating effect of culture in the relationship between trust and m-payment adoption. Particularly, it aims to answer:

- What are the types of trust in the m-payment context?
- To what extent does each type of trust influence consumer's m-payment adoption?
- What are the critical determinants for consumers' trust in m-payment adoption?
- To what extent does culture moderate the impact of trust on m-payment adoption?

3. A CONCEPTUAL MODEL

3.1 Theoretical Background

UTAUT was formulated based on unifying eight prominent models in technology adoption area which are the Theory of Reasoned Action, TAM, the Motivational Model, the Theory of Planned Behaviour (TPB), the combined TAM and TPB, the Model of PC Utilization, Diffusion of Innovation theory, and Social Cognitive Theory (Venkatesh et al. 2003; Venkatesh, Thong & Xu 2012). Accordingly, this model covers most variables necessary to study technology acceptance or behavioural intention to adopt a new system (Qasim & Abu-Shanab 2016). In addition, after collecting data for six months from four organisations, the analysis outcome revealed that UTAUT has an adjusted R^2 of 69 per cent, which outperforms the eight previous models (Venkatesh et al. 2003). Since its appearance, UTAUT has been widely and successfully adopted as a theoretical lens in a large number of studies of technology adoption or acceptance (Williams, Rana & Dwivedi 2015). Consequently, the authors adopt UTAUT as a theoretical background in this research.

The authors also adapt consumer trust in m-commerce from Siau and Shen's framework (2003) which posits that general consumer trust is based on mobile technology trust and mobile vendor trust because m-payment is considered as a subset of m-commerce. Applying Siau and Shen's framework to the context of m-payment, the vendor is not the seller or merchant, but should be the m-payment provider who provides m-payment service for consumers (Srivastava, Chandra & Theng 2010).

Hofstede's framework on culture is employed to hypothesise the moderating role of cultural variables between trust and m-payment adoption. Hofstede analysed the characteristics of culture around the world, and suggested five dimensions of natural culture, which are power distance, individualism/collectivism, uncertainty avoidance, masculine/feminine, and long-term/short-term orientation. Hofstede's cultural framework is one of the most important and influencing cultural studies which have been adopted widely in research in technology adoption (Baptista & Oliveira 2015).

Furthermore, a comprehensive review of related literature regarding the determinants of consumer trust in the adoption of e-commerce, m-commerce, mobile banking, and m-payment was conducted to support the background and hypotheses of this research. This is because: (1) m-payment is consider as an accelerator of payment method for m-commerce as well as e-commerce (Kumar 2013), i.e. m-payment is a subset of m-commerce as well as e-commerce, and mobile banking applications also can provide the payment functions; (2) there is no consensus and consistency of antecedents of trust in m-payment adoption due to a very limited numbers of studies in the literature. Obviously, a comprehensive review of related literature is necessary and significant.

3.2 The Proposed Conceptual Model and Hypotheses

Based on the comprehensive of related literature review of trust, four types of trust for m-payment adoption are proposed in this study.

(1) M-payment provider trust refers to the belief of consumers that the m-payment service provider will perform and complete the transaction even if there are risky or uncertain circumstances (Joubert & Belle 2009, 2013). Simply, m-payment provider trust indicates whether the provider of m-payment service can be trusted by customers or consumers using m-payment. Mingxing, Jing and Yafang (2014) highlighted the significance of m-payment service provider trust because it represents the extent to which users believe that a service provider can implement m-payment service correctly, fast, conveniently, and safely. Many authors also recognised the significant impact of service providers' roles on trust of consumers in m-commerce and m-payment adoption (Min, Meng & Zhong 2008; Xin, Techatassanasoontorn & Tan 2015). As a result, the authors argue that if consumers perceive that an m-payment provider is trustworthy, they are more likely to adopt m-payment.

(2) Technology trust or system trust refers to the degree to which the consumer believes that the underlying technology or system has the ability to work as expected and to process an m-payment transaction appropriately (Joubert & Belle 2013). This research focuses on the consumer perspective of system/technology trust, instead of the viewpoint of technical experts. Technology trust is another vital aspect of trust which has been adopted in various studies on technology or system adoption in e-commerce, m-commerce and m-payment (Joubert & Belle 2009, 2013; Min, Meng & Zhong 2008; Pennington, Wilcox & Grover 2003; Siau & Shen 2003; Srivastava, Chandra & Theng 2010). As a result, the authors argue that if consumers perceive that the underlying m-payment technology is trustworthy, they are more likely to adopt m-payment.

(3) Institution-based trust is the belief of consumers that necessary structural conditions for increasing the likelihood of gaining a successful outcome in an endeavour like m-payment, are present (McKnight, Choudhury & Kacmar 2002). These structural conditions are related to laws, regulations, institutions, legal protection, and the legal system, which contribute to the feelings of trustworthiness of an environment. Many researchers highlight that trust cannot be built without institutional infrastructures that set up and consolidate regulations in m-commerce and m-payment (Joubert & Belle 2009; McKnight, Choudhury & Kacmar 2002). Due to the importance of institution-based trust, many authors have employed it in research on e-commerce and m-commerce adoption (McKnight, Choudhury & Kacmar 2002; Min, Meng & Zhong 2008). As a result, the authors argue that if consumers perceive that they are protected by the third-party institutional mechanism, they are more likely to adopt m-payment.

(4) Seller trust is the degree to which the consumer trusts a community of sellers, and this is necessary for any e-commerce as well as social commercial activities (Lu, Fan & Zhou 2016). Andreev, Pliskin and Rafaeli (2012) pointed out that seller trust plays a vital role in m-commerce where there is an anonymous contact between sellers and buyers and a lack of formal contractual agreement, and found the significant impact of seller trust on willingness to accept m-payment of customers. Seller trust is adopted in many studies on e-commerce as well as m-payment adoption (Andreev, Pliskin & Rafaeli 2012; Lu, Fan & Zhou 2016; Pavlou & Gefen 2004). Obviously, a reputable seller must not only provide qualified goods, but also use a fast, accurate

and secured payment method. As a result, if customers trust reputable sellers accepting m-payment, customers are more likely to adopt m-payment.

The authors adopt these four types of trust for m-payment adoption, and propose the hypotheses below:

- *H1,2,3,4: M-payment provider trust, technology trust, institution-based trust, and seller trust positively influence m-payment adoption.*

Performance expectancy (PE) "is defined as the degree to which an individual believes that using the system will help him or her to attain gains in job performance" (Venkatesh et al. 2003, p. 447). The significant impact of PE on consumers' trust has been proven through many studies in e-commerce, m-commerce, and m-payment adoption (Li & Yeh 2010; Lin et al. 2014; Yan & Pan 2014; Yan & Yang 2014; Zhou 2011). As a result, the authors argue that if consumers perceive the usefulness or performance of m-payment, they may be more likely to trust m-payment technology and m-payment providers. This leads to the hypotheses:

- *H5,6: Performance expectancy positively influences m-payment provider trust and technology trust.*

Effort expectancy (EE) "is defined as the degree of ease associated with the use of the system" (Venkatesh et al. 2003, p. 450). Many studies in e-commerce, m-commerce, and m-payment have found that EE has significant impact on consumers' trust (Li & Yeh 2010; Yan & Pan 2014; Yan & Yang 2014; Zhou 2011). An easy to use m-payment application may reflect the ability and reliability of a m-payment provider and underlying technology. As a result, the authors argue that EE has a significant impact on m-payment provider trust and technology trust. This leads to the hypotheses:

- *H7,8: Effort expectancy positively influences m-payment provider trust and technology trust.*

Social influence (SI) is defined as "the degree to which an individual perceives that important others believe he or she should use the new system" (Venkatesh et al. 2003, p. 451). Basically, it conveys a notion that an individual's perception of society's expectations influences their behaviour. SI has been found to be an important driver for consumer trust in the adoption of mobile banking, online banking and e-commerce (Lu, Yao & Yu 2005; Malaquias & Hwang 2016; Montazemi & Qahri-Saremi 2015), for building institution-based trust in organisations (Bachmann & Inkpen 2011), and for seller trust in online shopping or e-commerce (Guo, Wang & Leskovec 2011; Lu, Fan & Zhou 2016; Pavlou & Gefen 2004). If a person perceives that people important to him/her trust m-payment applications and want him/her to use these, he/she is likely to generally trust m-payment including m-payment provider and technology. Similarly, citizens tend to trust sellers who have a good reputation in society. In addition, if m-payment is popular and trustworthy to citizens, the legal institutions must control and manage m-payment in order to ensure the legal rights of m-payment customers, and legal operations involved in m-payment. As a result, the authors argue that SI has a significant impact on m-payment provider trust, technology trust, institutional-based trust and seller trust of consumers in m-payment adoption. This leads to the hypotheses:

- *H9,10,11,12: Social influence positively affects m-payment provider trust, technology trust, institution-based trust, and seller trust.*

Disposition to trust (DT) refers "the extent to which a person displays a tendency to be willing to depend on others across a broad spectrum of situations and persons" (McKnight, Choudhury & Kacmar 2002, p. 339). The two studies of Joubert and Belle (2009) (2013) indicate the significant impact of DT on vendor trust, systems trust, and institutional-based trust of South African consumers in m-commerce adoption. McKnight, Choudhury and Kacmar (2002) identified the important effect of DT on institution-based trust when developing their web trust model of consumers in e-commerce. Meng, Min and Li (2008) suggested that DT has an important influence on mobile technology trust, mobile vendor trust, and institution-based trust. Pavlou and Gefen (2004) found out the significant impact of trust propensity on seller trust of e-commerce customers in Amazon's online auction marketplace. Lu, Fan and Zhou (2016) also recognised the important effect of DT on seller trust when researching trust and social commerce purchase intention in China. As a result, the authors argue that a person with high DT is more likely to have increased m-payment provider trust, technology trust, institutional-based trust, and seller trust in the adoption of m-payment. This leads to the hypotheses:

- *H13,14,15,16: Disposition to trust influence positively affects m-payment provider trust, technology trust, institution-based trust, and seller trust.*

Power distance (PD) reflects the inequality of power between managers and employees (Hofstede-insights 2018). In cultures with a high PD index, management decisions would be centralized and hierarchical, and people are more likely to comply with their managers' opinion. In contrast, in low PD societies, superiors and subordinates are more equal, therefore they are more interdependent. Interdependence is an important necessary condition for trust, therefore people in low PD societies tend to have more interpersonal trust than ones in high PD societies (Yoon 2009). Consequently, customers with high PD scores may have less trust toward m-payment adoption than ones with lower PD scores. This leads to the hypothesis:

- *H17. Power distance moderates the relationship between trust and m-payment adoption, in such a way that the relationship will be lower amongst people with higher power distance cultural values.*

Cultures with a long-term orientation (LTO) index are oriented toward future achievements when dealing with the challenges of the present and the future (Hofstede-insights 2018). Citizens with high LTO scores may be more likely to adopt m-payment because they are more aware of the long-term benefits of m-payment. As a result, customers with high LTO scores may have more trust toward m-payment adoption. This leads to the hypothesis:

- *H18. Long-term orientation moderates the relationship between trust and m-payment adoption, in such a way that the relationship will be stronger amongst people with long-term cultural values.*

People in individualistic cultures are expected to be more focused on themselves than with the group while ones in collectivistic cultures are sensitive to the group boundary (Hofstede 1993). As a result, citizens in collectivistic societies appreciate trusting members in a group, and trust less people outside their in-group. In contrast, individualistic citizens find it easier meeting new people, and tend to be more willing to rely on strangers (Yoon 2009). Consequently, people with individualist index may be more likely to have trust toward m-payment adoption than collectivists. This leads to the hypothesis:

- *H19. Individualism moderates the relationship between trust and m-payment adoption, in such a way that the relationship will be stronger amongst people with individualist cultural values.*

"The Masculinity side of this dimension represents a preference in society for achievement, heroism, assertiveness, and material rewards for success" (Hofstede-insights 2018). In a society with masculinity index, citizens tend to appreciate challenges, earnings, assertiveness, ambition, and dealing with facts (Minkov & Hofstede, 2010). People with high masculinity scores tend to adopt m-payment because they are more likely to value the benefits of m-payment more highly. This leads to the hypothesis:

- *H20. Masculinity moderates the relationship between trust and m-payment adoption, in such a way that the relationship will be stronger amongst people with masculine cultural values.*

"The Uncertainty Avoidance dimension expresses the degree to which the members of a society feel uncomfortable with uncertainty and ambiguity" (Hofstede-insights 2018). Cultures with high levels of uncertainty avoidance (UA) usually feel scared in uncertain situations (Ford, Connelly & Meister 2003). Consequently, citizens with high UA scores are expected to have a low rate of technology adoption and may have less trust toward m-payment adoption, because a new technology may be more risky than traditional payment methods. This leads to the hypothesis:

- *H21. Uncertainty avoidance moderates the relationship between trust and m-payment adoption, in such a way that the relationship will be weaker among people with higher levels of uncertainty avoidance values.*

Figure 1 below presents the overall model and the hypotheses.

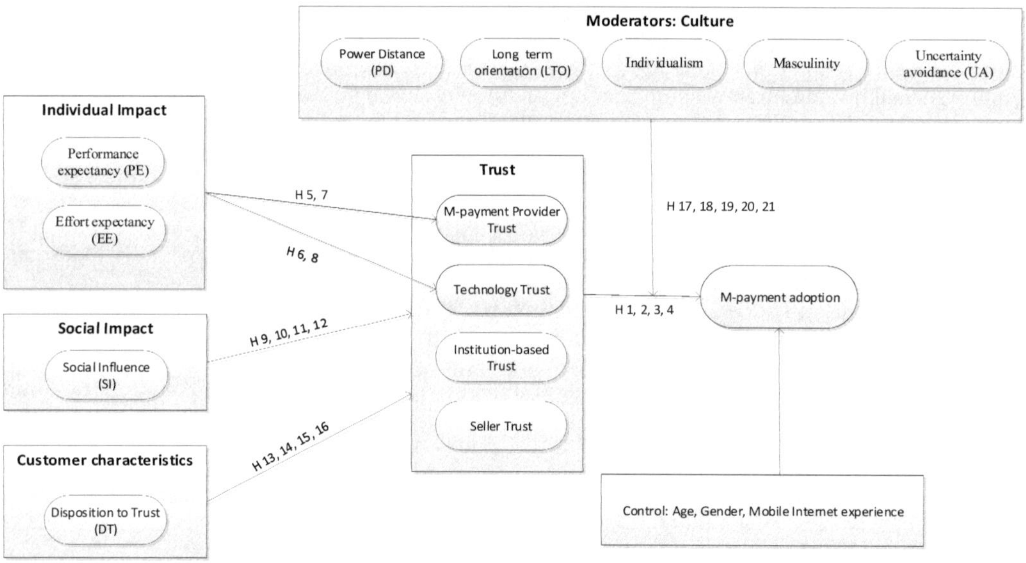

Figure 1. The conceptual model

4. CONCLUSION

M-payment benefits consumers, as well as, business due to the convenience, security, easier managing and monitoring of transactions, and improvement of the customer experience. As a result, m-payment should be considered as a powerful tool for both consumers and business performance. This research aims to address the issue of lacking understanding of the determinants of trust in m-payment adoption, and theorises trust as a multi-dimensional construct, with the consideration of the moderating role of culture on the four types of trust. This paper proposes a more comprehensive model of the critical determinants for trust in m-payment adoption, which may lead to more understanding for organisations, policy makers, m-payment services providers, and consultants to improve consumer trust when adopting m-payment. The model will be tested via an online survey in Vietnam and will be analysed using Structural Equation Modelling (SEM).

REFERENCES

Andreev, P, Pliskin, N & Rafaeli, S 2012, 'Drivers and inhibitors of mobile-payment adoption by smartphone users', *International Journal of E-Business Research (IJEBR)*, vol. 8, no. 3, pp. 50-67.

Bachmann, R & Inkpen, AC 2011, 'Understanding institutional-based trust building processes in inter-organizational relationships', *Organization Studies*, vol. 32, no. 2, pp. 281-301.

Baptista, G & Oliveira, T 2015, 'Understanding mobile banking: The unified theory of acceptance and use of technology combined with cultural moderators', *Computers in Human Behavior*, vol. 50, pp. 418-430.

Choi, J, Lee, HJ, Sajjad, F & Lee, H 2014, 'The influence of national culture on the attitude towards mobile recommender systems', *Technological Forecasting and Social Change*, vol. 86, pp. 65-79.

Coyle, D 2013, *The cost of mistrust*, OECD, viewed 14/12, <http://www.oecd.org/forum/the-cost-of-mistrust.htm>.

Eringa, K, Caudron, LN, Rieck, K, Xie, F & Gerhardt, T 2015, 'How relevant are Hofstede's dimensions for inter-cultural studies? A replication of Hofstede's research among current international business students', *Research in Hospitality Management*, vol. 5, no. 2, pp. 187-198.

Ford, DP, Connelly, CE & Meister, DB 2003, 'Information systems research and Hofstede's culture's consequences: an uneasy and incomplete partnership', vol. 50, no. 1, pp. 8-25.

Gao, L & Waechter, KA 2017, 'Examining the role of initial trust in user adoption of mobile payment services: an empirical investigation', *Information Systems Frontiers*, vol. 19, no. 3, pp. 525-548.

Guo, S, Wang, M & Leskovec, J 'The role of social networks in online shopping: information passing, price of trust, and consumer choice', ACM, pp. 157-166.

Hofstede-insights 2018, *NATIONAL CULTURE*, Hofstede-insights, viewed 27/12, <https://www.hofstede-insights.com/models/national-culture/>.

Hofstede, GH 1993, 'Cultures and organizations, software of the mind', *Administrative Science Quarterly*, vol. 38, pp. 132-134.

Jia, L, Hall, D & Zhu, S 2015, 'Trust building in consumer learning process and its effect on consumers' behavioral intention toward mobile payments', vol.

Jimenez, N, San-Martin, S & Azuela, JI 2016, 'Trust and satisfaction: the keys to client loyalty in mobile commerce', *Academia Revista Latinoamericana de Administración*, vol. 29, no. 4, pp. 486-510.

Joubert, J & Belle, J-PV 2009, 'The importance of trust and risk in M-commerce: A South African perspective', *PACIS 2009 Proceedings*, vol., p. 96.

Joubert, J & Belle, J-PV 2013, 'The role of trust and risk in mobile commerce adoption within South Africa', *International Journal of Business, Humanities and Technology*, vol. 3, no. 2, pp. 27-38.

Kolaki, M 2017, 'Mobile Payment Use and Mobile Payment Transactions by Older Adults: A Qualitative Study', thesis.

Kumar, B 2013, 'A Study on Mobile payment in Mobile Commerce', *International Journal of Enhanced Research in Management*, vol., pp. 1-8.

Lani, J 2018, *Moderator Variable*, Statistics solutions, viewed 12/12, <https://www.statisticssolutions.com/directory-of-statistical-analyses-general-moderator-variable/>.

Li, Y-M & Yeh, Y-S 2010, 'Increasing trust in mobile commerce through design aesthetics', *Computers in Human Behavior*, vol. 26, no. 4, pp. 673-684.

Lin, J, Wang, B, Wang, N & Lu, Y 2014, 'Understanding the evolution of consumer trust in mobile commerce: a longitudinal study', *Information Technology and Management*, vol. 15, no. 1, pp. 37-49.

Liu, B 'Understanding Consumers' Intention to Use Mobile Payment Services: The Perspective of University Students in Northern Jiangsu Area', IEEE, pp. 257-260.

Lu, B, Fan, W & Zhou, M 2016, 'Social presence, trust, and social commerce purchase intention: An empirical research', *Computers in Human Behavior*, vol. 56, pp. 225-237.

Lu, J, Yao, JE & Yu, C-S 2005, 'Personal innovativeness, social influences and adoption of wireless Internet services via mobile technology', *The Journal of Strategic Information Systems*, vol. 14, no. 3, pp. 245-268.

Lu, Y, Yang, S, Chau, PY & Cao, Y 2011, 'Dynamics between the trust transfer process and intention to use mobile payment services: A cross-environment perspective', *Information & Management*, vol. 48, no. 8, pp. 393-403.

Malaquias, RF & Hwang, Y 2016, 'An empirical study on trust in mobile banking: A developing country perspective', *Computers in Human Behavior*, vol. 54, pp. 453-461.

McKnight, DH, Choudhury, V & Kacmar, C 2002, 'Developing and validating trust measures for e-commerce: An integrative typology', *Information systems research*, vol. 13, no. 3, pp. 334-359.

Meng, D, Min, Q & Li, Y 'Study on trust in mobile commerce adoption-a conceptual model', IEEE, pp. 246-249.

MerchantSavvy 2019, *30 Amazing Stats Demonstrating The Unstoppable Rise of Mobile Payments Globally*, <https://www.merchantsavvy.co.uk/mobile-payment-stats-trends/>.

Min, Q, Meng, D & Zhong, Q 'An empirical study on trust in mobile commerce adoption', IEEE, pp. 659-664.

Mingxing, S, Jing, F & Yafang, L 'An empirical study on consumer acceptance of mobile payment based on the perceived risk and trust', IEEE, pp. 312-317.

Montazemi, AR & Qahri-Saremi, H 2015, 'Factors affecting adoption of online banking: A meta-analytic structural equation modeling study', *Information & Management*, vol. 52, no. 2, pp. 210-226.

Patil, P, Rana, N, Dwivedi, Y & Abu-Hamour, H 'The role of trust and risk in mobile payments adoption: a meta-analytic review',

Pavlou, PA & Gefen, D 2004, 'Building effective online marketplaces with institution-based trust', *Information systems research*, vol. 15, no. 1, pp. 37-59.

Pennington, R, Wilcox, HD & Grover, V 2003, 'The role of system trust in business-to-consumer transactions', *Journal of management information systems*, vol. 20, no. 3, pp. 197-226.

Phonthanukitithaworn, C, Sellitto, C & Fong, M 2015, 'User intentions to adopt mobile payment services: A study of early adopters in Thailand', *Journal of internet Banking and Commerce*, vol. 20, no. 1.

Qasim, H & Abu-Shanab, E 2016, 'Drivers of mobile payment acceptance: The impact of network externalities', *Information Systems Frontiers*, vol. 18, no. 5, pp. 1021-1034.

Siau, K & Shen, Z 2003, 'Building customer trust in mobile commerce', *Communications of the ACM*, vol. 46, no. 4, pp. 91-94.

Slade, E, Williams, M, Dwivedi, Y & Piercy, N 2015, 'Exploring consumer adoption of proximity mobile payments', *Journal of Strategic Marketing*, vol. 23, no. 3, pp. 209-223.

Srivastava, SC, Chandra, S & Theng, Y-L 2010, 'Evaluating the role of trust in consumer adoption of mobile payment systems: An empirical analysis', *Communications of the Association for Information Systems*, vol. 27, pp. 561-588.

Stringfellow, A 2018, *What is a mobile payment?*, viewed 3/01, <https://www.tccrocks.com/blog/what-is-a-mobile-payment/>.

Venkatesh, V, Morris, MG, Davis, GB & Davis, FD 2003, 'User acceptance of information technology: Toward a unified view', *MIS quarterly*, vol., pp. 425-478.

Venkatesh, V, Thong, JY & Xu, X 2012, 'Consumer acceptance and use of information technology: extending the unified theory of acceptance and use of technology', *MIS quarterly*, vol., pp. 157-178.

Williams, MD, Rana, NP & Dwivedi, YK 2015, 'The unified theory of acceptance and use of technology (UTAUT): a literature review', vol. 28, no. 3, pp. 443-488.

Xin, H, Techatassanasoontorn, AA & Tan, FB 2015, 'Antecedents of consumer trust in mobile payment adoption', *Journal of Computer Information Systems*, vol. 55, no. 4, pp. 1-10.

Yan, H & Pan, K 'Examine User Adoption of Mobile Payment Using the TAM: A Trust Transfer Perspective', p. 55.

Yan, H & Yang, Z 'An Empirical Examination of User Adoption Mobile Payment', IEEE, pp. 156-162.

Yoon, C 2009, 'The effects of national culture values on consumer acceptance of e-commerce: Online shoppers in China', *Information & Management*, vol. 46, no. 5, pp. 294-301.

Zhou, T 2011, 'The effect of initial trust on user adoption of mobile payment', *Information Development*, vol. 27, no. 4, pp. 290-300.

Zhou, T 2014, 'Understanding the determinants of mobile payment continuance usage', *Industrial Management & Data Systems*, vol. 114, no. 6, pp. 936-948.

DATA TRANSFER PROTOCOLS FOR BUSINESS SOCIAL NETWORKING

Venko Andonov, Valentin Kisimov, Tsvetana Stoyanova and Nikolay Sterev
University of National and World Economy, Sofia, Bulgaria

ABSTRACT

The next generation technologies are based on the smart communication between different users and product and services providers. Thus, the sharing economy could be explained as a process of continuous exchange of the information and data packages between different stakeholders. In these terms, the global economy is described as a global computer network and unstoppable data transfer between each two elements – global Business Social Network (BSN).

As the smooth Social Networking needs RULES for data transfer, the paper focuses not just on defining Business Social Networking requirements but on the main protocols for sharing information and for exchange data packages among the corporate participants of the BSN. Thus, the paper uses already defined three layers of the corporate BSNs as: Core layer of BSN, economic layer of BSN; social layer of BSN. **1.) Core Layer of Business Social Network (BSN)** defines the elements for logical protocol of data transfer that are similar to Traditional Social Network (TSN), but works outside a single corporation. Core of the BSN is the cooperation, project specific teaming, and business and solution generation discussions inside in a corporate division from one side or between particular divisions from the other. **2.) Economic Layer of Business Social Network (BSN)** express these elements of quantitative and qualitative indices of the business goals that are based on the function of the BSN. These indices are very important for the functioning of the contemporary sharing corporation and they could be neglected in the traditional corporations as: time saving; information partaking; social group participation and etc. **3.) Social Layer of Business Social Network (BSN)** gives the image of BSN as "talking structure" that allows to the users to exchange their opinions, emotions and behavior that are usually forbidden for expression at the traditional corporate networking.

The structure of the paper covers the next 4 elements: **Introduction**: the definitions of the sharing economy and digital platform's solutions are given as well as the explanation of the framework of BSN is presented. **1. Business-to-Business (B2B) communication protocols**: the architecture design of the BSN is explained and the main sets of communication protocols are given. Technical solution for the main B2B objects and their integration in BSN are proposed. **2. Web Social BSN protocols**: these protocols are elements of the interaction of the partners BSNs and they are specific in digital era. They allow social network be accepted as a interoperable service that is decentralized and distributed across distinct BSN's actors. **Conclusions**: the main results of the research are summarized in given architecture solution for a B2B BSN with two business partners participating in a non-centralized, distributed social network. Some limitations of the Electronic Data Interchange (EDI) are also discussed.

KEYWORDS

Business Social Network (BSN), B2B, Cross- Corporate BSN, BSN Logical Protocol, Web Social Protocol

1. INTRODUCTION

The expansion of the social networking (SN) nowadays is based on the opportunities that SNs provide to people for establishing connections with colleague or friends or for developing new friendships by person-to-person communications [Roberts and Roach, 2009 in Barczyk C., D. Duncan, 2011]. The SNs development is based on introduction of new generation of social media as a set of Internet-based applications that allow free exchange of User Generated Content through them. [Kaplan and Haenlein, 2010 in Barczyk C., D. Duncan, 2011; Benkler 2006].

The advantages of this virtualization of the person-to-person and resp. business-to business (B2B) relations is based on the main characteristics of digital networks: non-technical users, social type of users, and establishment of interpersonal relations [Agarwal and Mital, 2009 in Barczyk C., D. Duncan, 2011]. The future digitalization of B2B relations are based on further development of web applications and services that could introduce substantial changes to communication between businesses and different stakeholders as social and business communities, and individuals (clients) [Siricharoen, 2012].

The business accepts the Business Social Networks as an opportunity for instant messaging that make business more and more interactive as well as an opportunity for real time revision and update of the given information through social media channels [NMC, 2007 in Siricharoen, 2012]

Furthermore, business network is defined as a set of interconnected business relationships [Anderson et al., 1994 in Škarpová and Grosová, 2015]. Thus, business social network (BSN) is a set of people, preferably with a broad array of experience and knowledge, to which an individual is connected and with which the individual is in periodic contact. Ideally, any member of this BSN represent different stakeholders [Byham, 2008].

Thus, the BSN is established on three different layers: social; economic and core layers (Figure 1.)

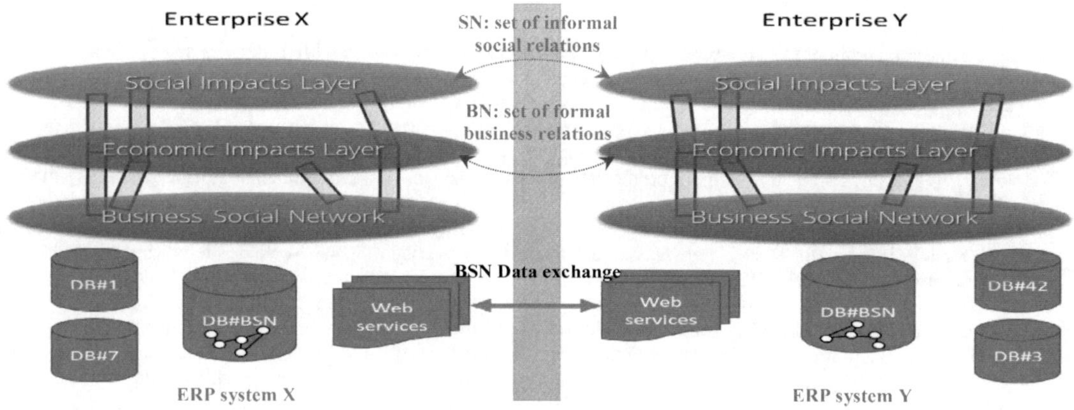

Source: Sterev, Kisimov, Stoyanova, Andonov, 2018a, 2018b

Figure 1. The data exchange for the B2B BSN communication through standard Internet-based web applications

The **Business Social Network Core Layer** defines the elements for logical protocol of data transfer:

- the objects, the relationships between them and how they are stored and processed, including the rules and constraints defined by the business requirements;
- the interlayer relationships between the defined objects and the indicators in the economic and social impact layers;
- the cross-business relationships between the objects defined as part of the communication protocol between any given business entities.

The abstract object types of the **BSN core layer** include:

- an **AGENT** – a user or automated process, participating in the Business Social Network; forms relationships with other Agents or other Content objects;
- a **CONTENT ITEM** – any object that might be shared in the BSN as part of the discussion and collaboration between the Agents; forms relationships with other Content items and different Agents;
- a **DYNAMIC DATA STRUCTURE** – contains a definition of a data structure that is populated manually or automatically during the collaboration and cross-teaming effort; forms relationships with other data structures, content items and agents;
- a GROUP – an object which unites multiple Agents, Content items and Dynamic data structures under a specific unique identity with its own permission structure; forms relationships with other Groups, Agents, Content items and Dynamic data structures.

In order to manage the digital data transfer among BSN, the architecture of the BSN Core layer follows these 5 principles:

- The network consists of multiple nodes (each business enterprise might have their own node).
- The nodes are dependent of each other only as much as defined in the security and privacy protocol configuration.
- There is no central authority that manages the whole network of multiple business entities – each node is feature-complete and is capable to function properly on its own.

- The inclusion of a new node in the business network consists of two main steps: defining its own security and privacy configuration; each of the other nodes in the network should add the new node with their own proper security and privacy configuration.
- It is possible for a given node to participate in different business networks with different security and privacy configurations

2. BUSINESS-TO-BUSINESS (B2B) COMMUNICATION PROTOCOLS

As the BSN is distributed on multiple nodes, typically in separate business enterprises (the concrete implementation might vary), there is no central server that would encapsulate the whole network since such a network requires strict security and privacy rules as discussed above. Furthermore, a central authority would require a centralized management of the system, which would be a significant organizational and managerial overhead for a system that tries to improve and optimize the business processes and communication between separate business entities.

Our view of a B2B BSN is as a distributed system of multiple nodes without a central authority, which communicate with each other over a strict set of protocol rules in order to achieve information sharing within the bounds of the defined objects and relationships.

Physically, the nodes might be single servers, server clusters, cloud servers or any other solution that might fit the technological organization of a given business entity. Each person within the given business entity accesses only their own service, which, on the other hand, communicates with the other nodes in the predefined social network in order to perform a requested operation. This architecture allows for federated machine learning as well – the ability to train ML models on separate nodes without sharing the raw data.

2.1 RPC - Remote Procedure Calls

Historically, especially until the mid-90s, most computers interacted with each other using **Remote Procedure Calls (RPC)**. This is client-server interaction model, where a client executes a procedure on a remote server in order to perform a specific operation and optionally receive results back [Baer, 2018].

The idea is to allow the developer to treat the procedures in the remote environment as if they were local, of course considering the network overhead and unreliability. Since it is unconstrained by the structure of data, highly specialized methods can be written for clients that request and retrieve exactly the information needed which can result in minimal network overhead and smaller payloads. The local and the remote systems are tightly coupled, the boundaries between the local and the remote code are lost [Baer, 2018]. This might lead to many types of difficulties in the management, maintenance and further development and this is one of the main reasons the standard RPC are considered obsolete nowadays.

- **gRPC** is a modernized alternative of the classical RPC approach. It is an open source, high performance RPC framework that can run in any environment. Initially, it was developed within Google for internal use. It can efficiently connect services (usually microservices) with pluggable support for load balancing, tracing, health checking and authentication. **gRPC** can be used also to connect devices, mobile applications and browsers to backend services. It is usually implemented for communication between services in a microservices style architecture; for connecting mobile devices and browser clients to backend services; for generating efficient client libraries [gRPC Network, 2019].

2.2 Web Services

- **SOAP** (Simple Object Access Protocol) is a protocol specification for XML based communication between applications (typically distributed). It has been created to address some of the practical problems and difficulties of RPC, by creating a well-structured foundation for complex web services. The enforceable contracts in the WSDL and WADL between the client and server guarantee predictable, type-safe results, and the WSDL can be used to generate documentation or to create integrations with IDEs and other tools. The most significant downside of SOAP is that it is very verbose and in practice, requires sophisticated tools in order to develop and debug systems based on it. Tools are necessary for testing, for inspection, parsing the data. There are still many systems operating with SOAP nowadays, but it is typically not recommended for new projects since it is considered impractical and too verbose [Baer, 2018].

- **REST** (Representational State Transfer), unlike SOAP, does not use client-server contracts, is much more concise and does not require special tools. It uses the HTTP (Hypertext Transfer Protocol) like verbs and URIs to reference and perform operations on a resource in some hierarchy of data. REST completely and explicitly changes API design from modeling interactions to modeling the data of a domain. Being fully resource-oriented when working with a REST API, the developer does not have to know anything about the implementation of the backend services.

REST services typically take multiple round trips between client and server to get enough data to render an application. This cascade of requests has devastating performance impacts, especially on mobile. Another problem with REST services is that the send way more information than is needed. There are a lot of projects that attempt to fix the shortcomings: HAL, Swagger/OpenAPI, OData, JSON API and more.

- In **GraphQL**, on the server, the data is described as a graph of interconnections, and the client asks specifically for the subset of the data that it needs [Baer, 2018]. This approach solved two of the most significant drawbacks of the classical REST services – generating too many requests and responses for related data entities, as well as transferring data that is irrelevant to the current context. Currently, it is considered to be the state-of-the-art approach for distributed applications communication, as it proposes solutions for the shortcomings of the earlier standards.

2.3 Other Client-Server Protocols

File Transfer Protocol (FTP) is a protocol for computers connected through the Internet (and other TCP/IP networks) to securely transfer files between each other [ArcESB, 2019]. FTP is used for many types of file transfer, for example, website updates and bulk file transfers. FTP is the most widely used file transfer protocol, but due to security issues, most organizations only use FTP for transferring files within the organization. The big drawbacks are that it doesn't encrypt data in transit and uses separate command and data channels [ArcESB, 2019].

Often, businesses connecting through FTP use a virtual private network (VPN), which provides an extra layer of security around transactions.

- **SFTP** is an enhanced version of FTP with a different security layer - SSH. This security layer encrypts the messages while in transit and decrypts the messages upon arrival. SFTP requires the server to authenticate the client computer. All commands and data are encrypted to prevent passwords and other sensitive information from being exposed to the network in plain text. Unlike FTP, SFTP does protect data during transmission and doesn't use separate command and data channels - it transfers data and commands in formatted packets with one secure connection.
- **FTPS** is also an alternative approach - FTP over SSL/TSL - adds a secure encryption layer (Secure Sockets Layer) around the FTP protocol to secure the commands and data transferred between client and server.
- **Odette File Transfer Protocol (OFTP)** is a communications technology built specifically for B2B document exchange. Unlike the basic FTP protocols, it can provide digitally signed electronic delivery receipts and provides multiple security features – transport security with TLS, file encryption, partner authentication [ArcESB, 2019; Odette, 2019].

3. SOCIAL NETWORKING PROTOCOLS

3.1 Definition of Social Networking Protocols

A distributed (also called federated) social network is an interoperable service that is decentralized and distributed across distinct entities. A social website participating in a distributed social network is interoperable with the other sites in the same network and is in federation with them. Communication among them is conducted over social networking protocols [Esguerra, 2011]. There have been numerous different standards over the years since this is a popular issue in the public space because of the privacy concerns with the centralized social networks (like Facebook, Twitter and others).

The Social Web Protocols are a collection of standards which enable various aspects of decentralized social interaction on the Web [W3C, 2017]. People and the content they create are the core components of the social web; they make up the so called "social graph". The Social Web Protocols describe a way in which people can: create, update and delete social content; connect with other people by subscribing to their content; interact with other peoples' content; be notified when other people interact with their content. regardless of what that content is or where it is stored [W3C, 2017]. These components are core building blocks for interoperable decentralized social systems. Each of these components can be implemented and extended to meet domain-specific requirements, such in the case of distributed B2B communication.

The Social Web Protocols define the following structures: Social Data Syntax - A JSON-based syntax to allow the transfer of social information; Social API - defines a specification for a client-side API that lets developers embed and format third party information; Federation Protocol - allows the federation of activity-based status updates and other data (such as profile information) between heterogeneous social systems [W3C, 2017].

- **ActivityStreams 2.0** is the recommended syntax and vocabulary for social data. It represents content and interactions as Objects and Activities. The ActivityStreams vocabulary defines a finite set of common Object and Activity types and properties, as well as an extension mechanism for applications which want to expand on or specialize these [W3C, 2017].
- **ActivityPub** provides two layers: a server to server federation protocol (so decentralized websites can share information); a client to server protocol (so users, including real-world users, bots, and other automated processes, can communicate with ActivityPub using their accounts on servers, from a phone or desktop or web application) [W3C, 2018]. ActivityPub uses ActivityStreams for its vocabulary.

ActivityStreams includes all the common terms that are typically needed to represent all the activities and content flowing around a social network. If this vocabulary is not enough for a given use case, it is possible to use JSON-LD to extend it.

ActivityPub uses authentication for two purposes; first, to authenticate clients to servers, and secondly in federated implementations to authenticate servers to each other. ActivityPub clients authenticate against a server using OAuth 2.0 bearer tokens. Server to server federation is authenticated using HTTP Signatures in conjunction with the signing key from the actor's publicKey field. The keyId should link to the actor so that the publicKey field can be retrieved. At minimum, the digest field should be included in the set of headers being signed. For most forms of delivery, HTTP Signatures is enough. However, some objects may be passed around the network, whether being shared, forwarded, or otherwise referenced at a future time. In this case it is important to be able to verify that the actors specified in the actor and attributedTo fields really did author the objects they are being claimed to have authored. In such a case we need to be able to verify the integrity of the object being passed around, and so we must sign the object itself. For this we use Linked Data Signatures to sign the object with the publicKey of the actor that is the actor or attributed to of the object being passed around the network.

Servers should not trust client submitted content, and federated servers also should not trust content received from a server other than the content's origin without some form of verification. They should also implement protections against denial-of-service attacks from other servers. This can be done using rate limiting mechanisms or algorithms for anomaly detection. Servers should be especially careful to implement this protection around activities that involve side effects.

Working implementations of these standards are Mastodon[1] and Friendi.ca [2], which are both free and open source software products for distributed, decentralized social networking.

[1] https://joinmastodon.org/

[2] https://friendi.ca/

3.2 Security and Privacy Configuration of a B2B-BSN: Node and Network

The security and privacy configuration of a node consists of a strictly formatted, machine-readable description of the permissions of each object type related to a specific other connected node.

Zot is a web standard and framework for implementing secure decentralized communications and services [Hubzilla, 2019]. The main difference with other communication standards is that it is built on top of a decentralized identity and authentication framework. The authentication is similar to OpenID conceptually but is insulated from DNS-based identities. Remote authentication should be silent and invisible to the end-user of the system. This provides a mechanism for internet scale distributed access control which is unobtrusive [Hubzilla, 2019]. Zot supports a wide array of background services in the grid, from friend suggestions to directory services. New content and data updates are propagated in the background between the nodes in the network according to access control lists and permissions specified by both sender and receiver channels.

Zot's identity layer allows each of the business partners to provide granular permissions to any content - social or source business document - and these permissions extend across the partner network. Access can be granted or denied for any resource, to any channel, or any group of channels; anywhere within the B2B network.

4. B2B - BSN SOLUTION AND CONCLUSION

Summarizing the main rules for architecture and protocols organization of B2B Business social networking the main web solution for BSN with two business partners participating in a non-centralized, distributed social network is presented on Figure 2.

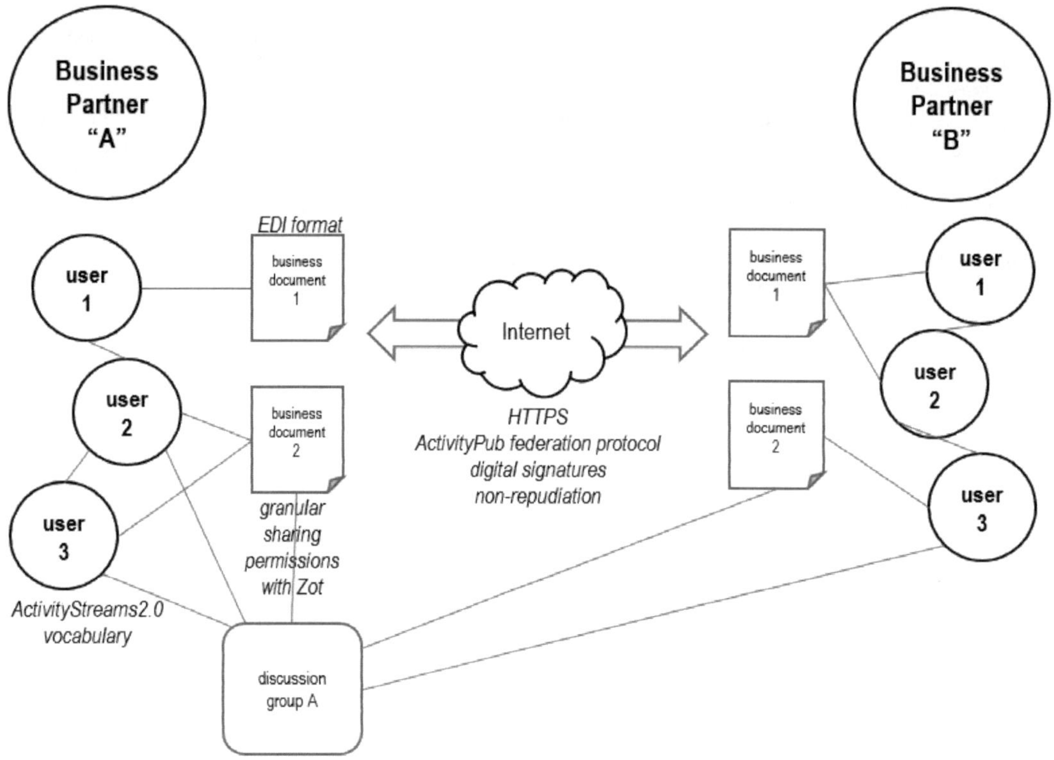

Figure 2. B2B – BSN Web solution

The given on Figure 2 data transfer between 2 business enterprises in web based BSN needs to explain furthermore main data transfer formats.

Electronic Data Interchange (EDI) is a communications technology and a group of standards used to exchange business documents and information between organizations. It can handle multiple types of data, including but not limited to orders, invoices, quotes, shipment data, insurance information [ArcESB, 2019]. The goal of EDI is to replace the manual, often paper-based, B2B communications, such as postal mail, fax and email. Documents are sent directly from the sender's computer system to the receiver's system. These systems might be ERP-s, CRM-s, SCM-s or any type of business information system. There are a variety of EDI standards for various industries, regions and use cases - each with different versions, so EDI partners must use the same standard and version. Popular standards include: ANSI X12 in the United States, UN/EDIFACT globally and industry-specific standards, such as HIPAA (health insurance in the U.S.), HL7 (for international healthcare data exchange), EANCOM (in the retail sector), ROSETTANET (electronics) and others. This diversity creates a significant implementation difficulty as the software developers should cover multiple protocols and the possibility of conversion. Typical documents transferred through EDI are: orders, quotes, invoices, shipping notices, product information, pricing and other depending on the specific industry.

EDI protocols are the different descriptions of data and communication formats that might be used to transfer data securely from one company to their partner. Each protocol reflects a set of universal guidelines that dictate how the data is encrypted and configured while in transit [3]. In direct EDI, also known as point-to-point EDI, each business partner connects directly to the other. An alternative approach is an indirect connectivity – using the so-called Value-Added Networks (VAN), which act as middlemen for the data exchange and help with the setup and the conversions between the different protocols.

- The **AS1 (Applicability Statement 1)** EDI Protocol describes methods to use the e-mail protocols to transfer data in a secure and reliable way. The AS1 protocol is based on SMTP and S/MIME. It was the first AS protocol developed and uses signing, encryption and message delivery notifications conventions. Files are sent as attachments in a specially coded S/MIME email message [ArcESB, 2019].
- **AS2** is the second-generation EDI protocol - it is the most widely used EDI standard nowadays [ArcESB, 2019]. AS2 defined how to transfer the business documents over the Internet using the HTTP (more specifically – HTTPS). An envelope of the transferred data is created so it can be sent securely - using digital certificates, signatures and encryption. It also supports signed receipts to ensure that the business partner actually received the message. Since the AS2 protocol operates over ordinary HTTP, it can easily pass through firewalls and utilize optional transport level SSL encryption and HTTP authentication. The digital certificates are used to encrypt the documents sent over the public Internet, with digital signatures to guarantee integrity and non-repudiation [Ruparathna, 2017].
- **AS3** is built on File Transfer Protocol (FTP). It also enables the business partners to securely send and receive documents. AS3 enables push and pull FTP capabilities, similar to setups in asynchronous and bi-synchronous environments. It is not used as much as AS2 and AS4. As discussed above, the standard FTP can be replaced by FTPS or SFTP for a more secure data transfer.
- **AS4** is a web-services (more specifically SOAP) update to AS2, built largely on the OASIS ebMS framework. The Message Service Specification (ebMS) describes a communication-neutral mechanism that must be implemented in order to exchange business documents [OASIS 2019, ArcESB 2019]. ebMS is built as an extension on top of the SOAP with Attachments specification. The SOAP message contains the metadata required to exchange the business document in a secure and reliable manner, while the business payload is attached to the SOAP message [OASIS 2019]. AS4 can transport any type of document as defined by the EDI standard. It maintains the integrity and the confidentiality of the business data by using the WS-Security standard. It provides password authentication, digital signatures and encryption; transport security with TLS; authenticity verification of the sender; ensures messages are unaltered in transit; provides non-repudiation.

ACKNOWLEDGEMENT

The paper is prepared as a part of the research activities under the project "Knowledge Economy based on business platforms and enterprises' networks" (DN 05/17/2016), financed by the Bulgarian National Science Fund.

REFERENCES

Agarwal, S., Mital, M., 2009, An exploratory study of Indian university students'' use of social networking web sites: Implications for the workplace, *Business Communication Quarterly*, 105, March. 2009

Anderson, C. J., Håkansson, H., Johanson, J., 1994, Dyadic Business Relationships Within a Business Network Context. *Journal of Marketing*, 58 (4) / 1994, 1-15.

ArcESB, 2019, *What is EDI*? The Complete Guide to Electronic Data Interchange, [Online]. Available: https://www.arcesb.com/resources/edi/. [Accessed 2019].

Baer E., 2018, *A GraphQL Primer: Why We Need A New Kind Of API* (Part 1), Smashing Magazine, January 2018. [Online]. Available: https://www.smashingmagazine.com/2018/01/graphql-primer-new-api-part-1/.

Barczyk C., D. Duncan, 2011, Social Networking Media as a Tool for Teaching Business Administration Courses, *International Journal of Humanities and Social Science*, Vol. 1 No. 17 / 2001

Benkler Y., 2006, *The wealth of networks: how social production transforms markets and freedom*, New Haven, Conn: Yale University Press, pp.528.

Byham W.C., 2008, *Business Networking: A Necessary Third Millennium Skill*, White Paper Development Dimensions International, Inc., https://www.ddiworld.com/ddi/media/white-papers/BusinessNetworkingbyham_wp_ddi.pdf

Esguerra E. R., 2011, *An Introduction to the Federated Social Network*, Electronic Frontier Foundation (EFF), 2011. [Online]. Available: https://www.eff.org/deeplinks/2011/03/introduction-distributed-social-network.

gRPC Network, 2019, *About gRPC*, [Online]. Available: https://grpc.io/about/. [Accessed 2019].

Hoffman C., 2019, *How HTTP/3 and QUIC Will Speed Up Your Web Browsing*," How-To-Geek, September 2019. [Online]. Available: https://www.howtogeek.com/442047/how-http3-and-quic-will-speed-up-your-web-browsing/.

Hubzilla, 2019, *Zot Protocol*, [Online]. Available: https://zotlabs.org/help/en/developer/zot_protocol. [Accessed 2019].

Kaplan, A. and Haenlein, M., 2010, Users of the world, unite! The challenges and opportunities of social media, *Business Horizons*, 53(1), pp. 59-68.

OASIS, 2019, *About ebXML*," [Online]. Available: http://www.ebxml.org/geninfo.htm.

Odette, 2019, *OFTP2*, [Online]. Available: https://www.odette.org/services/oftp2 [Accessed 2019].

Roberts, S. and Roach, T., 2009, Social networking web sites and human resource personnel: Suggestions for job searches, *Business Communication Quarterly*, pp. 110-114.

Ruparathna R., 2017, *AS2 Protocol for Business Data Interchange via HTTP*, DZone Devada Media, 2017. [Online]. Available: https://dzone.com/articles/as2-protocol-for-business-data-interchange-via-htt.

Siricharoen W. V., 2012, Social Media, how does it Work for Business? International Journal of Innovation, *Management and Technology*, Vol. 3, No. 4, August 2012

Škarpová L., G.Stanislava, 2015, The Application of Business Network Approach for Small and Medium Enterprises (SME) with regard to their Buying Behavior, *Journal of Competitiveness*, Vol. 7, Issue 3, pp. 62-74, September 2015

Sterev, Kisimov, Stoyanova, Andonov, 2018a, Multidimencial Framework for Crosscorporate Business Social Network (BSN), *Proceedings of 11th IADIS International Conference on Information Systems (IS 2018)*, Lisbon, Portugal 14- 16 April 2018

Sterev, Kisimov, Stoyanova, Andonov, 2018b, INDUSTRY 4.0 NEEDS of Business Social Network (BSN)), *Proceedings of ICEIRD 2018,* Doha, Qatar, 28-30 Oct 2018

The New Media Consortium (NMC), 2007, The "Third place," and The Evolution of Communication. [Online]. Available: http://creativecommons.org/licenses/by-sa/3.0/us/.

W3C, 2017, *Social Web Protocols*, World Wide Web Consortium (W3C), December 2017. [Online]. Available: https://www.w3.org/TR/social-web-protocols/.

W3C, 2018, *ActivityPub*, World Wide Web Consortium (W3C), January 2018. [Online]. Available: https://www.w3.org/TR/activitypub/.

WATER BALANCE OPTIMIZATION: CASE STUDY BY THE FAO PENMAN-MONTEITH MODEL IN APPLE TREE CULTIVATION (MALUS DOMESTICA BORKH) SUPPORTED BY WEB, BIO-BIO, CHILE

Marcos Lévano[1], Camilo Friz[2] and Billy Peralta[3]
[1]*Computer Engineering Department, Catholic University of Temuco*
Ave. Manuel Montt 56, Mailbox 15-D, Temuco, Chile
[2]*Software Development Consultant, Los Angeles, Chile*
[3]*Departamento de Ciencias de la Ingeniería, Universidad Andres Bello*
Antonio Varas 880, piso 6, Providencia, Región Metropolitana, Chile

ABSTRACT

This paper proposes a framework for water resource optimization by balanced use, where a case study by the FAO Penman-Monteith model is presented in the cultivation of apple fruit (Malus Doméstica Borkh) in a region of Chile called "Bio-Bio". A technological support by Web is proposed for water balance in calculating the evapotranspiration (evaporation and transpiration) as an important variable in an abundant irrigation activity. The results generate recommendations to Chilean authorities in agriculture about how to care for water in these times of water shortages for rational use.

KEYWORDS

Water Optimization, Productivity Increasing, Web Technology, Apple Fruit

1. INTRODUCTION

The amount of water that a crop needs through its different stages of vegetative development, a term that is expressed as use-consumption or evapotranspiration (Sanjay & Lakshman, 2020), is a fundamental antecedent in the determination of irrigation rates, in the irrigation planning both at property and regional level, in the design of method and structures of irrigation, distribution of water, etc. However, use-consumption values determined in one place have a limited extrapolation area because this factor is strongly influenced by the place climatic characteristics for a specific crop (Tosso, 1976). On the other hand, the use-consumption measurements require several years of experimentation so that they are representative, requiring, in addition, equipment and specialized personnel. According to Xiaojie (Xiaojie et al., 2019) and (Sanjay & Lakshman, 2020), it is possible to make estimates of evapotranspiration knowing the relationship between both parameters (use-consumption and evaporation) in the different stages of the crop vegetative development. This relationship is known as evapotranspiration K coefficient.

In this paper the water resource balance for the apple tree (Malus Doméstica Borkh) was made, the evapotranspiration was estimated manually and with support of computational program by Web technology through the Penman-Monteith model (Penman, 1948; Monteith, 1965; Sanjay & Lakshman, 2020).

Drought, desertification and degraded soil, 76% of the country's surface is affected by drought, desertification and degraded soil. This is 57.5 million hectares. There live 11.6 million inhabitants: 65% of the national population. 22% of the country's surface shows desertification signs to some degree, 80% show soil degradation signs and 72% of drought effects. That is the diagnosis with which Chile is updating its strategy and 2016-2030 national plan before the UN Convention to combat Desertification and Drought. The combined action of the three problems affects 76% of the national territory: 57.5 million hectares where 11.6 million people live (65% of the national population) (Schneider et al., 2007; BM, 2011; CONAMA, 2010).

The ozone layer destruction is the result of that according to what is estimated in 2009 in the country generated 16.9 million waste tons, of which 6.5 million corresponded to municipal waste and 10.4 million to industrial waste, excluding the massive mining waste (CONAMA, 2010).

Climate change has caused global warming, which in some areas is causing a great water shortage for people, as well as their own crops that are their main source of food.

In Chile there are few studies on the subject. Internationally, changes are expected in temperate and tropical zones that would negatively affect, for example, wheat (Triticum vulgare L.) and corn cultivations (Zea Mays L.)

Water resources management under scarce conditions is a complex challenge and it's of vital importance for the development of crops in Chile and in the rest of the world (Schneider et al., 2007; BM, 2011, MMA, 2011). For this reason it is extremely urgent to find and develop tools that better enable us to optimize the water resource used in crops. It is here that information technologies are a perfect formula for the crop efficiency and profitability. Where management and irrigation are the ones that make a crop obtain the best results through the use of data (meteorological, crop and ground). All these data must be managed by software that manages and provides relevant information for the optimum result of the crop.

The apple tree (Malus domestica Borkh) (Lobos and Yuri, 2006) is one of the first trees cultivated by man, tracing its domestication to the tenth century; Its center of origin is in Asia being introduced to Europe by the Romans and brought to America by the English in the seventeenth century. In Chile apple tree is the second fruit species in planted area, with about 37,000 ha mainly in the VI and VII region. Production is estimated at 700,000 tons, and exports at about 620,000 tons (Falvey and Garreaud, 2009). The apple tree for its cultivation needs certain climatic requirements (thermal, wind and evapotranspiration and crop coefficient), being the most important evapotranspiration since it must start the crop with an abundant irrigation activity that allows the roots to begin the new season.

Evapotranspiration (ET) is a main input of the framework to estimate water consumption of a crop. The most used methodology to estimate water resource consumption in a crop is the one recommended by Allen et al. (Allen et al., 1998), where ET is estimated as a function of actual evapotranspiration (ETr) and a crop coefficient (kc). ETr is calculated using the Penman-Monteith equation (Penman, 1948; Monteith, 1965; Sanjay & Lakshman, 2020) which requires simultaneous measurements of temperature, humidity, wind speed and solar radiation. In this methodology there are errors associated with the values of the crop coefficient, since they cannot be used generically and require a greater calibration, (Simonne et al., 2010).

For this reason, a model of optimization of the water resource in technified irrigation crops for the Apple tree (Malus Doméstica Borkh) is proposed, using a systematic framework: Web technology and the mathematical model FAO Penman-Monteith (Tosso, 1986; Lobos and Yuri, 2006) in the Region of Bío-Bío Chile.

The paper presents a section of introduction, theoretical framework, proposal framework, results, conclusions and references.

2. THEORETICAL FRAMEWORK

The main meteorological factors that determine evapotranspiration are:

2.1 Evaporation

Evaporation is the process by which liquid water turns to water vapor (vaporization) and it's removed from the evaporating surface (vapor removal) (Allen et al., 1998; Zotarelli et al., 2010). Water evaporates from a variety of surfaces such as lakes, rivers, roads, soils and wet vegetation. To change the water molecules state from liquid to vapor requires energy. Direct solar radiation and, to a lesser extent, the ambient air temperature, provide this energy. The driving force to remove water vapor from an evaporating surface is the difference between the water vapor pressure at the evaporating surface and the water vapor pressure of the surrounding atmosphere. Therefore, radiation, air temperature, atmospheric humidity and wind speed are climatic parameters to be considered when evaluating the evaporation process (Zotarelli et al., 2010).

2.2 Transpiration

Transpiration consists of the vaporization of the liquid water contained in the tissues of the plant and its subsequent removal into the atmosphere (Zotarelli et al., 2010). Crops lose water predominantly through the stomata. These are small openings in the plant leaf through which gases and water vapor flow through the plant into the atmosphere. Water, along with some nutrients, is absorbed by the roots and transported through the plant. Vaporization occurs within the leaf, in the intercellular spaces and the exchange of vapor with the atmosphere is controlled by the stomatal opening. Almost all the water absorbed from the soil is lost by transpiration and only a small fraction becomes part of the plant tissues.

2.3 Evapotranspiration

Evaporation and transpiration occur simultaneously and there is no simple way to distinguish between these two processes. Apart from water availability in the surface horizons, the evaporation of a cultivated soil is mainly determined by the fraction of solar radiation that reaches the soil surface. This fraction decreases throughout the crop cycle as the crop canopy projects more and more shade over the soil (Zotarelli et al., 2010; Allen et al., 1998). In the early stages of cultivation, water is lost mainly by the soil direct evaporation, but with the development of the crop and, finally, when it completely covers the soil, transpiration becomes the main process.

2.4 Penman-Monteith Equation

Penman combined the energy balance with the mass transfer method and derived an equation to calculate the evaporation of an open surface of water from standard weather data for sun hours, temperature, atmospheric humidity and wind speed (Zotarelli et al., 2010). This method known as combined was subsequently developed by many researchers and extended to cultivated surfaces by means of the introduction of resistance factors. The nomenclature on resistance distinguishes between aerodynamic resistance and surface resistance. The surface resistance parameters are often combined in a single value, that of the total surface resistance that is combined in series with the aerodynamic drag. The surface resistance (rs) describes the resistance to vapor flow through the stomata, the total leaf area and the soil surface. Aerodynamic drag (ra) describes the resistance in the part immediately above the vegetation and includes the friction that the air undergoes when flowing on vegetative surfaces. Although the vegetation exchange process is too complex to be fully described by the two resistance factors mentioned above, good correlations are obtained between the measured and calculated evapotranspiration values, especially in the case of a uniform pasture surface (Zotarelli et al., 2010; Tosso, 1976; Penman, 1948; Monteith, 1965; Sanjay & Lakshman, 2020), equation 1,

$$ET_{sz} = \frac{0.408\Delta(R_n - G) + \gamma\frac{C_n}{T+273}u_2(e_s^0 - e_a)}{\Delta + \gamma(1 + C_d u_2)},$$

Where, ET_{sz} is standarized evapotranspiration in units over time mmd^{-1} to 24 hrs of day or mmh^{-1} during 1 hour. C_n is the crop type constant numerator. C_d is the constant denominator for the reference crop type. G is the density of the soil heat flux MJ $m^{-2}d^{-1}$. e_s is the saturation vapor (KPa). e_a is the current vapor pressure (KPa). R_n is the net radiation on the crop surface MJ $m^{-2}d^{-1}$. u_2 is the wind speed at 2 meters high, ms^{-1}. Δ is the slope of the vapor pressure curve, kPa°C^{-1} . γ is the psychrometric constant, kPa°C^{-1} . T is the air average temperature at 2 meters high, °C.

3. DEVELOPMENT

3.1 Methodology

Iterative and incremental development is carried out (Sommerville, 2016), being the software base the most important, which is the calculation and estimation of variables with the model previously seen. Where it is contributed to the irrigation schedule, since it is intended to finish until the complete automation of a farm irrigation.

- Calculation of a crop evapotranspiration (Sanjay & Lakshman, 2020). This is the critical point. Although they have been investigated for years, some data and formulas are still experimental, but they are recognized by FAO (Zotarelli et al., 2010), so they have international scientific support. In addition, existing meteorological data should be used, and those calculated with moving averages
- Calculation of water volume to be applied by irrigation. At this point the crop and soil variables must be used. It is also essential that the values are correct, because with this point is delivered how much water needs the crop to not lose water by applying it unnecessarily, or to apply less water and pass the crop by water stress.
- Calculation of water scheduling to be applied by irrigation. This step is the one that generates the dates to apply the irrigation, delivering the optimal point of water application.

3.2 Design and Coding

In the case of design and coding, the following stages must be followed in software development:

3.2.1 System Requirements

Within the system functional requirements (Sepúlveda et al., 2015), there is the generation of an irrigation calendar, in which it gives the date of the next irrigations and the amount of water to be applied to the required crop with the use of climatic variables, soil and type of technical irrigation. Also within the non-functional requirements, is to facilitate the entry of data, in relation to the locality to be evaluated, the type of technified soil and irrigation, so that an untrained user can use the system functions without complications. For hardware requirements, this system must be deployed on a low-fault-tolerant infrastructure and with the minimum requirements for the use of a web server and database.

3.2.2 Use-Case Diagram

The following is the use case diagram (Figure 1), which analyzes the behavior and interaction of the user with the system.

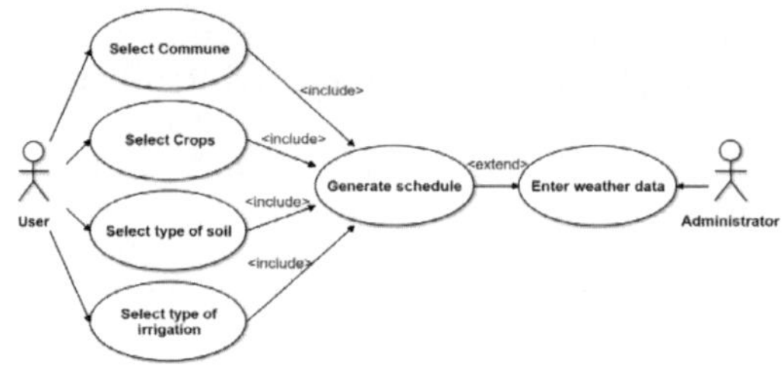

Figure 1. Use case diagram

Description:

- Select Commune: The commune is selected to obtain weather data.
- Select Crop: The crop to be irrigated is selected.
- Type of soil: The soil type is selected to obtain estimated data of the soil physical conditions.
- Select type of irrigation: The type of irrigation is selected to obtain estimated data of the irrigation water efficiency.
- Generate schedule: daily weather data are entered.

3.2.3 Flowchart

This provides a visual description of the activities involved in a process, showing the sequential relationship between them and facilitating a quick understanding of each activity and its relationship with others. The flow diagram of the irrigation scheduling system (Figure 2) is presented below.

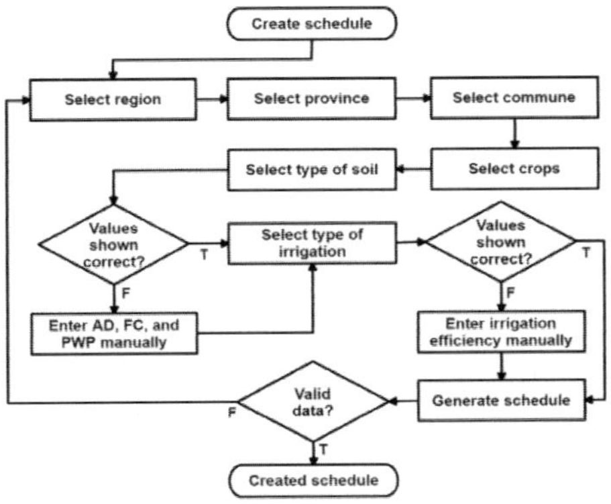

Figure 2. System Flowchart

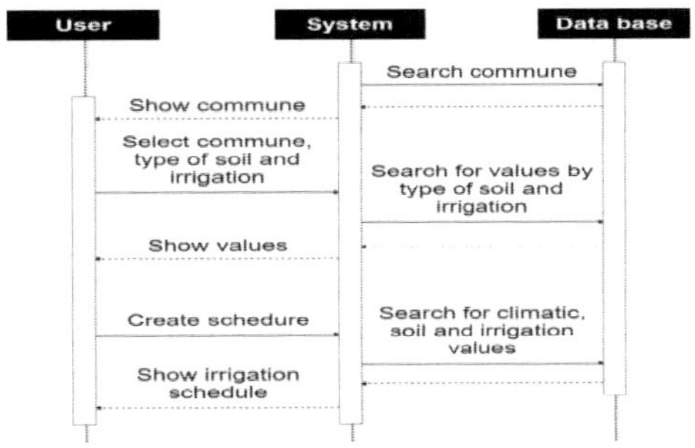

Figure 3. System Sequence Diagram

3.2.4 Sequence Diagram

A sequence diagram shows an interaction, which represents the sequence of messages between instances of classes, components, subsystems, or actors. The following diagram analyzes the interaction that occurs between the user, the system and the database (Figure 3).

3.2.5 Design and Data Model

The development of the system has data from the Meteorological Station of the Agriculture and Forestry High School "El Huertón" from Los Ángeles city of Bio-Bio Region in Chile, which since January 1, 2002 have stored the data obtained daily. From the beginning they have the following data: date, 9 o'clock temperature, 21 o'clock temperature, minimum daily temperature, maximum daily temperature, cold hours, rainfall, sunshine hours, minimum relative humidity, maximum relative humidity.

Since February 6, 2003, the evaporation value of the tray has been used, which is a necessary value for the calculation of the crop evapotranspiration.

The variables of temperature, precipitation and radiation are the critical variables to work with. This is mainly due to that field to field; city to city; region to region are changing, and in some cases are significant figures, so having the most real data to the area where the schedule is intended helps to generate accurate and reliable information.

In the following database model (Figure 4) the data mentioned above are presented as data for each culture. It also takes into account the communes and regions of Chile and the the soil physical and chemical characteristics.

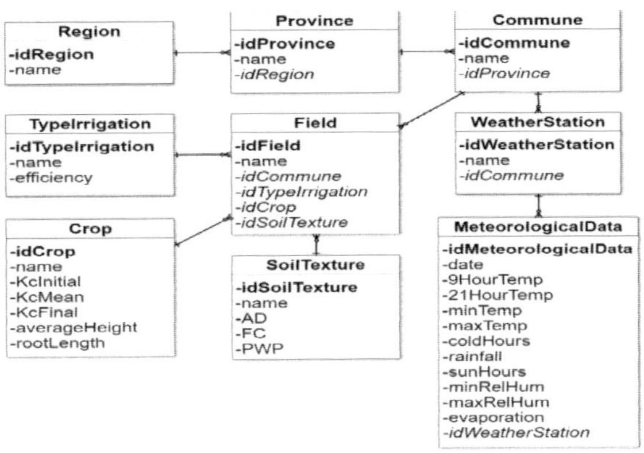

Figure 4. Database Model

3.2.6 Web System

The dialog structure diagram represents the windows and dialogs that the end user needs to complete all the tasks, and the necessary selections to move from one window to another. In the case of the web system would be as shown in figure 5.

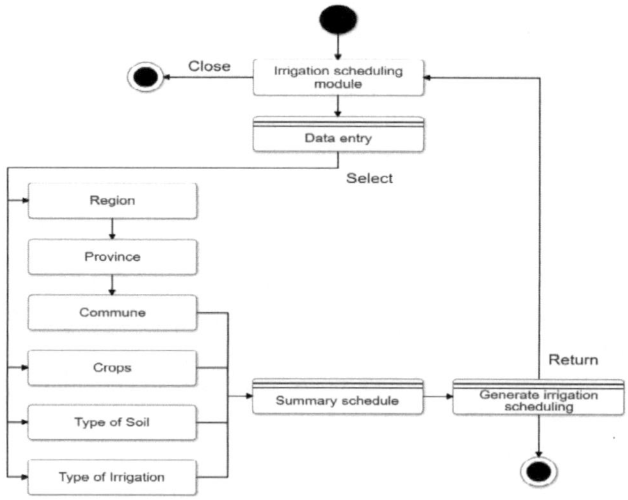

Figure 5. Web portal Diagram

4. RESULTS

The FAO Penman-Monteith equation that models evapotranspiration is more accurate to measure the water balance of a crop which gives us more accurate data. Calculations made with the water amount to be added to crops were consistent with the reality of traditional crops in Los Angeles city, Chile. We compared the risk data of a real plantation of Apple tree (Malus Doméstica Borkh) of 2014, in addition to the differences of irrigation obtained by the developed web system with the real data calculated by agronomists in the same way but with monthly averages and in a traditional way are very low, arriving at 10 days of differences between irrigations.

Figure 6 shows the comparison of the water resources applied in cubic meters calculated manually and with the software (web system). Observing the curves it is clear that manual calculation gives an irrigation every 5 days, which leads to the use of 28,000 cubic meters of water to the crop, instead the web system delivers a wide difference of days, applying four irrigations per month, being 19800 cubic meters of applied water. Saving 30% of water per month.

Without the help of soil samples at the moment of irrigation, it would not be possible to know exactly which of the two methods has a greater efficiency in the irrigation scheduling of the apple tree. With the help of agronomist engineers there is an instance of conducting studies in the experimental field and testing in situ the veracity of the data made using the water amount and the periodicity delivered by the web system. In order to complete the only data needed to perform a crop irrigation schedule are: soil type, drip irrigation and a watering threshold.

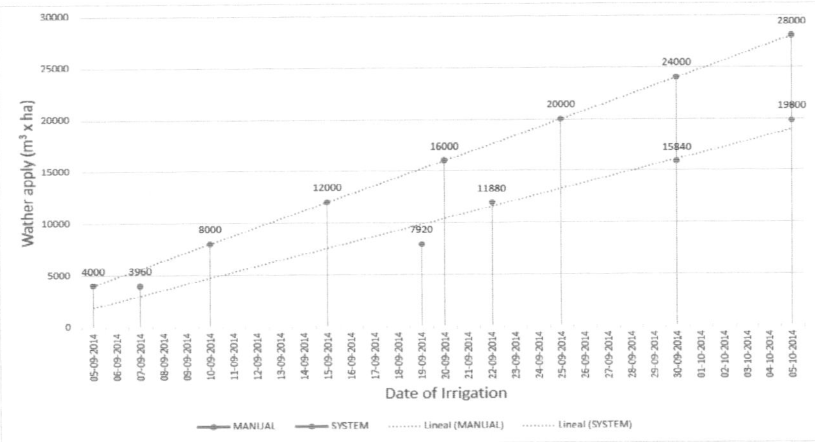

Figure 6. Comparison of irrigation manually and with the web system

5. CONCLUSIONS

The use of the web system in which the agricultural irrigation scheduling can be generated using real data, mainly favors the use of resources in an optimal way, such as irrigation, water, nutritional and human equipment.

The obtained results cannot be compared to irrigations carried out in a crop with manual calculations and monthly, unless experiments be carried out, since soil samples must be taken at the moment of irrigation, to know if it is necessary to do so or if the values delivered are far from reality.

There are few projects of this type in Chile, which contradicts the messages of the authorities, such that water must be care for in these times of water scarcity, since agriculture is where the waste of this vital resource is mostly produced (MMA, 2011), therefore, it is necessary to take advantage of the social interest in the area of care of water resources and to present a tool that is an aid to the farmer, in addition to the use of qualified personnel that show users the potential that the framework has for them to choose according to their growing needs.

The research centered on proof of concept and with the knowledge provided by computer engineering and agronomics, generates a tool, which at a first stage wants to reach all farmers to improve their way of irrigation, giving you fast, timely and accurate information, in addition, will be a teaching tool for future agricultural technicians of the country.

Dealing with computer technology today as support system allow the technicality scale traceability of measuring behavior of using water as the apple tree plantations.

ACKNOWLEDGEMENT

In the process of making this paper, I would like to thank the support from Vice-Rectory for Research and Postgraduate of the Catholic University of Temuco, by the project 2019EM-ML-08.

REFERENCES

Allen, R.G., L.S.Pereira, D. Raes, and M. Smith. 1998. Crop evapotranspiration: guidelines for computing crop water requirements. Irrigation and Drainage Paper No. 56, Food and Agriculture Organization of the United Nations, Rome, Italy.

BM, Banco Mundial. (2011). Diagnóstico de la gestión de los recursos hídricos. Departamento de Medio Ambiente y Desarrollo Sostenible Región para América Latina y el Caribe.

CONAMA: Comisión Nacional del Medio Ambiente, 2010. Primer reporte sobre manejo de residuos sólidos en Chile. Santiago, Chile: CONAMA.

Falvey, M. and Garreaud. R., 2009. Regional cooling in a warming world: Recent temperature trends in the southeast Pacific and along the west coast of subtropical South America (1979-2006). Journal Geophysical Research, 114. doi:10.1029/2008JD010519.

Ian Sommerville Ian: IEEE Software and Professional Development. IEEE Software 33(2): 90-92 (2016).

Lobos, G. A. and Yuri, J. A. (2006). Flower induction and differentiation of four Apple cultivars in Chile. Agricultura Tcnica (Chile) 66(2): 141-150.

MMA: Ministerio del Medio Ambiente, 2011. Catastro de sitios con presencia de dioxinas y furanos asociados al uso de pentaclorofenol en aserraderos fase II. Metodología de investigación confirmatoria y estimación preliminar de riesgos ambientales. Preparado por Ingeniería Alemana. Santiago: MMA.

Monteith, J. L. 1965. Evaporation and Environment. In: The state and movement of water in living organism. 19th Symp. Soc. Exptl. Biol. P. 205-234.

Penman, H. L. 1948. Natural evaporation from open water, bare soil and grass. Proceedings of the Royal Society of London. Series A, Mathematical and Physical Sciences, Vol. 193, No. 1032, p. 120-145.

Sanjay Shekar N C & Lakshman Nandagiri (2020) A Penman-Monteith evapotranspiration model with bulk surface conductance derived from remotely sensed spatial contextual information, International Journal of Remote Sensing, 41:4, 1486-1511.

Schneider S. H. et al. (2007). Assessing key vulnerabilities and the risk from climate change. Contribution of working group II to the Fourth Assessment Report (AR4) of the IPCC. http ://www:ipcc:ch/publicationsanddata/.

Sepúlveda S., Cravero A., Bustamante M. Identification of non-functional requirements for electronic voting systems: a systematic mapping. IEEE Latin America Transactions, vol.13, 1577-1583, 2015.

Simonne, E.H., M.D. Dukes, and L. Zotarelli. 2010. "Principles and Practices of Irrigation Management for Vegetables," p. 17-26, In: S. M. Olson and E. Simonne. eds. Vegetable Production Handbook for Florida 2010-2011. IFAS, Gainesville, FL.

Tosso J. and Torres Juan. (1986). Plant - water relations in grapevines, under different irrigation levels, using drip, sprinkler and furrow irrigation. II. Effect on vegetative growth and production. Agricultura Técnica (Chile) 46(3): 283-289, Chile.

Tosso, Juan. (1975). A new formula to determine evapotranspiration in Chile. Agricultura Tcnica, RESEARCH ARTICLES, Volume 35, Issue 3, Pages 139-147, Chile.

Tosso, Juan. (1976). Determination of Evapotranspiration and K Coefficients for Several Crops. Agricultura Tecnica (Chile) 36(4): 151-155.

Xiaojie Li, Shaozhong Kang, Jun Niu, Zailin Huo, Junzhou Liu, Improving the representation of stomatal responses to CO2 within the Penman–Monteith model to better estimate evapotranspiration responses to climate change, Journal of Hydrology, Volume 572, 2019, Pages 692-705.

Zotarelli L., Dukes M, Romero C., Migliaccio K., and Morgan K. (2010). Step by Step Calculation of the Penman-Monteith Evapotranspiration (FAO-56 Method). Agricultural and Biological Engineering Department, UF/IFAS Extension. U.S.

MATURITY ANALYSIS TO ASSESS THE CAPABILITY OF AN ORGANIZATION TO INNOVATE

Marc Adam, Marco Peter and Stella Gatziu Grivas
University of Applied Sciences Northwestern Switzerland

ABSTRACT

Globalization creates a highly competitive environment for organizations. To be successful in this environment in the long term, organizations need the capability to innovate and produce ongoing innovations. However, many organizations do struggle to do so despite their innovation efforts. Therefore, it is important to determine the factors of a company's innovation capability. This research paper answers the question of how a method should be designed in order to assess an organization's capability to innovate. To answer this question, extensive literature research on the topics of innovation, existing innovation models, and organizational behavior, as well as expert interviews with people from different industries, were conducted. Thus, this paper follows a design science strategy with a qualitative approach. The analysis of the literature showed that several factors determine the innovation capability of an organization. However, existing models sometimes focus on a single factor or contain several factors, which are not described sufficiently. Furthermore, the possibility for organizations to assess themselves using the models is largely missing. Based on the data from the literature and the interviews, a maturity assessment, consisting of a model of seven dimensions and 27 indicators, and a corresponding questionnaire to assess these indicators, was developed. The research findings suggest that the developed maturity assessment with its Organizational Innovation Capability model is a suitable and comprehensive method that can be used to support organizations by assessing their current innovation capability in order to define the necessary further measures. This research argues that the additional dimensions and indicators are needed in order to provide a comprehensive overview of the innovation capability maturity of an organization. Further, the experts emphasized the value of creating awareness within an organization and providing a good foundation for further discussions and actions by means of the maturity assessment.

KEYWORDS

Innovation, Innovation Capabilities, Innovation Capability Assessment, Maturity Assessment

1. INTRODUCTION

Innovation is everywhere, in the world of goods as well as in the world of words (Benoit, 2008). Innovation is therefore not only discussed in technical literature but also in social sciences such as history, sociology, management, and economics as well as in the humanities and arts. Nowadays, innovation has become a symbol of our society and is seen as a panacea for overcoming our problems (Benoit, 2008). However, today many consider innovation to be a technological and economic issue. This is reflected, for example, in the fact that most government studies such as the OECD's Oslo Manual (OECD, 2005) focus exclusively on innovation in enterprises.

The fast-paced technological progress has led to the integration of the world's economies into a single market within the last quarter of the 20th century and further has become a major factor in the process of change known as globalization (Akis, 2015). Globalization and the resulting fusion of world markets have created an extremely competitive and dynamic environment for organizations (Akis, 2015). To stay competitive in this environment, organizations need the capability to innovate (Ceausu et al., 2017), or as Urbancova (2013) states, are organizations at risk of lagging behind if they are not capable of introducing innovations on an ongoing basis. Already Tushman and Nadler (1986) stressed the importance of not only managing the success of the daily business but rather simultaneously creating innovation for tomorrow. Further, they mentioned that the management of innovation could be the most urgent managerial challenge. Today, this view seems to be still valid, as innovation is still regarded as an essential driver of economic performance not only in academic papers (Tohidi and Jabbari, 2012; Urbancova, 2013) but also by the maturity of CEOs as a survey of Accenture reveals

(Alon, Elron and Jackson, 2015). The importance of innovation can be explained by the fact that goals such as increased productivity and profitability, the penetration of new markets, and the improvement of existing market shares are achieved through innovation activities, which are the reason for companies to commit to developing their capability to innovate (Dereli, 2015). As Tohidi and Jabbari (2012) state: "Innovation is the success key for organizations."

According to Tohidi and Jabbari (2012), innovation is not only the most important but at the same time, one of the most difficult issues organizations have to confront today. This point is supported, by an innovation survey of Alon et al. (2015), which results show that companies are very confident in their capability to innovate, which is not justified when compared to their actual innovation performance. They furthermore mention that this misjudgment leads to negative effects, since organizations, who believe themselves to be innovators, are less likely to take actions to improve their capability to innovate and that their leaders are also less likely to recognize the complexity in innovation. Another survey by Loewe and Dominiquini (2006) provides a more self-critical image of organizations, which, nonetheless, also struggle in developing their innovation capabilities. According to Loewe and Dominiquini (2006), the reason for the struggle is that most organizations do only treat the symptoms or single root causes of their innovation issues and that this procedure is ultimately likely to fail since isolated measured proof to be inefficient. Instead, organizations need to tackle innovation with a systematic and holistic approach (Loewe and Dominiquini, 2006). The results of these surveys are supported by Ceausu et al. (2017), who mention that despite the importance of innovation only a few companies have mastered managing it.

Concluding, to be a successful innovator an organization must first understand which factors determine its innovation capabilities. In addition, organizations need to be able to assess their current organizational innovation capability before planning specific measures to achieve the desired state. However, this paper's research has revealed the existence of a gap in the literature regarding the existing organizational innovation capability models. Each model analyzed is missing at least one of the following properties: holistic focus instead of just one specific dimension, clear definition and explanation of its dimensions, and appropriate self-assessment tool. Thus, existing models make it difficult for organizations to improve their organizational innovation capabilities. These challenges should be overcome by developing a method to assess organizational innovation capability. Therefore, this paper aims to identify the relevant factors that define the capability of an organization to innovate and to develop a maturity assessment method to assess the capability of an organization to innovate with the goal to create awareness of its strong and weak points as well as possible areas of improvement.

In order to fulfill this paper's objective, the following research question needs to be answered: How should a method be designed in order to assess an organization's capability to innovate?

This paper continues with a literature review of the existing theories and related work about innovation, innovation models, as well as organizational behavior by analyzing what behavior does enable innovation within an organization. Further, the applied methodology and the created organizational innovation capability model and maturity assessment are presented and explained. Finally, this paper closes with the conclusion and suggests areas for further research.

2. EXISTING THEORIES AND RELATED WORK

2.1 Innovation and Existing Models

Creativity is defined as the generation of new ideas, which are useful or serve a purpose and the instantiation of these creative ideas are defined as innovation, thus, innovation can be seen as the successful implementation of creative ideas (Amabile et al., 1996). Organizational innovation is therefore defined as the successful implementation of creative ideas within the organizational context (Sarros, Cooper and Santora, 2008; Gumusluŏlu and Ilsev, 2009).

An organization's capability to innovate is vital as innovation has become one of the more powerful factors for growth, performance, and valuation (Salavou, Baltas and Lioukas, 2004; Barsh, Capozzi and Davidson, 2008). Therefore, the question arises on how an organization can improve its innovation performance. Within the literature many organizational factors can be found, which support the innovation performance such as the organizational structure (Hunter and Cushenbery, 2011; Robbins and Judge, 2016), the organizational culture

(Maughan, 2012; Szczepańska-Woszczyna, 2014) and appropriate leadership (Agbor, 2008; Sarros, Cooper and Santora, 2008; Gumusluŏlu and Ilsev, 2009). However, according to Loewe and Dominiquini (2006), it is not effective to adjust single factors but instead do organizations need to address innovation in a systematic and holistic approach in order to improve the innovation performance. Likewise, Mumford and Hunter (2005) do suggest a holistic view of how to foster organizational innovation. They mention that creative ideas may be generated by individuals but that for the successful implementation of these ideas the individuals need to be considered within a team. Moreover, it needs to be considered that these teams do function within broader structures such as divisions, departments, and organizations. Hunter and Cushenbery (2011) add that the multilevel perspective provides a more accurate and useful perspective on the innovative performance and they furthermore note that creativity and innovation are complex and nonlinear phenomena that are the result of a complex set of activities, actions, and behaviors and in order to achieve successful innovation, attention must be paid to this complexity (Hunter and Cushenbery, 2011). The multilevel approach is further supported by Robbins and Judge (2016) who also share the opinion that all three organizational levels are needed in order to successfully implement ideas and therefore create innovation.

The literature review revealed three relevant innovation models for the objective of this research paper. The Innovation Effectiveness model by Loewe and Dominiquini (2006) defines the following four dimensions, which are relevant for the effectiveness of innovation within an organization: leadership and organization, culture and values, people and skills, and processes and tools. Unfortunately, their report does not provide a detailed definition of the model's dimensions or what sub-topics they cover. In addition, the provided simplified maturity check does not allow an analysis of the maturity of each dimension but instead only provides a vague overall score of maturity.

The second innovation model, the Profile of Innovation Culture model from Losane (2013), defines innovation culture as the culture which makes innovation its everyday life and therefore supports a company´s sustainability. This model consists of the five determinants values, strategy, structure, behavior and communication, and leadership for organizational culture and further provides, based on the determinants, the profile of innovation culture. Also, the model's author provides a definition of innovation culture as well as the characteristics based on an extensive literature review. However, the model is only focused on culture and it does not provide a deeper explanation of the characteristic or a possibility for a detailed self-assessment in order for an organization to determine its strengths and weaknesses.

This third innovation model, the Direct and Indirect Leadership Influence model from Hunter and Cushenbery (2011), focuses on leadership and its direct and indirect influences on the innovation process. The authors provide a multi-level innovation process and argue that innovation starts with a creative idea, which is born from individuals. These individuals do normally not operate alone and are part of a team. Within that team, ideas must be proposed and validated and if successful it may be adjusted or refined by the team and even be prototyped. If a prototype is viable, the next step is to implement it at the organizational level, where the project may shift to other teams within the organization for further refinement, testing, evaluation, or realization. In addition, Hunter and Cushenbery (2011) mention that these three stages are firstly not independent of each other and secondly, therefore, are not rigid. Also, they state that leaders can indirectly influence innovation by indirect methods such as creating an environment that allows novel thinking or that leaders can directly influence innovation by direct methods by e.g. allocating resources. The model from Hunter and Cushenbery (2011) is based on a solid literature base and reveals the importance of leadership as well as the methods which leaders can use to support innovation. However, its focus is only on leadership and furthermore does only partially explain how this leadership method can be used successfully. In addition, it lacks the possibility for an organization to assess itself.

2.2 Organizational Behavior

According to Robbins and Judge (2012) organizational behavior (OB) does examine the impact of individuals, groups, and structures on human behavior within an organization with the aim of influencing them positively and thereby increasing the effectiveness of the organization. Key elements of OB are therefore individual behavior, group behavior, and organization system behavior, which makes it a multi-level analysis of human behavior (Robbins and Judge, 2012).

Within this chapter, the subtopics related to group behavior and organizational system behavior are analyzed while focusing on innovation. Individual behavior is not part of this research, because it is not relevant for the creation of the organizational innovation capability model.

2.2.1 Group Behavior

Group behavior can be broken down into the topics of groups and teams, power and politics, and leadership.

Groups and Teams:

A group is two or more interdependent and interaction individuals who share common interests or objectives and it can be of formal or informal nature (Robbins and Judge, 2012). A team is a group with members of complementary skills, furthermore does this kind of group share a common mission, performance goal, and approach for which they hold themselves mutually accountable (Katzenbach and Smith, 1993). The differences between a group and a team are therefore that group members mainly interact to share information while team members interact in a collaborative way in order to perform a collective performance while utilizing positive synergies (Robbins and Judge, 2012). To increase the innovative performance of groups and teams the following characteristics are of importance:

- Diversity: According to Hirschberg (1999), teams consisting of people from different departments (cross-functional-teams) improve overall creativity and innovation (Hirschberg, 1999). The same seems to apply to cultural diversity. Multi-cultural teams achieve higher levels of creativity than their counterparts. A challenge that diverse teams face is that their heterogeneousness makes it more difficult to integrate processes and problem-solving processes (Gressgård, 2011). According to Gibson and Gibbs (2006), however, could a psychologically safe communication climate help to mitigate these challenges.
- Team size: In order to improve the innovation performance of teams the team size should be kept small since too many members limit the idea exchange between the individuals (Hunter and Cushenbery, 2011) and small teams increase the individual commitment and performance (Gressgård, 2011). The optimal team size tends to be between five to nine people (Robbins and Judge, 2017).
- Team compositions: According to Sethi, Smith and Park (2001), social bonds within teams above a certain level reduce their innovation performance. In order to prevent the decrease of the innovation performance of teams over time, it is necessary to modify team compositions or that team members are involved in several teams (Gressgård, 2011).
- Personality of members: According to Robbins and Judge (2016) do especially teams with a high level of conscientiousness and openness, based on the Big Five personality model, not only perform better but are also more innovative.

Power and Politics:

The ability to influence someone is called power (Homans, 1958). And politics can be defined by using power. Or in other words, if an employee converts his powers into action he is being engaged in politics (Robbins and Judge, 2012). Othman (2008) differentiates organizational politics into a negative and positive side. The negative side describes politics which involves convenient and illegal behavior. This kind of politics is disapproved due to its ethical dilemmas and the workplace conflicts it generates (Cacciattolo, 2015). Positive politics are seen as a social function that is important to the success of an organization (Othman, 2008). Cacciattolo (2015) describes organizational politics as positive when it serves the organization's vision and objectives, fosters collaboration and is ethically balanced. She further mentions that positive organizational politics sometimes is a constructive necessary to bring together different competing interest groups. Therefore, positive organizational politics provide a benefit to the organization.

An organization's culture can influence political behavior within the organization. Characteristics of cultures that intensify negative politics are low level of trust, rare and unclear performance evaluations, zero-sum reward allocation practices, self-serving senior managers and the scarcity of resources (Robbins and Judge, 2016). The effect of organizational politics on innovation performance is, according to Abbas and Raja (2014), not been examined by any studies. Their research provided first insights that negative politics do not only hinder the productivity but also the innovation capability of an organization.

Leadership:

According to Yukl (2006) leadership is the process of influencing others so in order to understand and agree on action to be taken and methods to be used, as well as the facilitation of individual and collective efforts to achieve common goals. The differences of power and leadership are that leadership uses power to achieve group goals and that power is directed downwards to influence the followers and not upwards or lateral. Leadership is seen as a significant factor for innovation (Gumusluŏlu and Ilsev, 2009; Hunter and Cushenbery, 2011). According to Ancona and Caldwell (1987) especially the leadership style transformational leadership does support and promote innovation. This is supported by several studies, which have shown the positive influences of transformational leadership on organizational innovation (Gumusluŏlu and Ilsev, 2009). According to Sarros et al. (2008), transformational leadership helps to build a strong culture and does positively influence a positive climate for organizational innovation and therefore influence innovative behavior. The transformational leadership style is defined by four components: vision, role model, individual support, and intellectual stimulation (Gumusluŏlu and Ilsev, 2009).

2.2.2 Organizational System Behavior

The topic of organizational system behavior consists of the topics of organizational structure, organizational culture, and organizational change.

Organizational structure:

The organizational structure defines the way tasks are divided, grouped, and coordinated. According to the model of Mintzberg (1979), there are nine design parameters that determine the design of an organizational structure. By design, it means how the division of labor and coordination mechanisms influence the flow of materials, authority, information, and decision-making processes through the organization (Mintzberg, 1979). There are two extremes when designing an organizational structure, the mechanistic model and the organic model. The mechanistic model focuses on high specialization, high formalization, high centralization, high standardization, strong and tall hierarchy, and low complexity, while the organic model is the exact opposite. It is characterized by cross-functional and cross hierarchical teams, decentralization, and low formalization (Mintzberg, 1979).

Organizations that focus on innovation need the flexibility of an organic structure defined by its loose structure, low specialization and formalization and decentralization (Robbins and Judge, 2017) which provides employees with the autonomy and freedom to achieve tasks the way they see fit (Losane, 2013). Conversely, mechanical designs like the bureaucracy have a negative impact on creativity and innovation because they limit employees in their freedom to do their work and therefore inhibit creativity and innovation (Hunter and Cushenbery, 2011; Maughan, 2012).

Organizational culture:

Organizational culture can be defined as shared perceptions of organizational work practices within organizational units, which may vary compared to other organizational units (Van Den Berg and Wilderom, 2004). Warrick and Mueller (2015) describe culture as the characteristic of a group of people defined by their beliefs, values, attitudes, behaviors, and practices. The term organizational culture is typically used to refer to the culture of a whole organization or any unit of people working together within an organization (Linnenluecke and Griffiths, 2010). Organizational culture is an important factor to drive and maintain innovation and therefore increase the innovativeness of an organization (Barsh, Capozzi and Davidson, 2008; Ceausu et al., 2017). According to Maher (2014), there are seven key dimensions to culture, which distinguish highly innovative organizations from others, which according to Szczepańska-Woszczyna (2014) can be used in order to assess and improve the organizational culture for innovation. The seven key dimensions, defined by Maher (2014), are risk-taking, resources, knowledge, goals, rewards, tools, and relationships.

Organizational change:

There are two kinds of change in organizations: planned and unplanned (Nelson and Quick, 2011). The planned organizational change is a deliberate action to bring an organization from its present state to a desired future state (Harigopal, 2006). For this type of change, proactive and carefully planned action can be pursued (Nelson and Quick, 2011). According to Robbins and Judge (2016), innovations are a specialized kind of change. Therefore, all innovations imply change but not all changes need to be seen as an innovation. Furthermore, in order to create an innovative climate, an organization may develop a culture for change. This means a change of mindset where instead to adapt to change an organization focuses on a proactive approach and embraces change by transforming its culture.

3. METHODOLOGY

This paper uses the Design Science Research approach which is according to Hevner and Chatterjee (2010) suitable if the desired result is an artifact like a model or method, which is the case in this paper. Also, the approach allows developing the artifact in an iterative manner in order to include further insights from the data collection as soon as it is gathered, which for this research were done three iterations. Furthermore, it allows a qualitative data collection which is the data collection technique for this research.

In order to answer the research question of how a method should be designed in order to assess an organization's capability to innovate, this paper uses secondary and primary data. The secondary data consists of artifact and document studies, while the primary data is based on the results of nine semi-structured expert interviews. Eight of these interviews are conducted with five innovation experts in the fields of production, technology, banking, and consulting and one with an expert in applied organizational psychology. The semi-structured interviews with the innovation experts are used to improve and validate the Organizational Innovation Capability Model and its corresponding questionnaire while the interview with the expert in applied organizational psychology is used for the improvement and validation of the questionnaire from a usability perspective. As suggested by Saunders et al. (2009) the authors of this work used existing contacts from their own social networks to gain access to the intended interview partners.

4. ORGANIZATIONAL INNOVATION CAPABILITY MATURITY MODEL

The developed maturity model consists of the Organizational Innovation Capability Model and a corresponding questionnaire. The Organizational Innovation Capability Model and the questionnaire are based on the literature review and expert interviews and the final version has been reached after three development iterations. As illustrated in Figure 1, the model consists of seven dimensions with a total of twenty-seven indicators. The dimension Organizational Structure aims to evaluate if an organization provides the necessary structures needed in order to support innovation. The dimension Leadership assesses if the current leadership style motivates and supports people in order to create innovation. The third dimension Power & Politics does analyze if politics within an organization support innovation or hinder it. The dimension Collaboration evaluates the way people within an organization work together. The dimension Organizational Change assesses the attitude of an organization towards change. The dimension Organizational Innovation Management does analyze how an organization manages the innovation process inside and outside of the organization. The last dimension is called Organizational Culture and assesses the maturity by using Maher's (2014) model and its seven key dimensions for an organizational culture for innovation.

The comparison with the existing models from the literature revealed that the developed model provides a more detailed and comprehensive set of indicators to analyze the organizational innovation capability of an organization, while also covering all indicators of the existing models, except for three indicators, which did not match the requirements for the Organizational Innovation Capability Model.

The maturity model provides four maturity levels, one to four while one is the lowest and four the highest. The maturity level of an organization is determined by the answers given in the questionnaire. The questionnaire does not work with the common Likert scale but instead uses a single indicator description for each indicator and provides four level descriptions for the user to choose from. This approach allows the user to simply pick the level description, which fits the most to his or her current situation. An excerpt from the questionnaire is shown in Table 1.

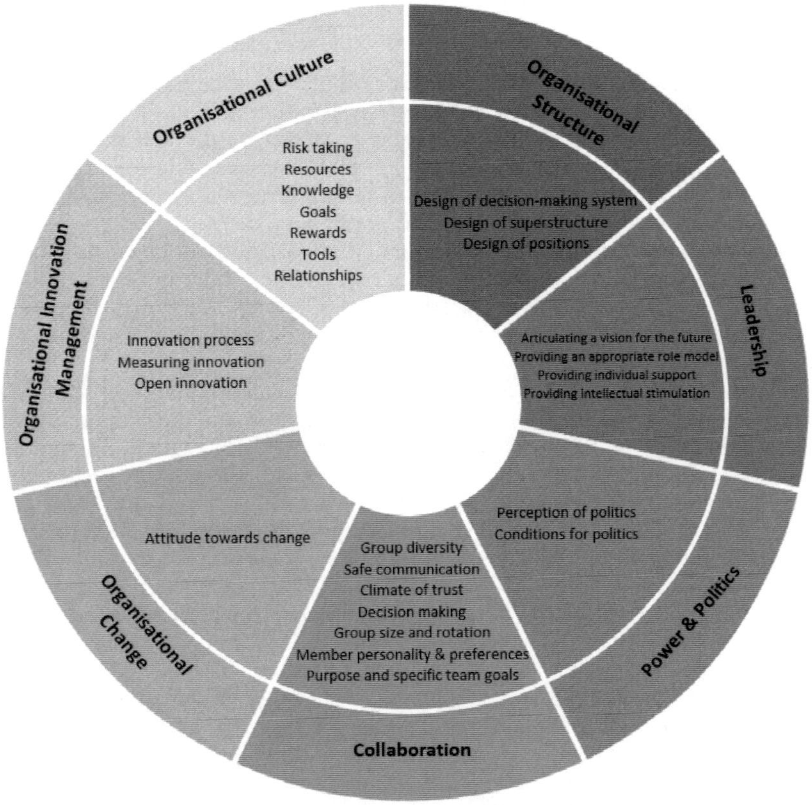

Figure 1. Organizational Innovation Capability Model

Table 1. Example excerpt of the questionnaire

Dimension	Indicator	Description	Level 1	Level 2	Level 3	Level 4
Organi-sational Structure	Design of positions	Describes how much freedom do people have in the way they perform their jobs.	Job are highly specialised and standardised.	The organisation is on the way to reduce job standardisation and enriched jobs.	Jobs require broad knowledge and skillset and encourages employees to come up with their own solutions.	Employees can have several roles within the organisation and are actively encouraged to acquire new skills.

Once the individual or better several employees from different units of an organization have completed the questionnaire, it can be evaluated. The evaluation provides an overview of each dimension and its corresponding maturity level. The maturity level of each dimension is calculated by the average score of the underlying indicators. Each indicator on maturity level 1 achieves one point, on maturity level 2 two points and so on. The evaluation across all dimensions dispenses with an overall maturity level, as the various dimensions have different numbers of indicators.

The feedback during the expert interviews for the testing cycle was positive. The interviewees mentioned that the model and questionnaire are very comprehensive and that especially due to the possibility of comparing the maturity of different units within the organization this model provides significant value for an organization. Furthermore, the interviewees mentioned that this analysis can be useful for organizations to create awareness for the topic of innovation and to provide a good starting point for further discussions and actions throughout the company.

5. CONCLUSION

The literature research has identified that the analyzed existing innovation models have several weaknesses, be it the lack of a holistic focus, the lack of precise and understandable indicators, or the lack of appropriate self-assessment tools. Therefore, the objective of this paper was to develop an organizational innovation capability maturity model, which helps organizations to assess their innovation capability and with that supports their innovation efforts and to thereby answers the following research question.: How should a method be designed in order to assess an organization's capability to innovate?

Based on the literature review and expert interviews the Organizational Innovation Capability Model was developed, including seven dimensions with a total of twenty-seven indicators. Furthermore, a corresponding questionnaire with a total of twenty-seven questions has been developed. For each indicator, a question exists, which defines the maturity level of this indicator. The combination of the model and the questionnaire results in the maturity assessment of organizational innovation capability.

The research was able to answer the research question and could therefor successfully achieve the research objective. The results show that the developed model and questionnaire not only cover all dimensions and almost all indicators of the existing models from the literature but further provides additional dimensions and indicators. This research argues that the additional dimensions and indicators are needed in order to provide a comprehensive overview of the organizational innovation capability maturity of an organization. Further was the validity and value of the maturity model confirmed during the expert interviews. The questioned experts especially emphasized its value for creating awareness within an organization and providing a good foundation for further discussions and actions.

The authors of this paper suggest the following two further areas of research. Firstly, future studies could examine the relationships of dimensions and their mutual influence in more detail. Particularly interesting would be to find out which dimensions and indicators are active variables (do influence others) and which are passive variables (are influenced by others). This would allow a better understanding of the impact of each dimension and indicator on the innovation capability of an organization. This knowledge would help to identify the most critical indicators and provide valuable indications of where measures should be taken. Secondly, future studies could research how specific measures could be proposed to organizations based on their maturity level. This would enhance this maturity model by providing organizations not only with a maturity assessment but further with clear instructions on how to improve. The need for this future research is given by the expert interview results, where this feature was mostly mentioned as a useful future extension of the model. The extraordinary challenge here will be that, as Maughan (2012) mentioned, there is no silver bullet for innovation, due to the huge differences between organizations and their environment.

REFERENCES

Abbas, M. and Raja, U. (2014) 'Impact of Perceived Organizational Politics on Supervisory-Rated Innovative Performance and Job Stress: Evidence from Pakistan', *Journal of Advanced Management Science*, 2(2), pp. 158–162. doi: 10.12720/joams.2.2.158-162.

Agbor, E. (2008) 'Creativity and innovation: The leadership dynamics', *Journal of Strategic Leadership*, 1(1), pp. 39–45.

Akis, E. (2015) 'Innovation and Competitive Power', *Procedia - Social and Behavioral Sciences*. Elsevier B.V., 195, pp. 1311–1320. doi: 10.1016/j.sbspro.2015.06.304.

Alon, A., Elron, D. and Jackson, L. (2015) *Innovation: clear vision, cloudy Execution*, *Accenture*. Available at: https://www.accenture.com/t20160412T084615Z__w__/us-en/_acnmedia/PDF-10/Accenture-Innovation-Research-ExecSummary.pdf#zoom=50.

Amabile, T. M. *et al.* (1996) 'Assessing the Work Environment for Creativity', *The Academy of Management Journal*, 39(5), pp. 1154–1184.

Ancona, D. G. and Caldwell, D. F. (1987) 'Management issues facing new product teams in high technology companies', in *Advances in Industrial and Labor Relations*. JAI Press Inc., pp. 199–221.

Barsh, J., Capozzi, M. M. and Davidson, J. (2008) 'Leadership and innovation', in *The McKinsey Quartlerly*, pp. 38–47.

Benoit, G. (2008) *Innovation: the History of a Category*, *Project on the Intellectual History of Innovation Working*.

Van Den Berg, P. T. and Wilderom, C. P. M. (2004) 'Defining, measuring, and comparing organisational cultures', *Applied Psychology*, 53(4), pp. 570–582. doi: 10.1111/j.1464-0597.2004.00189.x.

Cacciattolo, K. (2015) 'Organisational Politics: the Positive & Negative Sides', *European Scientific Journal*, 11(1), pp. 1857–7881.

Ceausu, I. *et al.* (2017) 'The Organizational Culture As a Support of Innovation Processes', *International Journal of Advanced Engineering and Management Research*, 2(6), pp. 2392–2403. Available at: www.ijaemr.comhttp://ijaemr.com/.

Dereli, D. D. (2015) 'Innovation Management in Global Competition and Competitive Advantage', *Procedia - Social and Behavioral Sciences*. Elsevier B.V., 195, pp. 1365–1370. doi: 10.1016/j.sbspro.2015.06.323.

Gibson, C. B. and Gibbs, J. L. (2006) 'Unpacking the concept of virtuality: the effects of geographic dispersion, electronic dependence, dynamic structure, and national diversity on team innovation', *dministrative Science Quarterly*, 51(3), pp. 451–495.

Gressgård, L. J. (2011) 'Virtual team collaboration and innovation in organizations', *Team Performance Management*, 17(1), pp. 102–119. doi: 10.1108/13527591111114738.

Gumusluŏlu, L. and Ilsev, A. (2009) 'Transformational leadership and organizational innovation: The roles of internal and external support for innovation', *Journal of Product Innovation Management*, 26(3), pp. 264–277. doi: 10.1111/j.1540-5885.2009.00657.x.

Harigopal, K. (2006) *Management of Organizational Change: Leveraging Transformation*. 2. SAGE PUBN.

Hevner, A. and Chatterjee, S. (2010) *Design Research in Information Systems*. New York: Springer.

Hirschberg, J. (1999) *The creative priority: Putting innovation to work in your business*. New York: Harper-Business.

Homans, G. C. (1958) 'Social Behaviour as Exchange', *American Journal of Sociology*, 63, pp. 597–606.

Hunter, S. T. and Cushenbery, L. (2011) 'Leading for innovation: Direct and indirect influences', *Advances in Developing Human Resources*, 13(3), pp. 248–265. doi: 10.1177/1523422311424263.

Katzenbach, J. R. and Smith, D. K. (1993) 'The Discipline of Teams', *Harvard Business Review*, 71, pp. 111–120.

Linnenluecke, M. K. and Griffiths, A. (2010) 'Corporate sustainability and organizational culture', *Journal of World Business*. Elsevier Inc., 45(4), pp. 357–366. doi: 10.1016/j.jwb.2009.08.006.

Loewe, P. and Dominiquini, J. (2006) 'Overcoming the barriers to effective innovation', *Strategy and Leadership*, 34(1), pp. 24–31. doi: 10.1108/10878570610637858.

Losane, L. (2013) 'Innovation Culture – Determinant of Firms ′ Sustainability', *World Academy of Science, Engineering and Technology International Journal of Social, Behavioral, Educational, Economic, Business and Industrial Engineering Vol:7, No:10, 2013*, 7(10), pp. 2755–2760.

Maher, L. (2014) 'World Hospitals and Health Services', *The Offical Journal of the International Hospital Federation*, 50(1), pp. 4–6.

Maughan, C. (2012) *Organisational Innovation: A review of the literature*. Working Paper CW001. doi: 10.1142/9789813220607_0010.

Mintzberg, H. (1979) *The structuring of organizations*. Prentice-Hall. Available at: http://citeseerx.ist.psu.edu/viewdoc/download?doi=10.1.1.383.6417&rep=rep1&type=pdf.

Mumford, M. D. and Hunter, S. T. (2005) 'Innovation in Organizations: A Multi-Level Perspective on Creativity', *Research in Multi-Level Issues*, 4(October), pp. 9–73. doi: 10.1016/S1475-9144(05)04001-4.

Nelson, D. L. and Quick, Ja. C. (2011) *Organizational Behavior - Science, the Real World, and You*. 7. Mason, OH 45040: South-Western Cengage Learning.

OECD (2005) 'The measurement of scientific and technological activities', *Oslo manual*, pp. 1–92. Available at: http://www.oecd.org/science/inno/2367614.pdf.

Othman, R. (2008) 'Organisational politics: The role of justice, trust and job ambiguity', *Singapore Management Review*, 30(1), pp. 43–53.

Robbins, S. P. and Judge, T. A. (2012) *Essentials of Organizational Behavior*. 12. Essex: Pearson Education.

Robbins, S. P. and Judge, T. A. (2016) *Essentials of Organizational Behavior*. 13. Essex: Pearson Education Limited.

Robbins, S. P. and Judge, T. A. (2017) *Organizational Behavior*. 17. Essex: Pearson Education Limited.

Salavou, H., Baltas, G. and Lioukas, S. (2004) 'Organisational innovation in SMEs: The Importance of Strategic Orientation and Competitive Structure', *European Journal of Marketing*, 38(9/10), pp. 1091–1112. doi: 10.1108/03090560410548889.

Sarros, J. C., Cooper, B. K. and Santora, J. C. (2008) 'Building a Climate for Innovation Through Transformational Leadership and Organizational Culture', *Journal of Leadership & Organizational Studies*, 15(2), pp. 145–158.

Saunders, M., Lewis, P. and Thornhill, A. (2009) *Research Methods for Students*. 5., *Research methods for business students*. 5. Essex: Pearson Education Limited. doi: 10.1007/s13398-014-0173-7.2.

Sethi, R., Smith, D. C. and Park, C. W. (2001) 'Cross-functional product development teams, creativity and the innovativeness of new consumer products', *Journal of Marketing Research*, 38(1), pp. 73–85.

Szczepańska-Woszczyna, K. (2014) 'The importance of oranizational culture for innovation in the company', *Forum Scientiae Oeconomia*, 2(3).

Tohidi, H. and Jabbari, M. M. (2012) 'The important of Innovation and its Crucial Role in Growth, Survival and Success of Organizations', *Procedia Technology*, 1, pp. 535–538. doi: 10.1016/j.protcy.2012.02.116.

Tushman, M. and Nadler, D. (1986) 'Organizing for Innovation', *California Management Review*, 28(3), pp. 74–92. doi: https://doi.org/10.2307/41165203.

Urbancova, H. (2013) 'Competitive Advantage Achievement through Innovation and Knowledge', *Journal of Competitiveness*, 5(1), pp. 82–96. doi: 10.7441/joc.2013.01.06.

Warrick, D. D. and Mueller, J. (2015) 'Understanding, Building and Changing Organization Culture', in *Lessons in changing cultures: Learning from real world cases*, pp. 1–16.

Yukl, G. (2006) *Leadership in organisations*. 6. London: Pretice Hall.

TAILOR-MADE IT PROJECT MANAGEMENT

Ariel I. La Paz[1] and Rodrigo I. López[2]
[1]*Faculty of Economics and Business, Universidad de Chile, Chile*
[2]*Departamento de Ciencias de la Computación, Pontificia Universidad Católica de Chile, Chile*

ABSTRACT

IT project management has been studied and documented over recent decades. Topics studied tend to cover the tools, methods and cases of technological developments and systems implementations. In spite of the advances in the knowledge base of project management, still, high rates of failure can be found along with the unmet goals of the IT investments and wasted resources mainly by poor management of technological innovations. The article explores what are the methods, tools and techniques for project management that better fit the diverse and varied initiatives known as IT projects implemented in diverse organizational contexts. In order to manage and systematically analyze the complexity of projects and organizations, ontological frameworks are introduced, and a set of tools and techniques for project management are associated with the different contexts. With a sample of 183 capstone projects developed in an undergraduate senior course for IS design, the authors identified customized sets of tools and methods for project management that adapt to the characteristics of each project.

KEYWORDS

Project Management, Ontological Frameworks, Toolset for IST Project, IT Project

1. INTRODUCTION

IT project management methods and tools formally sprung over the last three decades, since the publication of standards and methods for IT project management such as the Project Management Book of Knowledge (PMBOK), Projects in Controlled Environment (PRINCE) (Matos and Lopes, 2013), KANBAN, more recently SCRUM (Takeuchi and Nonaka, 1986, Cockburn and Highsmith, 2001), and many variations of these and other methods for project management. The methods and standards for IT project management appeared as a response to the development and implementation of Information Systems and Technologies (IST) and software development in organizations all over the world, and are based on project management methods aiming to standardize tools, practices and roles since the late 1950s (Garel, 2013). The emergence, sophistication and effectiveness of the IT project management methods and models have not proven to follow the same pace of the technological evolution or the increasing demands of companies adopting IST (Hoffman, Ahlemann and Reining, 2020; Mir and Pinnington, 2014). The former translates into poor statistics of IT project success, high rates of delay and cost overruns, not to mention the user's frustration and corporate value losses (Papke-Shields et al., 2010). Several publications reveal success rates in the implementation of projects below 30%, associating such rates to several reasons, with most causes rooted in the mismanagement of project planning and execution, rather than failures explained by technological issues (Nelson, 2007).

Project management methods vary from structured to agile, descriptive to prescriptive, rigid to flexible (Špundak, 2014) and include management dimensions or areas such as budget, people, risk, communications, documentation, or scope (Radujković and Sjekavica, 2017). The management dimensions suggest the use of tools and techniques to plan and monitor the use of resources, as well as to verify the accomplishment of the project objectives for the client, assisting the project manager in achieving more predictable results (Joslin and Müller, 2015). In spite of a sound theorization of IT Project management, failure rates do not seem to decrease (Nelson, 2007, Mir and Pinnington, 2014). Improving the methods, techniques and use of tools for IT Project management is critical in an increasingly demanding scenario of technological transformations in all types of organizations, and the imminent advent of even more expectedly pervasive technologies such as 5G, quantum computing, artificial intelligence, and sensors that pave the road for Industry 4.0 (Rao and Prasad, 2018, Lasi et al., 2014).

Scholars in the field argued that there is a strong relationship between the use of good practices and success in project management. Joslin and Müller (2015) found that the application and use of comprehensive methodologies lead to higher levels of success. Academic publications in IT project management present case studies, methods comparisons, or history and trajectory of methods, revealing the need for adapting project management methods and tools to improve the management process itself, as well as the final product success (Garel, 2013). In spite of some general directions to choose methods (for example, according to size and complexity), there is neither a unified theory of project management (Garel, 2013, Špundak, 2014), nor concrete ideas of how to customize and apply methods and tools to the different project characteristics, so that the probability of success increases. Even though the current success rates are rather low compared with the amounts of investments and technological potential, it is good and positive to have a variety of methods and approaches to manage IT projects where project managers can choose from. Then, choosing the right method or approach to manage a given project is as critical as it is to choose the right technology. Nelson (2007) synthesizes the postmortem learning from ten failed IT projects and concludes that most failure causes relate first to the IT project management process, second to issues with stakeholders and people involved in the project, and just a minority of causes relate to technology. Hence, our motivation is to better understand how the selection of methods, approaches and tools for IT project management can be adapted for the effective and efficient management of IST adoption. The research question we aim to answer is: How can the selection of methods and tools for IT project management be systematically formulated to improve the probability of success? The premise behind the pursued answer is that the mere existence of methods and certifications for IT project management does not suffice for success, but that the strategic selection and application of tools could be an alternative approach to customize the toolkit for project managers.

To answer our research question, two ontological frameworks are presented in section 2, in order to seize the complexity of IST project management and organizational context, and to explore the feasibility to use them to systemically and systematically characterize a given project, and then choose the right tools for its management. Section 3 explains how the ontological frameworks are used to analyze a set of IST projects. The main findings of this research, presented in section 4, are not yet conclusive, but open alternative avenues to study the mechanisms for failure and success in IST projects, as well as to customize the set of tools used in the management of IST projects, as explained in section 5.

2. ONTOLOGICAL MODELING

Complex phenomena are usually modeled by simplification and reduction of the variables that represent the causes, correlations and effects. IST project management methods have been modeled by stages and dimensions, or according to the structured or agile approaches towards the project. Such analyses provide general rules for the association of methods and projects, indicating what methodologies better suit the project type according to the size of a project, available time to completion, the experience of a company conducting technological projects, or the organizational understanding of the purpose. This research applies ontological modelling to the key areas of project management, in a similar fashion as it has been developed in other areas of IST (Vasquez and La Paz, 2019; La Paz et al 2019)

However, the complexity of a project to be managed under a particular organizational context is for much larger than generic dimensions, stages and traditional tools, being the dimensions a subject of study for project success (Papke-Shields et al., 2010). On one hand, there are many different things called IST projects, from the very technical integration of software architectures, or back-office migration of data, to the strategic implementation of business analytics tools to support decision-making processes. On the other hand, the organizations where these IST projects are implemented also present multiple characteristics and differences as well, for example, industry, size, maturity or organizational structure. Both entities (project and organization) present complexities and particularities that affect the selection and the effectiveness and efficacy of methods and tools for the management of the resources and the achievement of objectives (Serrador and Turner, 2015). The following sub-sections introduce ontological frameworks to describe systematically the complexities of projects and organizations.

2.1 IST Project Ontology

Essentially, FTP is a client-server protocol that facilitates the transfer of files between two IST projects are hardly standardized. The implementation of the same software in two companies in the same industry, and with similar conditions may find diverse difficulties and produce very different results. A project may start from scratch, while others start from an installed infrastructure with processes, data and applications already in use, implying pros and cons to be differently managed in each case. With an ontological framework, we organize the dimensions lifecycle stage, acquisition strategy, operation objective, and the IT structure to systematically characterize an IST project. Each dimension is represented by a column containing a taxonomy and arranged to be read from left to right to form phrases describing a given IST project. The taxonomies are taken from generic available descriptions in the Management Information Systems (MIS) field.

Table 1. IST project ontological framework

Lifecycle stage		**Acquisition strategy**		**Operation objective**	**IT structure**
Planning	*of a/an*	In-house development	*To*	Create	Software
Analysis		Packaged software purchase		Read	Hardware
Design		Outsourcing		Update	Networks
Implementation		Cloud service		Delete	Data
					Persona
					Process
					Policy

The IST project ontological framework presented in Table 1 contains 448 possible combinations to describe any particular project. One example of the combinations for a project is "Planning of an in-house development to create software", while a second different combination is "Implementation of a cloud service to delete policy". The first example takes the first element from each taxonomy, and the second example takes the last element from the taxonomies. Other 446 different elements can be built by concatenating the elements from the columns and connectors. One project could use more than one element from each dimension to characterize itself, and with its particular definition, choose and apply methods and tools for effective and efficient management.

2.2 Organizational Context Ontology

A second ontological framework is presented in this subsection to represent the complexity of organizational context, which significantly impacts the implementation of IST. Different studies have portrayed the organizational complexity by the analysis of constructs such as size, culture, country, and industry (See a summary of measures used in project management in Papke-Shields et. al (2010). Our study captures the organizational complexity and variability by defining taxonomies for Company size, Maturity, Structure type, and Industry. Other constructs such as culture type, focus on efficiency, sustainability, customer satisfaction, or operations scope could be included, but in order to preserve the parsimony of the ontological framework, and to use of well-known taxonomies, we decided to use only four main concepts. The reader could modify the framework to make it more comprehensive by adding new columns or terms to the taxonomies if s/he needs to make an even more precise characterization of the organizational context, but the logic of the representation is presented here in Table 2.

The ontological framework introduced to represent the organizational context contains 1,500 different combinations, calculated as the multiplication of the elements of each dimension that form the instances of the ontology as one selects one element from each column and combines with the connecting phrases and the elements of subsequent columns. A few examples of different organizational contexts are:

- *Small emergent company, with hierarchical structure in finance & insurance*
- *Large structured company, with matrix structure in manufacturing*
- *Medium initial company, with linear structure in educational services*
- *Large optimized company, with divisional structure in retail trade*
- *Small integrated company, with inverse structure in professional, scientific & technical services*

Implementing the same IST project in each illustration -for example, a payroll system-, would need different tools, techniques and methods for project management, given the specific labor norms that may apply to each industry and country, the contract types that each organization offers to their employees, the number of employees or the organizational culture, to name a few differentiating aspects that affect the implementation of a payroll system.

Table 2. Organizational context ontological framework

Company size	**Maturity**		**Structure Type**		**Industry**
Small	Initial		Linear		Agriculture, forestry, fishing and hunting
Medium	Emergent		Matrix		Mining, quarrying, oil & gas extraction
Large	Structured	*Company with*	Hierarchical	*Structure in*	Utilities
	Integrated		Divisional		Construction
	Optimized		Inverse		Manufacturing
					Wholesale trade
					Retail trade
					Transportation and warehousing
					Information
					Finance & insurance
					Real estate and rental & leasing
					Professional, scientific and technical services
					Management of companies and enterprises
					Administrative and support and waste management a remediation services
					Educational services
					Health care and social assistance
					Arts, entertainment and recreation
					Accommodation and food services
					Public administration
					Other services

2.3 Relation of Tools with Projects and Organizational Contexts

The two ontological frameworks present fairly large numbers for IST project types and organizational contexts, even with relatively small ontological frameworks. Combining the numbers of both frameworks, we could calculate the even larger product (448 x 1,500 = 672,000) that reveal an exponential complexity of the IST project management, given that each of the 448 types of projects could be executed in any of the 1,500 different organizational contexts. These numbers could be increased or reduced by adding, refining or removing components in the taxonomies, but the message and point the authors make is that complexity and variety of projects is by far larger than the number of methods, tools and techniques for IST project management.

The revealed variety, indirectly indicates that any particular method for project management containing subsets of tools and techniques, most likely not fit all the possible combinations of projects and contexts. Likely, some methods and approaches support better certain projects and contexts, and some other projects and contexts require different sets of tools, techniques, approaches or methods for their better execution. It is to say that given the particularities of a project and the organization executing it, it may be more effective to use lean and agile methods, taking advantage of reduced costs and time, while in some other context it is more convenient to use more traditional and comprehensive methods with multiple tools and at a higher monitoring cost. In between the extremes of the different methods for IT project management, intermediate projects may need particular combinations of the methods, tools and techniques, balancing the effectiveness and efficiency of particular sets of tools. With such logic, we surveyed the most used methods, in their original versions, to identify their classic tools and techniques, finding a list of 122 tools contained in the widely used methods for project management, and commonly applied during the execution of IT projects.

It should be noted that the tools present different levels of application, and some tools contain or use other tools as components (Figure 1 presents an example of main tools and subcomponents). The identification of the tool's subcomponents facilitates its use, by making sense to the users and stakeholders of the project, and allows projects with a smaller budget to focus the resources on those tools that maximize the effectiveness of management on the project.

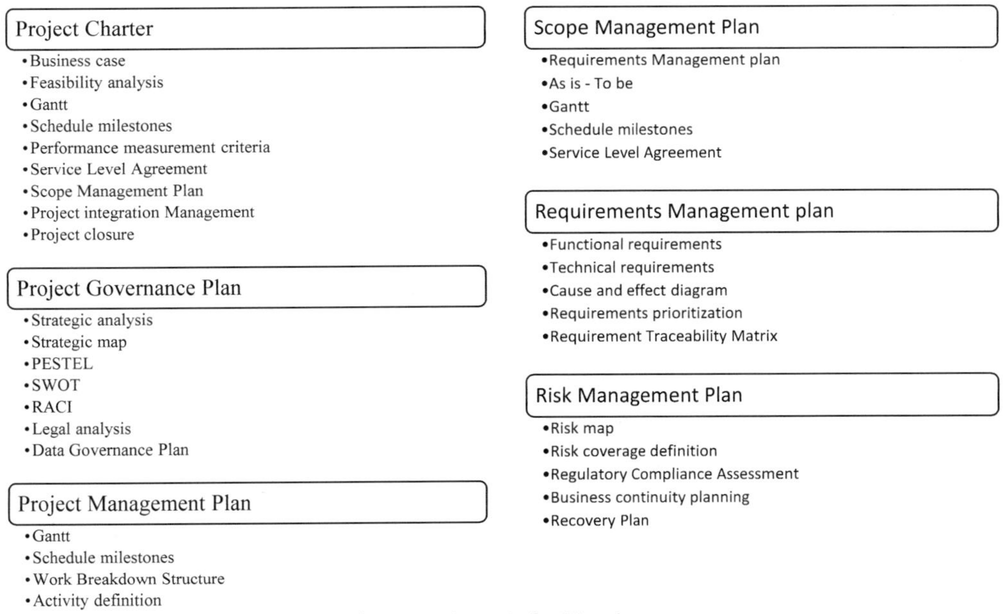

Figure 1. Main composite tools for IT project management

The task was then to associate tools and techniques to particular combinations of IST project types and organizational contexts to systematically analyze and identify trends or patterns to customize sets of tools according to the project and context types.

3. METHOD FOR THE ONTOLOGICAL ANALYSIS

A main expected result, is to deliver contextualized – tailor-made – information to the IST project management teams, according to the stage/size/complexity of the project, by selecting a set of relevant tools that significantly, effectively and efficiently assist the project manager in monitoring, tracking, and executing the project with his/her team and the stakeholders. By using the ontological frameworks as lenses to analyze the particularities of projects and organizations, it is possible to systematically characterize the different instances for the implementation of IST projects and specifically recommend and choose tools, techniques and methods for project management. Given the number of combinations from the ontologies, the authors prepared partial combinations of ontological dimensions to represent by extension the projects and contexts in which tools for management are required. Then assigned, by using expert judgment, the most appropriate tools from the list of 122 items to each instance identified.

Several iterations of tools' assignment to the partial dimensions of the ontologies were made, and subsequently integrated as the combinations of the ontologies were reconstructed. First the union of all combinations, and then the intersection of combinations and tools allowed us to assign particular sets of tools and techniques for project management in specific organizational contexts, and for each type of IST project.

In order to test the validity of the tools assignment to such a large number of combinations, a sample of 183 capstone projects developed by senior students in an undergraduate course of Information Systems Design were analyzed and mapped onto the ontological frameworks by the authors of this article. In these projects, students design information systems prototypes for companies with real-life problems and document the analysis process. Each project was characterized and mapped onto the ontologies with the information available from project reports and presentation records. Finally, the sets of tools and techniques associated with each project were retrieved from the initial assignment of tools and techniques for IST project management to the ontological frameworks.

4. RESULTS

In the projects mapped, the ontological analysis suggested an average of 75 tools, a maximum of 104, and a minimum of 44 tools subsets. Although some tools are recommended in a large proportion of the capstone projects, the composition of the sets of tools differs according to the characteristics of each project and the context of each organization. Table 3 illustrates toolsets recommended for 2 projects, which have similar characteristics in terms of producing prototypes at initial stages of IST projects, but that have different stages in the systems development cycle, organizational contexts, and project characteristics. The illustrations have been selected to present the project wit minimum and maximum number of tools recommended from the ontological analysis.

Table 3. Examples of sets of tools recommended for IT project management

Project Id 87: Design of a Balanced Scorecards for a private nursery			
The project belongs to a preschool education company, which provides the services of nursery and kindergarten, the company presents problems in the management of his data and information, these are scattered in multiple digital files and under multiple formats, making decision making and management difficult. The proposed solution includes the design of a central data model, the integration of multiple data sources and the construction of a Balanced Scorecard.			
Planning	**Analysis**	**Design**	**Implementation**
Business case Business Expert judgment Business Recovery Plan Communication protocols Decision maker Feedback Detractors identification Economic Value Added Financial planning Incentive program Legal analysis Monte Carlo simulation Net Present Value Payback Policies for distribution and access to information Procurement Management Plan Regulatory Compliance Assessment Requirements Management plan Risk coverage definition Strategic analysis Total Cost Ownership Zone of possible agreement (ZOPA)	Business case Business Expert judgment Business Recovery Plan Communication protocols Cost Management Plan Decision maker Feedback Detractors identification Financial planning Legal analysis Monte Carlo simulation Policies for distribution and access to information Procurement Management Plan Requirements Management plan Resource Management Plan Risk coverage definition Strategic analysis Total Cost Ownership Training program identification Zone of possible agreement (ZOPA)	Business Expert judgment Incentive program Total Cost Ownership Training program identification Zone of possible agreement (ZOPA)	Cost Management Plan Regulatory Compliance Assessment Resource Management Plan
Integration			
Benchmark Brand design Budget Change Control System Change management Data dictionary	Financial indicators Focus group Implementation Plan Meeting Agenda Meetings Mentoring	Performance Incentive Plan Project Charter Project Management Plan Recruitment and selection Staffing Stakeholder Engagement Plan	Stakeholder matrix Talent development program

In the sample of capstone projects analyzed, some projects require large numbers of tools, numbers that may exceed the budget assigned for the administration of such technological initiatives in these types of organizations. A more detailed review of these projects confirmed that they tend to correspond to organizations with weak organizational definitions, minimum experience or maturity to manage or develop IST projects that translate into insufficient strategic definitions, absence of documentation and process mapping procedures, insufficient staffing, among other characteristics. Organizations with those features may need to use larger sets with multiple tools as a way to face their weaknesses. Given the need to use more tools to manage a project, and considering the usual budget constraints it is foreseeable that these projects would present more difficulties for their completion, beyond the project definition, that reduces its chances to succeed. On the other hand, projects with reduced complexity and with proper strategic definitions may need a smaller but agile and economic set of tools than a traditional method may indicate.

Table 3. Examples of sets of tools recommended for IT project management (continued)

Project Id 60: Financial and operational control system in a Spa			
The project presents an aesthetic center dedicated to non-invasive treatments in the body and facial area, the company faces high competition in the sector, which drives it to seek new forms of differentiation, unfortunately, it lacks automated systems that support the management of the business operation, so it is proposed as a solution the design of an operational and financial control system.			
Planning	**Analysis**	**Design**	**Implementation**
Budget execution Business case Business continuity planning Business Expert judgment Business Recovery Plan Canvas Communication protocols Decision maker Feedback Detractors identification Economic Value Added Incentive program Job definition Legal analysis Monte Carlo simulation Net Present Value Payback Policies for distribution and access to information Procurement Management Plan Project closure Regulatory Compliance Assessment Requirements Management plan Risk coverage definition Service Level Agreement Strategic analysis Strategic map Test Plan Total Cost Ownership Zone of possible agreement (ZOPA)	Activity definition Brainstorming Business case Business continuity planning Business Expert judgment Business Recovery Plan Canvas Cases of use Communication protocols Cost Management Plan Data flow diagram Decision maker Feedback Detractors identification Flowchart Functional requirements Identification of Users Job definition Legal analysis Performance analysis Policies for distribution and access to information Process engineering Process indicators Procurement Management Plan Requirement Traceability Matrix Requirements Management plan Requirements prioritization Resource Management Plan Risk coverage definition Standards Check Strategic analysis Strategic map Systems architecture Test Plan Total Cost Ownership Training program identification User roles User segmentation User stories Zone of possible agreement (ZOPA)	Activity definition Brainstorming Business Expert judgment Canvas Cases of use Data flow diagram Employee role definition End user Feedback Flowchart Functional requirements Identification of Users Incentive program Interaction Guide Job definition Job description Process engineering Process indicators Product Recovery Plan Prototypes Requirement Traceability Matrix Requirements prioritization Standards Check Systems architecture Technical requirements Technological Expert judgment Total Cost Ownership Training program identification User modeling User role definition User roles User segmentation User stories Wireframe Zone of possible agreement (ZOPA)	Budget execution Cost Management Plan End user Feedback Functional requirements Interaction Guide Performance analysis Product Recovery Plan Project closure Prototypes Regulatory Compliance Assessment Requirement Traceability Matrix Resource Management Plan Service Level Agreement Standards Check Systems architecture Technical requirements Technological Expert judgment Test Plan User modeling User segmentation User stories Wireframe
Integration			
Appendix As is - To be Benchmark Brand design Budget Change Control System Change management Communication Management Plan Data dictionary Data Governance Plan Expert judgment Feedback	Financial indicators Focus group Gantt Implementation Plan Interaction Plan Interview key people IT Infrastructure Metadata Knowledge Management Plan Meeting Agenda Meeting minutes Meetings Mentoring	Minute of Agreement Negotiation Performance Incentive Plan Process Mapping Project Charter Project Governance Plan Project Management Plan Quality Management Plan RACI Recovery Plan Recruitment and selection Risk Management Plan	Risk map Schedule milestones Scope Management Plan Staffing Stakeholder Engagement Plan Stakeholder matrix Talent development program Training Management Plan Work Breakdown Structure

Problems in the management of IST projects are subsequently attributed to the technology, its management, or the chosen management methodology when some of these issues can be solved or minimized with a better selection of tools and techniques for project management.

Figure 2 shows the grouping of the tools recommended to the 183 capstone projects into word clouds. In this figure, the word clouds have been grouped around the IS lifecycle stages, planning, analysis, design and implementation, and added an integration category. The size of the tool's names illustrate the frequency of assignments by expert judgment applied into the ontological design. Considering tools with a higher frequency, and cases where the purposes and objectives of the projects are clear and shared by the company, the Regulatory Compliance Assessment, the Risk Coverage definition and a Legal analysis help diagnose and assess project risks. The Zone of possible agreements for negotiation and the Functional and Technical requirements for the IST project help to define the scope of the project and manage the expectations of stakeholders. Finally, the prevalence of the Change Control System and Stakeholder Engagement Plan as tools for integration provide the management team a way to control the adjustments to the project during its life cycle, taking into account the stakeholders and the way in which they get involved. These tools and methods identified from the ontological design, are not usually recommended from the traditional methodologies (Papke-Shields et al., 2010).

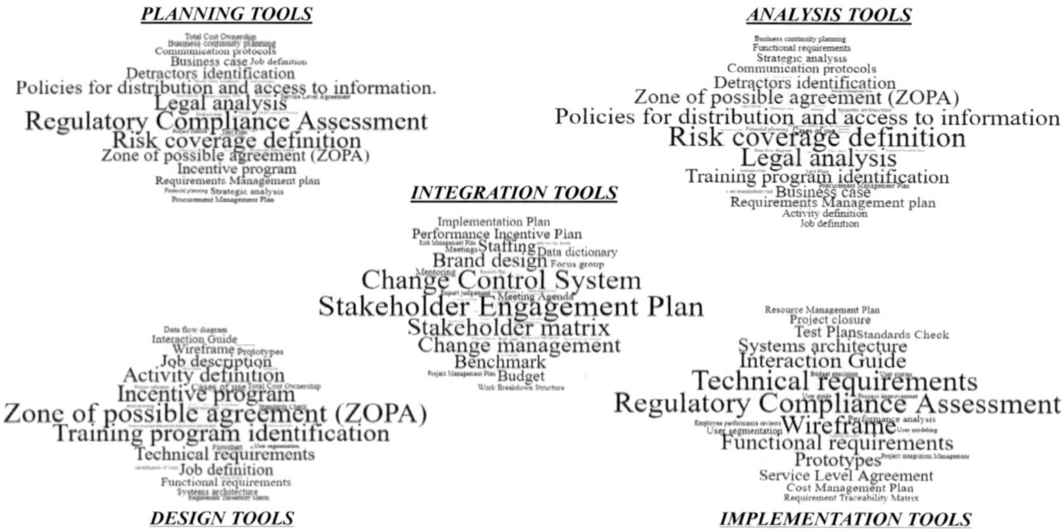

Figure 2. Recommended tools word clouds

5. CONCLUSIONS

The complexity of project management is usually approached with the development of specific methods, thought as standardized products out of the best practices. The complexity of the IST projects analyzed and revealed in this study, by means of representing the variety of projects and organizational contexts, reinforces the view of the authors about the difficulties to standardize with a few methods, the management of an increasing number and types of information systems and technology projects. Then, the association of the appropriate sets of tools, techniques or methods to each particular project needs a more precise definition of the project and context to be recommended to a large variety of projects.

The ontological frameworks represent practical tools to describe projects and contexts, and the association of tools and techniques for project management to a large number of combinations contained in the frameworks facilitates the customized selection of the corresponding sets that assist the strategic effective, efficient and economic use of tools and methods. In our study, the association of tools and projects and contexts is based on the expert judgment of the authors, which has been pre-designed and incorporated into the ontological modeling and analysis. Simultaneously, the tailor-made association of these tools, permits to discard the use of methods that are expensive and ineffective under the wrong context of a project. No tool or method will be complete or sufficient for all projects, and hence the need to customize their selection and use to improve the current rates of success and to optimize the costs of their management. Our analyses present such differences in the number and type of tools required for effective and efficient IT project management contrasting the elements in table

3 for two projects, and later in Figure 2, it is represented how some tools are recommended in more projects. The emphases in recommendations of tools and techniques should be directed by the nature of the project and organizational context, hence, customizing in each case the toolkit for the manager and his team. In some cases, it is expected that the set of tools and techniques could be assimilated with some method (i.e., agile, lean, or structured), while in some other cases, the recommended toolkit may be a composite method mixing tools, techniques and good practices from different approaches towards IT Project management.

The present study can be improved by increasing the number of projects analyzed and including in the sample other projects that can be evaluated ex post, after the successful or failed use of traditional methods. With a larger and more diverse sample of IST projects covering the whole IS lifecycle and IT project Lifecycle, more tools could be analyzed and prioritized. As future research, the tools could be systematically analyzed and prioritized according to some degree of contribution for the improvement of the success rates on each IST project.

REFERENCES

Cockburn, A. & Highsmith, J. (2001). Agile software development: The people factor. *Computer*, 131-133.

Garel, G. (2013.) "A history of project management models: From pre-models to the standard models. *International Journal of Project Management* (31), 663-669.

Hoffmann, D., Ahlemann, F., & Reining, S. (2020). Reconciling alignment, efficiency, and agility in IT project portfolio management: Recommendations based on a revelatory case study. *International Journal of Project Management*, 38(2), 124-136, doi:https://doi.org/10.1016/j.ijproman.2020.01.004.

Joslin, R. & Müller, R. (2015.) Relationships between a project management methodology and project success in different project governance contexts. *International Journal of Project Management* (33), 1377-1392.

La Paz, A., Merigó, J., Powell, P., Ramaprasad, A., & Syn, T. (2019). Twenty-five years of the Information Systems Journal: a bibliometric and ontological overview. *Information Systems Journal*. https://doi.org/10.1111/isj.12260

Lasi, H., Fettke, P., Kemper, H.-G., Feld, T. & Hoffmann, M. (2014.) Industry 4.0. *Business information systems engineering* (6), 239-242.

Matos, S. & Lopes, E. (2013.) Prince2 or PMBOK–a question of choice. *Procedia Technology.* (9), 787-794.

Mir, F. A. & Pinnington, A. H. (2014.) Exploring the value of project management: linking project management performance and project success. *International journal of project management (*32), 202-217.

Nelson, R. (2007) IT project management: Infamous failures, classic mistakes, and best practices. *MIS Quarterly executive* (6)

Papke-Shields, K. E., Beise, C. & Quan, J. (2010.) Do project managers practice what they preach, and does it matter to project success? *International journal of project management* (28), 650-662.

Radujković, M. & Sjekavica, M. (2017.) Project management success factors. *Procedia engineering* (196), 607-615.

Rao, S. K. & Prasad, R. (2018.) Impact of 5G technologies on industry 4.0 *Wireless personal communications* (100), 145-159.

Serrador, P. & Turner, R. (2015.) The relationship between project success and project efficiency. *Project management journal* (46), 30-39.

Špundak, M. (2014.) Mixed agile/traditional project management methodology–reality or illusion? *Procedia Social Behavioral Sciences* (119), 939-948.

Takeuchi, H. & Nonaka, I. (1986.) The new product development game. *Harvard business review* (64), 137-146.

Vásquez, J., & La Paz, A. (2019). The Knowledge Body of Requirement Engineering in IST Innovations: An Ontological Analysis. *Journal of technology management & innovation*, 14(4), 78-84.

COMPARATIVE ANALYSIS OF SOFTWARE DEVELOPMENT METHODOLOGIES FOR SECURITY REQUIREMENT ANALYSIS: TOWARDS HEALTHCARE SECURITY PRACTICE

Prosper K. Yeng[1], Stephen D. Wolthusen[1,2] and Bian Yang[1]
[1]*Information Security and Communication Technology, Norwegian University of Science and Technology (NTNU) Gjøvik, Norway*
[2]*School of Mathematics and Information Security, Royal Holloway, University of London, Egham, United Kingdom*

ABSTRACT

Reducing time to market (TTM), dynamic requirement changes and increasing profit to service providers are some of the features that are most interesting to software developers, in their look-up for software development methodologies. Security requirement features in system development methodologies are often not the primary concern of developers until now. Due to the increasing rate of data breaches in healthcare, software engineers in healthcare are desiring for suitable methods which have been incorporated with security requirement activities, for effective security requirement analyses.

This study surveyed on existing software development methodologies and assessed their suitability for security requirements gathering and analysis towards enhancing information security assurance in healthcare. Security requirement activities were obtained from software security engineering standards and guidelines. The security activities were then assessed in existing software development methods to determine their extend of incorporation towards secure software development in healthcare. In this review, the traditional software development methods, including the Waterfall Model, were realized to have more integration of security requirement capturing activities than the agile methods.

KEYWORDS

Security Requirement, Security Assurance, Software Development Methods, Healthcare

1. INTRODUCTION

Security in software development methodologies is considered a non-functional requirement and is often not handled with the needed attention like the functional requirements (El-Hadary & El-Kassas, 2014). There are various software development methodologies such as Agile, Spiral, Rapid application development and Waterfall methods. These methods are primarily used to efficiently elicit the system requirements as desired by the users(Keramati & Mirian-Hosseinabadi, 2008). Reducing time to market (TTM), dynamic requirement changes and increasing profit to service providers are some of the features that are most interesting to software developers, in their look-up for software development methodologies(Keramati & Mirian-Hosseinabadi, 2008). Security requirement features in system development methodologies are often not the primary concern of developers until now. According to the 2019 Version's data breaches report, about 52% data breaches were caused by hacking activities, 21% were as a result of errors, and authorized users' misuse contributed to 15%(Verison, 2019).

Within the healthcare, data breaches continue to increase globally. In 2017, about 5million health records were compromised but this figure tripled to about 15million in 2018, in about 503 attacks (HealthITSecurity, 2019; Verison, 2019). As at the middle of 2019, the number of compromised records in healthcare were more than 25 million(HealthITSecurity, 2019). Greater proportion of the breaches (59%) were perpetrated by insiders (Verison, 2019) who are authenticated users of the systems (Zhang, Mehotra, Liebovitz, Gunter, & Malin, 2013). The number of data breaches in healthcare has significantly exceeded that of the financial sector and now in competition with other public sector entities (Verison, 2019).

The European Union, recognizing the essential role of Network and Information Systems (NIS) in economic and social activities, provided directives for member states to adopt appropriate security measures towards ensuring Confidentiality, Integrity and Availability (CIA) of critical sectors including the healthcare(council, 2019). Good knowledge on the suitability of software methodologies in relation to how they support security requirement gathering and analysis, would support healthcare information security professionals in their choice of methods towards secure application development.

Some studies have attempted in suggesting suitable software development methods for healthcare information technology professionals towards enhancing security in healthcare, but some critical aspects were not considered. For instance, Al-Dahmash et al proposed Software Engineering Methodology for Healthcare Applications development ((SEMHTA) towards solving healthcare related software related challenges including security (Al-Dahmash & El-Masri, 2013). Additionally, Moratidis et al proposed the extension of a software development method known as Tropos, towards secure healthcare software development (Mouratidis & Giorgini, 2007).

Tropos was designed for analyzing multiagent related systems but lacks analyzing security constraints of actors and lack of security modelling during the early requirements analysis stage (Al-Dahmash & El-Masri, 2013). To this end, Mouratidis et al suggested for these security lapses to be incorporated in Tropos for secure healthcare system development. SEMHTA took into consideration the healthcare background of the end user and the impact on the development activities but the study did not refer to any security requirement standards such as the NIST' security requirement analysis standards or ISO 19977 and this makes it hard to rely on their proposed method for secure application development (Al-Dahmash & El-Masri, 2013). Also, Mouratidis considered some gaps in Tropos but various standards and regulations in healthcare were not adopted.

The objective of this study is to therefore compare existing software development methodologies as to how they are incorporated with security requirement gathering and analysis towards healthcare professional security practices. Such results would provide knowledge to information security professionals in healthcare in their choice of software development methodologies for secure healthcare application development. Section two provides the background on software development methods and security requirement, followed with the approach in section 3. Section 4 presented the literature survey which was followed with the presentation of the findings in section 5. Section 6 and 7 respectively discussed and concluded on the findings.

1.1 Research Problem and Contribution

Healthcare data is classified to be among the most sensitive personal data which require special security measures (e-helse, 2018; ISO, 2016; Yeng, Yang, & Snekkenes, 2019). This has led to the development of a special security standard for healthcare sector ISO 27799:2016(ISO, 2016). But the conventional software development methodologies are still being used to develop healthcare related software. So, to develop healthcare application and other mission critical systems, which of the software methodologies can best help in capturing and analyzing security requirements? The contribution of this study was to compare existing software development methodologies in their suitability for security requirement analysis.

2. BACKGROUND

Due to the huge data breaches in healthcare, there have been concerted research efforts towards improving the security practice in healthcare (Kandabongee Yeng, Yang, & Arthur Snekkenes, 2019; Nweke, Yeng, Wolthusen, & Yang, 2019; Prosper Kandabongee Yeng, 2019; Yeng et al., 2019). Such security practices include the conscious care security practice of various user group such as healthcare professionals, healthcare information communication technology (ICT) professionals and healthcare administrative staff (Kandabongee Yeng et al., 2019; Nweke et al., 2019; Prosper Kandabongee Yeng, 2019; Yeng et al., 2019). In the security practices of healthcare ICT professionals within the context of secure software development, suitable software methodologies are to be adopted. But what software methodologies are more appropriate for secure software development in critical systems like healthcare? This study therefore reviewed common software development methodologies to provide knowledge on the extend of which each method incorporates security requirement analysis in their respective framework.

2.1 Software Development Methodologies

Software development Life Cycle (SDLC) consists of layout stages in which each stage involves undertaking some activities in a manner that would meet some software development objectives (Demirors, Demirors, Kolukısa Tarhan, & Yildiz, 2000; Khong, Yu Beng, Yip, & Fun, 2012). According to ISO/IEC 12207, the stages required in developing and maintaining software are analysis and planning, requirement definitions, architecture design, implementation development, product testing and operational and maintenance (Demirors et al., 2000; Khong et al., 2012) (Stoica, Mircea, & Ghilic-Micu, 2013). Various type of agile methods exists. These methods share the common ideas and values but with subtle characteristics between them. For instance, Some of these objectives include meeting software product quality and customer requirements, decreasing development time, reducing software product development cost while increasing revenue and investments on return (Everett & McLeod, 2006; Stoica et al., 2013). As an example, while crystal methodology focuses on team building, collaboration and communication to enhance quality delivery of non-critical software(Hanssen, Yamashita, Conradi, & Moonen, 2009), Scrum method concentrates on project management in which initial requirements are deemed fuzzy (Schwaber & Beedle, 2001).

The traditional software development methods include Waterfall model, Rational Unified Process (RUP) and Spiral methods (Nikiforova, Nikulsins, & Sukovskis, 2008). The traditional software development methodologies are characterized with sequential series of steps, defining and documenting requirements. The traditional methods are also based on predictive approach where all activities are strictly based on the initial requirement analysis and planning. Software change requirements in the traditional methods must pass through established change management process.

One of the key features of agile approaches to software development is the adoption of adaptive methods (Vijayasarathy & Turk, 2008). There are no detailed planning in the initial phase and the scope of tasks are primarily restricted to only the current functionalities of the specified software (Hazzan & Dubinsky, 2008). So, the agile methods rely on early client involvement, incremental and iterative approach whereby the software development life cycle activities are iteratively visited based on customer feedback and desires (Everett & McLeod, 2006; Hazzan & Dubinsky, 2008; Khong et al., 2012; Stoica et al., 2013). The agile approach involves frequent testing and constant open communication with clients and closed team collaboration but involves minimal documentation and reduced risks of major faults in ongoing activities (Everett & McLeod, 2006; Hazzan & Dubinsky, 2008; Khong et al., 2012; Stoica et al., 2013).

2.2 Security Requirement

Required security practices are specified in security engineering (Wäyrynen, Bodén, & Boström, 2004), which involves some activities towards ensuring secured systems(Hefner, Monroe, & Hsiao, 1996). Security requirements can be decoupled into functional and non-functional requirements and security assurance (Hefner et al., 1996; Jones & Rastogi, 2004; Raj, Singh, & Bansal, 2014). The functional security requirements are description of the security functions which the software must possess (Hefner et al., 1996; Jahl, 1991; Jones & Rastogi, 2004; Raj et al., 2014). The functional security requirement is a repository of security specifications of a system consisting of threats, risks and the system's environment which is termed as the security targets of the system. Examples include access control, data integrity, authentication and wrong password entry logout functional behaviors. Non-functional security requirements consist of the descriptions of the quality of the security of the software (Hefner et al., 1996; Jahl, 1991; Jones & Rastogi, 2004; Raj et al., 2014). The non-functional security requirements often relate to uptime and auditability. Confidence level of satisfaction of security needs in a system is a measure of its security assurance (Wäyrynen et al., 2004). The security assurance of a system is usually presented with some assurance arguments such as structured or support statements to explain how the security needs were met. The arguments also include assurance evidence such as test results and documentation of code reviews.

Various security standards exist to provide guidelines and measures to ensure systems' security. The Common Criteria(CC) (Jahl, 1991), ISO 15408 and Systems Engineering Capability Maturity Model (SE-CMM) security standards are mostly relied on by organizations in developing secure systems (Han & Zheng, 2000; Regulwar, Gulhane, & Jawandhiya, 2010; Wäyrynen et al., 2004). Particularly, SSE-CMM was designed for assessing the capabilities of organizations to develop secure systems. SSE-CMM has some primary practices which are classified into process areas (PA). The PA in SSE-CMM include assess security risks, assess threat, assess vulnerability, provide security input, verify and validate security. The CC is a structured method for expressing security needs of a system and their development processes. The assurance aspect of CC outlines activities and processes to meet evaluation assurance levels (EAL). The EAL objective measures the level of design, testing and verification in a structured, formal and functional way.

In a related context, The National Institute of Standards and Technology (NIST) also provided basic framework which consists of 5 phases of SDLC to provide guidance for the development of security in Information Technology Systems (Hefner et al., 1996; Jahl, 1991; Jones & Rastogi, 2004; Raj et al., 2014). The SDLC phases are Initiation, Development or acquisition, Implementation, Operation or maintenance and Disposition. The initiation stage is associated with identification of security leads and stakeholders, feasibility study and high-level requirement gathering. The development or acquisition stage involve threat modeling, risk management, asset identification and security assurance measures. The implementation stage deals with coding management, security testing, installation, security training and documentation among others. The security disposition includes information preservation, media sanitization and software disposal.

There are various security activities in the various phases of the SDLC of information security development. Within the SDLC phases as shown in Figure 1, there are security requirement gathering and management activities which are being carried out. These security related activities include,

- Identification of related key information security team and stakeholders: The security team and the stakeholders initially gather high level security requirements.
- Requirements Gathering: Involves conducting workshops and interviews to understand the security needs of the business.
- Risk Assessment: The security team performs the risk assessment, by analyzing, measuring, and establishing acceptable level of risks for the system.
- Asset Identification and Valuation. Both tangible and intangible assets are identified and valued for the purpose of cost-benefit analysis of security controls.
  Threat Modeling. This involves identifying and mitigating security threats and vulnerabilities to the system components such as assets
- Risk Mitigation. The vulnerabilities and threats identified are analyzed and Corrective Control, Deterrent Control, Detective Control or Preventive Controls measures are taken.
- Cognizance of Security Risks: The whole team is orientated on security risks with the guide of the security policy, standards, guidelines, and procedures of the organization.
- Secure Coding: Appropriate secured coding should be adopted to mitigate the identified threats and vulnerabilities
- Testing: Appropriate security testing methods and standards should be adopted for security assurance. Testing should include, assurance testing, unit testing and penetration testing.
- Within the operational and maintenance phase, various activities such as monitoring and reviewing logs, documenting security information, security patches, conducting security training and managing cryptographic materials are carried out to maintain security.
- When systems are retired or during disaster situation, the disposition of the information, software and hardware, should be appropriately handled.

To enhance security in application development, the processes in the software development frameworks need to be able to support these outlined security considerations. So, this study examines the extend of which the existing software development methodologies, provide mechanisms for conducting these security requirement activities.

Figure 1. Security Requirement

In brief, the security considerations of SDLC in an information system project should identify and recruit security related stakeholders to gather security requirements, identify assets, perform threat modeling, manage risks, orientate the entire project team on security risks, manage secure coding and conduct security tests. Some of the security requirements considerations are shown in Table 1.

Table 1. Security considerations in SDLC

Security Consideration (SC) #	Security Consideration
SC1	Security Requirement gathering and analysis
SC2	Identification of Assets
SC3	Threat modeling
SC4	Risk management
SC5	Security Orientation
SC6	Manage secure coding
SC7	Security Testing
SC8	Security maintenance and operation
SC9	Security Disposition

3. METHOD

A literature survey was conducted to determine the suitability of software development methods for information security requirement gathering and analysis in software development. IEEE Explore, Google Scholar, Elsevier and Science Direct were explored for the related literatures. Key words such as "security requirements", "Software development methodologies", "Software development framework", "Traditional Software Development Methods" and "Agile software Development Methods" were appropriately combined with Boolean operators of "AND", "NOT" and "OR", to identify only literatures which focused on elucidating security requirement gathering abilities in various software development methodologies.

Some security requirement standards such as CC (Davoud Mougouei, Sani, & Almasi, 2013; Wäyrynen et al., 2004), SSE-CMM, SQUARE (Mead, Viswanathan, & Padmanabhan, 2008; Ray, 2013) and NIST recommendations on information security requirement considerations, were identified in the survey and explored for security requirement activities (Jones & Rastogi, 2004; Raj et al., 2014). The suitability of the software development methodologies, regarding information security requirement development in software, were then assessed by using the security requirement activities as a reference point.

3.1 Criteria Used to Analyze the Literature

As outlined in in section 2.1, the various security requirement activities in Initiation, Development or acquisition, Implementation, Operation or Maintenance and Disposition stages of SDLC were identified. The security requirement activities in each software development methodology which were identified in the literature survey, were then compared with the security requirement activities in each stage of the SDLC. Each software development methodology and how it suits in identifying a particular security activity were scored with '+' (suitable), '/' (not completely suitable) and '–' (not suitable).

4. LITERATURE SURVEY

This section presents security requirements in both agile and traditional software development models.

4.1 Security Requirement in Agile Software Development Methods

In a contribution towards enhancing the security of software products, Wayrymen et al., assessed extreme programming (XP) method (Wäyrynen et al., 2004). The goal was to analyze the security characteristics of XP method to determine its fitness for the development of security critical applications. The security traits of the XP were analyzed based on security considerations in relation to common criteria (CC) and SSE-CMM security standards. Both CC and SSE-CMM are deemed to complement each other. Their combination provides better coverage of the security considerations of functional and non-functional requirements and security assurance. In the study, Wayrymen et al., discovered that XP does not have security engineering support for many areas, relating to specifying security needs and Assurance. Though XP was realized to support some evaluation assurance levels (EAL) such as structural testing, but structural testing require documentation. Furthermore, XP partly addresses assurance requirements which are specified in Evaluation Assurance Level (EAL) 3 and EAL 4 as listed in Table 2. Specifically, XP does not have formal and semi-formal design and verification documentation for EAL5, EAL6 and EAL7.

Table 2. CC's assurance levels and their objectives

Evaluation Assurance Level	Objectives
EAL1	Functionally tested
EAL2	Structurally Tested
EAL3	Methodically tested and checked
EAL4	Methodically designed, tested and checked
EAL5	Semi formally designed and tested
EAL6	Semi formally designed, verified and tested
EAL7	Formally verified, designed and tested

In a related study into Scrum framework (Davoud Mougouei et al., 2013; Ghani, Azham, & Jeong, 2014), the agility of Scrum partly depends on its reduced documentation of development activities. Scrum does not also have explicit lay-down activities for security analysis and design (Chivers, Paige, & Ge, 2005; Wäyrynen et al., 2004). According to Ghani et al, (Ghani et al., 2014) Scrum do not have adequate features to support secure software development. Siponen et al., noted the following as activities in Scrum which do not support security requirement gathering practices (Siponen, Baskerville, & Kuivalainen, 2005):

- Release cycle in Scrum is too short and does not give adequate time for the team to address security requirement.
- Scrum development team do not specify security expert and this contributes to inability to gather security needs(Siponen et al., 2005).
- Unlike in conventional system development life cycles, there are no guidelines for gathering security requirements in Scrum(Ge, Paige, Polack, & Brooke, 2007).

In addition, Scrum was also observed to lack risk management activities, threat identification, threat analysis and also had no decision on security controls (Azham, Ghani, & Ithnin, 2011).

Furthermore, Dynamic System Development Method (DSDM), was also found not to be suitable for secured application development (N. R. Mead, V. Viswanathan, & D. Padmanabhan, 2008). DSDM is a traditional agile model, which was extended from Rapid Application Development (RAD). DSDM relies on the knowledge of people and tools such as prototyping to achieve project schedule and it require active user involvement, fitness for business purpose of deliverables and collaborative approach between stakeholders. Initial high-level requirement, Iterative and incremental development, testing and frequent delivery of products are among DSDM's core principles. There are no clear provisions for capturing and analyzing nonfunctional requirements in DSDM. So, security related projects cannot be developed with DSMD.

4.2 Security Requirements in Traditional Software Development Method

The Rational Unified Process (RUP) was analyzed in context of Security Quality Requirements Engineering (SQUARE) method. This was to analyze the security requirements in RUP towards integrating SQUARE in RUP. RUP consists of inception phase, elaboration phase, construction phase and transition phase. The elaboration phase involves revising and prioritizing the risks and requirements identified in the initial phase. The architecture of the project is also specified at this stage. Major coding occurs in the construction stage and it involves development of the designed components. Transition stage deals with moving product to client, training and testing to meet user's desires. RUP support eliciting and analyzing methods and manage requirements by adopting Unified Modeling Language (UML) for communicating requirements, architecture, and designs.

RUP (N. R. Mead, V. Viswanathan, & J. Zhan, 2008) uses sound software engineering principles which enables it to capture non-functional requirements in addition to the functional requirement specifications in the elaboration phase. This makes RUP more suitable for security critical projects since detailed information is captured at its early phase to address security concerns. Also, RUP has a risk driven feature and risk is identified in every phase (N. Mead, V. Viswanathan, & J. Zhan, 2008). Therefore, risks relating to security are identified. So, vulnerabilities are then identified, and their likelihood of exploitation can be assessed.

In the spiral model, a partial list of the objectives, alternatives and constraints (Ray, 2013) are initially obtained. The model usually begins with this incomplete requirement but with add on functionalities as it progresses in its various stages. The second phase is the "evaluate alternatives, identify and resolve risks" (Boehm, 1988). In this phase, risk management is used to identify risks which serves as input and guidelines for building the prototype. Develop and verify next-level product, is another phase in which models are devised for future development work and software requirements are elicited and validated to meet user needs. Plan next phase is the final phase which only involves developing plans towards guiding the next iteration. Finalizing requirements, development of the application design, and integration and test processes for application implementation are some of the planning activities in this phase. The spiral model assesses risk analysis with each iteration step and assesses security measures to be updated and applied in each iteration since requirement and software products can change in each iteration.

Waterfall model is characterized with more formal approach in which the system requirements are well elucidated from identified stakeholders of the business. The requirements are gathered at high level as well as detailed manner. The developers can infer into the requirements to assess risks and feasibility of the system with regards to technology and regulatory requirements. Requirements are then modelled, designed and implemented. The system then undergoes vigorous testing and maintenance. There are a lot of documentations involve in collecting as much information as possible. The detailed information also helps in traceability of requirements to stakeholders and through the entire development process. Changes have to go through established change request procedure. These characteristics of the Waterfall model makes it more aligned for security requirement management since, requirements and designs are well understood in the initial phases. Waterfall model is predictable due to the involvement of detailed planning of its architecture software (Petersen, Wohlin, & Baca, 2009). In this regard, security requirement phases and activities can be properly woven into Waterfall and other traditional models. The software development methodologies and how they incorporate security requirement activities in their framework are shown in Table 3.

5. RESULTS AND FINDINGS

Based on the review in section 4, the suitability of these methods for security requirement gathering and analysis were indicated in Table 2. The suitability of the software development methods was rated based on reviews of their characteristics regarding security requirement activities.

Table 3. Security Requirement activities and their suitability in software development methods: '+' means suitable '/' means not completely suitable and '–' means not suitable

Security Activities	Software Development Life Cycle Methods					
	XP	Scrum	DSDM	Waterfall	RUP	SPIRAL
Initiation						
Security lead and Stakeholders identification	-	-	-	+	-	-
High level requirement gathering	/	/	/	+	+	+
Feasibility Study	/	/	-	+	+	+
Development or acquisition						
Requirement gathering and analysis	/	/	/	+	+	+
Identify Assets	-	-	-	+	+	+
Threat Modeling	-	-	-	+	+	+
Risk Management	-	-	-	+	+	+
Security Orientation	-	-	-	-	-	-
Functional and non-functional Security requirement analysis	-	-	-	+	+	+
Security Assurance Requirement Analysis	/	-	/	+	+	+
Security Control development	-	-	-	+	+	+
Security test and evaluation development	-	-	-	+	+	+
Implementation						
Manage Secure Coding	+(Through pair programming	-	-	+	+	+(through iteration)
Security Testing	/(Through user specification)	/(Through user specification)	/	+	+	+
Installation	+	+	+	+	+	+
Acceptance testing	+	+	+	+	+	+
Initial user training	+	+	+	+	+	+
Documentation	-	-	-	+	+	+
Operations and Maintenance						
Configuration Management and Control	-	-	-	+	+	+
Continuous Monitoring	-	-	-	+	+	+
Disposition						
Information Preservation	-	-	-	-	-	-
Media Sanitization	-	-	-	-	-	-
Hardware and Software Disposal	-	-	-	-	-	-

With reference to Table 3, the traditional software methods incorporated most of the security requirement activities in their framework as compared to the agile methods. But none of the application development methods incorporated security requirement activities under disposition phase of security system development life cycle.

6. DISCUSSION

A survey was conducted into software development methodologies (SDLC) to assess their fitness for security requirement gathering and analysis in healthcare context. Alongside, software security requirement frameworks and standards were explored for security considerations which are desired in existing software development methods. Security requirement considerations of functional and non-functional requirements and security assurance were derived from CC, SSE-CMM (Davoud Mougouei et al., 2013; Wäyrynen et al., 2004), SQUARE and NIST's security requirement considerations as shown in Table 1. The software development methods which were assessed are Extreme Programming (XP), Scrum, Dynamic System Development Method (DSDM), Spiral, Rational Unified Process (RUP) and Waterfall Model. These methods were in the category of both traditional methods (Spiral, Rational Unified Process (RUP) and Waterfall Model) and agile methodologies (XP, Scrum, DSDM).

From Table 3, aside security considerations in the disposition phase, most of the security requirement activities were included in the traditional software development methodologies as compared to the agile methods. While agile merely had installation, testing and training activities in their framework, the traditional software development methods included all the security development methods excepts security orientation. The traditional software development methods indicated the higher suitability based on the argument that, most of the information security development methodologies relied on the traditional software development models to create these security requirement frameworks. The agile development framework was not considered during the development of these security guidelines and standards. This makes current security requirement guidelines unsuitable for agile methods. So, the way forward could be to develop security frameworks or guidelines in the perspective of agile framework in order for agile methods to be able to adopt to security requirement activities.

The swiftness in agile methods are due to lightweight documentation, usage of basic requirement for application development, frequent involvement of product owners and frequent testing and verification (Davoud Mougouei et al., 2013; Ghani et al., 2014). It is of the viewed that, some of the features of agile methods are rather inimical to software security requirement activities. For instance, the lightweight documentation does not provide room for adequate requirement gathering on the onset of the system development process. This makes it difficult for identification of threats and vulnerabilities at the onset and therefore, security needs become an after-math thought. Additionally, the agile method do not have formal approach for stakeholder identification and planning and therefore security teams are not identified into the development team of the system. The lack of security knowledge in the agile development methods also inhibits adequate security requirement gathering and analysis. However, because agile method adopts frequent engagements with product owners and conducts frequent tests and verification, Evaluation Assurance Level (EAL 2,3 and 4, are partly addressed. But EAL of semi-formal and formal design and verification are not addressed. Another pattern in Table 3 indicates that none of the application development frameworks is suitable for security requirement activities in the disposition phase. This is due to the point that all the software development methods aimed towards creating software to meet customer needs. The retirement phases of these software are not provided in these software development methods (Demirors et al., 2000; Khong et al., 2012).

In summary, none of the software development methods in both agile and traditional systems is completely suitable with the incorporation of all the outlined security requirement activities for secure healthcare system development analysis. But the traditional software development methods are more suitable, particularly, the Waterfall model. In comparing the agile methods, XP is more suitable since it incorporates secure coding management activity through pair-wised programming.

6.1 Conclusion

The review was towards assessing software development methodologies regarding how suitable they incorporate security requirement analysis activities for secure healthcare software development. The traditional software development methods were more suitable, particularly, the Waterfall model. In comparing the agile methods, XP was more suitable since it incorporated secure coding management activity through pair-wised programming. The traditional methods were more suitable because the security requirement analysis methods were developed to be more tailored to the traditional software development methods. Healthcare professionals could be guided in their choice of software development methods for secure systems. Also, the findings can guide the development of a new system software development framework for healthcare context.

REFERENCES

Al-Dahmash, A., & El-Masri, S. (2013). A New Proposed Software Engineering Methodologyfor Healthcare Applications Development. *Int. J. Mod. Eng. Res, 3*(3), 1566-1570.

Azham, Z., Ghani, I., & Ithnin, A. P. D. N. (2011). Security backlog in Scrum security practices. doi:10.1109/MySEC.2011.6140708

Boehm, B. W. (1988). A spiral model of software development and enhancement. *Computer, 21*(5), 61-72. doi:10.1109/2.59

Chivers, H., Paige, R., & Ge, X. (2005). *Agile Security Using an Incremental Security Architecture.*

council, E. p. a. o. t. (2019). *concerning measures for a high common level of security of network and information systems across the Union.* Official Journal of the European Union: Official Journal of the European Union Retrieved from https://eur-lex.europa.eu/eli/dir/2016/1148/oj

Davoud Mougouei, Sani, N. F. M., & Almasi, M. M. (2013). S-Scrum: a Secure Methodology for Agile Development of Web Services. *World of Computer Science and Information Technology Journal (WCSIT), 3*(1), 15-19.

Demirors, O., Demirors, E., Kolukısa Tarhan, A., & Yildiz, A. (2000). *Tailoring ISO/IEC 12207 for instructional software development* (Vol. 2).

Code of conduct for information security and data protection in the healthcare and care services sector, (2018).

El-Hadary, H., & El-Kassas, S. (2014). Capturing security requirements for software systems. *J Adv Res, 5*(4), 463-472. Retrieved from https://www.ncbi.nlm.nih.gov/pubmed/25685514. doi:10.1016/j.jare.2014.03.001

Everett, G., & McLeod, R. (2006). The Software Development Life Cycle. In (pp. 29-58).

Ge, X., Paige, R. F., Polack, F., & Brooke, P. (2007). *Extreme programming security practices.* Paper presented at the Proceedings of the 8th international conference on Agile processes in software engineering and extreme programming, Como, Italy.

Ghani, I., Azham, Z., & Jeong, S. R. (2014). Integrating Software Security into Agile-Scrum Method. *KSII Transactions on Internet and Information Systems, 8*, 646-663. doi:10.3837/tiis.2014.02.0019

Han, J., & Zheng, Y. (2000). *Security characterisation and integrity assurance for component-based software.*

Hanssen, G., Yamashita, A., Conradi, R., & Moonen, L. (2009). *Maintenance and Agile Development: Challenges, Opportunities and Future Directions.*

Hazzan, O., & Dubinsky, Y. (2008). Introduction to Agile Software Development. doi:10.1007/978-1-84800-198-5_1

HealthITSecurity (Producer). (2019, 2019-07-23). The 10 Biggest Healthcare Data Breaches of 2019, So Far. Retrieved from https://healthitsecurity.com/news/the-10-biggest-healthcare-data-breaches-of-2019-so-far

Hefner, R., Monroe, W., & Hsiao, D. (1996). Experience with the Systems Security Engineering Capability Maturity Model. *INCOSE International Symposium, 6*, 1069-1074. doi:10.1002/j.2334-5837.1996.tb02124.x

ISO. (2016). ISO 27799:2016(en), Health informatics â" Information security management in health using ISO/IEC 27002. In.

Jahl, C. (1991). *Common Criteria for Information Technology Security Evaluation.*

Jones, R., & Rastogi, A. (2004). Secure Coding: Building Security into the Software Development Life Cycle. *Information Systems Security, 13*, 29-39. doi:10.1201/1086/44797.13.5.20041101/84907.5

Kandabongee Yeng, P., Yang, B., & Arthur Snekkenes, E. (2019). Healthcare Staffs' Information Security Practices Towards Mitigating Data Breaches: A Literature Survey. *Studies in health technology and informatics, 261*, 239-245. Retrieved from http://ebooks.iospress.nl/publication/51543. doi:10.3233/978-1-61499-975-1-239

Keramati, H., & Mirian-Hosseinabadi, S. (2008, 31 March-4 April 2008). *Integrating software development security activities with agile methodologies.* Paper presented at the 2008 IEEE/ACS International Conference on Computer Systems and Applications.

Khong, L., Yu Beng, L., Yip, T., & Fun, T. (2012). *Software Development Life Cycle AGILE vs Traditional Approaches.*

Mead, N., Viswanathan, V., & Zhan, J. (2008). Incorporating Security Requirements Engineering into Standard Lifecycle Processes. *International Journal of Security and Its Applications, 2*(4), 67-80.

Mead, N. R., Viswanathan, V., & Padmanabhan, D. (2008, 28 July-1 Aug. 2008). *Incorporating Security Requirements Engineering into the Dynamic Systems Development Method.* Paper presented at the 2008 32nd Annual IEEE International Computer Software and Applications Conference.

Mead, N. R., Viswanathan, V., & Zhan, J. (2008, 24-26 April 2008). *Incorporating Security Requirements Engineering into the Rational Unified Process.* Paper presented at the 2008 International Conference on Information Security and Assurance (isa 2008).

Mouratidis, H., & Giorgini, P. (2007). Secure Tropos: A Security-Oriented Extension of the Tropos methodology. *International Journal of Software Engineering and Knowledge Engineering, 17.* doi:10.1142/S0218194007003240

Nikiforova, O., Nikulsins, V., & Sukovskis, U. (2008). *Integration of MDA Framework into the Model of Traditional Software Development*.

Nweke, L. O., Yeng, P., Wolthusen, S. D., & Yang, B. (2019, 23-24 April 2020). *Understanding Attribute-Based Access Control for Modelling and Analysing Healthcare Professionals' Security Practices.* Paper presented at the strategic foresight, security challenges and innovation, Kyungdong University, South Korea.

Petersen, K., Wohlin, C., & Baca, D. (2009, 2009//). *The Waterfall Model in Large-Scale Development.* Paper presented at the Product-Focused Software Process Improvement, Berlin, Heidelberg.

Prosper Kandabongee Yeng, A. S., Bian Yang, Einar Arthur Snekkenes. (2019). Framework for Healthcare Staffs' Information Security Practice Analysis: Psycho-Socio-Cultural Context.*JMIR.*

Raj, G., Singh, D., & Bansal, A. (2014, 25-26 Sept. 2014). *Analysis for security implementation in SDLC.* Paper presented at the 2014 5th International Conference - Confluence The Next Generation Information Technology Summit.

Ray, L. L. (2013). Security considerations for the spiral development model. *International Journal of Information Management, 33*(4), 684-686. doi:10.1016/j.ijinfomgt.2013.03.003

Regulwar, G. B., Gulhane, V. S., & Jawandhiya, P. M. (2010, 17-19 Sept. 2010). *A Security Engineering Capability Maturity Model.*Paper presented at the 2010 International Conference on Educational and Information Technology.

Schwaber, K., & Beedle, M. (2001). Agile Software Development With Scrum.

Siponen, M., Baskerville, R., & Kuivalainen, T. (2005). *Integrating Security into Agile Development Methods.*

Stoica, M., Mircea, M., & Ghilic-Micu, B. (2013). Software Development: Agile vs. Traditional. *Informatica Economica, 17*, 64-76. doi:10.12948/issn14531305/17.4.2013.06

Verison. (2019). *Data Breaches Report.* Retrieved from https://www.key4biz.it/wp-content/uploads/2019/05/2019-data-breach-investigations-report.pdf

Vijayasarathy, L. E. O., & Turk, D. A. N. (2008). Agile software development: A survey of early adopters. *Journal of Information Technology Management, 19.*

Wäyrynen, J., Bodén, M., & Boström, G. (2004, 2004//). *Security Engineering and eXtreme Programming: An Impossible Marriage?* Paper presented at the Extreme Programming and Agile Methods - XP/Agile Universe 2004, Berlin, Heidelberg.

Yeng, P., Yang, B., & Snekkenes, E. (2019, 15-19 July 2019). *Observational Measures for Effective Profiling of Healthcare Staffs' Security Practices.* Paper presented at the 2019 IEEE 43rd Annual Computer Software and Applications Conference (COMPSAC).

Zhang, H., Mehotra, S., Liebovitz, D., Gunter, C., & Malin, B. (2013). Mining Deviations from Patient Care Pathways via Electronic Medical Record System Audits. *ACM Transactions on Management Information Systems (TMIS), 4.* doi:10.1145/2544102

HEDGING STRATEGIES IN THE ADOPTION AND USE OF E-GOVERNMENT SERVICES

Sharif Khan, Salah Kabanda and Adedapo Mobee
University Cape Town,
Department of Information Systems, South Africa

ABSTRACT

Despite the anticipated benefits of efficiency, cost savings, inclusion and overall citizens' satisfaction; adoption and use of ICT and related technologies in government (e-Gov) remains low in developing countries. One of the main challenges has been trust. It is believed that the online environment poses a series of risk and uncertainties which user's find difficult to navigate through and develop trust. In such uncertain situations, users engage in hedging strategies to shield from the risks that they would be exposed to and ensure themselves from any loss. This study seeks to explore what hedging strategies online users employ to guard against risks associated with the use of e-Gov services. Following an interpretive paradigm and semi-structured interviews as a means of data collection, the study identifies three hedging strategies associated with the adoption of e-Gov services in the Western Cape of South Africa.

KEYWORDS

E-Government, Trust, Hedging

1. INTRODUCTION

Governments globally realize that e–Government (eGov) has the potential to improve service delivery and is now considered the instrument through which citizens use to measure government performance (Mutula and Mostert 2010). To date, many governments are advocating for eGov as a means to, among other benefits, reduce cost, enhance citizen trust of government and improve efficiency (Picazo-Vela et al 2012). Despite these benefits and opportunities, the successful implementation is dependent on citizen's willingness to adopt these services (Shareef et al 2011). Rashid and Othman (2010) state that 'although it is clear that the citizen is the main user of eGov services, there are only few studies conducted on the issue specific to citizen adoption of the online service'; and even if studies are done, adoption remains low, implying that we have not adequately understood what factors influence adoption (Lallmahomed et al 2017). Further, the majority of the studies report from a developed economy context, where their contextual challenges and opportunities differ significantly to those present in developing countries. For example, developed economies cite the characteristics of the services themselves as being highly influential for the decision to not use eGov; and that 'technological shortcomings like data security or a lack of usability only play a subordinate role' (Distel 2018). These findings are in contrast for most developing countries were technology related factors are still seen as being significant to citizen's adoption of eGov. The plethora of studies have shown that the most influencing factors include issues of privacy and security risks posed online (Munyoka and Maharaj 2019); performance and time risks associated with e-services as well as quality of services such as system, service and information quality (Alzahrani et al 2018). Prior studies have also identified trust in online IT systems as one of the main predictor of adoption and continued use of online systems (van Esterik-Plasmeijer and van Raaij, 2017).

Alzahrani et al (2018) reiterates that a lack of trust in eGov is the main inhibitor of adoption, mainly due to the inherent risks of online interactions and transactions, and its dependence on the context (Chen et al 2015). The online context presents two conditions which makes trust impotent: uncertainty and vulnerability risk (Mellouli et al 2016). In the face of these conditions, people tend to develop hedging mechanism as a means of self-protection (Reich and Wheeler, 2016). According to D'cruz (2015), hedging is "a defensive posture in the face of uncertainty, a method of mitigating the severity of feared negative outcomes by expending resources to protect oneself in the event" (472). Understanding hedging as a coping strategy when trust is not completely conferred in an eGov service is important, as the findings would help developers have better insights into users' needs to improve the design and implementation of online services (Bhattacharya et al, 2012) and consequently increase adoption and usage of eGov services. This study seeks to explore what hedging strategies online users employ to guard against risks associated with the use of e-Gov services.

This study examines this phenomenon in the South African context. Although countries in Africa are seen to lag behind the world in eGov adoption, South Africa is amongst the six African countries, which show a high E-Government Development Index (EGDIs) and possess a high E-Participation Index. As a country that is featured in the top fiftieth percentile along with countries that have EGDIs above the world average of 0.549 (E-government Survey, 2019); South Africa is seen as a good case study for this study.

2. RELATED WORK

2.1 E-Government

E-Government is traditionally seen as the use of the Internet by government agencies to provide (i) informational services such as policy information to downloadable forms for automobile license renewal; and (2) transactional services to citizens such as filing taxes and conducting online transactions (Venkatesh et al 2016). In this way, the government 'improves transparency, accountability and governance of the public sector services and in so doing it can improve government performance and create new public value for citizens and businesses' (Al-Hujran et al 2015). Currently, the literature is rich on studies on citizen adoption of eGov services. Yet adoption and usage of eGov services remains low, specifically in developing countries who are also now embarking on the use of ICTs to deliver their services. For example, Mauritius is one of the first country in Sub Saharan Africa to obtain a high score on the UN E-Government Development Index for 2014 (Lallmahomed et al, 2017) and is the second top most E-Government ready country in Africa behind Tunisia (UN E - Goverment Survey, 2016). In South Africa, several eGov services are noted such as the electronic filing system, which delivers a means to submit tax returns using internet; as well as the National Traffic Information System (Mutula and Mostert, 2010). Several authors have attributed the lack of adoption to citizen's mistrusts of eGov (Bélanger and Carter 2008).

Chen et al (2015) divides trust in two categories: trust in the entity providing the service, (the government), and trust in the tools used to deliver the service, (the technology). Whilst the former "arises if citizens have confidence in the government, reinforcing perceptions of integrity and reliability; the latter arises when online users trust the tools to be used to deliver the service - especially considering ongoing security and privacy concerns that hinders e-government use" (253). Studies in tools used to deliver the service, have shown that if citizens perceive that using eGov will be easy to use, it will influence the decision to adopt (Shareef et al 2011). For instance, Lallmahomed et al (2017) notes that factors such as performance expectancy, facilitating conditions and perceived value showed significant positive relationship with behavioural intention to use eGov services. These two categories of trust are perceived to be significant factors in influencing trust in the usage of e-Gov services due to potential risk and uncertainties posed online (Chen et al 2015). Alzahrani et al (2016) identify citizen's disposition to trust, demographic factors such as age and internet experience as important aspects influencing trust in eGov. Previous studies have also identified eGov awareness as an important factor for citizen's intention to use eGov services. This is because awareness can translate into recognition of the perceived benefits and may influence adoption (Joseph and Du Plessis, 2015). In addition to awareness of the services offered, Liu and Carter (2018) posits that an individual's awareness of and familiarity with organizational information privacy practices and an eGov system are important as these can potentially influence adoption.

2.2 Hedging

Several studies have shown that trust is an essential element of a relationship when uncertainty, or risk, is present (Bélanger and Carter 2008). It is therefore imperative to understand how online users manage during uncertainty. One strategy identified to be used by those in uncertainty situation is hedging - a "strategy of insuring oneself against a loss" (D'cruz, 2015). Hedging is perceived to be one of the most important risk management decisions (Dorfman and Karali 2010) and as such has drawn the attention of policy makers and scholars alike (Koga 2017). Jackson (2014) posits that the concept of mistrust gives one of the dominant explanations for hedging. When individuals fail to trust the trustee, they involve themselves in hedging strategies to shield from the risk that the trustee presents. There are several hedging strategies in literature, however, these tend to be concentrated within the financial sector context to examine risk management (Taušer and Čajka, 2016); and others who examine hedging at international political macro level to influence policymaking (Salman, 2017). The former has also been widely used in the context of farming, to manage risks associated with farming by presenting farmers with information on "how to hedge, how much to hedge, when to hedge, etc., by a wide variety of ''experts" (Dorfman and Karali, 2010).

Rao et al (2011,555) notes that although hedging is a powerful tool, "it has not been studied in computing systems to handle the uncertainties" such as those that exist in the operation. Attempts to use the hedging concept in information systems is by Hariguna and Berlilana (2017) who shows that: "if an e-commerce on social media has reliability on the quality of system, quality of information and quality of service, it will greatly affect the number of visits to e-commerce which will certainly be a hedge against the quantity of purchases on e-commerce". Trust, therefore is an important attribute of hedging. Although there are plethora of studies on trust and e-government, few have explored hedging in the context of e-government and specifically from an employee or citizen perspective.

3. METHODOLOGY

To explore hedging strategies used by online users to guard against risks associated with the use of e-Gov services, this study followed an interpretive approach. The study was inductive in nature given that "hedging" as a concept has not been well researched and theorised in the information systems discipline. Using interviews as a means of data collection, the researchers sought to engage participants with e-Gov, specifically their experiences in engaging with online services offered by government and strategies they use if any, of mitigating risks associated with consuming online services. Data was collected from government employees in the Western Cape of South Africa. The motivation to focus on government employees was firstly because, whilst there have been several studies on citizen adoption, few have examined public sector adoption and use of eGov services. This is a limitation given the employee's organizational contextual constraints towards their adoption and usage. Also, focusing on the employee could also provide insights into how best to develop systems that are address both citizen and public employee concerns. This can be achieved through, for example co-design of the systems in the initial phase of the innovation (Ruiz Ben et al 2017).

The Western Cape province of South Africa is one of the provinces which boasts as the tech hub of Africa, with Cape Town as the New Silicon Valley (https://www.siliconcape.com/). The province is the second-highest contributor to South Africa's GDP and therefore serves as a good context. In total, sixteen interviews were conducted and thematic analysis was employed to study the interviews to identify patterns associated to the phenomenon of interest. Firstly, the data was transcribed the transcribed interviews became the data corpus through which the main data analysis was performed from. Then, initial reading and rereading of each transcribed document was done with the purpose of identifying key words that spoke towards the research problem and goal of the study. These key words became the first step towards the development of initial codes for the analysis. The codes were then compared and instances where the codes appeared to point to the same meaning, these codes were grouped together to form a theme. For example, initial codes identified as "physically seeking assistance", "call in to seek help", and "log a call online" were grouped together to form one major theme titled *Use of multichannels for e-Gov services*. This process was iterative in nature, as it required going back to the themes and codes to ensure the aggregation of the theme does reflect what the codes intend, and that the codes correspond to the data extract. Three main themes were identified: use of multichannels to access e-Gov services, friends with benefits and "blessers"; and Limited use of eGov services. These themes are discussed below.

4. FINDINGS AND DISCUSSION

4.1 Demographic Findings

Sixteen respondents participated in the study as shown in Table 1. All respondents, with the exception of $Resp_{16}$ had used eGov services, with some identifying themselves as frequent users ($Resp_{1,2,3,7,8,10,11,12,13,14,15}$); others as infrequent users ($Resp_{4,5,6,9}$). It is interesting to note that the majority of the younger respondents identified as frequent users of eGov services. Our findings are in line with Gupta et al (2017) who posits that "old aged employees are generally not comfortable with computers and ICT, and hence reluctant towards adopting e-government, as com-pared to young ones". Nine of the respondents had a national certificate or a diploma as their highest education qualification. Six respondents identified as female and the remaining identified as male.

Table 1. Respondent demographic Profile

Respondent	Gender	Age	Education	Government
$Resp_1$	Male	31	National Certificate/Diploma	Municipality
$Resp_2$	Male	33	National Certificate/Diploma	Municipality
$Resp_3$	Male	20	National Certificate/Diploma	Municipality
$Resp_4$	Female	26	National Certificate/Diploma	Municipality
$Resp_5$	Male	40	National Certificate/Diploma	Municipality
$Resp_6$	Male	42	National Certificate/Diploma	Municipality
$Resp_7$	Male	42	Master's Degree	Municipality
$Resp_8$	Male	44	National Certificate/Diploma	Municipality
$Resp_9$	Female	52	Higher Diploma	Department of Home Affair
$Resp_{10}$	Male	38	Postgraduate certificate	Department of Home Affair
$Resp_{11}$	Male	27	Bachelor's degree	South Africa Revenue service
$Resp_{12}$	Male	27	Postgraduate certificate	South Africa Revenue service
$Resp_{13}$	Female	45	National Certificate/Diploma	Department of Justice
$Resp_{14}$	Female	39	National Certificate/Diploma	Supply chain management
$Resp_{15}$	Female	28	Honors Degree	Department of labor
$Resp_{16}$	Female	60	Higher Diploma	Social Security Agency

4.2 Hedging Strategies

4.2.1 Use of Multichannels for e-Gov Services

Most respondents in this study were educated – possessing a national certificate or diploma as minimal qualification. They however, identified literacy as a factor of consideration when using e-Gov because the content presented online is difficult to understand. To avoid the risk of continuing with the online task, due to lack of understanding what is required, they reverted to traditional channels of communicating with government as $Resp_8$ explains:

> *reading and comprehending technology language is different from reading and comprehending non IT language. When it comes to following instructions on how to use online services, it is difficult to understand and I would prefer to have someone physically guiding me. When online filling a form, iam usually confused (chuckles), so I go to their offices personally, and sometimes I phone them. This is easier for me.*

The use of technological jargon increases *confusion* and has the potential to develop computer anxiety amongst users (Oluwalola 2015). Although this jargon emanates from the developers who come from different disciplines, it is imperative that it is contained during development as it can lead to misunderstandings (Blanson Henkemans, 2015), and the ramification observed during adoption. $Respondent_{15}$ agrees and indicates that *this problem is bigger for those whose English is not their first language or are older... they not going to know what to do*. Several authors have called for the need to understand how technological media influence contexts and forms of expression and communication because "language technologies vary dramatically and being literate in one mode does not imply being literate in all modes" (Chun 2016).

Although there were some citizens who were aware of the services (awareness) and able to understand the technical jargon presented to them (literacy), there was a perception that there was a need from service providers to explain in detail how to start using a particular service and the various activities involved in the consumption of the service. For example, most respondents identified the tax process as being tedious and complicated. One of the respondents ($Resp_{12}$) explains:

> *there are a lots of tax payers who need to be educated on how it works, they feel like they being robbed. You must be aware of the processes. Where does it start, what signatures do I need when I reach which phase of the process, what it consists of, how do I know I have reached the end? People do not know so they visit the offices physically – simply because they failed to understand the tax process.*

The use of multichannel was also employed to confirm the details presented online because according to $Resp_2$ *you cannot trust everything online. Some individual can pose as the municipality of Cape Town when they are sitting in some island ready to trick you. I call the numbers they have given me to verify and also go in myself to actually see that it is indeed them.* The findings therefore show that citizens would use multichannel approach (such as revert to traditional channels of access when they fail to understand how to consume an online services or require to confirm the actual existence of the eGov service), as a hedging strategy to respond to the uncertainties presented when consuming an eGov service.

4.2.2 Friends with Benefits and "Blessers"

A consistent claim from respondents was the fear of not completing the online task correctly due to poor digital competencies, and in so doing *jeopardize my money – imagine I had already paid and everything (gasps)! ($Resp_3$).* Understanding the technical language used online was one challenge, and the other was having the skill set and competency required to engage with the technology itself. Whilst most respondents indicated that they have access to ICTs, they noted that they do not have the specialized skills to complete an online service without assistance as $Resp_4$ explains:

> *I mostly* ask *my friend to help me out. Most of us do these transactions when we are at work because it cheaper that way, and when we stuck we ask friends who have these sophisticated skills. Of course you have to trust the friend, and having a friend with benefits helps.*

Several respondents called for the government to invest in all employees instead of *investing only in administrators and managers because some employees do not have the skills and are now forced to find alternatives means that are not safe* ($Resp_6$). According to McLeod and Savoy (2015) major benefits can be derived from an introductory level computer courses designed and structured in a way to provide the basic steps to becoming technologically literate. Neves et al (2018) identified digital literacy – a user's ability to have prior and current digital skills to navigate online – as an instrumental factor that can facilitate but also hinder adoption of eGov services. Whilst friends with benefits were used to assist in navigating the online platform, they were also used when access to eGov services was not possible due to lack of data. Access to the device such as a computer or a mobile phone that allows usage of online services was not a problem; but access to data, which was usually associated with high costs was problematic as $Resp_5$ explains:

> *Data wise I don't have a problem, no access problems. I can afford. But what about others who can't? Most people cannot afford and they turn to friends who loads them with credit – sometimes, if not most time, at a cost in kind. Government must put procedures in place as this can lead to blessers here because we have young employees coming in.*

A "blesser is defined as "an older rich man who tend to entice young women with money and expensive gifts in exchange for sexual favours" (Mampane 2018). When users become weary of risking to lose their finances or incur costs when completing a task online, they indulge in *friends with benefits* or *blesser* hedging strategies. That is, having friends with benefits or blessers is perceived by some respondents as a potential means of cushioning oneself of any risk posed by the use of online services. This is not new in the South African context as Masenya (2017,121) explains that "while many a young person, (cf. especially girl children in the context of the South African sugar daddies/male 'blessers' and sugar mummies/female blessers) get entangled in such relationships due to poverty (in some cases even being supported by parents), many of them are motivated by the materialistic context of globalization". This is further compounded by the "Fear of Missing

Out and the ubiquitous nature of 'being on', in case we miss something" (Andrews, 2018). To address some of these challenges, so as to appear connected and relevant "the emergence of blessers seems to be an escaping route" (Thobejane et al 2017).

4.2.3 Limited Use of eGov Services

Most respondents identified the ease of using online service and the convenience it provides. $Resp_{12}$ comprehensively explains:

> *If it is during tax season, the process of completing the tax invoice traditionally can take long, you have to take leave from work sometimes and you go to the main office. But it does not take long online and you don't have to take leave from work. Most of my accounts are on line. I download the apps so when I get paid I just transfer the money, I don't have to go to the office. , download apps, don't have to queue just transfer.*

Yet, despite these conveniences, most opt to use eGov services less frequently.Two reasons were presented. Firstly, that "*no one can confidently confirm, everything that is online is true and works...like there is no campaign about it like other government initiative have* ($Resp_2$). Whilst they perceived the conveniences and benefits associated with eGov services, they adopted a limited-use hedging strategy to mitigate risk. The lack of awareness of eGov services and respondents lack of observing many people who have used eGov services was the main factor influencing the adoption of limited-use hedging strategy. For example, $Resp_9$ notes that *most people are not aware of these services, including myself. I was not aware you could apply for a passport online. I became aware of it after working here [in government].* $Resp_7$ echoes similar sentiments, *I was not initially aware that I can use the on line service. I become aware of it only last year almost by accident – from a work mate in another department.* According to $Resp_{15}$, lack of awareness is driven by government's lack of strategic digital marketing tools because *online services are not advertised, not on social media, billboards, or on other tv channels. Instead it's normally done on traditional SABC channels – who watches them?* The perception was that government's marketing initiative should employee new digital tools and techniques to be able to reach all citizens. These findings echo those in literature, highlighting that to provide better public services through the adoption and use of eGov, marketing remains an obstacle (Otniel, 2015). Teerling and Pieterson (2010) advocate for the application of different marketing strategies to lead citizens to electronic channels and thus increase the usage of eGov services.

The second reason was the quality associated with eGov services. System quality in this study was perceived as availability (online) and responsiveness of the system. Most respondents argued that *online systems do not work and it is frustrating* ($Resp_{13}$) when for example *you uploading documents. It does not upload properly and you spending a lot of time on line, and this translates into unnecessary costs which were supposed to be an advantage of online in the first place* ($Resp_{15}$). Previous studies have also called for eGov services "to be available as much as possible, preferably 24/7, without technical or organizational issues, ensuring the citizen a constant and problem-free access to the portal, regardless of time or geographic location" (Sá et al, 2017). According to $Resp_8$ *the problem here is that the online system sometimes is not working properly, they are offline and therefore not dependable. You can't trust it.* These findings of service availability and responsiveness, have been reported in earlier studies and are amongst other technical performance features, important criterion for determining the quality of eGov services (Jansen and Ølnes, 2016). To avert the risks imposed by system quality (service availability and responsiveness in this case), respondents engaged in limited-use hedging strategies of eGov services.

5. CONCLUSION

The purpose of this study was to explore hedging strategies online users employ to guard against risks associated with the use of e-Gov services in South Africa. The study identified three key hedging strategies. The multichannel hedging strategy was used in instances when users faced technological language or jargon that increased confusion and has the potential to develop computer anxiety amongst users; when confirmation of information and also when the consumption of an e-Gov services was perceived to be difficult. The friends-with benefit/blesser hedging strategy was employed when users perceived the cost associated with e-Gov services was high; and when they perceived themselves to have limited digital competencies to engage with e-Gov services. In this instance, the risk, if incurred at all, would befall the friends-with benefit/blesser. The limited-use hedging strategy was adopted and influenced by the perception of low quality delivery of e-Gove services, lack of awareness of availability of e-Gove services due to, among others, no digital marketing of these services. These findings, provide an alternative explanation as to how online users in the South African context manage the risk and uncertainty present online. Using these results, developers are able to develop eGov services that meet user's needs amidst their contextual challenges they face. The study has some limitation, mainly from the sample used. By understanding the phenomenon of hedging from government employee's perspective alone, and only from one province in South Africa, does not provide a holistic view, and therefore cannot be generalized to other population groups in South Africa. Future work can expand on this study and understand the phenomenon from a wider audience of e-Gov users.

REFERENCES

Al-Hujran, O., Al-Debei, M. M., Chatfield, A., & Migdadi, M. (2015). The imperative of influencing citizen attitude toward e-government adoption and use. *Computers in human Behavior*, 53, 189-203

Alzahrani, L., Al-Karaghouli, W., & Weerakkody, V. (2018). Investigating the impact of citizens' trust toward the successful adoption of e-government: A multigroup analysis of gender, age, and internet experience. *Information Systems Management*, 35(2), 124-146.

Andrews L (2018). #YouthReport2018: Being a teenager in 2018, more pressure than peer pressure. Retrieved from https://www.bizcommunity.com/Article/196/347/181580.html

Bélanger, F., & Carter, L. (2008). Trust and risk in e-government adoption. *The Journal of Strategic Information Systems*, 17(2), 165-176

Ruiz Ben, E., Scholl, M., & Ehrlich, P. (2017). Exploring the Adoption of E-Government Tools with WISE Work Index.

Bhattacharya, D., Gulla, U., & Gupta, M. P. (2012). E-service quality model for Indian government portals: citizens' perspective. *Journal of Enterprise Information Management*, 25(3), 246-271

Blanson Henkemans, O. A., van Empelen, P., Paradies, G. L., Looije, R., & Neerincx, M. A. (2015) Lost in persuasion: a multidisciplinary approach for developing usable, effective, and reproducible persuasive technology for health promotion. *In Proceedings of the 9th International Conference on Pervasive Computing Technologies for Healthcare*, 49-56

Chen, J. V., Jubilado, R. J. M., Capistrano, E. P. S., & Yen, D. C. (2015). Factors affecting online tax filing–An application of the IS Success Model and trust theory. *Computers in Human Behavior*, 43, 251-262

Chun, D., Kern, R., & Smith, B. (2016). Technology in language use, language teaching, and language learning. *The Modern Language Journal*, 100(S1), 64-80

D'cruz, J. (2015). Trust, Trustworthiness, and the Moral Consequence of Consistency. *Journal of the American Philosophical Association*, 1(3), 467-484

Distel, B. (2018). Bringing Light into the Shadows: A Qualitative Interview Study on Citizens' Non-Adoption of e-Government. *Electronic Journal of e-Government*, 16(2), 98-105

Dorfman, J. H., & Karali, B. (2010). Do farmers hedge optimally or by habit? A Bayesian partial-adjustment model of farmer hedging. *Journal of Agricultural and Applied Economics*, 42(4), 791-803

E-government Survey. https://publicadministration.un.org/egovkb/Portals/egovkb/Documents/un/201 8-Survey/E-Government%20Survey%202018_FINAL%20for%20web.pdf Retrieved March 2019

Gupta, K. P., Bhaskar, P., & Singh, S. (2017). Prioritization of factors influencing employee adoption of e-government using the analytic hierarchy process. *Journal of Systems and Information Technology*, 19(1/2), 116-137

Hariguna, T., & Berlilana, B. (2017). Understanding of Antecedents to Achieve Customer Trust and Customer Intention to Purchase E-Commerce in Social Media, an Empirical Assessment. *International Journal of Electrical and Computer Engineering*, 7(3), 1240

Jackson, V. (2014). Power, trust, and network complexity: three logics of hedging in Asian security. *International Relations of the Asia-Pacific*, 14(3), 331-356

Jansen, A., & Ølnes, S. (2016). The nature of public e-services and their quality dimensions. *Government Information Quarterly*, 33(4), 647-657

Joseph, B. K., & Du Plessis, T. (2015). Consumers' Awareness of the Value of e-Government in Zambia: Empirical Evidence. *International Journal of Electronic Government Research (IJEGR)*, 11(3), 1-23

Koga, K. (2017). The concept of "hedging" revisited: the case of Japan's foreign policy strategy in East Asia's power shift. *International Studies Review*, 20(4), 633-660

Lallmahomed, M. Z., Lallmahomed, N., & Lallmahomed, G. M. (2017). Factors influencing the adoption of e-Government services in Mauritius. *Telematics and Informatics*, 34(4), 57-72

Liu, D., & Carter, L. (2018) Impact of citizens' privacy concerns on e-government adoption. *In Proceedings of the 19th Annual International Conference on Digital Government Research: Governance in the Data Age* (p. 27).

Mampane, J. N. (2018). Exploring the "Blesser and Blessee" Phenomenon: Young Women, Transactional Sex, and HIV in Rural South Africa. *SAGE Open,* 8(4), 1–9, 2158244018806343

Masenya, M. (2017). Reading Proverbs 7 in the context of female'blessers' and sugar mamas in South Africa. *Scriptura, 116*, 120-132.

McLeod, A., & Savoy, A. (2015). The Building Blocks for Enhanced Technological Literacy. *CTE Journal*, 3(2), 2-14.

Mellouli, M., Bentahar, O., & Bidan, M. (2016). Trust and e-government acceptance: The case of Tunisian on-line tax filing. *The Electronic Journal Information Systems Evaluation*, 19(3), 197-212.

Munyoka, W., & Maharaj, M. S. (2019). Privacy, security, trust, risk and optimism bias in e-government use: The case of two Southern African Development Community countries. *South African Journal of Information Management,* 21(1), 1-9

Mutula, S. M., & Mostert, J. (2010). Challenges and opportunities of e-government in South Africa. *The electronic library,* 28(1), 38-53

Oluwalola, F. K. (2015). Effect of emotion on distance e-learning—The fear of technology. *International Journal of Social Science and Humanity*, 5(11), 966-970

Otniel, D. (2015). The challenges of e-government 2.0 projects in Romania: An insight. *Annals-Economy Series*, 4, 24-29

Picazo-Vela, S., Gutiérrez-Martínez, I., & Luna-Reyes, L. F. (2012). Understanding risks, benefits, and strategic alternatives of social media applications in the public sector. *Government information quarterly*, 29(4), 504-511

Rao, L., Liu, X., Xie, L., & Pang, Z. (2011). Hedging against uncertainty: A tale of internet data center operations under smart grid environment. *IEEE Transactions on Smart Grid*, 2(3), 555-563

Rashid, M. A. A., & Othman, M. N. A. (2010). User adoption and use of e-government online service. *Gading Journal for the Social Sciences*, 14(01)

Reich, T., & Wheeler, S. C. (2016). The good and bad of ambivalence: Desiring ambivalence under outcome uncertainty. *Journal of Personality and Social Psychology*, 110(4), 493

Sá, F., Rocha, Á., Gonçalves, J., & Cota, M. P. (2017). Model for the quality of local government online services. *Telematics and Informatics*, 34(5), 413-421

Salman, M. (2017). Strategic Hedging and Unipolarity's Demise: The Case of China's Strategic Hedging. *Asian Politics & Policy*, 9(3), 354-377

Shareef, M. A., Kumar, V., Kumar, U., & Dwivedi, Y. K. (2011). e-Government Adoption Model (GAM): Differing service maturity levels. *Government information quarterly*, 28(1), 17-35

Taušer, J., & Čajka, R. (2016). Hedging techniques in commodity risk management. *Agricultural Economics,* 60(4), 174-182

Teerling, M. L., & Pieterson, W. (2010). Multichannel marketing: An experiment on guiding citizens to the electronic channels. *Government Information Quarterly*, 27(1), 98-107

Thobejane, T. D., Mulaudzi, T. P., & Zitha, R. (2017). Factors leading to "blesser-blessee" relationships amongst female students: The case of a rural university in Thulamela Municipality, Limpopo Province, South Africa. *Gender and Behaviour*, *15*(2), 8716-8731.

UN E - Goverment Survey. https://publicadministration.un.org/egovkb/en-us/reports/un-e-governmentsurvey-2016.

van Esterik-Plasmeijer, P. W., & van Raaij, W. F. (2017). Banking system trust, bank trust, and bank loyalty. *International Journal of Bank Marketing*, 35(1), 97-111

Venkatesh, V., Thong, J. Y., Chan, F. K., & Hu, P. J. (2016). Managing citizens' uncertainty in e-government services: The mediating and moderating roles of transparency and trust. *Information Systems Research*, 27(1), 87-111

SOCIAL NETWORK SENTIMENT ANALYSIS TOOLS FOR THE DETECTION OF MENTAL ILLNESS: A SYSTEMATIC MAPPING

Ariel Altamirano[1], Daniel Avila[1] and Graciela Guerrero[1,2(0000-0002-0903-734X)]
[1] *Universidad de las Fuerzas Armadas ESPE , Avenida General Rumiñahui, 171103 Sangolquí, Ecuador*
[2] *Universidad de Castilla – La Mancha*
Departamento de Sistemas Informáticos, campus universitario s/n 02071, Albacete, España

ABSTRACT

The growing demand of users on the Internet and their dependence on it has caused websites such as Twitter or Facebook to become a source of personal information for each user, which is why, within the psychological context, one can take advantage of it by analyzing the publications of each of these users; on the other hand, the importance of detecting mental disorders in a person has grown exponentially, so that in recent years several analysis tools have been developed to detect a person's mental state. This systematic mapping work details relevant information about the analysis tools and their importance to society, as well as describing the methodology used in this article, its results, conclusions and proposals for future work.

KEYWORDS

Feelings Analysis, Social Network Analysis, Mental Illness, Social Networks, Anxiety

1. INTRODUCTION

According to (Wongkoblap, et al., 2017), mental illness is becoming a serious global health problem, with a growing number of patients suffering from depression, anxiety and other disorders. This issue should be highlighted and given importance because out of 350 million patients worldwide suffering from mental disorders, it also impacts the world economy at a cost of US $2.5 trillion in 2010 and an estimated expenditure of US $6 trillion by 2030.

Anxiety is the most common mental health condition in children and adolescents, with prevalence rates ranging from 5% to 10% in children and up to 25% in adolescents (Glover & Fritsch, 2018). Adolescents are the most likely to suffer from anxiety disorders which, according to (Gerez, et al., 2016) are the most pervasive mental health problems and despite the devastating effects of anxiety disorders (ADS) worldwide, debates about causes and remedies have not solved the psychologist's riddle: should they be treated and how? Anxiety disorders have consequences for an individual's mental health, which leads to a certain insecurity and inferiority when it comes to offering professional advice. According to (Deepali, et al., 2018) unlike physical illness, in mental illness the symptoms are not evident in the early stages, for this reason psychologists look for different ways to understand the patient in treatment, so, according to (Jia, 2018) with the popularity of social networks it is feasible to take advantage of these data for stress and detection of depression and anxiety.

Over the past 10 years, social networks have become an important component of young people's lives, with the use of a peak in 16-24 years (Glover & Fritsch, 2018). Today, the use of social networks and other popular microblogging tools has become an everyday activity since in addition to being a means of communication it is a source of information and according to (Miks & Aurel, 2019) they allow individuals to express their opinions, feelings and thoughts on a variety of topics in the form of short text messages or tweets. When published on social network platforms, the day-to-day feelings or thoughts of each user become valuable information and according to (Manikonda & De Choudhury, 2017) is self-revelation by the user. Although there is a debate about the excessive use of social networks, whether they are for personal benefit or harm, since it is not possible to control what type of information is true within social networks or whether personal information is completely secure; according to (Park, et al., 2015) there are recent studies that have used data from online social networks to predict the well-being of the individual.

Several published articles have studied mental illness and recommended various free tools for the analysis of feelings, however, no systematic mapping articles like the one presented in this article have been found. According to (Cooper, 2016) systematic mappings are critical, but they do not discuss the findings. They are based on the concept that published articles not only represent findings, but, indirectly, represent the activity related to the finding. Therefore, this article will provide an overview to help psychologists and software developers to have a clear and comprehensive idea of sentiment analysis and social network tools.

This article is structured as follows: i) Section 2: introduction of the methodology to be used, research guidelines, response to research questions and data analysis and extraction. ii) Section 3: the results of the study and its limitations are presented. iv) Section 4: the results obtained are discussed. Finally, iv) Section 5 presents the conclusions obtained.

2. METHOD

In this section, the research methodology used is detailed, as well as the interest of the research in which the reason for the proposed subject matter is stated, research guidelines in which the research questions are stated, source selection in which the research databases used are stated, formulation of the search chain in which the structure of the chain used is detailed, exclusion and inclusion criteria, data collection and the search process.

2.1 Research Methodology

2.1.1 Research Interest

There are several reasons for conducting this systematic mapping review. The first is to conduct a broad review of the literature related to sentimental analysis or social network tools for the detection of mental illness, with the aim of providing summaries of which tools have been used according to two specific criteria: sentimental analysis or social network analysis. The second reason, if possible, is to identify what kind of complications exist in the detection of mental illness when using sentimental analysis tools or social networks to provide facilities for psychologists, academics and software developers to plan future research in this area. The third reason is to identify topics and areas for future systematic reviews of the literature that will cover smaller areas of research after analyzing the literature in depth.

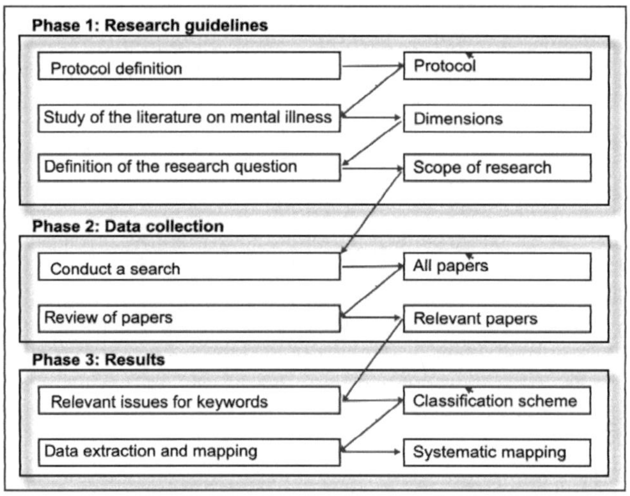

Figure 1. Systematic mapping review process applied at work

To guide this empirical study, the "Template for a Mapping Study Protocol" proposed by (EBSE-RG, 2009) was taken into consideration. As shown in Figure 1, the research protocol has three phases: (1) Research guidelines that define the protocol applied for this study, identify which dimensions should be analyzed, and determine which research questions should be answered throughout the work. (2) Data collection identifies relevant documents, according to the inclusion and exclusion criteria defined in the protocol. (3) The results phase leads to the mapping of the existing literature, according to the defined criteria and the respective analysis to answer the proposed research questions.

2.1.2 Research Directives

In this section, the first phase of the systematic mapping review. The process is introduced, where the protocol and research questions are defined.

The protocol includes the subject of the study (sentimental analysis tools or social networks for the detection of mental illness); its rationale (explained above); preliminary research questions; and the search strategy, selection criteria, and form of data extraction. An overview of the empirical screening approaches found in the selected articles is also provided. Finally, the protocol includes an overview of the selected articles in terms of their publication locations and years.

The three research questions (RQ) for this study and their rationale are

RQ1. How many articles have been published on sentiment analysis tools or social networks for the detection of mental illness? What is their temporal trend?

As argued in the Introduction section, mental illness can be understood as mental health conditions such as anxiety and depression, which are most diagnosed in adolescents and children. From this context, a first step might be to determine the number of articles that have been published on sentimental analysis tools or social networks for the detection of mental illness and second, whether there is any temporal trend (increasing or decreasing) in the publication of these articles.

RQ2. What types of mental illness are investigated with sentimental analysis tools or social networks? What characteristics do these analysis tools possess?

As is known, there are several types of mental illness, however, it is necessary to know which mental illnesses are investigated or sought to be detected when using any sentiment analysis or social network tool. Likewise, understanding the characteristics that these different tools have.

RQ3. What type of analysis has been used for the detection of mental illness and on what social network platforms have these tools been developed?

It is necessary to find out which type of analysis is the most used when detecting a mental illness. Similarly, to know on which social network platform these tools are applied or used more, to know the reason for this situation or to distinguish if there is any reason for privacy, number of users, security for which such an effect occurs; if it exists.

2.2 Data Collection

Data collection should lead to the inclusion of relevant documents and the exclusion of irrelevant documents. The search strategy used was to query relevant databases, create search strings and enter the selected databases, evaluate the results obtained and finally apply inclusion and exclusion criteria. All researchers were involved in the execution of data collection.

2.2.1 Source Selection and Search String

In order to avoid the loss of information, the consultation was carried out in three relevant databases: Scopus (Elsevier), ACM (Association for Computing Machinery) and IEEE (Institute of Electrical and Electronics Engineers).

From the research questions, the key words in the search string were identified. Synonyms and relationships of the keywords were identified to form the search string that is connected to OR and AND respectively. The search string entered in the different databases is as follows: (Mental Health OR Anxiety OR Depression OR Moods) AND ((Social Network Analysis OR Sentiment Analysis) AND (Application OR Tool)).

The first part of the search string consists of words related to mental illness, while the second part consists of words related to sentiment analysis and social network analysis, and finally the third part consists of tools for sentiment analysis. Each part is related to AND connectors.

2.2.2 Inclusion and Exclusion Criteria

The inclusion and exclusion criteria for filtering the articles were

- Inclusion criteria

I1. Articles published between 2014 and 2020

I2. Articles that include the selected keywords within the title and are in turn within the keywords of each article.

- Exclusion criteria

E1. Words like "Education", "Big Data" and their synonyms are within the titles and keywords of the articles.

E2. Articles with themes and areas outside the context of the research.

E3. Articles repeated among the three databases.

2.2.3 Search Process

As shown in Figure 2 the search string was entered in each of the above-mentioned databases and different item numbers were obtained from each of them, making a total of 4142.

Applying the inclusion criteria (E1, E2 and E3) to the 4142 articles, each researcher reading the summary of each article ruled out those that were not in the context of the investigation, in case the researcher was unsure of keeping the article decided to read the introduction and conclusion of the article and together with the opinion of the other researcher the article in question was included or discarded. At the end of the analysis, 15 articles were obtained as a result at this stage.

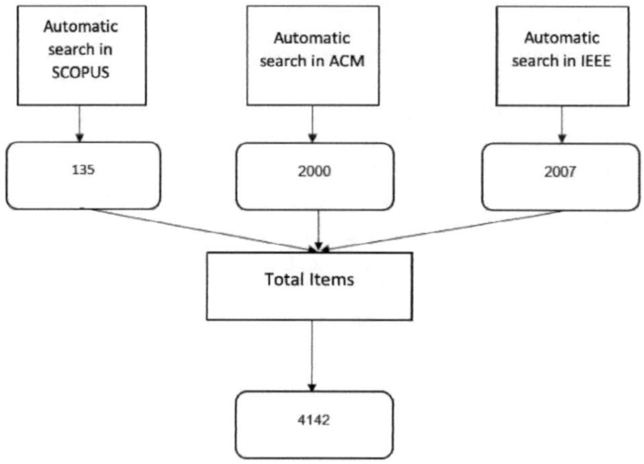

Figure 2. Result of the search for articles in each of the databases applying the inclusion I1 and I2

Figure 3 shows the number of articles selected among all the articles shown in figure 2. You can appreciate the importance of searching in different databases since by searching in only one you run the risk of losing information from other articles.

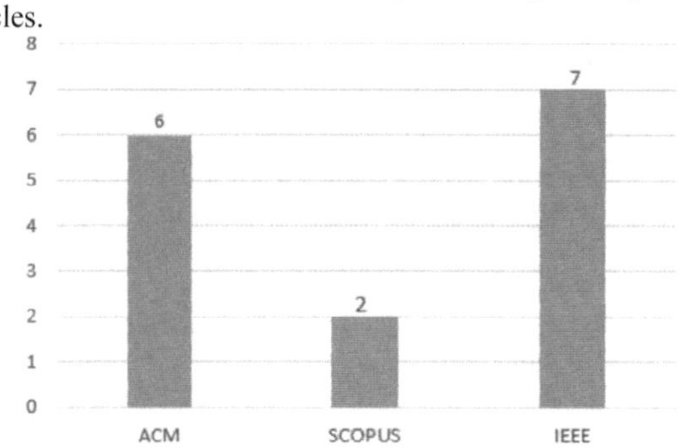

Figure 3. Results of the articles obtained by applying the criteria of E1, E2 and E3

3. RESULTS

Finally, 15 articles have been selected according to the process described above. Then, descriptive statistics and frequency analysis were used to answer the research questions. An overview of the articles and the answers to the three research questions are shown in the following subsections.

3.1 Summary of Selected Articles

The summary of the selected articles was presented in terms of their locations and years of publication.

3.1.1 Journal and Conference Publications

Figure 4 shows the journals where more articles have been published on the use of sentiment analysis tools or social networks for the detection of mental illness

Figure 4. Articles published in journals and conferences according to the topic of research

3.1.2 RQ1. How Many Articles have been published on Sentiment Analysis Tools or Social Networks for the Detection of Mental Illness? What is their Temporal Trend?

In the study period from January 1, 2014 to December 30, 2019, a total of 15 published articles on sentiment analysis tools or social networks for the detection of mental illness were found. An upward temporal trend was observed from 2014 to 2018 as shown in Figure 5., where it is intuited that this behavior occurs, in proportion to discarding the Big Data theme as an exclusion criterion.

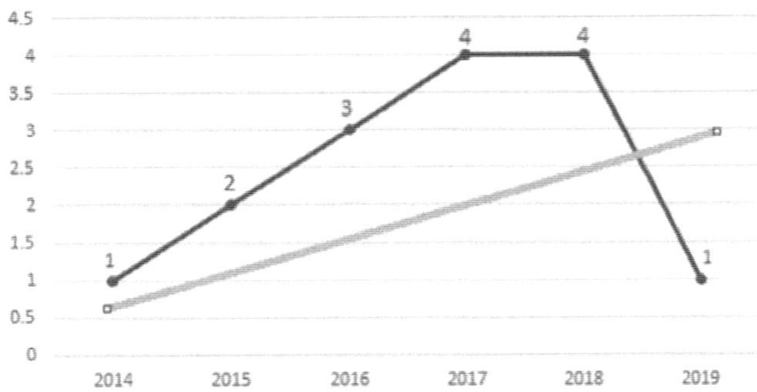

Figure 5. Temporal Trend (2014 – 2019)

3.1.3 RQ2. What kind of Mental Illnesses are investigated in the Tools Of Analysis of feelings or Social Networks? What Characteristics do These Analysis Tools have?

Among the different types of mental illness or mental health states, the most studied in relation to the number of people who are diagnosed with such a mental state are anxiety, depression and stress. Figure 6 shows the type of mental illness studied and its importance and prominence within the articles selected in the period described above. The characteristics of social network analysis tools are shown in Table 1. Similarly, the characteristics of feeling analysis tools are shown in Table 2, which compares OSAT with the other feeling analysis tools (Sharma, et al., 2016).

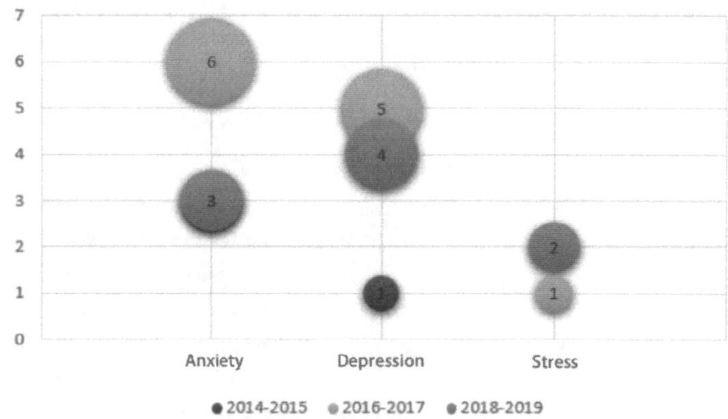

Figure 6. Type of mental illness where tools for detection are made or linked

Table 1. Characteristics of the functioning of social network analysis tools

Software	Type	Platform	Calculation Time	Number of Nodes
NETWORKX	Library	Python	Fast	1 million
IGRAPH	Library	Biblioteca Python/R/C	Fast	1 million
GEPHI	Independent	Windows	Fast	0.15 million
PAJEK	Independent	Windows	Medium	1 million

Table 2. Characteristics of the functioning of social network analysis tools

Software	Accuracy	Precision
Sentic Net	0.59	0.94
Sentic Word Net	0.63	0.79
Senti Strength	0.81	0.78
LIWC	0.68	0.84
OSAT	0.85	0.9

3.1.4 RQ3. What Type of Analysis has been used for the Detection of Mental Illness and on what Social Network Platforms have these tools been developed?

As established in this paper, two types of analysis can be used for the detection of mental illness. Sentimental analysis is defined as the process of extracting the polarity of a subjective sentence, where it is classified into three main categories: lexical-based method, automatic learning method, hybrid method (Rathan, et al., 2017). Social network analysis is defined as the way to identify, analyze, visualize or simulate nodes and edges of various types of input, including mathematical models of social networks (Akhtar, 2014). However, it was found that when any tool is used to link it to the detection of mental illness, only sentiment analysis tools have been used, which capture three general feelings (negative, neutral and positive).

The social media platforms where this type of opinion analysis tools or social networks are most used are Facebook and Twitter; are the most mentioned platforms in all selected articles, where for both cases facilities are exposed and difficulties in obtaining data. However, Twitter is the social network platform most used for this type of opinion analysis, because unlike Facebook, Twitter users' posts are public, so you don't need permissions to access them and perform the respective analyses.

4. DISCUSSION

This article shows the literary background for the development of a future software. The articles researched between the years 2014-2019 have produced results, which have been presented in the answers to the research questions.

Figure 7 shows a representation of the citations of each article that was used for the development of this work.

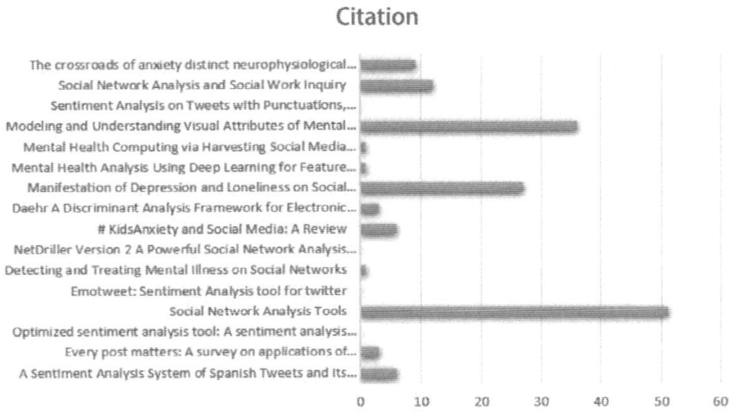

Figure 7. Number of quotations of the selected articles

As for the tools researched, we found two types to differentiate, which are: tools for the analysis of feelings in social networks and tools for the analysis of social networks despite the existence of a large number of software tools, (Akhtar, 2014) defines social network analysis as to identify, analyze, visualize or simulate nodes and edges of various input types, including mathematical social media models and recommends four analysis tools that are: Gephi, NetworkX, igraph and Pajek; this tools are describe on table 1; recommends them for being tools of free use and that can handle large graphic size. On the other hand, (Afra, et al., 2018) propose NetDriller2 as a powerful tool for the analysis of social networks, explaining that this tool covers the lack of other tools by building a network of raw data using data mining techniques.

With regard to sentiment analysis; (Abhijit, et al., 2016) emphasize that sentiment analysis is much better at capturing general feelings (negative, neutral or positive) expressed in star ratings. On the other hand, (Cao, et al., 2014) define sentiment analysis as the mining of affective information from data and the recognition of the polarity of feeling contained in the information; they also stress that most studies of sentiment analysis have focused on the English language.

5. CONCLUSIONS AND FUTURE WORK

According to (Cerón Gúzman & León Gúzman, 2016), thanks to platforms such as Facebook and Twitter, profound changes have taken place in the paradigm of information generation and consumption. However, it should be noted that by using tweets as a source of data, there would be no problem with the privacy of such information, since this information is public. When using data provided by Facebook there are problems, since this information is private to the user and sometimes users decide not to lend their Facebook information.

According to (Wongkoblap, et al., 2017) social network data are a valuable source of information for predicting mental health problems. Understanding the factors associated with symptoms of mental illness can contribute to early detection and treatment of network users with poor mental health.

In the selected articles, screening for mental illness is only done with sentimental analysis tools, so a future job could be to carry out screening work for mental illness using only social network analysis tools or to use both types of analysis.

Finally, it was determined that anxiety and depression are the most researched types of mental illness in the last 5 years; related to the early detection of them.

REFERENCES

Abhijit, J. P., Kshama, K. & Kotrappa, S., 2016. Emotweet Sentiment Analysis tool for twitter. IEEE Xplore, pp. 157-159.

Afra, S., Ozyer, T., Rokne, J. & Alhajj, R., 2018. NetDriller Version 2 A Powerful Social Network Analysis Tool. *IEEE Explore,* pp. 1475-1480.

Akhtar, N., 2014. Social Network Analysis Tools. IEEE Explore, pp. 388-392.

Cao, J. y otros, 2014. Web-Based Traffic Sentiment Analysis Methods and Applications. IEEE Xplore, pp. 844-853.

Cerón Gúzman, J. A. & León Gúzman, E., 2016. A Sentiment Analysis System of Spanish Tweets and Its Application in Colombia 2014 Presidential Election. IEEE Xplore, pp. 250-257.

Cooper, D., 2016. What is a "mapping study?". JMLA, pp. 76-78.

Deepali, J., Makhija, J., Nabar, Y. & Nehet, N., 2018. Mental Health Analysis Using Deep Learning for Feature Extraction. ACM, pp. 356-359.

EBSE-RG, 2009. Durham University Community. [Online] Available at: http://community.dur.ac.uk/ebse/resources/templates/MappingStudyTemplate.pdf [Last access: November,11-2019].

Gerez, M. y otros, 2016. The crossroads of anxiety: Distinct neurophysiological maps for different symptomatic groups. SCOPUS, pp. 159-175.

Glover, J. & Fritsch, S., 2018. #KidsAnxiety and Social Media: A Review. SCOPUS, pp. 171-182.

Jia, J., 2018. Mental Health Computing via Harvesting Social Media Data. ACM, pp. 70-70.

Manikonda, L. & De Choudhury, M., 2017. Modeling and Understanding Visual Attributes of Mental Health Disclosures in Social Media. ACM, pp. 170-181.

Miks, Q. & Aurel, J., 2019. Sentiment Analysis on Tweets with Punctuations, Emoticons, and Negations. ACM, pp. 266-270.

Park, S., Kim, I., Won, S. & Yoo, J., 2015. Manifestation of Depression and Loneliness on Social Networks: A Case Study of Young Adults on Facebook. ACM, pp. 557-570.

Rathan, Hulipalled, V., Murugeshwari & Sushmitha, 2017. Every Post Matters A Survey on Applications of Sentiment Analysis in Social Media. IEEE Xplore, pp. 709-714.

Sharma, N., Sharma, C., Indu & Chugh, P., 2016. Optimized Sentiment Analysis Tool A sentiment analysis tool to study cognitive inclinations. IEEE Xplore, pp. 2589-2592.

Wongkoblap, A., Vadillo, M. & Curcina, V., 2017. Detecting and Treating Mental Illness on Social Networks. IEEE Explore, p. 330.

CONTEXTUAL CONTRADICTIONS TO THE SCALING -UP OF MOBILE HEALTH IN ARMED-CONFLICT SETTINGS OF NORTH-EASTERN NIGERIA: A CASE STUDY OF ALMANACH

Nakama David[1], Muhammadou Kah[2], Jennifer Tyndall[3] and Olumide Longe[4]
American University of Nigeria, Nigeria
[1]+2348038013255
[2]+2348149228426
[3]+2348077092830
[4]+2348160900893

ABSTRACT

Developing countries are undergoing an unprecedented growth on the adoption of ICT's. Mobile technologies, digital platforms and services for health care are gaining acceptance and use for detection and response for disease outbreaks, support of the healthcare value chains to facilitate improvements of public health care delivery and services. This study through a case study examines how m-Health platforms and services produce positive results in the context of Sub-Saharan Africa, specifically investigating the challenges of m-Health adoption and use in the Boko Haram settings in Adamawa State, North Eastern Part of Nigeria. Our study also explores the challenges that impede the successful scale-up of m-Health intervention in armed conflict settings of Adamawa State in the North Eastern region of the Federal Republic of Nigeria. We examined the use of ALMANACH in five local government areas (LGAs) namely; Yola south, Girei, Mubi-South, Mubi-North, and Maiha located in the armed-conflict (Boko Haram) settings of Adamawa State, Nigeria. Nineteen PHCs where ALMANACH has been deployed, primarily conducted in children clinics. A m-Health: "Algorithm for the Management of Acute Childhood Illnesses" (ALMANACH) was introduced as a clinical decision support tool into the child health system to aid the management of common acute illnesses in children between 2 months and 5 years. The ALMANACH is an electronic version of the integrated management of childhood illnesses (IMCI) running on mobile tablets. The lens of activity theory has guided the study to unearth the emergence of some developments in ALMANACH adoption and use in our study setting. Activity theory (AT) was used as the analytical lens because it is central for understanding challenges in adoption and use which can present in the form of contradictions. Thus, our findings suggest several challenges in the form of contradictions that can impede the successful scale-up of ALMANACH in peculiar settings of Boko Haram. Hence, a key contribution to the literature from our study is uncovering that contradictions are critical to achieving mHealth scale-up in our study setting.

KEYWORDS

mHealth, Healthcare Services, Armed-Conflict, ALMANACH, Contradictions

1. INTRODUCTION

Armed-conflict zones usually present some of the most precarious health systems with poor human capacity and significant governance challenges. There is also an acute shortage of human resources for health care service delivery in conflict and post-conflict settings due to the migration of large numbers of qualified health workers, as well as the destruction of educational and health facilities (Devkota & van Teijlingen, 2010; Woodward et al., 2014) . These challenges have contributed greatly to the poor child health outcomes as well as the high child mortality rates especially in developing countries. In 2015, about 6 million children between age 0 and 5 died of curable and preventable illnesses in conflict-affected countries like Syria, Nigeria, and Niger (Asi & Williams, 2018). In an attempt to augment these healthcare deficiencies, mobile health (mHealth) solutions have witnessed a high number of implementations in many disadvantaged regions of the world including conflict and post- conflict regions (Woodward et al., 2014). mHealth can have a resounding and positive effect on health care delivery in the most disadvantaged regions around the world (Chigona et al., 2012; Motamarri et al., 2014), if it is properly implemented and effectively scaled-up. Such is especially the case in the areas of reproductive, maternal and child health (Chigona et al., 2012). By leveraging on mobile technologies to improve child health outcomes, mHealth has experienced unprecedented growth in recent years with about 500 distinct pilot implementations globally, the majority of these developments have taken place in developing countries (Tomlinson et al., 2013). This approach has been found to overcome widespread health system barriers such as health professional shortages, reliance on untrained and/or informal providers, cost of service and transportation, and lack of sources of reliable information (WHO,2011). Regardless of the enthusiasm around mHealth and its great potentials in improving the health care landscape of developing countries (Motamarri et al., 2014; Schmied et al., 2010), the majority of mHealth interventions are faced with challenges which hampers the scale-up of such interventions (Bilandzic & Venable, 2011; Chigona et al., 2012; Fanta & Pretorius, 2018; Mangone et al., 2016).

Related studies have illuminated on mHealth scale-up with some wide range methods, outcome measures, and scope (Dehzad et al., 2014; Sanner et al., 2012). While these studies were successful in exploring the different measures of taking mHealth pilots to full scale-up across diverse settings, experts in the field have acknowledged the relative absence of a rigorous scholarly approach of how mHealth scale-up can be achieved (Tomlinson et al., 2013). There is also, the need to study the challenges of mHealth implementations in developing countries (Kruse et al., 2019). Thus, this study aims to explore the challenges that impede the successful scale-up of mHealth intervention in developing countries. Particularly, armed conflict settings. Such studies are scarce in literature. Hence, knowledge from this study will contribute to extant literature on mHealth implementations. The study may serve as a valuable tool for intervention donors and policymakers to consider when planning or designing imminent mHealth projects. Findings from this study will also strengthen the chances of long-term, sustainable scale-up of mHealth in armed conflict settings of developing countries. This study was conducted within a child health care program in the armed conflict settings (Boko Haram) of North-East (NE) Nigeria. A mHealth: "Algorithm for the Management of Acute Childhood Illnesses" (ALMANACH) was introduced as a clinical decision support tool into the child health system to aid the management of common acute illnesses in children between 2 months and 5 years. Activity theory (AT) was used as the analytical lens because it is central for understanding challenges in practice which can present in the form of contradictions (Shidende, 2014). With that understanding, the following research question is addressed: how can the challenges faced by mHealth systems in armed conflict settings affect its scale-up?

2. THEORETICAL FOUNDATION

Activity theory is a *social-psychological* theory that is based on the work of the Russian psychologist Leo Vygotsky during the first half of the 20th century (Leontiev et al., 1981). AT is a theory that seeks to understand who is doing what, why they are doing it and how the activity is done in a social context. Engeström (2001) describes AT as "a theory of object-driven activity". In the sense that, it provides scholars with a holistic framework and explanation for all the meaningful things people do to produce a change in practice. The basic unit of analysis in AT is the *activity performed by humans* (Kaptelinin et al., 2018; Ngoma et al., 2011). From the perspective of AT, an activity occurs when a "**subject**" uses certain tools to achieve an object. A subject could be an individual or an organization working together as a team with the aim of achieving an object (Kaptelinin et al., 2018). **Objects** are set goal (s) needed to be achieved by the subjects with the aid of certain tools. These **Tools** can be tangible or intangible. Examples of tangible tools are the hammer, spanner, mobile phone, or computer while intangible tools comprises ideas, signs or language (Ngoma et al., 2011). These concepts are interrelated and form part of an activity system. Hence, the nature of AT holds a relational ontology (Armstrong, 2011). The interrelationships among these concepts has the potentials of producing dynamic and conflicting perceptions through continuous interaction between and among these components in goal-directed activity (Wolff-Piggott & Rivett, 2016a).The dynamic perceptions can be controlled by rules and a clear division of labor. **Rules** are the guiding principles that govern how and why a person acts within the activity system while. **Division of labor** defines specific roles and responsibilities of an individual subject in an activity system

Activity Theory believes that the cultural-historical context of activity is key to understanding the dynamic nature and characteristics of an activity (Engeström, 2001; Wolff-Piggott & Rivett, 2016b). This aspect of activity theory is an important when studies are done in the context of developing countries where activity systems are influenced by the societal and organizational context in which the activity exists (Karanasios & Allen, 2013). Another fundamental concept in Activity Theory that is relevant to this study is contradiction. Contradictions are not simply problems or conflicts, they are "historically accumulating tensions among and between activity systems". Contradiction is an important principle in activity theory because it can lead to change and development (Brown, Allen et al., 2013). Contradictions are identified from empirical data in form of breakdowns and recurrent problems. They manifest in *primary, secondary, tertiary and quaternary* levels (Engeström, 2001). *Primary contradictions* are found within a component of an activity system. For example, conflicting rules may occur in situations where a physician may be forced, because of the economic strength of his patient, to prescribe cheaper and less effective drugs over the best (Riechert et al., 2016). *Secondary contradictions* manifest between components of an activity system. Secondary contradiction emerges when some elements like the division of labor or rules collide with new set of rules or roles. *Tertiary contradictions* are found "between the object of the central activity system and object of a more cultural advanced activity system". *Quaternary contradictions* appear in a network of activity systems between some components of the main activity system and the components of another activity system. Thus, activity systems change and develop by resolving their historically evolving contradictions (Engeström, Y, 1999). Furthermore, activity theory acknowledges contradictions as inevitable in the functioning of any activity system and identifies them as useful sources for developments in a system (Igira & Aanestad, 2009).

3. RESEARCH CONTEXT

The setting of this research comprises selected PHCs in the Boko Haram affected areas of Adamawa State, Nigeria. Adamawa state is located in the North-Eastern (NE) region of Nigeria. The Boko Haram movement became militant in NE Nigeria in 2009. Consequently, Nigeria has been described as home to the deadliest armed conflict actors in Africa and was ranked as the third unsecured terrorized country in Africa (Ekhator-Mobayode & Abebe Asfaw, 2019). Boko Haram is based on the Takfiri Islamic belief system, which opposes western education and views it as Haram (forbidden). Although a peaceful movement at inception, Boko Haram became violent in 2009 when the movement clashed with the Nigerian government because the government was against the ideology of Boko Haram (Badau & Abdulrasheed, 2015). Boko Haram insurgency has displaced about 10,000 people in Borno and Adamawa states Most of the internally displaced people(IDPs) are from six Local Governments in Adamawa and Borno - Madagali, Gwoza, Michika, Gombi, Hong, Mubi North and Mubi south. This forceful movement has negative social and health impacts on the people of Adamawa state, especially children (Adamawa State Emergency Management Agency, 2014).

The research investigates the effectiveness of ALMANACH program in Adamawa State, Nigeria. ALMANACH was piloted in Adamawa state in December 2016 through a tripartite collaboration among the Adamawa State Primary Healthcare Development Agency (ADPHDA), the SWISS-TPH, and the International Committee of the Red Cross (ICRC). The ALMANACH is an electronic version of the integrated management of childhood illnesses (IMCI) running on mobile tablets. IMCI is a regulatory guideline that is in line with WHO's policy for improving the quality of child healthcare against the commonest child killer diseases in developing countries (malaria, measles, pneumonia, diarrhea, and malnutrition). Consequently, the ALMANACH was deployed as a clinical decision support tool to enhance the activities of the PHC workers during clinical consultations of children under the age of 5 by ensuring adherence to the IMCI guidelines. The ALMANACH provides a step-by-step process that guides the PHC worker to make accurate diagnosis and to administer correct dosage. It also suggests whether a patient needs referral to a higher care facility when necessary. The collaboration among the ADPHCDA, ICRC, and SWISS TPH is consistent with the ICRC Health Strategy, and complementary to the *United Nations Sustainable Development Goals 3* (SDG3) (on ensuring good health) and SDG17 (pursuing partnerships to meet the goals). The long-time vision of the ALMANACH project is to scale up its application to all supported Primary Healthcare (PHC). This study seeks to provide additional insights that will help ALMANACH stakeholders realize their vision of a wide-scale-up.

4. RESEARCH METHODOLOGY

A case study design was used to examine the use of ALMANACH in five local government areas (LGAs) namely; Yola South, Girei, Mubi-South, Mubi-North and Maiha. All the selected LGAs are located in armed-conflict (Boko Haram) parts of Adamawa State, Nigeria. Nineteen PHCs where ALMANACH has been deployed were studied, and the study was conducted mainly in children clinics. A conceptual understanding was developed by drawing insights from the Activity Theory in interpreting the data. A case study data collection procedure was used because the approach is suitable for investigating complex phenomena like mHealth (Yin, 2003).

The data collection took place through different but overlapping fieldwork phases. Data collection was done from March 2019 to July 2019 and from September 2019 to November, 2019. The ethnographic approach inspired the data collection methods adopted. The data collection procedure was guided by the activity theory principle of contradictions. Ethnography helps researchers to have a deep insight and describes how subjects utilize tools to accomplish an object in practice (Kaptelinin & Nardi, 2018). We visited ten children clinics in different PHC centres in the state and observed clinical consultations. We collected the requisite data we need for the study and stored it in a database. We further reviewed clinical records (hospital cards) and the ALMANACH mobile tablet. We also participated in two steering committee meetings where all activities around ALMANACH were discussed with relevant stakeholders. A total of seventeen observation sessions were made across all selected PHCs with each session lasting between 1 to 3 hours. Interview was the main source of data collection techniques we deployed. A total of thirty-seven. Semi-structured interviews were conducted to have an understanding of work practices around ALMANACH. In some cases, focused group interviews were conducted for subset of health workers involved in the ALMANACH activity. This was augmented with one-on-one interviews where necessary. The interviews were conducted in Hausa and English languages. During observations and interviews, we interacted with three nurses, fifteen facility managers, nine CHEWs, and two laboratory technicians. However, because this type of interaction often leads to bias in sample selection, purposive sampling was used to select participants for the study. The participants were selected because they have met the inclusion criteria outlined for the conduct of the research. The criteria include being a member of ALMANACH team, experience in handling the ALMANACH system for at least six months and the ALMANACH must be deployed in an armed conflict zone of Adamawa State, Nigeria. Participants must also be 18 years of age and above before they eligible to participate in the study.

The data collection and analysis were guided by the Vygotsky's principles of contradictions which have been discussed in the previous section. Notes were taken during the focus group and interview sessions. In total, 22-page notes of qualitative data were collected, grouped, and analyzed using (Braun and Clarke (2006) principles of thematic analysis. This included careful and repeated readings of the data to get a summary of the main themes discussed by the participants. Next, a set of themes and relevant quotations from interviews were produced with relation to Vygotsky's principles of contradictions.

5. ANALYSIS AND DISCUSSION

Vygotsky's' principle of contradictions was used as the framework for the case study analysis. This was adopted in order to understand the challenges of using mHealth at PHCs in the selected study sites. These challenges manifested in the form of contradictions. Some of these contradictions have led to changes/ developments in the original activity system. Contradictions in ALMANACH system are then discussed.

5.1 Contradictions within ALMANACH Systems (Primary Contradictions)

The ALMANACH is deployed at the PHCs with the assumption that all clinical consultations of children under the age of 5 will be done using the ALMANACH. The present reality does not fit this assumption, as only one ALMANACH is assigned to each PHC and as it takes a long time to complete the process of a single clinical consultation (i.e. one child). The consequence to this is that facilities with a high turn-out of patients have developed other means of using the ALMANCAH whenever they have many patients awaiting consultation.

The strategy the PHCs have employed is that while one health worker is using the ALMANACH to consult, another health worker records the vital signs of patients on a hard copy clinic card. In such scenario problem arises as some health workers sometimes forget to transfer all the data into the ALMANACH. Also, quality of care can be compromised thereby affecting the overall outcome of child healthcare, since some of the health workers work based on assumptions. For example, we witnessed discrepancies associated with data quality when we tried to compare entries made on the hard copy IMCI card and data recorded on the ALMANACH on some specified dates.

In some PHCs ALMANACH were powered off at the time there was electricity supply at the facilities. A health worker confessed to our team that they used the ALMANACH in their facility for only a month and since then they have been having problems whenever they try to use it again. Another staff said he feels the problem is that they do not understand how to use it. This highlights the lack of self-efficacy which was supported by the comment below:

"How can we even know how to use it properly when the person that was trained on how to use the ALMANACH is not a serious person and cannot use it herself?"

Another contradiction observed among the subjects (health workers) is related techno-phobia. Techno-phobia among health workers was confirmed at some facilities where some health workers stated that they no longer attend to children under the age of 5 since ALMANACH was deployed at their facility. This is because they would have to use the mobile tablet (ALMANACH) which they do not like. Therefore, they only consult adults and children above the age of 5 since they do not need any form of technology to attend to the medical needs of these populations. They said their decision not to consult children under the age of 5 was in agreement with all other staff of the facility.

The next sub-section presents contradictions that arise from the interaction of the ALMANACH activity system with other components within the activity systems.

5.2 Secondary Contradictions

Interactions among the sub-components of the ALMANACH produced some contradictions in the ALMANACH activity system, which could serve as potential threats to its scalability. The identified contradictions are elaborated in this sub-section.

There is no Internet network connectivity in some communities where the ALMANACH was deployed. This is especially the case at the Boko Haram host communities. As a result, facilities affected by this challenge devised a means through which they can overcome the problem. The facilities temporarily save all their information entered into the ALMANACH system and then travel to the nearest community with Internet connectivity to upload the data. This is done once in a week across all PHCs with similar problems. However, this development is further challenged by finance even though the sum of one thousand naira is included in their monthly budget. The money is to cover the purchase data bundle per month. A committed health worker narrated how their facility is trying hard to overcome this challenge in the following comment:

"This facility does not provide us with either money to buy a data bundle or the data bundle subscription. I have been using my money to buy data of about 200 naira weekly, and I have to also fuel my motor cycle to enable me to travel for about 2 kilometers to where I can be connected to internet service that will allow me to send our report. To be honest with you, I cannot promise you that I will continue to do this".

Delays in uploading of generated data at PHCs level could further have an impact on the disease surveillance system or other real-time analysis.

Other forms of secondary contradiction emanated from the rule and the division of labor components of the ALMANACH activity system. The rule guiding the use of ALMANACH states that only health worker is allowed to use the ALMANACH for medical consultations of children under the age of 5. But we found out that some laboratory technicians use the ALMANACH during clinical consultations of children. Such scenarios were seen at the Boko Haram host communities due to shortage of manpower. This contradiction led to a form of informal change in the division of labor in the facility. We have also observed that it has established a relationship between healthcare facilities. The laboratory technician had this to say:

"if not because of my presence here, this facility would have been under lock and key and the people here will have to travel some distance to receive any health care emergency needs".

Also observed was the contradiction between tool and subject. This was made manifest during our interview sessions with the health workers where they mentioned that malaria was the most common disease in their communities and that it is one of the most dangerous killers of children under the age of 5. They also said that in their context, there are more than one different species of malaria and that, some malaria species cannot be seen when a blood sample is subjected to a particular type of malaria investigation. They have expressed their dissatisfaction with the ALMANACH arguing that ALMANACH recommends only a rapid diagnostic test (RDT) laboratory investigation to query malaria in a patient. A health worker at a different facility narrated his ordeal:

"A woman walked into this office crying and looking disappointed. She said to me that I had killed her daughter for her! She further said to me that, you should have told me that you don't know your job! My daughter died of severe malaria after you told me that there was nothing wrong with her".

There was also evidence of a contradiction between the clients and the subject. Some clients are of the view that subject (health workers) use the ALMANACH only because they are incompetent. Some health workers told us that some of their clients were bold to tell them the only reason they come to the clinics is that they have no other options. The facility had to organize orientation and sensitization sessions during antenatal, postnatal and immunization days to make the clients understand the reasons why the ALMANACH is used during clinical consultations of their children. These sessions somewhat changed the perceptions of many of the clients towards the use of ALMANACH. The clients also understood why they would have to go through all the processes involved before a prescription is made. This activity produced some visible positive outcomes.

5.3 Quaternary Contradictions

There were other protocols and programs for the management of children under the age of 5 across all the facilities visited. Other program protocols such as the standing order, IMCI chard, and save one million lives were deployed in the PHCs. A health worker said to us during an interview session with him that other protocols like the standing order covers many other illnesses which illnesses, which are not included on the ALMANACH. Again, even though, the ALMANACH is an electronic version of the IMCI, the IMCI chart is more detailed. As a result, some external evaluators and assessors score us high on other protocols in comparison to the ALMANACH system. The assessors often complain that the records we have on ALMANACH do not provide relevant information such as the client's address and phone number. They said they need this information to track the clients and to get feedback from them. For these reasons, we now ask for phone numbers of our clients and their addresses. Though we know there is no provision for it on the ALMANACH, we record it on the hard copy cards that we use. In this regard, a health worker said:

"In this clinic alone, we have been trained on the management of under 5 children by different intervention donors and each sponsor has a different approach to the management of children under the age of 5. The sponsors encourage us to use their program because as far as they are concerned, it is the best and so their supervision team always come around and we are always caught in-between one or more protocols".

6. DISCUSSION AND CONCLUSION

This study examined the challenges of mHealth in practice in the Boko Haram settings Adamawa State, NE of Nigeria. Findings from the study have uncovered several challenges in the form of contradictions that can impede the successful scale-up of ALMANACH in peculiar settings of Boko Haram. Hence, the findings of the study respond to concerns in the literature that uncovering contradictions are critical to achieving mHealth scale-up (Brown, Allen et al., 2013; Igira & Aanestad, 2009).

The contradictions identified in the study were categorized into primary, secondary and quaternary contradictions. Following the Engeström (2009) principle of contradictions. The primary contradictions that were identified in the study are similar to others that were previously reported (e.g Ngoma, Faraja T. Igira, 2014; Kenny, Heavin, et al., 2017; Kenny, O'Connor, et al., 2017; Kruse et al., 2019) where mHealth is challenged by poorly trained health workers and poor data quality. Contrary to the findings of Kenny, O'Connor, et al (2017), a negative attitude towards mHealth was discovered in this study. Primary contradictions that were also discovered at the PHC level in this study include insufficient availability of mobile tablets (ALMANACH) and increased consulting time. Secondary contradictions were discovered from interactions between components of the ALMANACH activity system. The secondary contradictions are poor internet connection. This is mostly the case in the areas that have either been attacked by the Boko Haram or areas that are still experiencing attacks by Boko Haram. Poor funding policy at the PHC level, restrictions on certain laboratory investigations, shortage of healthcare workers especially in Boko Haram host communities, poor clients' knowledge and perception on mHealth were all secondary contradictions that were uncovered in the study. A quaternary contradiction was discovered from interactions among the ALMANACH system with other external systems. For instance, there were overlapping protocols for the management of children under the age of 5 from other intervention donors like UNICEF and the save one million lives intervention.

Insights from activity theory has guided the study to unearth the existence of some developments in ALMANACH practice (Igira & Aanestad, 2009). Examples of such include: a form of a new division of labor, uploading of data to the main database has been rescheduled, an alternate source of funding has been created, rules limiting consultations at PHCs to only CHEWs have been changed to include laboratory technicians in the process of consultations using ALMANACH. Also, other malaria tests were done concurrently with RDT to satisfy contextual needs and CHEWs engaged some clients in conversations that changed their perception of ALMANACH.

Finally, in suggesting areas for future studies, the limitations of this study are acknowledged. The study was limited to a single case study. However, the study overcomes these limitations by the strength of qualitative data in providing deep insights (Abubakar & Dasuki, 2018), into the experiences of health workers as it relates to the challenges of ALMANACH in practice. In conclusion, the study has made both practical and theoretical contributions. Activity theory helped in conceptualizing challenges as contradictions thereby exposing potential threats to achieving scale-up of ALMANACH to provide more insight into the pathways towards achieving scale-up of mHealth in armed conflict settings, our future study will examine the processes and outcomes of implementing ALMANACH.

REFERENCES

Abubakar, N. H., & Dasuki, S. I. (2018). Empowerment in their hands: Use of WhatsApp by women in Nigeria. *Gender, Technology and Development*, *22*(2), 164–183. https://doi.org/10.1080/09718524.2018.1509490

Armstrong, A. (2016). *The Impact of Traditions and Traditional Birth Attendants on Maternal Mortality: A Case Study of Nyakayojo sub-County, Mbarara District, Uganda*. 68.

Asi, Y. M., & Williams, C. (2018). The role of digital health in making progress toward Sustainable Development Goal (SDG) 3 in conflict-affected populations. *International Journal of Medical Informatics*, *114*, 114–120. https://doi.org/10.1016/j.ijmedinf.2017.11.003

Badau, K. M., & Abdulrasheed, O. (2015). Management of Emergency Peace Education Programmes for Boko Haram Internally Displaced Persons in Yola Refugee Camp of Adamawa State Nigeria. *Journal of Social Science Studies*, *2*(2), 36. https://doi.org/10.5296/jsss.v2i2.7138

Bilandzic, M., & Venable, J. (n.d.). *Towards Participatory Action Design Research: Adapting Action Research and Design Science Research Methods for Urban Informatics*. 24.

Braun, V., & Clarke, V. (2006). Using thematic analysis in psychology. *Qualitative Research in Psychology*, *3*(2), 77–101. https://doi.org/10.1191/1478088706qp063oa

Brown, Allen, A., Karanasios, S., Leeds University, & Norman, A. (2013). How Should Technology-Mediated Organizational Change Be Explained? A Comparison of the Contributions of Critical Realism and Activity Theory. *MIS Quarterly*, *37*(3), 835–854. https://doi.org/10.25300/MISQ/2013/37.3.08

Chigona, W., Nyemba, M., & Metfula, A. (2012). A review on mHealth research in developing countries. *The Journal of Community Informatics*, *9*(2). http://ci-journal.net/index.php/ciej/article/view/941

Dehzad, F., Hilhorst, C., de Bie, C., & Claassen, E. (2014). Adopting Health Apps, What's Hindering Doctors and Patients? *Health*, *06*(16), 2204–2217. https://doi.org/10.4236/health.2014.616256

Devkota, B., & van Teijlingen, E. R. (2010). Understanding effects of armed conflict on health outcomes: The case of Nepal. *Conflict and Health*, *4*(1), 20. https://doi.org/10.1186/1752-1505-4-20

Ekhator-Mobayode, U. E., & Abebe Asfaw, A. (2019). The child health effects of terrorism: Evidence from the Boko Haram Insurgency in Nigeria. *Applied Economics*, *51*(6), 624–638. https://doi.org/10.1080/00036846.2018.1502871

Engeström, Y. (1999). *Innovative learning in work teams: Analysing cycles of knowledge creation in practice. In Y. Engeström, R. Miettinen, & R.-L. Punamäki (Eds.), Perspectives on Activity Theory*. UK: Cambridge University Press.

Engeström, Y. (2001). Expansive Learning at Work: Toward an activity theoretical reconceptualization. *Journal of Education and Work*, *14*(1), 133–156. https://doi.org/10.1080/13639080020028747

Fanta, G. B., & Pretorius, L. (2018). A Conceptual Framework for Sustainable Ehealth Implementation in Resource-Constrained Settings. *South African Journal of Industrial Engineering*, *29*(3). https://doi.org/10.7166/29-3-2055

Igira, F., & Aanestad, M. (2009). Living with Contradictions: Complementing Activity Theory with the Notion of "Installed Base" to Address the Historical Dimension of Transformation. *Mind, Culture, and Activity*, *16*(3), 209–233. https://doi.org/10.1080/10749030802546269

Kaptelinin, V., Kuutti, K., & Bannon, L. (n.d.). *Activity theory: Basic concepts and applications*. 13.

Karanasios, S., & Allen, D. (n.d.). *Activity Theory in Information Systems Research*. 5.

Kruse, C., Betancourt, J., Ortiz, S., Valdes Luna, S. M., Bamrah, I. K., & Segovia, N. (2019). Barriers to the Use of Mobile Health in Improving Health Outcomes in Developing Countries: Systematic Review. *Journal of Medical Internet Research*, *21*(10), e13263. https://doi.org/10.2196/13263

Leontiev, A. I., Mostinsky, I. L., Polonsky, V. S., Styrikovich, M. A., & Chernika, I. M. (1981). Experimental investigation of the critical heat flux in horizontal channels with circumferentially variable heating. *International Journal of Heat and Mass Transfer*, *24*(5), 821–828. https://doi.org/10.1016/S0017-9310(81)80005-1

Mangone, E. R., Agarwal, S., L'Engle, K., Lasway, C., Zan, T., van Beijma, H., Orkis, J., & Karam, R. (2016). Sustainable Cost Models for mHealth at Scale: Modeling Program Data from m4RH Tanzania. *PLOS ONE*, *11*(1), e0148011. https://doi.org/10.1371/journal.pone.0148011

Motamarri, S., Akter, S., Ray, P., & Tseng, C.-L. (2014). Distinguishing "mHealth" from Other Healthcare Services in a Developing Country: A Study from the Service Quality Perspective. *Communications of the Association for Information Systems*, *34*. https://doi.org/10.17705/1CAIS.03434

Ngoma, C., Chawani, M. S., & Herstad, J. (2011). Adaptation of Mobile Application to Improve Flow of Birth Information from the Community to the District Level. In R. Popescu-Zeletin, I. A. Rai, K. Jonas, & A. Villafiorita (Eds.), *E-Infrastuctures and E-Services for Developing Countries* (Vol. 64, pp. 79–92). Springer Berlin Heidelberg. https://doi.org/10.1007/978-3-642-23828-4_8

Riechert, J., Durst, C., & Wickramasinghe, N. (2016). *The Application of Activity Theory to Explain Collaborative Technology Use in Healthcare: The Case of a Chemotherapy Ordering System*. 989–997. https://doi.org/10.1109/HICSS.2016.126

Sanner, T., Roland, L. K., & Braa, K. (2012). *From Pilot to Scale: Towards a Mhealth Typology for Low Resource Contexts*. 13.

Schmied, V., Mills, A., Kruske, S., Kemp, L., Fowler, C., & Homer, C. (2010). The nature and impact of collaboration and integrated service delivery for pregnant women, children and families: Collaboration in universal child and family health services. *Journal of Clinical Nursing*, *19*(23–24), 3516–3526. https://doi.org/10.1111/j.1365-2702.2010.03321.x

Shidende, N. H. (2014). Challenges in Implementing Patient-centred Information Systems in Tanzania: An Activity Theory Perspective. *The Electronic Journal of Information Systems in Developing Countries*, *64*(1), 1–20. https://doi.org/10.1002/j.1681-4835.2014.tb00455.x

Tomlinson, M., Rotheram-Borus, M. J., Swartz, L., & Tsai, A. C. (2013). Scaling Up mHealth: Where Is the Evidence? *PLoS Medicine*, *10*(2), e1001382. https://doi.org/10.1371/journal.pmed.1001382

WHO Global Observatory for eHealth, & World Health Organization. (2011). *MHealth: New horizons for health through mobile technologies.* World Health Organization. http://www.who.int/goe/publications/goe_mhealth_web.pdf

Wolff-Piggott, B., & Rivett, U. (2016a). An *Activity Theory Approach to Affordance Actualization in mHealth : A Case of MOMCONNECT*..

Woodward, A., Fyfe, M., Handuleh, J., Patel, P., Godman, B., Leather, A., & Finlayson, A. (2014). *Diffusion of e-health innovations in 'post-conflict' settings: A qualitative study on the personal experiences of health workers*. 10.

Yin, R. K. (2003). *Applications of Case Study Research*. SAGE.

A KNOWLEDGE-AS-A-SERVICE SUPPORT FRAMEWORK FOR AMBIENT LEARNING IN KENYA

Lucy Waruguru Mburu, Richard Karanja and Simon M. Nyaga
KCA University
P.O. Box 56808 – 00200 Nairobi Kenya

ABSTRACT

Knowledge as a Service (KaaS) is a relatively new model, albeit one that is rapidly gaining popularity within cloud computing environments. Over the recent years, learners have experienced a constant need to access on demand knowledge that is fully aligned with the paradigm of cloud computing. This need stems from the knowledge that users will be able to access applications and the information therein on demand, without the restrictions that are usually imposed by time and space. The KaaS model terms knowledge as the understanding of information based on its relevance to a specific context and problem area, thus forming a valuable resource for the human decision-making process. As motivated by the global sustainable development goal of ensuring inclusive and equitable quality education to promote learning opportunities for all, this research has developed a framework that is hinged on KaaS and utilizes knowledge from ambient learning systems. The main aim is to provide a platform for disseminating and exploiting the available knowledge to aid the learning process and, thus, to improve the quality of education on the ambient learning system. The research further explores how collaborative effort can be used to form a knowledge network that allows access to heterogeneous sources of knowledge. The research outcomes will benefit knowledge consumers such as the developers of ambient learning systems.

KEYWORDS

Actionable Knowledge, Ambient Learning, Cloud Computing, Decision Trees, KaaS

1. INTRODUCTION

Knowledge as a Service (KaaS) has emerged as a popular paradigm for knowledge acquisition though the cloud. According to de Sousa et al. (2016), conventional knowledge management practices are limited in the information age where we are experiencing exponentially growing data, heavy reliance on digital tools and a general shift towards open data and big data. The rigidity of the traditional stand-alone platforms of the client-server architecture renders such platforms incapable of staying at par with information requirements. An effective and efficient solution to this limitation has been cloud computing (Armbrust et al., 2012, Grover et al., 2018). Cloud based information management has changed the landscape of operation by leveraging cloud-operand resources and enabling integration of increasing information value and support for critical processes (Kathuria et al., 2018). Cloud computing is a distributed computing technology comprising three layers:

1) the Software as a Service (SaaS) layer that avails the high-level interaction platform and top-level functionality. This is the layer that a user of the learning platform interacts with directly.
2) the Platform as a Service (PaaS) layer that is responsible for processing of all relevant applications
3) the infrastructure as a Service (IaaS) layer that deals with low-level services such as database administration (Xu, 2012).

It is into this three-layer configuration that KaaS emerges, in this case to provide a platform for retrieving knowledge that can be leveraged from anywhere, anything and anyone within the distributed computing environment. KaaS has been viewed as a framework of lessons learned, best practices, proven workflows and case studies which allow knowledge to diffuse in an open cloud platform (Ssekakubo et al., 2013). The challenge for researchers now is to integrate KaaS models with technology-enhanced approaches such as ambient learning.

Ambient learning is a highly innovative integrated knowledge and learning management system which merges the e-learning provision with context-based knowledge management (Al-Busaidi, 2013). The approach of this research is to harness knowledge through information and communication technology (ICT) to realize knowledge gaps in the realization of quality education, in line with the sustainable development goals (SDGs, General Assembly, 2015).

1.1 Background

With the SDGs, global development has entered a new stage with clearer focus on current challenges and key means to counter them. This has invariably placed knowledge at the center of how development can be achieved. The SDG goal four focuses on the acquisition of foundational and higher order skills at all stages of education and development with greater and more equitable access to quality education. To date, this goal has not been fully realized in Kenya. The Kenya National Adult Literacy Survey revealed that only 61.5% of the adult and out-of-school youth above 15 years have attained minimum literacy level leaving 38.5% (7.8 million) adults illiterate (UNESCO, 2015). A majority of these are individuals from less fortunate backgrounds who have been left out of a chance to attain quality education either due to lack of resources or reading material. With the prevalence of mobile phones where Kenya has a national coverage of about 77% of the population, the mobile industry covers over 31 million people and is therefore the ideal platform that can be leveraged to bridge this gap to help enhance accessibility of learning materials (Kaliisa and Picard, 2017). A recent survey of 3500 mobile phone users across Africa revealed five major markets; South Africa, Nigeria, Kenya, Ghana and Uganda (IT News Africa, 2015). Kenya recorded a 34% rate of internet browsing and 19% rate of downloading software from the app stores. This rate has since gone higher in the subsequent years. The growing adoption of mobile technologies accompanied by ubiquitous connectivity, and the ever-increasing pervasiveness of information technology are changing the conditions for lifelong learning.

1.2 Problem Statement

Data is growing exponentially, such that 90% of the world's stored data has been created in the last two years alone and a major facilitator for KaaS is the huge proliferation of information which includes documents, data, government records, multimedia and tacit knowledge such as blogs that are available in digital format. The implication of this is that the potential for the availability of knowledge for development is huge with the only questions being who owns this knowledge, and how is shared. The idea therefore is to look at the vast data and see how a conceptual framework can be used to focus on inclusive and equitable education while leveraging ambient learning to help improve the livelihoods of the general population.

Despite the available infrastructure to support automated learning and content dissemination, initial observation indicates that little or no research has been conducted to evaluate the effectiveness and drivers of ambient learning. As a result, there are few theoretical models to describe how knowledge regarding education quality can be extracted from ambient learning systems.

2. THE AMBIENT LEARNING – RELEVANCE AND ARCHITECTURE

The SDG goal 4 aims to ensure that all people have access to quality education and lifelong learning opportunities. Ambient learning is viewed as the next generation of technology enhanced learning in mobile learning seeks to enable anytime, anywhere and anyhow access to customized and high-quality E-learning material (Mwendia et al., 2014). The technique focuses on the mobility of the learner, the design of learning spaces, lifelong learning and informal learning and describes a world in which technology is both implicit and anticipatory (Parsons, 2014). Ambient learning is thus an example of technology enhanced learning approaches that aims at enhancing access to quality education (Mwendia et al., 2014, 2016). Mobile phones are the most preferred choice for ambient learning because they are mostly available at almost every place and people move around with them most of the time. Globally, Africa, Latin America and Asia experience the largest usage of mobile learning. According to Ambient Insight (2013), 11 African countries had a predicted rate of 30% adoption for ambient learning as shown in Figure. 1.

2.1 The Ambient Learning Architecture

Two of the most common KaaS models include the Actionable Knowledge as a Service (AKaaS) Model (Depeige &Doyecourt, 2015) and the Collaborative Knowledge as a Service (CKaaS) model (Krolinger et al., 2015) as discussed below.

2.1.1 Actionable Knowledge as a Service

AKaaS is a knowledge management system deployed in the cloud computing environments that seeks to enable available knowledge assets to be gathered and customized according to the knowledge consumer's context and needs. This brings about an evolution from traditional KM that is oriented towards a global knowledge delivery to a model that emphasizes a personalized knowledge acquisition by users. This model can be applied in an ambient learning system like OMAL which at the moment does not give this actionable knowledge aspect on data gathered and analyzed from users.

2.1.2 Collaborative Knowledge as a Service

The CKaaS model integrates disparate cloud knowledge through collaboration among distributed KaaS entities with the goal of satisfying consumer knowledge needs (Krolinger et al., 2015).

This research borrows knowledge from the two models above to construct a cloud-based knowledge sharing system that incorporates resources from learning objects, open educational resources and mobile education. Learning analytics which correlate to patterns of student activity with learning outcomes will be derived to support students to reach their potential and the delivery of personalized learning.

3. METHODOLOGY

3.1 Research Design

The research design applied content analysis method and the creative process for service development. Content analysis includes both observation and document analysis to provide objective, systematic and quantitative description of the given content of communication. This is by asking questions to help describe characteristics of content and make inferences on the causes of the content through questions like what, why, who, and with what effect, thus comprehensively making valid and replicable inferences from data to its context (Prasad, 2004).

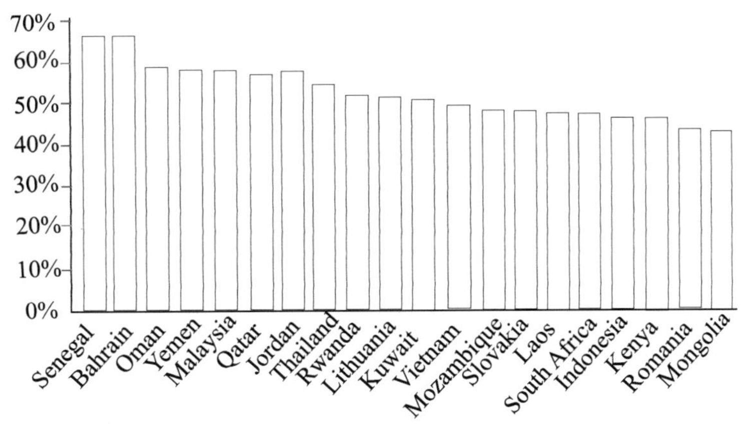

Figure 1. Projected Statistics of mobile learning per country (adopted from Ambient Insight, 2013)

3.2 Knowledge Base

The knowledge base was constructed using the OMAL ambient learning system that is piloted at KCA university, a higher learning institution in Kenya, East Africa. Usage statistics totaling 602 instances were recorded for four of the courses taught at the University, namely Java programming (314 instances), artificial intelligence (112 instances), research skills (42 instances) and management mathematics (134 instances) over a period of three months.

Data from an ambient learning system was used to capture knowledge through a knowledge discovery process known as Knowledge Discovery from Data. This involved combining an abstract model with an ambient learning system and extracting the knowledge through iterative processes consistent with Mwendia (2018). This research however extends Mwendia's approach by substituting the data warehousing approach that uses extract-transform-load (ETL) tools with a virtual data integration approach. This is a modern approach that avails current data on demand and avoids the need to constantly clean and update extracted data (Asano et al., 2018). Knowledge extraction applied the process shown in Figure 2.

3.3 Analysis Strategy

Data sets from the OMAL system were analyzed to discover new knowledge in the set of steps shown in Figure 3. Initial analysis of the extracted variables used descriptive statistics such as the measures of central tendency (mean, *min*, *max*, standard deviation) as well as the Pearson Chi square ($\mathcal{X}^2$) and Cramer's V tests. The Pearson $\mathcal{X}^2$ is a significance-based distribution free statistic for measuring group differences among qualitative variables (McHugh, 2013).

Cramer's V test was further used to test the significance levels of the Pearson $\mathcal{X}^2$ values. Variables that were determined to be significant were further measured using decision tree analysis. Decision tree learning helped to extract significant relationships that will help to strengthen the actionable knowledge for advising the improvement of the ambient learning system through customization and provision of suitable content on the cloud.

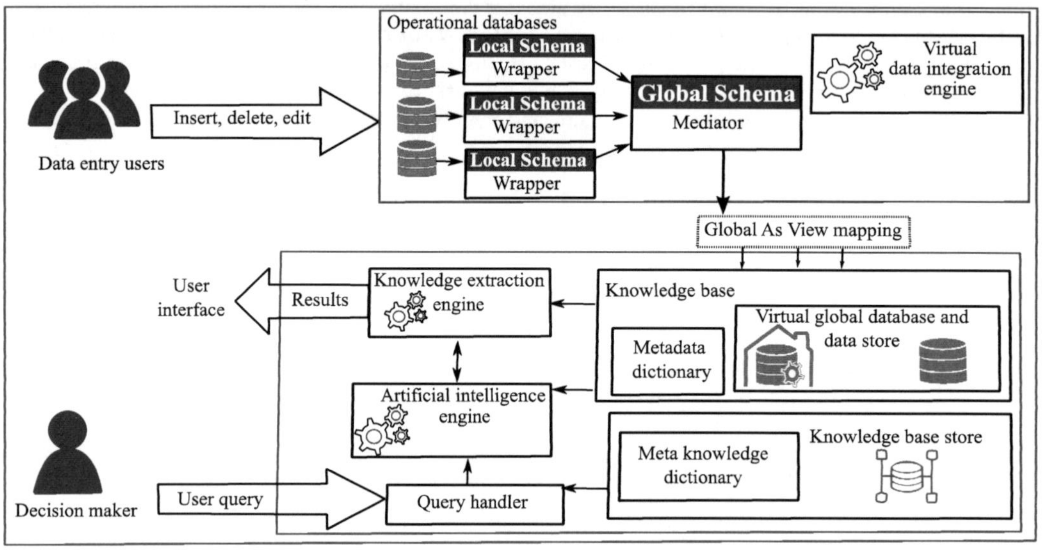

Figure 2. Knowledge extraction process using an ambient learning system

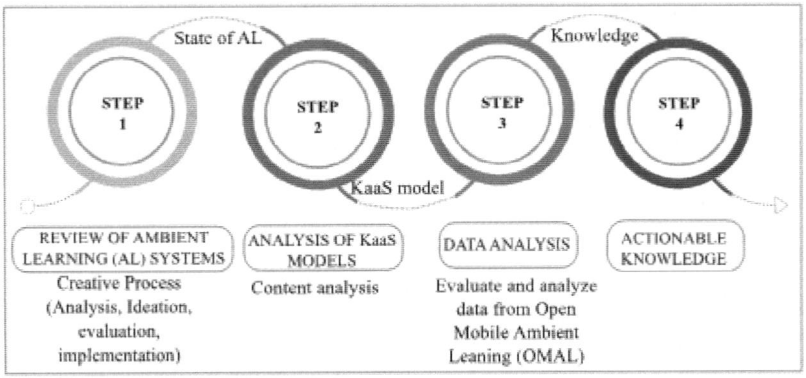

Figure 3. Steps for achieving actionable knowledge from an ambient service

4. RESULTS

This section provides results from the statistical analysis and interpretation of the data. In addition to descriptive analysis, we also provide results decision trees modeling with the sampled data.

4.1 Descriptive Analysis of Influential Learning Factors

After reviewing two of the common ambient learning (AL) models described above, a model combining the strengths of the two was used to extract knowledge from a developed AL system. Various factors were considered such as the course accessed, the mode of access (e.g. via Google Docs, YouTube, etc.), the stage of learning, day-of-week and time-of-day of access and the reason for accessing (e.g. to read text, watch video, collaborate, etc.)

As shown in Figure 4, Java programming was the course recording the highest usage statistics per week, especially through YouTube. Artificial intelligence had similarly high YouTube access. While Mathematics generally has low access, most of this access was though YouTube. Facebook seemed to be the least preferable access mechanism for ambient learners.

The course Artificial intelligence had the highest level of consistency between expected values and observed values as measured by the Pearson Chi-square statistic. Table 1 shows the summary of significant Chi-square outcomes for access to the Artificial Intelligence course on the ambient learning system. Generally, watching video had the highest frequency of usage, consistent with the descriptive analysis shown in Figure 4 above. Learners also recorded consistent results for reading text and accessing examples from the ambient learning service.

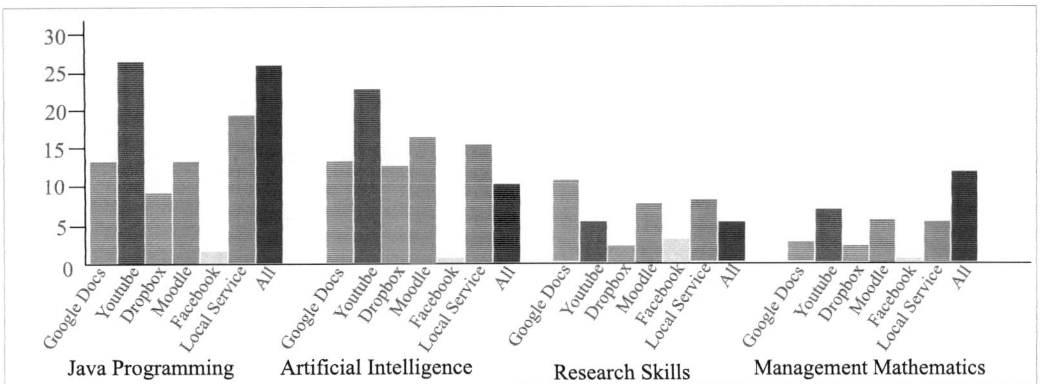

Figure 4. Steps for achieving actionable knowledge from an ambient service

Table 1. Summary of significant Chi-square outcomes for access to the Artificial Intelligence course

Rows: Usage Frequency Columns: Artificial Intelligence	RT	WV	AF	Co	AE	Row Margin
Weekly or less than weekly -- % of access	23.5	25.3	13.2	14.1	23.9	100
Usage frequency (%)	42.4	61.2	60.8	51.8	53.2	74.1
Pearson X^2 (%)	19.8	21.7	11.6	9.9	11.1	74.1
Cramer's V statistic	0.001	0.000	0.005	0.001	0.000	
Expected Frequency	25.2	23.5	9.7	11.4	13.2	83
More than weekly -- % of access	23.9	34.6	11.7	11.4	18.4	100
Usage frequency (%)	11.5	6.8	13.1	--	6.4	25.9
Pearson X^2 (%)	9.7	6.2	2.3	1.8	5.9	25.9
Cramer's V statistic	0.001	0.001	0.000	0.012	0.005	
Expected Frequency	10.5	7.8	2.1	5.5	3.1	29
Column Margin -- % of access	23.2	31.4	12.9	12.6	19.9	100
Usage frequency (%)	100	100	100	100	100	100
Pearson X^2 (%)	29.5	27.9	13.9	11.7	17	100
Cramer's V statistic	0.000	0.000	0.002	0.005	0.002	
Expected Frequency	32	24	17	18	21	112

RT= Read Text, WV= Watch Video, AF= Access Feedback, Co= Collaborate, AE= Access Example

4.2 Classification Results

Using a dataset from the Open Mobile Ambient Learning (OMAL) database that was reserved for validation, decision tree analysis was done with 10-fold cross validation resulting in predictions of usage frequencies for ambient learning across different variables. The most important variable was access frequency, and it was discovered that the course highly determines this frequency, with machine-based learning modules such as artificial intelligence being commonly accessed especially during the day and by student in the later learning stage. Mode of accessing AL content was also influential particularly for purposes other than to access feedback and examples.

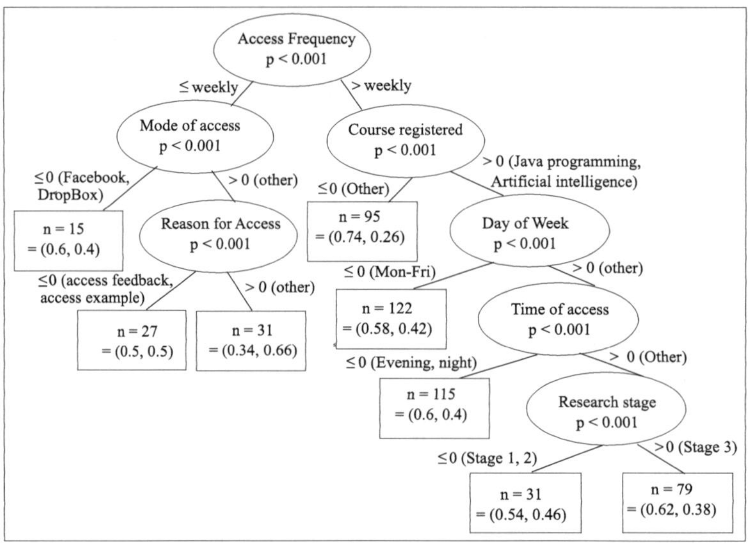

Figure 5. Outcomes from decision tree analysis of different ambient learning variables

5. CONCLUSION

The current research was focused on providing a resource of actionable knowledge through analysis of ambient learning usage statistics to advise improvement of knowledge provision on the cloud. This section offers the theoretical and industrial implications of the study, with its limitations and propositions for future direction.

5.1 Discussion

The research has demonstrated integration of the Open Mobile Ambient Learning (OMAL) system with a Knowledge as a Service (KaaS) model for extracting knowledge to advise decision-making processes of ambient learning system developers. The outcomes of this research can help address the issues facing quality and equitable lifelong learning approaches that are not limited by space and time.

Developing countries are increasingly improving their network infrastructures, and private ownership of smart mobile devices. Most learners in developing countries today are being provided with learning resources such as mobile phones, laptops and tablets. This avails a natural platform for ambient learning to thrive. With the convenient internet connection speeds, quality and life-long learning is possible. Additionally, the advanced education systems in developing countries become accessible to all, thus bridging the gap between learners in developed versus developing world.

As demonstrated by Mwendia (2018), the OMAL system provides multi-modal access for ambient learner, but it does not provide opportunities for gathering knowledge from data generated to be able to make changes or decisions. Therefore, this research is a major improvement on the OMAL system architecture since it enables dissemination of knowledge gathered on the knowledge-based system via the proposed cloud service and generates objective actionable knowledge. Such knowledge is more useful for ambient learning experts who can improve the ambient learning system and the general quality of education.

5.2 Limitations and Future Research Areas

Results from this study have substantial policy implications, but further work is needed before the procedures can be effective for practical use. First, analysis using a larger sample of data is necessary as the study has used a limited sample. Secondly particular attention should be made to how well the assumptions behind the credibility model are fulfilled and whether improved variables for the model can be found. Thirdly, the current research places focus on the content dissemination. Further research is necessary to evaluate the quality of education, such as by assessing the learning outcomes. A more relevant platform should also showcase how managed cloud services can aid learning.

Finally, future research can extend the current study by comparing results from the methods reported here with those reported among learners in other regions of both developed and developing economies, possibly from the design science methodological perspective. Nevertheless, the work reported in this paper provides valuable insight regarding the dissemination of knowledge to support ambient learning, particularly in areas with limited infrastructures to support conventional learning practices.

REFERENCES

Al-Busaidi, K.A. 2013. *An empirical investigation linking learners' adoption of blended learning to their intention of full e-learning*. Behaviour & Information Technology, Vol. 32, No. 11, pp.1168-1176

Ambient Insight 2013. *All Roads Lead Mobile*. Accessed from https://ambientinsight.wordpress.com/tag/worldwide/ (31/8/2019)

Asano, Y., Hidaka, S., Hu, Z., Ishihara, Y., Kato, H., Ko, H.S., Nakano, K., Onizuka, M., Sasaki, Y., Shimizu, T. and Tsushima, K., 2018. *A View-based Programmable Architecture for Controlling and Integrating Decentralized Data*. arXiv preprint arXiv:1803.06674.

Armbrust, M. Joseph A.D and Katz, K. 2009. *Above the Clouds: A Berkley View of Cloud Computing*. Wiley. New York.

de Sousa, L., Kanyimba, A.T. and Bothun, G.D. 2016. Data networks and sustainability education in African universities. International Journal of Sustainability in Higher Education, Vol. 17, No. 2, pp. 246-268.

General Assembly. 2015. *About the Sustainable Development Goals*. Accessed from https://www.un.org/sustainabledevelopment/sustainable-development-goals/ (23/8/19)

Grover, V., Chiang, R.H., Liang, T.P. and Zhang, D., 2018. Creating strategic business value from big data analytics: A research framework. Journal of Management Information Systems, 35(2), pp.388-423.

IT News Africa. 2015. *Study reveals African mobile phone usage stats*. Accessed from https://www.itnewsafrica.com/2015/04/study-reveals-african-mobile-phone-usage-stats/ (23/8/19)

Kaliisa, R. and Picard, M. 2017. *A Systematic Review on Mobile Learning in Higher Education: The African Perspective*. Turkish Online Journal of Educational Technology-TOJET, Vol. 16, No. 1, pp.1-18.

Kathuria, A., Mann, A., Khuntia, J., Saldanha, T.J. and Kauffman, R.J., 2018. *A strategic value appropriation path for cloud computing*. Journal of management information systems, 35(3), pp.740-775.

Mwendia, S.N., Wagacha, P.W. and Oboko, R., 2014. *Culture Aware M-Learning Classification Framework for African Countries*. In Cross-Cultural Online Learning in Higher Education and Corporate Training (pp. 98-111). IGI Global.

Mwendia, S.N., Waiganjo, P. and Oboko, R. 2016). Dynamic Heuristics: Greedy Search: A Mobile Information Retrieval Algorithm for Ambient Learning Systems. In *Proceedings of the First African Conference on Human Computer Interaction*, pp. 69-79. ACM.

Parsons, D., 2014. *The future of mobile learning and implications for education and training*. Increasing Access, 217.

Ssekakubo, G., Suleman, H. and Marsden, G. 2013). Designing mobile LMS interfaces: learners' expectations and experiences. Interactive Technology and Smart Education, Vol. 10, No. 2, pp.147-167.

UNESCO. 2015. *Kenya National Adult Literacy Survey report*. Accessed from https://www.eldis.org/document/A31868 (23/8/19)

Xu, X. 2012. *From cloud computing to cloud manufacturing*. Robotics and computer-integrated manufacturing, Vol. 28, No. 1, pp.75-86.

USING SYSTEM MODELS TO RESOLVE CO-REFERENCE IN TRANSLATING NATURAL LANGUAGE REQUIREMENTS INTO CODE

Brit Arnon[1,2], David Harel[1] and Michal Gordon-Kiwkowitz[3]
[1]*Weizmann Institute of Science, Rehovot, Israel*
[2]*Google LLC. Tel-Aviv, Israel*
[3]*Holon Institute of Technology, Holon, Israel*

ABSTRACT

One important quest in software development is to be able to translate natural language requirements into executable code. In this paper we address the issue of co-reference resolution, extending our previous work on a controlled natural language translation to live sequence charts. While domain-specific co-reference resolvers perform adequately, and state-of-the-art deep learning-based generic resolvers are emerging, in software development, especially for critical systems, a higher level of performance is required. We present an approach that incorporates system-model-based anaphora resolution. Using an annotated corpus for software requirements with system models, we show that while our approach reaches high accuracy, it is synergistic to generic resolvers and when combined with them it reaches higher accuracy. Our method shows that incorporating system models into the pipeline of requirements to code is a promising approach.

KEYWORDS

Requirements to Code, Live Sequence Charts, Co-Reference Resolution, Controlled Natural Language

1. INTRODUCTION

In an age when technology is all around and more people are involved in building software, simpler interfaces for development tasks are required [Stefanidi et al., 2018]. A long-term goal of software engineering is to develop tools that translate software requirements directly into executable code, skipping the "programming" phase. There are two approaches to reaching this goal, namely, processing natural language and making software languages more compatible with requirements.

The challenge with software requirements is that they are usually written in natural language (NL) and processing them is challenging. One approach is to use a "controlled natural language" (CNL), which imposes restrictions and rigor on the requirements. In [Bryant & Lee, 2002] the authors present a formal but natural-like language that can translate software requirements into Java code, while [Finucane et al., 2010] features a robot controller that transforms task specifications into direct motor commands to the robot.

However, the programming languages used in these attempts were not developed with requirements in mind. Behavioral programming languages, on the other hand, attempt to be compatible with how people think about software requirements; they are more event-driven and are often visual. One such language is live sequence charts (LSC), which is an extension of message sequence charts [Damm & Harel, 2001].

There have been attempts to create an NL interface for behavioral programming. In [Gordon & Harel, 2009], a novel approach was developed based on interaction with the user, whereas [Tsarfaty et al., 2014] features a machine-learning-based model for translating requirements written in the CNL of [Gordon & Harel, 2009] into LSCs.

One outstanding challenge with these approaches is the resolution of co-reference; that is, deciding which of two or more expressions that appear to refer to the same entity is the correct one. Co-reference resolution is challenging, because it deals with ambiguity. For example, *"when the car approaches the garage, it opens"*: does *it* relate to the car or the garage? While there have been many attempts to overcome this challenge [Shekhar & Kumar, 2018], only very few software requirement translating tools have succeeded

[Yang et al., 2011]. The task of resolving co-references for software requirements has strict demands, more so when the requirements are to be translated into executable code for critical systems. In this paper, we describe a method for co-reference resolution in the CNL interface described in [Gordon & Harel, 2009], translated into executable LSC.

The paper is organized as follows: Section 2 contains preliminaries. We discuss co-reference resolution, followed by a brief description of LSC, a CNL for the language of LSC, and the basics of co-reference resolution in natural language. In Section 3, we present our co-reference resolution method, and in Section 4 we present the results. We then conclude with related work and conclusions in Section 5.

2. PRELIMINARIES

2.1 Co-Reference Resolution

Research on co-reference resolution has focused on various domains separately [Shekhar & Kumar, 2018]. In [Rosiger & Teufel, 2014] the reference resolver of [Bjorkelund & Farkas, 2012] is adapted to the domain of scientific texts, and it is shown that adding domain specific training and knowledge drastically increases the success rate. In [Zheng et al., 2011] a co-reference resolution method that focuses on the clinical domain is reviewed, and [Uzuner et al., 2012] evaluates several such methods. The conclusion is that domain knowledge and semantics-related features are required for satisfactory co-reference resolution. While such features are not prominent in many reference resolution systems, our CNL-specific system presented here uses semantics-related features quite heavily; namely, the system model information.

Despite these advances, general co-reference resolution is still an unsolved problem [Peng et al., 2015]. More recent approaches use deep learning algorithms to address the problem. In [Lee et al., 2017] an end-to-end co-reference resolution model is presented, which uses a recurrent deep neural network. Expansions to this model appear in [Luo & Glass, 2018], where cross-sentence dependencies improve performance. Yet state-of-the-art performance is still below 80%.

Several approaches have focused on processing requirements written in a "free" natural language. In [Nanduri & Rugaber, 1995], a natural language parser is developed, which transforms requirements into an object oriented structure and thus enables some kinds of automatic validation. In [Roth & Klein, 2015] a semantic role labeler is used to convert natural language requirements into structured semantic representations. In [Chhabra et al., 2018], Petri nets and context based reasoning are used to transform natural language requirements into a more formal representation — expressive decision tables.

Our interest here is co-reference resolution in requirement documents. One approach to this appears in [Yang et al., 2011], where a human subject is used to help train a classifier for solving ambiguous co-references in requirement documents. As we shall see, our approach combines system knowledge with requirements parsing to boost the efficiency of co-reference resolution.

2.2 Controlled Natural Language for Live Sequence Charts

Live sequence charts (LSCs) [Damm & Harel, 2001] are a formal visual language for specifying programming scenarios of reactive systems. Each LSC is a diagram that describes a specific scenario of the system: a possible one, a necessary one or a forbidden one. A set of LSCs specifies the behavior of an entire system, and such a set can be directly executed, or compiled into conventional executable code that realizes that behavior [Harel & Marelly, 2003; Harel et al., 2010].

Let us begin with an example. Consider a system that simulates a “smart home”: a central unit that automatically controls the air conditioning and the lighting in the house. We may have certain expectations regarding such a system: for example, we can expect the lights in a room to turn on as people enter and to turn off when the room becomes empty; or we can expect the air conditioner to start and stop according to the current temperature in the room. Such requirements can be expressed easily using LSCs.

Formally, the behavioral requirements expressible in this language involve elements in the structural model of the system: objects, properties, methods and values. We represent these elements in a data structure called **the system model**. The system model contains all the classes and objects of the system. Each class has a set of properties and a set of methods that are associated with this class. Each object is an instance of a certain class, and it acquires the properties and methods of that class. For example, in the case of the smart home, the system consists of several objects: `rooms`, `lights`, an `air conditioner`, `blinds`, and so on. Each object has properties and methods. For example, a `blind` has a property `state` and methods `open()` and `close()`.

In [Gordon & Harel, 2009] a CNL was developed for expressing requirement scenarios that can be directly translated into LSCs. The language is a simplified version of English; it has a rigid grammar, but it is quite expressive. For example, requirements from the world of the "smart house" can be expressed as follows: *"When Alice enters the room, the light state is set to on"* or *"When Alice enters the room, if the room temperature is greater than 24, the air_conditioner starts"*.

The CNL of [Gordon & Harel, 2009] is structured as a context-free grammar. The terminal symbols in the grammar are of two types, static and dynamic. Static terminals are predefined in the grammar, and are words that describe the flow and the structure of the scenario; e.g., *when, then, if.* Dynamic terminals are not predefined, and can be written quite freely; they refer to the elements of the system. **Objects** are expressed by noun phrases: *Alice, the room, the light, the air conditioner.* **Properties** are expressed by compound noun phrases, composed of an object and another noun: *the light state, the room temperature.* **Constant values** can be expressed by several parts of speech. For example, *on* is a preposition and *24* is a number. Almost any word can be considered a constant value. **Messages**: the CNL distinguishes between two types of messages: method calls and property changes. A **method call** represents a call to an object's method; for example, the phrase *Alice enters the room* expresses a call to the method `enter()` of the object `the room`. The method is expressed by a verb. A **property change** is the event of setting the value of a property; for example, the phrase *the light state is set to on* indicates that the property `the light state` is assigned the value "`on`". It is actually a call to an object's setter method, but it is usually not expressed as such in the grammar.

We note that in this approach words can be ambiguous. For example, a noun may express either an object or a constant value. Moreover, many English noun forms can be interpreted as verbs (e.g., *light* is both a noun and a verb), so they may express objects, constant values or verbs. These inherent lexical ambiguities cause the language to be highly ambiguous. Yet, combining the CNL translation with LSCs means that we are able to generate executable code (see [Harel & Marelly, 2003]) out of textual requirements in a controlled subset of English.

2.3 Reference Resolution in Natural Language

Reference resolution is the task of determining which entity is referred to by a certain expression in the discourse. For example, in the sentence (taken from our "smart home" domain): *"When Alice enters the room, if **its** temperature is less than 24, the smart home opens all the blinds, otherwise **it** closes **them**."* In this example, *its* refers to *the room,* while *it* refers to the *smart home*, and *them* refers to *all the blinds*.

An expression that refers to an entity is called a **referring expression** or a **mention**, and the entity it refers to is called its **referent**. If two mentions refer to the same entity, we say that they are **co-referent**. In the sentence above the co-references are *the room* and *its*, the *smart home* and *it* and *all the blinds* and *them*.

Note that in the example sentence each model entity is first expressed explicitly, and only then is referred to by a pronoun. This type of reference, where the explicit mention appears before the pronoun, is called **anaphora**. The pronoun is said to be an **anaphoric pronoun**, and the explicit mention is said to be the **antecedent** of the pronoun. The explicit mention may appear after the pronoun, as in the following sentence: *"Whenever **she** enters the room, Alice opens the windows*". This phenomenon is called **cataphora**. It is less common than anaphora, and therefore in this paper we focus on the task of anaphora resolution.

We do not attempt to cover them here, but instead briefly mention some prominent principles in reference resolution that are frequently used, and which are relevant to our work. One is **grammatical agreement**: co-referent expressions should agree in **number** (singular/plural), **gender** (male/female/neuter) and **person** (1st/2nd/3rd). Another is **salience**: the more salient an entity is in the discourse, the more probable it is to be an antecedent of a pronoun. There are several methods for determining how salient a certain entity is in a given sentence [Jurafsky & Martin, 2009].

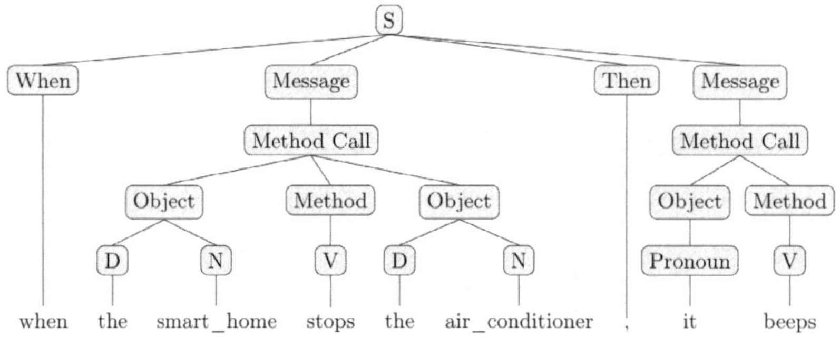

Figure 1. The parse tree (see [Jurafsky & Martin, 2009] for details) for the sentence: *"When the smart_home stops the air_conditioner, it beeps"*. The terminal *it* is generated from the non-terminal *pronoun*

3. ADDING CO-REFERENCE RESOLUTION TO THE CNL

In this section we present our approach to co-reference resolution in sentences written in our CNL. First, since the grammar in [Gordon & Harel, 2009] did not include pronouns, we have extended the grammar to include them. Since pronouns are used to refer to noun phrases, they should appear in the same contexts as noun phrases do, namely as objects and properties. The extension was quite straightforward: we added the non-terminal *pronoun*, which may generate any English pronoun; and the *object* and *property* non-terminals may generate a *pronoun*. As an example, Figure 1 shows the full parse tree of the sentence *"When the smart home stops the air conditioner, it beeps"*.

We note that pronouns in 1st or 2nd person (*I* or *you*) seldom appear in software requirement specifications, and therefore we support only 3rd person pronouns (*she*, *he*, *it*, *they* and their inflections).

Recall from subsection (2.2) that the system model is the collection of the classes and objects associated with methods and properties. As we mentioned in subsection (2.3), a principal technique in reference resolution is enforcing grammatical agreement between the co-referent expressions: they must agree on gender and number. In our approach we extend this, and enforce also "class agreement": co-referent mentions must be associated with the same class. The class can be deduced from methods and properties that are mentioned in the context.

For example, consider the following pair of requirements, written in the CNL: (a) *"When the smart home stops the air conditioner, **its** state changes to off."* (b) *"When the smart home stops the air conditioner, **its** message changes to "stopped the air conditioner"."* In (a), the referent of *it* must have a property named *state*; otherwise the requirement would be nonsensical. Therefore, *it* must refer to *the air conditioner*, which is the only object with such a property. Likewise, in (b), the referent of *it* must have a property named message, and therefore it must be *the smart home*. This constraint can be formulated as follows: **Property-Related Constraint:** If a pronoun p is immediately followed by a noun n, the referent of p is an object, which is an instance of a class that has a property named n.

The situation for methods is more complicated. In the CNL, methods can appear in three possible constructs: **(1) Object Method**. Example: *"the air_conditioner beeps"*. The pronoun in the phrase *"it beeps"* must refer to an object that has a method named *beep*. **(2) Object Method Property**. Example: *"the smart_home records the room temperature"*. The pronoun in the phrase *"it records the room temperature"* must refer to an object that has a method named *record*. **(3) Object Method Object**. Example: *"the smart_home stops the air_conditioner"*. Here a pronoun can replace either of the two objects. However, according to the CNL grammar, the "agent" of the method in this structure is always the second object. Thus, the *stop* method mentioned is a method of the *air_conditioner*.

This analysis can be formulated as the following constraint: **Method-Related Constraint**: For a pronoun p, if a verb v is associated with p, the referent of p is an object that is an instance of a class that has a method named v.

In the **system model inference** technique, we extract system-model-related attributes of the entities in the sentence, and then use them to impose constraints on potential co-referent entities. The attributes are methods and properties that are associated with the objects. We note that these considerations do not always suffice to determine the antecedent of a pronoun.

Our goal was to adapt the system of (Gordon & Harel, 2009), which translates requirements written in the CNL into LSCs, to be able to deal with sentences that include referring pronouns. The original system consists of two components: a parser and a semantic processor; We added an anaphora resolution component, which uses the system model inference technique. We now describe the operation of the anaphora resolver and the modifications we made in the other components.

The **parser** receives a single sentence in the CNL as input, and outputs the most probable parse tree for this sentence. Our parser also processes pronouns. The **semantic processor** interacts with the anaphora resolver. Whenever it encounters a pronoun, it requests the anaphora resolver to resolve it.

The **anaphora resolver** is our major contribution. Given a parsed sentence and a pronoun therein, the anaphora resolver outputs an appropriate antecedent. In order to do so, it maintains a set of all the explicit entities that have been extracted by the semantic processor. For a given pronoun, the anaphora resolver constructs a set of extracted entities that are compatible antecedents according to the system model constraints, and outputs one of them arbitrarily. (The optimal case is that the resulting set has only one element, which is the correct antecedent.) The algorithm is "system-model-based" (**SMB**) and is shown in Algorithm 1. Lines 3-4 enforce the method-related constraint on the object entities, and lines 5-6 enforce the property-related constraint on them. Notice that at most one of them is applied (since, grammatically, a pronoun cannot be both associated with a verb and immediately followed by a noun). Lines 8-9 handle property entities: since there are no constraints for properties, the algorithm simply outputs the first property entity.

This simple algorithm uses almost no considerations other than the system model constraints. As our analysis will show, its performance is encouraging. Furthermore, it adds a feedback mechanism: An additional benefit since for certain types of incorrectly parsed sentences it can detect the error by using the system model information. Having not found any appropriate antecedent for a pronoun in the sentence is an indication that the sentence's parse tree is incorrect. In such cases, the anaphora resolver notifies the parser, which then selects another parse tree, and the semantic processing is restarted. This feedback mechanism allows for a higher accuracy of the entire system.

Algorithm 1: System-model-based (SMB) anaphora resolution algorithm

Input: a parsed sentence *s*, and an anaphoric pronoun *p* from *s*.

Denote by $O = \{o_1, \ldots, o_k\}$ the set of extracted objects, and denote by $R = \{r_1, \ldots, r_k\}$ the set of extracted properties. Assume that the entities are sorted according to their order of appearance in the sentence.

1: **if** *p* is parsed as an object in *s* **then**
2: construct a set *O'* which is a copy of *O*.
3: **if** a verb *v* is associated with *p* **then**
4: remove from *O'* any object that does not have a method named *v*.
5: **else if** *p* is immediately followed by a noun *n* **then**
6: remove from *O'* any object that does not have a property named *n*.
7: **return** the first entity in *O'*.
8: **else if** *p* is parsed as a property in *s* **then**
9: **return** the first entity in *R*.

4. RESULTS

As far as we could tell, there is no corpus of requirement specification texts with reference annotations. Therefore, we built and annotated our own dataset. The collection consists of several sets of LSC programs and the CNL sentences that correspond to them. We replaced recurring mentions in these sentences with pronouns. In some cases we joined closely-related sentences into a paragraph, or replaced a word with a synonym in order to make the sentence clearer. However, we made sure not to alter the grammatical structure of the sentences, so that the resulting dataset is an accurate reflection of the original collection.

The dataset consists of 68 paragraphs, which include 107 pronouns, and we mapped each pronoun to its antecedent. We considered several variants of anaphora resolution algorithms and compared their performance on our dataset. Each system received a binary score on each pronoun, indicating whether the system outputs the correct antecedent for it.

As a baseline, we used a known reference resolution system, developed by [Lee et al., 2011], which is a part of the Stanford CoreNLP toolkit [Manning et al., 2014]. It has two variants: a statistical one (machine-learning-based) and a deterministic one (rule-based). Note that the system output is not a pronoun-antecedent mapping, but a set of clusters of co-referent mentions, so it had to be adapted for the needs of our evaluation. We added an antecedent selection layer: for each pronoun, the layer finds the cluster that contains it and selects the cluster's first mention (by order of appearance in the text) to be the antecedent. We denote the statistical and deterministic variants by **SST**[1] and **SDE**[2], respectively.

We considered several variants of our system-model-based algorithm. The first is the SMB[3] algorithm described in the previous section..

Next, recall that this basic algorithm filters out incompatible antecedent candidates, and then selects one of the remaining candidates arbitrarily. The selection phase is completely naive, since the system model information can be used to reject candidates but not to score the remaining ones. In order to make the selection phase more sophisticated, we extended the algorithm by "consulting" the Stanford CoreNLP systems, in the following way. In the selection phase the extended algorithm examines two sets: the candidate set constructed in the filtering phase, and the set of mentions that the Stanford system variant considers to be co-referent with the given pronoun. If possible, the mechanism outputs a mention that is included in both sets. This method refines the candidate set, and thus we expected it to improve the accuracy of the selection phase. We used two variants, one that consults the Stanford deterministic system, denoted **SMBcSDE**[4], and one that consults the statistical system, denoted **SMBcSST**[5]. Note that SMB uses only system model knowledge, while the Stanford systems use various syntactic and structural features. This makes the two types of systems complementary, and therefore their integration is expected to be beneficial.

Table 1 compares the performance of the three anaphora resolution algorithms. The SMB variants outperform SDE significantly, and the "consulting" variants outperform the "non-consulting" one. One could claim that the main reason for this is that SMB has been specifically developed to handle the grammar in which the requirements are written. However, we claim that incorporating system model information directly is especially beneficial. To support this claim, we examined the impact of incorporating the system model inference into SDE. (For more details on SDE, see [Lee et al., 2011].)We enriched SDE's pronominal co-reference model so that it enforces agreement regarding two additional attributes: (1) the type of the mention: object, property or value; and (2) the set of possible classes of which the mention can be an instance, if it is an object. Two mentions are considered to agree on these attributes if they share their type and if their class sets intersect. This agreement enforcement was implemented using the same scheme by which the grammatical agreement enforcement is implemented in the original system.

Another necessary modification was in the mention extraction process. As described in [Lee et al., 2011], at the beginning of the process the model scans the text and extracts all noun phrases that it considers to be candidate mentions. The extraction is fairly strict: it skips noun phrases that are less likely to refer to world entities, such as phrases that are preceded by quantifiers, like *all* and *every*. These considerations are very suitable for general texts, but less suitable for requirement specifications. We modified the mention extraction process, making it more relaxed for noun phrases that are typically used in requirement specifications.

We incorporated the system model information into SDE, and not into SST, since the way to adapt SST would be by training it on an appropriate dataset, which should be sufficiently large. We hope that such a dataset will be constructed in the future.

[1] SST - Stanford Statistical Variant.
[2] SDE – Stanford Deterministic Variant.
[3] SMB – System Model Based Variant.
[4] SMBcSDE – System Model Based consulting the Stanford Deterministic Results
[5] SMBcSST – System Model Based consulting the Stanford Statistical Results.

Table 1 also shows the performance of three variants of SDE: the original one, one that has relaxed mention extraction, denoted SDE-R[6], and one that has relaxed mention extraction and uses system model inference, denoted SDE-R-SM[7]. Incidentally, the accuracy of the variant that uses system model inference with the original strict mention extraction was similar to the original SDE version, since the correct antecedents were not extracted as mentions, and hence were not considered as antecedents. It is therefore omitted from the table. The relaxed mention extraction allows for more mentions to be extracted and assigned as antecedents, thus improving the accuracy. For example, SDE produces an incorrect result when applied to the paragraph *"When the traffic light status is set to "green", all cars with speed 0 resume. When **they** resume, **their** speed is set to the controller speed"*. In contrast, SDE-R gives the correct result on it, since it extracts *all cars with speed 0* as a mention and considers it as an antecedent to *they* and *their*.

Table 1. The accuracy of the anaphora resolution algorithms on the left and of the three variants of the Stanford deterministic reference (SDE) resolution combinations with the system model on the right. The table shows the percentage of correct outputs out of 107

System Model Based Algorithm Variants	% correct
SMB[3]	81.3
SMBcSDE[4]	82.24
SMBcSST[5]	87.85

SDE Variants	% correct
SDE[2]	44.85
SDE-R[6]	54.2
SDE-R-SM[7]	68.22

The system model inference technique allows for selecting more accurate antecedents. For example, SDE-R is incorrect on the sentence *"When the smart home stops the air conditioner, **its** state is set to off."*, while SDE-R-SM is correct on it: it does not allow *the smart home* to be co-referent with *it*, since the smart home does not have a property state, and therefore *the air conditioner* is correctly recognized as co-referent with *it* and as its antecedent. We thus see that adapting SDE to the domain and incorporating system model information improves its performance.

5. CONCLUSION

We have presented a novel integration of a controlled natural language parser with a system model-based technique for anaphora resolution. While several methods have been proposed for co-reference resolution [Rosiger & Teufel, 2014; Zheng et al., 2011], they are usually domain-specific, and very rarely address software requirements [Roth & Klein, 2015]. However, there are several generic co-reference resolution methods [Lee et al., 2011, 2017], and our approach is synergistic with these, as we have demonstrated with the out-of-the-box Stanford Core toolkit resolver [Lee et al., 2011].

We have shown that augmenting a generic resolver with our system model based resolver drastically improves performance. Hence, we suggest that state-of-the-art algorithms can also benefit greatly from our approach. One limitation is that the current work was tested on a CNL that may not be appropriate for all domains.

Another direction for future work, stems from work like that of [Arora et al., 2016], where a method is proposed for extracting the model of a system from its requirements. We can use such a method in the future to extract the system model automatically, instead of constructing it manually as we did. And in a totally different direction, in [Mitkov et al., 2007] it is shown that deploying an anaphora resolution module can improve the performance of other NLP applications. This encourages us to believe that our anaphora resolution mechanism is the first step in extending our CNL-to-LSC system with more advanced features.

In summary, co-reference resolution in requirements engineering must be precise, since the end goal is an executable system. The presented method, built upon a controlled natural language and a co-reference resolution algorithm based on the system model, appears to be a promising new approach.

[6] SDE-R – Stanford Deterministic Variant with Relaxed mention extraction

[7] SDE-R-SM – Stanford Deterministic Variant with Relaxed mention extraction and uses System Model inference

REFERENCES

Arora, C., Sabetzadeh, M., Briand, L., & Zimmer, F., 2016. Extracting domain models from natural-language requirements: approach and industrial evaluation. *Proc. of the ACM/IEEE 19th Int. Conf. on Model Driven Engineering Languages and Systems*. Saint-malo, France, pp. 250-260.

Bjorkelund, A. & Farkas, R., 2012. Data-driven Multilingual Coreference Resolution using Resolver Stacking. Joint Conf. on EMNLP and CoNLL - Shared Task. Jeju Island, Korea, pp. 49–55.

Bryant, B. R. & Lee, B.-S., 2002. Two-level grammar as an object-oriented requirements specification language. *Proc. of the 35th Annual Hawaii Int. Conf. on System Sciences (HICSS)*. Hawaii, pp 280.

Chhabra, A., Sangroya, A., & Anantaram, C., 2018. Formalizing and Verifying Natural Language System Requirements using Petri Nets and Context based Reasoning. *MRC@ IJCAI*. Stockholm, Sweden, pp. 64–71.

Damm, W. and Harel, D., 2001, LSCs: Breathing Life into Message Sequence Charts. *Formal Methods in System Design*, Vol. 19, No. 1, pp 45-80.

Finucane, C., Jing, G., and Kress-Gazit, H., 2010, LTLMoP: Experimenting with language, temporal logic and robot control. *Proc. of the IEEE/RSJ Int. Conf. on Intelligent Robots and Systems (IROS)*. pp 1988-1993.

Gordon, M. and Harel, D., 2009, Generating Executable Scenarios from Natural Language. *Proc. of the 10th Int. Conf. on Computational Linguistics and Intelligent Text Processing (CICLing)*. Mexico, pp 456-567.

Harel, D., et al., 2010. PlayGo: Towards a Comprehensive Tool for Scenario Based Programming. *Proc. of the 25th IEEE/ACM Int. Conf. on Automated Software Engineering (ASE)*. Antwerp, Belgium, pp. 359-360.

Harel, D. & Marelly, R., 2003. *Come, Let's Play: Scenario-Based Programming Using LSCs and the Play-Engine*. Springer-Verlag.

Jurafsky, D. & Martin, J. H., 2009. *Speech and Language Processing: An Introduction to Natural Language Processing, Speech Recognition, and Computational Linguistics*. Prentice-Hall.

Lee, H., Peirsman, Y., Chang, A., Chambers, N., Surdeanu, M., & Jurafsky, D., 2011. Stanford's Multi-Pass Sieve Coreference Resolution System at the CoNLL – 2011 Shared Task. *Proc. of the Conf. on Natural Language Learning (CoNLL)*. Portland, Oregon, USA, pp. 28-34.

Lee, K., He, L., Lewis, M., & Zettlemoyer, L. S., 2017. End-to-end Neural Coreference Resolution. *Proc. of the 2017 Conf. on Empirical Methods in Natural Language Processing, EMNLP*. Copenhagen, Denmark, pp. 188-197.

Luo, H. & Glass, J., 2018. Learning Word Representations with Cross-Sentence Dependency for End-to-End Co-reference Resolution. *Proc. of the 2018 Conf. on Empirical Methods in NLP*. Brussels, Belgium, pp. 4829–4833.

Manning, C. D., Surdeanu, M., Bauer, J., Finkel, J., Bethard, S. J., & McClosky, D., 2014. The Stanford CoreNLP Natural Language Processing Toolkit. *Proc. of the 52nd Annual Meeting of the Association for Computational Linguistics (ACL): System Demonstrations*. Baltimore, Maryland, pp. 55-60.

Mitkov, R., Evans, R., Orasan, C., Pekar, V., & others, 2007. Anaphora resolution: To what extent does it help NLP applications? *Discourse Anaphora and Anaphor Resolution Colloquium*. Lagos, Portugal, pp. 179–190.

Nanduri, S. & Rugaber, S., 1995. Requirements Validation via Automated Natural Language Parsing. *Journal of Management Information Systems*. Vol. 12, No. 3, pp. 9–19.

Peng, H., Khashabi, D., & Roth, D., 2015. Solving Hard Coreference Problems. *Proc. of the 2015 Conf. of the North American Chapter of the ACL: Human Language Technologies*. Denver, Colorado, pp. 809-819.

Rosiger, I. & Teufel, S., 2014. Resolving Coreferent and Associative Noun Phrases in Scientific Text. *Proc. of the Student Research Workshop at the 14th Conf. of the European Chapter of the Association for Computational Linguistics (EACL)*. Gothenburg, Sweden, pp. 45–55.

Roth, M. & Klein, E., 2015. Parsing Software Requirements with an Ontology-based Semantic Role Labeler. *Proc. Of the 1st Workshop on Language and Ontologies (ACL)*, London, UK.

Shekhar, S. & Kumar, U., 2018. Review on the Techniques of Anaphora Resolutions. *Int. Journal of Latest Trends in Engineering and Technology*, Vol. 8, No. 2, pp. 37–40.

Stefanidi, E., et al., 2018. Programming Intelligent Environments in Natural Language: An Extensible Interactive Approach. *Proc. of the 11th Pervasive Technologies Related to Assistive Environments Conf.* Greece, pp. 50–57.

Tsarfaty, R., et al., 2014. Semantic Parsing Using Content and Context: A Case Study from Requirements Elicitation. *Proc. Int. Conf. on Empirical Methods in Natural Language Processing (EMNLP)*. Doha, Qatar, pp. 1296–1307.

Uzuner, O., Bodnari, A., Shen, S., Forbush, T., Pestian, J., & South, B. R., 2012. Evaluating the state of the art in coreference resolution for electronic medical records. *J. of the American Medical Informatics Ass*. Vol. 19, No. 5.

Yang, H., de Roeck, A., Gervasi, V., Willis, A., & Nuseibeh, B., 2011. Analysing anaphoric ambiguity in natural language requirements. Requirements Engineering. Vol. 16, No. 3, pp. 163.

Zheng, J., Chapman, W. W., Crowley, R. S., & Savova, G. K., 2011. Coreference resolution: A review of general methodologies and applications in the clinical domain. J. of Biomedical Informatics. Vol. 44, No. 6, pp. 1113-1122.

QUALITY SCALE ADAPTATION APPLIED TO A COMMUNICATION PLATFORM FOR PRIMARY HEALTH CARE ANALYSIS

Galba Freire Moita[1, 2, 3] and Galba Freire Moita Júnior[4,5]
[1]*Ministério da Saúde (MS) – Brasília (DF), Brasil,* [2]*Fundação Oswaldo Cruz (Fiocruz) – Fortaleza (CE), Brasil and* [3]*Universidade de Coimbra (UC), Faculdade de Economia, Centre for Business and Economics Research (CeBER) – Coimbra, Portugal*
[4]*Universidade Federal do Ceará – Fortaleza (CE), Brasil*
[5]*Omnielmaster Hem., Repr., Com. e Serv. em Saude, Consultoria, Trein. e Educ. Prof. Ltda*

ABSTRACT

Nationally based opinion polls showed population dissatisfaction ranging from 54 to 93% (CFM, 2014, 2015, 2018). And yet, that high percentages of Brazilians evaluate public health as bad or terrible, which increased from 61% in 2011 to 75% in 2018 (CNI, 2012, 2018), which revealed a supposed dissatisfaction in public and supplementary health of Brazil. In an integrative bibliographical research on quality measurement and health user satisfaction in Brazil, the results obtained are timid and there are no records of standardization of quality and satisfaction measurement systems in Brazilian Health System whose acronym in Portuguese is SUS (Sistema Único de Saúde). Thus, the outlined objective was to adapt an international model by transliterating and revalidating the 22 questions on the Servqual scale (Berry, Parasuraman, Zeithaml, & Adsit, 1994; Parasuraman, Berry, & Zeithaml, 1991a), for quality assessment and satisfaction in health services to support the development of a virtual platform to capture the experience of SUS users. In a world where data is what most matter, which generate information and knowledge and can be a basis for new strategies, methodologies for its collection, manipulation, transformation and visualization enable diagnoses, solutions to help users' perceptions of a system in relation of quality of provided services. This study involved 220 managers and professionals (stakeholders) as well as 506 users for the cross-cultural translation and validation of the Servqual scale constructs for the SUS context and presents a way of extracting knowledge of specialists and users through the cross-cultural adaptation of Servqual Scale, which resulted in the instrument QUALITY SAÚDE (Health quality in portuguese) of measuring expectation and perception from users of Brazilian health system (SUS), measuring their satisfaction. Data were extracted from a relational database in order to be consulted in an organized way, quickly and mainly without unnecessary use of repeated data, bringing integrity. Data were manipulated and transformed using a BI tool, which allowed visualization in an analytical and synthetic way, being able to be analyzed in a micro (small samples of data) and macro (large samples of data), facilitating decision making process, proposing improvements, making diagnoses, proposing solutions.

KEYWORDS

Business Intelligence, Servqual Scale, User Satisfaction, Health Quality, Brazilian Health System

1. INTRODUCTION

Evaluating quality of services is an essential factor when you want to measure customer satisfaction, retain customers and having a broad vision from the consumer perspective of a service. There is a need to evaluate services provided in public health sector as a measure to assist resources management.

In reality in Brazil, two nationally-based opinion polls from the Federal Council of Medicine (CFM) (2014, 2015; 2018) and from the National Confederation of Industry (CNI) (2012, 2018) were identified, with the most renowned institutes Brazilian research workers, Datafolha and Ibope, respectively, with data from 2011 to 2018, which reveal the importance of assessing quality and satisfaction. In the meantime, they point out population dissatisfactions ranging from 54 to 93% (CFM, 2014, 2015, 2018). And yet, that high percentages of Brazilians evaluate public health as bad or very bad, which increased from 61% in 2011 to 75% in 2018 (CNI, 2012, 2018), which vary according to the perspective of analysis and addressing these researches, especially regarding the recent use of services, whether in public or supplementary health.

However, some robust bibliographic analyzes (G. F. Moita, 2019; Volpato, 2014) showed that there is no record of standardized models or systems for measuring quality and satisfaction in SUS, in addition to the incipient theme. A systematic search in the main databases of scientific articles in Brazil (Medline; Lilacs; Scielo), in addition to obtaining extremely scarce results, no robust methodology for assessing quality and satisfaction was identified through standardized and validated and / or wide instruments use in the Brazilian health context. In a previous study (G. F. Moita, 2019) it was shown that there is no validated scale for SUS, but that the proposal of the Gespública initiative (Brasil, 2014) had many similarities with the five dimensions and with the 22 questions of the original Servqual scale (Berry et al., 1994; Parasuraman et al., 1991a). In this scope, there are three small works of application of Servqual in specific contexts (Hercos & Berezovsky, 2004; BORGES, et al., 2006; CRUZ & MELLEIRO, 2007). Three other works were also identified with systematization of the Servqual scale for application in hospital environments, but with simplified translations and adaptations and application in a short sample in hospitals in Brazil (Aharony & Strasser, 1993 apud Esperidião e Trad, 2005: 304).

These mentioned surveys help to understand that they do not serve its purposes well, because scientific methods with methodological rigor were not applied to structure models that really approximate reality. In this purpose an international scale named Servqual was selected as a proposal for translation and adaptation of Servqual scale in a new instrument named QUALITY SAÚDE (Health Quality in portuguese), which is based on the translation field of knowledge in which consolidated theories are targets of transliteration in social actors involved experiences (Barbosa & Neto, 2017 apud Clavier et al, 2011; Hartz et al, 2008). Thus, in present study, it was based on a collaborative process aimed at establishing the constructs (ideals-forces) to synthesize and apply knowledge aimed at improving services in order to fill knowledge gaps and instruments to transform policies and practices for SUS services management. The applied process can be expanded to other public services, aiming at structuring and validating specific quality scales. Thus, was created the following problem question: Is it possible to use BI techniques to analyze the adaptation of the ServQual scale in the Brazilian health system?

Servqual questionnaire model is a selection of quality concepts in the service with a broader understanding, with the objective of basing customer's expectation against the perception of the same client about a service. However, there are no records of standardization of quality and satisfaction measurement systems in SUS. The aim of this article was to treat data obtained through a research that proposes the cross-cultural adaptation of Servqual scale for health quality evaluation, to evaluate services rendered in Brazilian public health, presenting information to assist in decision-making. The following specific objectives have been proposed: i. Define a data model that makes it possible to store collected data in an organized way; ii. Apply processes of extraction, transformation and loading of collected data; iii. Keep the data in a relational database; iv. Produce solutions to visualize collected data presenting them in a way that can accurately evidence obtained results.

Exploratory research was used and for formulation of necessary information for analysis of this work we searched for references in service evaluation area, mainly on Servqual model. This was used in research prototype applied under a PhD thesis developed by Moita (G. F. Moita, 2019) with initial results, which resulted in the proposal of QUALITY SAÚDE Scale, a measurement instrument of perceived quality (satisfaction and suitability for use) by users, duly adapted to the context of SUS.

The data model was developed based on adaptation made of Servqual scale. Extract, Transform and Load (ETL) processes were applied, which deals with data cleaning coming from several sources to be inserted in Data Warehouse (DW). This process was carried out in three stages: Data extraction; Transformation of data to correct, standardize and eliminate inconsistencies; Loading data into a database. With data available in DW, visualization was prepared in QlikView tool, enabling creation of reports and interactive dashboards.

There is a need to evaluate services provided in public health area as a measure to assist resources management. To that end, Moita (Galba Freire Moita, Barbosa, & Raposo, 2019b) states that it is necessary to evaluate quantity of health services or products (care, examinations, surgeries, hospitalizations) produced by health system or health units, but that requires efficient resource management, that is, it is intended to measure and monitor decisive impact on patients health, society and health system, since it is often perceived that mobilized resources are not monitored from an operative point of view.

2. SERVQUAL QUESTIONNAIRE MODEL

The two nationally based opinion polls from the Federal Council of Medicine (CFM, 2014, 2015, 2018) and from the National Confederation of Industry (CNI, 2012, 2018) not use an effective research method to assess quality of public health services provided to population. Current research does not serve its purpose well, because a rigorous methodology is not applied to sketch results that really approximate reality.

Servqual questionnaire model is a selection of quality concepts in deepening service, with the objective of basing client's expectation in counterpoint with the perception of same about a service. American researchers Parasuraman, Zeithaml and Berry (Parasuraman, Berry, & Zeithaml, 1988, 1991b), developed it. Its research method evaluates five aspects defined as dimensions, which are: Reliability; Safety; Empathy; Tangibles; Responsiveness. The questions can be adapted according to service, but the questionnaire applied must meet basic premises to reach its objective of collecting information. They are i. engaging the participant; ii. communicating appropriately with participant; iii. make participant develop their responses; iv. avoid creating biases or trends of any kind; v. promotes interviewer's task easily; vi. seek automated processing of responses.

In the initial research (Galba Freire Moita, Barbosa, & Raposo, 2019a) the questions on the Servqual scale were studied in order to validate constructs (ideas-forces) representative of the 22 original questions. The data were the basis for the construction of a new structured questionnaire with 20 closed questions, validated by pilot groups (195 experts) and then consolidated by a field survey with 506 SUS users, in care in 15 health units in the metropolitan region of Fortaleza - Ceará. Then, a virtual platform was developed for online application in multicenter groups of SUS users.

In addition to highlighting which points (13 sub-dimensions and six macro-dimensions of quality) that should be reviewed by public managers and add value to the satisfaction surveys offered to health organizations, for presenting real results and interpretations of the users' experience, according to the trend (Patient Reported Outcome Measures- PROMs) (Patrick et al., 2011; Reeve et al., 2013; Wild et al., 2005).

Original 22 questions of Servqual scale were adapted for health services (Babakus & Mangold, 1992) and asked the group to suggest and ponder in what dimensions each original question was appropriate and which personal constructs could be better adapted to SUS patients' reality. Afterwards, a questionnaire of 20 questions and a questionnaire of 14 questions were adapted and pondered in the panel of experts and pilot groups, where in these cases the last question represents the patient general satisfaction, through reliability and validity analyzes (through correlation and exploratory factor analysis) concluded that the QUALITY SAÚDE scale is reliable and valid in the hospital environment and in other health services.

About 2,547 respondents were interviewed, where 701 answered 40 constructs, 2,547 answered 20 questions and 2,547 answered the 14 questions, with responses from users of 81 primaries, secondaries and tertiaries health units from four cities in the state of Ceará, immediately after the effective care received. n this research data was stored in a relational database, and for this research PostgreSQL (2018) was chosen. On analysis of obtained results, 9,063 responses to each of the items of QUALITY SAÚDE scale were obtained in groups of 195 specialists in pilot groups with answers from 10 Brazilian states: Bahia, Ceará, Federal District, Goiás, Maranhão, Mato Grosso, Pará, Piauí, Rio Grande do Norte and Rondônia, besides 506 SUS users with analysis via software application R, version 3.3.2. For R Project (2017) it is a programming language with a focus on statistics and graphics; is a General Public License (GNU) project and is under open source license and performs a wide variety of functions.

There is no control of participants who are chosen randomly and as consequence people's grade who did not even receive service at that time, the research questions are considered superficial because they do not approach a topic deeply. As a result, the research results are unsatisfactory, since it does not assist managers in decision-making. Based on this, a satisfaction survey was carried out in order to evaluate public health services quality provided to Brazilian population, adapted from parameters of Servqual scale, which resulted in a new instrument adapted to SUS context, named in Portuguese Escala QUALITY SAÚDE (Quality Health Scale).

3. BI IN SERVQUAL SCALE ADAPTATION

A large amount of data is generated daily and data usage is minimal. Due to this factor, many opportunities to leverage health services in Brazil are lost. In order to control and manage care provided by SUS, information systems developed by Brazilian health ministry are used in most cases, which has one of its goals to define standards for collection and transfer of health information, aiming at databases operational integration and systems developed and implemented within the scope of SUS. This same system served as a model for similar program initiative in Peru. According to Datasus (2017b) it is essential for health management to know about health situation with quality and speed. This information, if it is easy to access and available with quality, becomes a great help for decision making in any area of activity, such as strategic planning, sectoral, control and evaluation, audit, epidemiological investigation. It is in this context that Business Intelligence can be applied in public health, making it possible to obtain excellence in data stored using in various information systems for knowledge production.

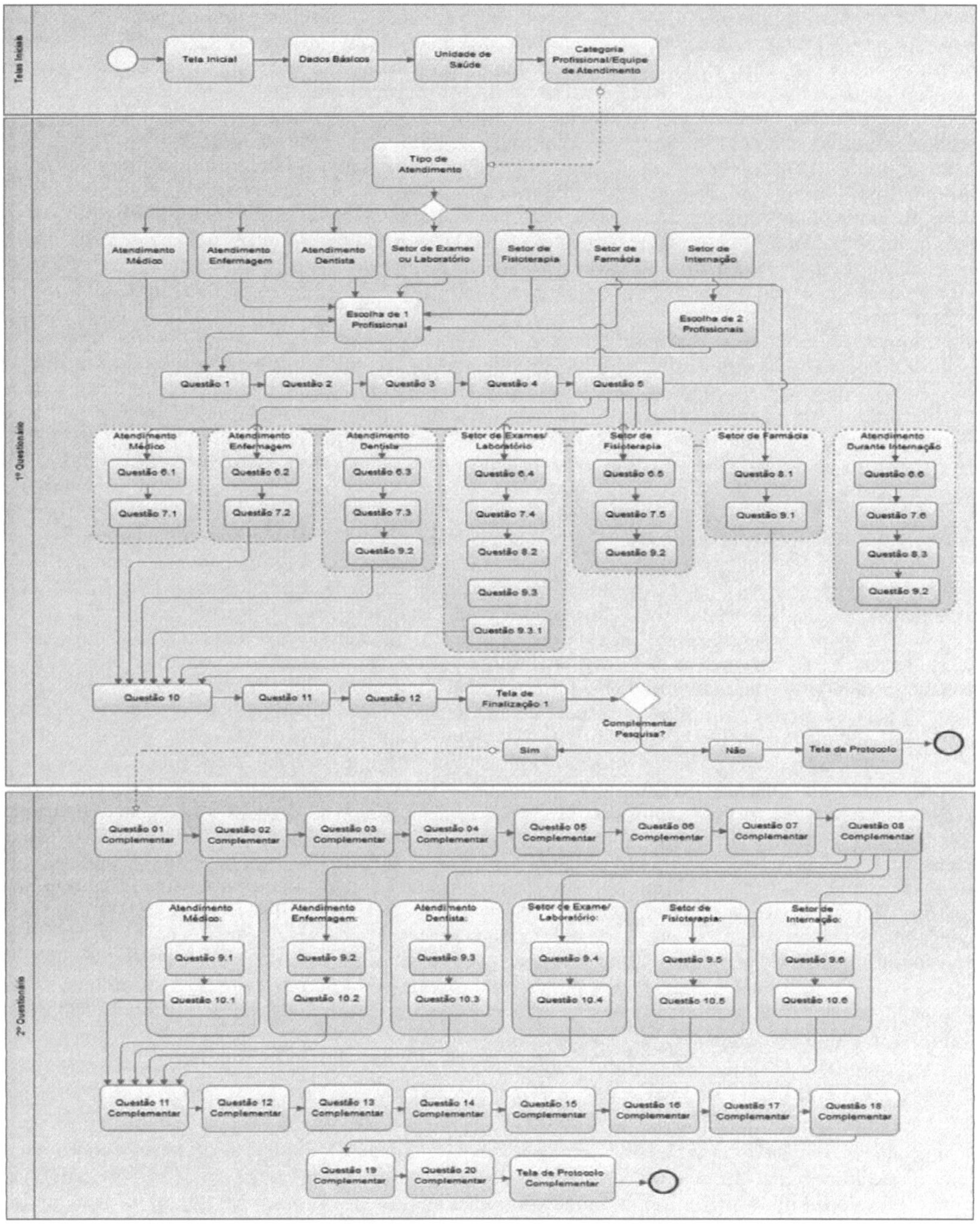

Figure 1. Flowchart for modeling the functionality of QualitySaude screens

Data obtained in first moment were not able to pass accurate information to interested parties, since they are often inconsistent, mainly due to lack of standardization. In order to avoid these inconsistencies, it was necessary standardize collected data so that this information could be crossed and sketched obtained results. QUALITY SAÚDE scale proved to be efficient because significant data were collected and with great potential for analysis. However, it is necessary to maintain a quality standard in information so that there is also quality in information interpretation, providing correct strategies for decision-making. Gross information is not considered useful, data must always be intact, in order to have quality in information.

Then, a virtual platform was developed for online application in multicenter groups of SUS users. According to Vidal (2000), figure 2 (in Portuguese) shows the cognitive process and its interrelationships with the perceptual and motor processes. In cognitive terms, the human being transforms information of a physical nature into information of a symbolic nature and, from this, into actions on interfaces. Its conception is from the field of cognitive sciences, which aims to study virtual knowledge, that is, it focuses on the set of minimum structural and functional conditions that allow to perceive, represent, recover and use information. These "Cognitive Ergonomics" principles were used to build a graphical interface.

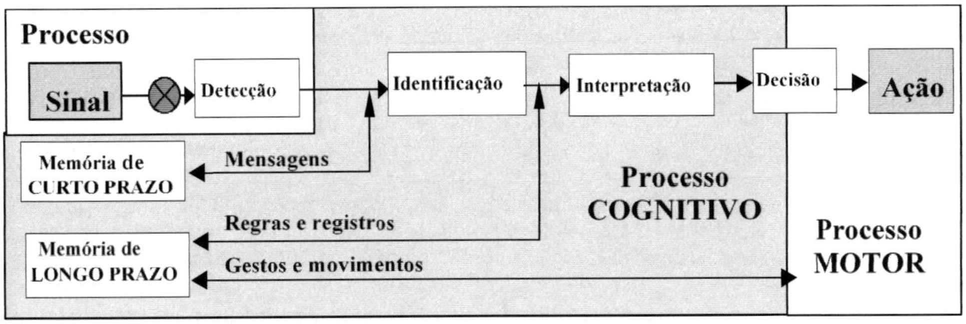

Figure 2. Perceptual, Cognitive and Motor Process

Moita et al. (2018) proposed the use of Business Intelligence (BI) tools and techniques to support the application of the 20 scenario questions. It should be noted that the application of BI techniques can guarantee the generation of quality information and allow a powerful visualization of the fundamental points to improve decision making. Figure 1 shows the Flowchart for modeling the functionality of QualitySaude screens.

Figure 3. Basic data record screen

Figure 3 is the initial screen of user satisfaction questionnaire proposed in this research where the interviewee is allowed to inform his basic data. Such personal identification is not mandatory. Data in screen are written in Portuguese.

Figure 4 presents screen with one of the 14 questions of the web QUALITY SAÚDE platform. In it are presented five figures representing grades attributed to interviewee expectation in relation to service performed, the grade 1 for lowest expectation and 5 grades for highest expectation. The same happens for grades attributed to interviewee satisfaction in relation to performed service. Data in screen are written in Portuguese.

For the treatment of analyzed results two tools (free license versions) were used: 1. PowerDesigner (Sybase, 2017) has support for several activities such as business process modeling, data modeling, multidimensional data modeling, which stores, and controls developed models. PowerDesigner brings impact analysis, design time change management, and metadata management techniques to your user. 2. QlikView (QlikTech, 2017), which covers BI techniques, enables an interactive visualization of information and can be defined as a tool for decision-making. QlikView compresses data and keeps it in its memory, where it is available for use by multiple users. In the case of data sets too large to be stored in memory, this tool connects directly to data source and provides an associative experience for all data used for analysis, regardless of where they are stored.

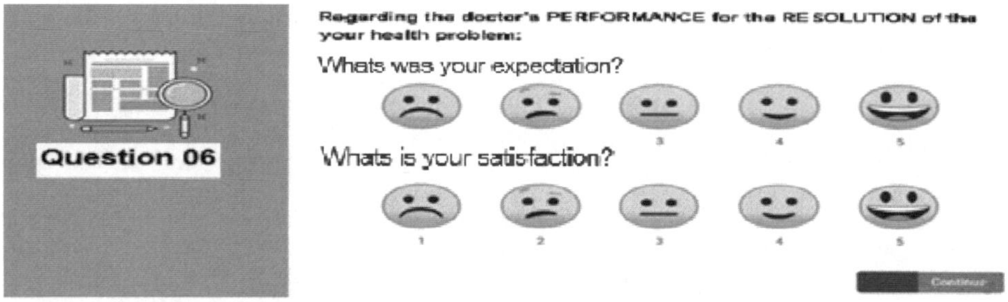

Figure 4. Response screen in relation to interviewee's expectation and satisfaction

Data treatment was performed based on data standardization. For this purpose, an ER model (entity-relationship model) describing interrelated things of interest in this specific domain of knowledge was created aiming at standardizing tables, in order to maintain data consistency. Initial analysis demonstrated need for data abstraction, placing Institution table as the main entity of the model, because it ends up being related to all other entities.

Afterwards, ETL - Extraction, Transformation and Load processes were applied in data, being applied using programming language R, where they were kept in PostgreSQL database. Data extraction is presented in figure 5, transformation of imported data with R is presented in Figure 6 and data load imported with R is shown in Figure 7.

```
notas.14Q.CEOREG <- `NOTAS-14Q-CEOReg`[5:44, ]
names(notas.14Q.CEOREG) <- `NOTAS-14Q-CEOReg`[4, ]
temp <- `NOTAS-14Q-CEOReg`[57:93, ]
names(temp) <- `NOTAS-14Q-CEOReg`[4, ]
notas.14Q.CEOREG <- bind_rows(notas.14Q.CEOREG, temp)
temp <- `NOTAS-14Q-CEOReg`[106:145, ]
names(temp) <- `NOTAS-14Q-CEOReg`[4, ]
notas.14Q.CEOREG <- bind_rows(notas.14Q.CEOREG, temp)
temp <- `NOTAS-14Q-CEOReg`[158:198, ]
names(temp) <- `NOTAS-14Q-CEOReg`[4, ]
notas.14Q.CEOREG <- bind_rows(notas.14Q.CEOREG, temp)
temp <- `NOTAS-14Q-CEOReg`[211:250, ]
names(temp) <- `NOTAS-14Q-CEOReg`[4, ]
notas.14Q.CEOREG <- bind_rows(notas.14Q.CEOREG, temp)
temp <- `NOTAS-14Q-CEOReg`[263:302, ]
names(temp) <- `NOTAS-14Q-CEOReg`[4, ]
notas.14Q.CEOREG <- bind_rows(notas.14Q.CEOREG, temp)
```

Figure 5. Data Extraction using R language

```
TD_INSTITUICAO <- sqldf(
  "select
  CO_CNES||grupo||subgrupo as ID_INSTITUICAO,
  case when `No. CNPJ` = 999 then NU_CNPJ_MANTENEDORA else `No. CNPJ` end as CNPJ,
  NO_RAZAO_SOCIAL, CASE WHEN `RazÃ£o Social InstituiÃ§Ã£o` IS NULL OR
  `RazÃ£o Social InstituiÃ§Ã£o` = 999 THEN  NO_FANTASIA ELSE `RazÃ£o Social InstituiÃ§Ã£o` END
  AS NO_FANTASIA ,
  `SIGLA Instit.`,
  NO_LOGRADOURO || ' ' || ' ' || NU_ENDERECO || ' ' || ' ' || NO_BAIRRO ||' '
  || NO_COMPLEMENTO || ' ' || Cidade || '-' || UF AS ENDERECO,
  `Cod. Mun.`,CO_CEP,
  case when `CNPJ_Gestor Unid. Agrup.` = 999
  or `CNPJ_Gestor Unid. Agrup.` is null then 'Não Informado'
  else `CNPJ_Gestor Unid. Agrup.` end as `CNPJ_Gestor Unid. Agrup.`,
  case when `RazÃ£o Social Gestor Unid. Agrup.` = 999
  or `RazÃ£o Social Gestor Unid. Agrup.` is null then 'Não Informado'
  else `RazÃ£o Social Gestor Unid. Agrup.` end `RazÃ£o Social Gestor Unid. Agrup.`,
  case when `SIGLA Gestor Unid. Agrup.` = 999
  or `SIGLA Gestor Unid. Agrup.` is null then 'Não Informado'
  else `SIGLA Gestor Unid. Agrup.` end
  `SIGLA Gestor Unid. Agrup.`,
  Grupo,SubGrupo,`Tipo_Agrup.`,Fase_PesqS,CO_CNES,`Nivel AtenÃ§Ã£o`,`Nivel Complex.`,
  Etapa_PesqS,`Tipo Instit.`,`Classif. Unid.`,CASE WHEN `Classif. Serv. Atend.` IS NULL THEN 0 ELSE `Classif.
  FROM x
  where CO_CNES is not null"
)
TD_INSTITUICAO <- distinct(TD_INSTITUICAO)
```

Figure 6. Data transformation imported by R

To data visualization, QlikView BI tool was used, the information was crossed, and interactive dashboards were created. According to Gartner (2017), Figures 7 to 10 present some results obtained in this research. In Figure 7, initial dashboard analysis reveals that, when Servqual model was applied in a total of responses obtained in an expert groups, an average of 25 responses per question was obtained in selected phases, and from that average, about 2.30% of answers were scores equal to 1, the mean number of grades 2 was 10.10%, the mean for grades 3 was 19.10%, the mean for grades 4 was 26.88% and the mean score for 5 was 41.70%. Thus, in the stage and phases selected (steps 4, phases 1 and 2), the most received grade was 5, in addition to being able to understand that on average the mean number of grades 1 (lowest grade) is lower than the mean of grade 5 (highest grade).

```
################instituicao##############################
TD_INSTITUICAO[TD_INSTITUICAO$id_class_servico_atendido == 0, "id_class_servico_atendido"] <- -1
TD_INSTITUICAO[TD_INSTITUICAO$id_municipio == '530040', "id_municipio"] <- 530010
TD_INSTITUICAO <- TD_INSTITUICAO[,-19]

dbWriteTable(con, c("dfdwp", "td_instituicao"), value = TD_INSTITUICAO,append = T,row.names = F)
rm(TD_INSTITUICAO)

################TELEFONE##############################

TELEFONE <- select(TD_TELEFONE,id_participante = ID_PARTICIPANTE,
                             nu_telefone = TELEFONE)

dbWriteTable(con, c("dfdwp", "td_telefone"), value = TELEFONE,append = T,row.names = F)
rm(TELEFONE,TD_TELEFONE)
```

Figure 7. Data load imported by R

On the central chart and on the smaller chart, you can see the number of responses received grouped by grade, to give a more detailed view of data being analyzed. Initial dashboard is the starting point for other views, working just like an application, where user can navigate from one screen to another using buttons.

After initial data analysis, where general data are observed without a large level of detail, it is possible to observe more specific data, using filters to reach final objective. Several items can be selected in filters, allowing the manager to view information about all institutions that concern him.

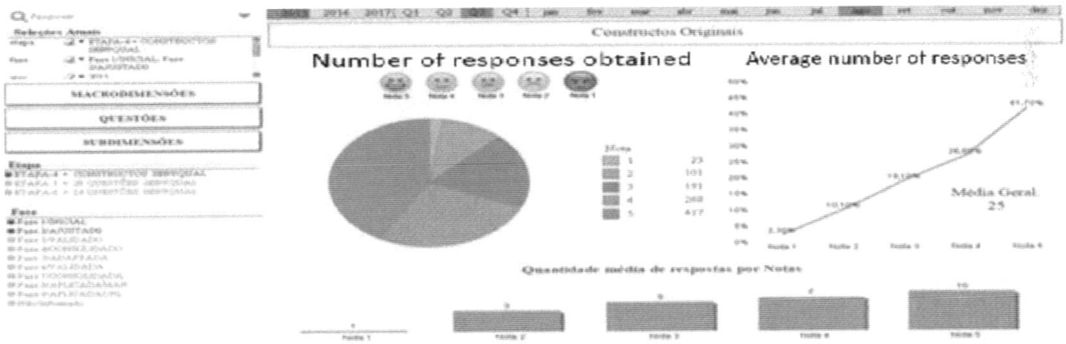

Figure 8. Dashboad QlikView

On the larger bar graph it is possible to compare the average of grade received by institution or set of filtered institutions (General average) in relation to the group that it belongs to, managing entity, microregion and macroregion, grouped by macro dimensions (Tangibility, Reliability, Empathy, Security, Readiness, Access / Accessibility).

The graph at the bottom right is common to all screens because it allows you to see how many responses are being analyzed. The bar chart on the lower left shows the difference between perceived grades and expectations, the red line indicates this difference, and represents a very important analysis within Servqual.

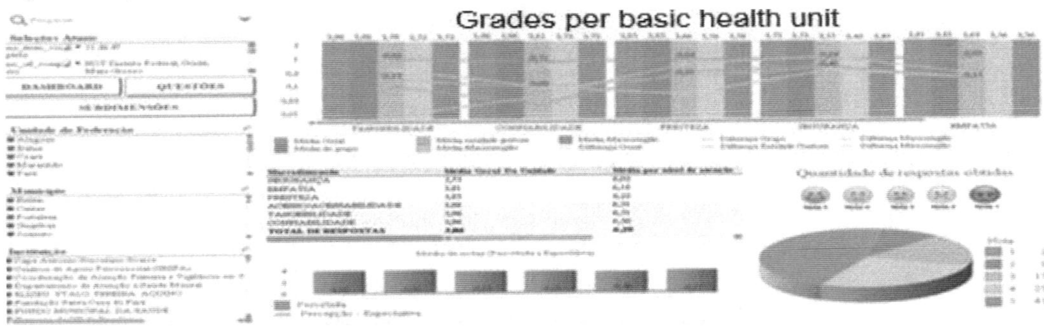

Figure 9. Grade by macro dimension QlikView

Figure 9 shows visualization with a higher level of detail, in this screen averages of grades are grouped by questions / constructs, where it is possible to see, for example, quantity of grades 1 that the institution received, or if a filter is not made by data refer to the number of responses for all units that belong to the step and phase selected in dashboard (Figure 10), this table becomes useful when there are a greater number of answers being the object of analysis, in this work we are only showing a sample of data as you can see in pie chart in the upper right corner of the view.

In the above view, it is possible to observe a further level of detail of grades' mean, and in this case mean notes that were obtained by one or more institutions are grouped by sub-dimensions. The central chart and the table present the mean of grades in each sub-dimension, always comparing the institution with the group, managing entity, microregion and macro-region in which that institution belongs.

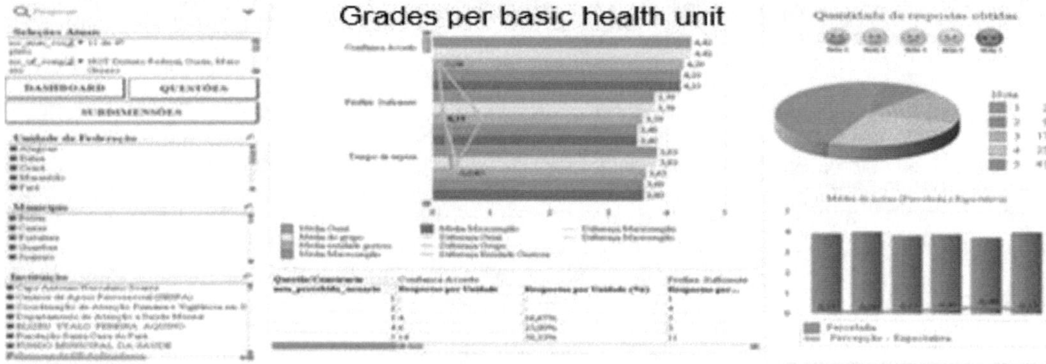

Figure 10. Note by question QlikView

4. CONCLUSION

Based on what was presented in this research, it can be seen that evaluating quality of services provided to public is of utmost importance. Evaluation of services provided in Brazilian public health with using a scientific method is practically non-existent, which makes it difficult to define strategies to improve services.

Applying BI techniques to a data set such as those generated by satisfaction surveys is of the utmost importance to ensure that collected data can generate quality information. Its application (web QUALITY SAÚDE platform) is a focus of this research, in order to allow public managers a powerful visualization of points in which they really need attention, improving strategic decision making and factor management, instrumentalizing governance of quality factors of health units, positively impacting all public health services. From the analysis of these data it is possible, for example, to invest financial resources in areas where the average evaluation was below user's expectation.

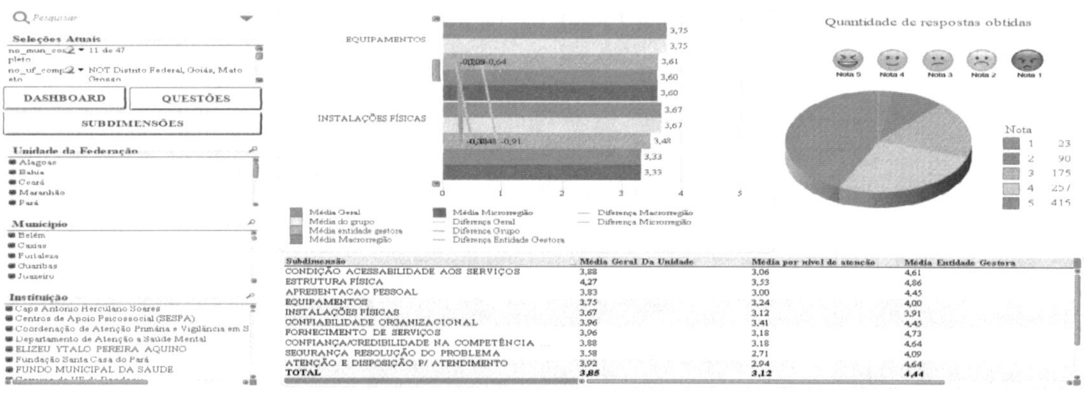

Figure 11. Grades by subdimension QlikView

Solutions presented in this paper demonstrate a small possibility of analysis for data initially collected; however, in addition to looking at the data in a general and grouped way, comparisons between institutions, municipalities, management entities, macro-regions, microregions, among other possibilities may be useful to assist in the decision-making. Among the possibilities of future works on this research is the creation of articles that can further detail the obtained results with the analysis of dashboards presented here, as well as others that may be created. Foremost, we notice a need to create a software to serve as input of data that are objects of analysis of this work, with main characteristic of being able to be implemented in any platform. Adapting Servqual scale with the objective of evaluating services provided in Brazilian public health allows user perception to be viewed in counterpoint to their expectation, presenting results that really approximate reality, besides highlighting which points should be reviewed by public managers, and can add value in the satisfaction surveys offered by Brazilian Ministry of Health for presenting real results and interpretations.

REFERENCES

Aharony, L., & Strasser, S. (1993). Patient satisfaction: what we know about and what we still need to explore. *Medical Care Review, 50(1),* 31.

Babakus, E., & Mangold, G. (1992). Adapting SERVQUAL Scale Hospital Service: Na empirical Investigation. *Health Services Research, 22.*

Barbosa, L., & Neto, A. P. (2017). Ludwik Fleck (1896-1961) e translação do conhecimento: considerações sobre a genealogia de um conceito. *Saúde Debate, 41(Especial),* 13.

Berry, L. L., Parasuraman, A., Zeithaml, V., & Adsit, D. (1994). Improving service quality in America: Lessons learned; Executive commentary. *The Academy of Management Executive, 8*(2), 21.

Borges, J. B. C., Carvalho, S. M. R., & Silva, M. A. M. (2006). Qualidade do serviço prestado aos pacientes de cirurgia cardíaca do Sistema Único de Saúde – SUS. *Revista Brasileira de Cirurgia Cardiovascular, 25(2).*

Brasil. (2014). *Governos Estaduais no Federalismo Brasileiro*. Brasilia: Instituto de Pesquisa Econômica Aplicada

CFM. (2014). Pesquisa revela que 92% da população está insatisfeita com a saúde no Brasil. Retrieved from http://portal.cfm.org.br/index.php?option=com_content&view=article&id=24984:datafolha-revela-93-da-populacao-esta-insatisfeita-com-a-saude-no-brasil&catid=3

CFM. (2015). Para 93% da população, a saúde Brasil é considerada péssima, ruim ou regular. Retrieved from http://portal.cfm.org.br/index.php?option=com_content&view=article&id=25807:2015-10-13-14-55-36&catid=3

CFM. (2018). *Opinião dos brasileiros sobre o atendimento público na área de saúde (2018).* Retrieved from http://portal.cfm.org.br/images/PDF/datafolha_sus_cfm2018.pdf

Clavier, C., Sénéchal, Y., & Potvin, L. (2011). A theory - based model of translation practices in public health participatory research. *Sociology of Health and Illness, 34(5),* 16.

CNI, C. N. d. I.-. (2012). *Retratados da sociedade brasileira: saúde publica (2011).* Retrieved from Brasília: http://admin.cni.org.br/portal/data/files/00/FF80808134CE96AF0134D22242451D75/Retratos%20da%20Sociedade%20Brasileira%20Sa%C3%BAde%20P%C3%BAblica%20Janeiro%202012.pdf

CNI, C. N. d. I.-. (2018). *Retratados da sociedade brasileira: saúde publica (2018).* Retrieved from Brasília: https://bucket-gw-cni-static-cms-si.s3.amazonaws.com/media/filer_public/18/7f/187f1473-2603-4b06-a8a1-070486293e98/retratosdasociedadebrasileira_44_saude.pdf

Cruz, W. B. S., & Melleiro, M. M. (2007). Análise da satisfação dos usuários de um hospital privado. *Revista Escola de Enfermagem da USP.*

Datasus. 2017a. *Health informations notebook (in Portuguese).* Available in: <http://www.datasus.gov.br>. Acessed in 21 oct. 2017.

Datasus. 2017b. *System developed by Datasus serves as model for initiative in Peru Program (in Portuguese).* Available in: <http://datasus.saude.gov.br/noticias/atualizacoes/406-sistema-desenvolvido-pelo-datasus-serve-de-modelo-para-iniciativa-de-programa-no-peru>. Acessed in 15 oct. 2017.

Esperidião, M., & Trad, L. A. B. (2005). Avaliação de satisfação de usuários. *Ciência e saúde coletiva [online], 10,* 10.

Gartner. 2017. *Gartner Recognizes Qlik® as a Leader in BI and Analytics - Magic Quadrant for Business Intelligence and Analytics Platforms.* Available in: < https://community.qlik.com/docs/DOC-18134>. Acessed in: 04 dec. 2017.

Hartz, S., & John, J. (2008). Contribution of economic evaluation to decision making in early phases of product development: A methodological and empirical review *International Journal of Technology Assessment in Health Care, 24*(4), 9. doi:10.1017/S0266462308080616

Hercos, B. V. S., & Berezovsky, A. (2004). *Qualidade do serviço oftalmológico prestado aos pacientes ambulatoriais, do Sistema Único de Saúde – SUS.* Paper presented at the XV Congresso Norte-Nordeste de Oftalmologia, Belo Horizonte, Minas Gerais – Brasil.

Moita, G. F. (2019). *Avaliação Integrativa de Performance Multidimensional e Decisão Multicritério: Um Proxy de Painel de Indicadores de Eficiência, Efetividade e Qualidade para Governação de Organizações Hospitalares e Serviços de Saúde no Brasil [Integrating Evaluation of Multidimensional Performance and Multicriterary Decision: A Panel Proxy of Efficiency, Effectiveness and Quality Indicators for Governance of Hospital Organizations and Health Services in Brazil].* (Doutoramento Doctoral). Universidade de Coimbra, Coimbra.

Moita, G. F., Barbosa, A. C. Q., & Raposo, V. M. R. (2019a). Quality Saúde – uma adaptação transcultural multicêntrica dos constructos da escala Servqual de satisfação para o SUS, por translação de conhecimento de especialistas e usuários *Rev. Serv. Público Brasília, 70(2),* 325-364. Retrieved from https://revista.enap.gov.br/index.php/RSP/article/view/3142/2291

Moita, G. F., Barbosa, A. C. Q., & Raposo, V. M. R. (2019b). Quality Saúde – uma adaptação transcultural multicêntrica dos constructos da escala Servqual de satisfação para o SUS, por translação de conhecimento de especialistas e usuários *Rev. Serv. Público, 70(2),* 325-364. Retrieved from https://revista.enap.gov.br/index.php/RSP/article/view/3142/2291

Oliveira, Douglas T.; Pereira, Otacilio J. Um estudo do Business Intelligence no ambiente empresarial. 2008. Disponível em: <http://www.uvv.br/portais/cienciacomputacao/pdf/2008/UM%20ESTUDO%20DO%20BUSINESS%20INTELLIGENCE%20NO%20AMBIENTE%20EMPRESARIAL.pdf> Acesso em: 29 jun. 2010.

Parasuraman, A., Berry, L. L., & Zeithaml, V. A. (1988). SERVQUAL:A Multiple-Item Scale for Measuring Consumer Perceptions of Service Quality. *Joumal of Retailing, 64*, 29.

Parasuraman, A., Berry, L. L., & Zeithaml, V. A. (1991a). Refinement and Reassessment of the SERVQUAL Scale. *Journal of Retailing, 67*(4).

Parasuraman, A., Berry, L. L., & Zeithaml, V. A. (1991b). Understanding costumer expectation of service. *Sloan Management Review, 31*, 10.

Patrick, D. L., Burke, L. B., Gwaltney, C. J., Leidy, N. K., Martin, M. L., Molsen, E., & Ring, L. (2011). Content Validity—Establishing and Reporting the Evidence in Newly Developed Patient-Reported Outcomes (PRO) Instruments for Medical Product Evaluation: ISPOR PRO Good Research Practices Task Force Report: Part 2—Assessing Respondent Understanding *Value in Health, 14*, 978–988. doi:10.1016/j.jval.2011.06.013

PostgreSQL. 2018. *The PostgreSQL global development group.* Available in: https://www.postgresql.org/ Acessed in 18 jan. 2018.

QlikTech, 2017. *Introdution to QlikView.* Available in <https://www.qlik.com/pt-br/products/qlikview> Acessed in 01 nov. 2017

Reeve, B. B., Wyrwich, K. W., Wu, A. W., Velikova, G., Terwee, C. B., Snyder, C. F., . . . Butt, Z. (2013). ISOQOL recommends minimum standards for patient-reported outcome measures used in patient-centered outcomes and comparative effectiveness research. *Qual Life Res, 22*, 1889–1905. doi:10.1007/s11136-012-0344-y

R Project, 2017. *R language introdution.* Available in: <https://www.r-project.org/> Acessed in 23 oct. 2017.

Rud, O.P. 2009. *Business intelligence success factors: tools for aligning your business in the global economy.* John Wiley & Sons, Inc. New Jersey, USA.

Sybase. *SAP PowerDesigner: Enterprise Architecture tools for digital transformation success.* Available in: <https://www.sap.com/products/powerdesigner-data-modeling-tools.html>. Acessed in 01 nov. 2017.

Vidal, M. C. (2000). *Introdução à Ergonomia* (G.-G. d. E. e. N. Tecnologias Ed.). Rio de Janeiro: CESERG - Curso de Especialização Superior em Ergonomia. COPPE-UFRJ.

Volpato, L. F. (2014). *Utilização de uma ferramenta para análise da qualidade nos serviços públicos de saúde.* (Doctoral). Universidade estadual de campinas, Piracicaba

Wild, D., Grove, A., Martin, M., Eremenco, S., McElroy, S., Verjee-Lorenz, A., & Erikson, P. (2005). *Principles of Good Practice for the Translation and Cultural Adaptation Process for Patient-Reported Outcomes (PRO) Measures: Report of the ISPOR Task Force for Translation and Cultural Adaptation.* Retrieved from https://www.ispor.org/workpaper/research_practices/PROTranslation_Adaptation.pdf

SHORT PAPERS

TOWARDS A CYBERSECURITY CULTURE TOOL THROUGH A HOLISTIC, MULTI-DIMENSIONAL ASSESSMENT FRAMEWORK

Kanaris Bounas, Anna Georgiadou, Michalis Kontoulis, Spiros Mouzakitis and Dimitrios Askounis
National Technical University of Athens
Iroon Politexniou 9, Zografou, Greece

ABSTRACT

Cyber-security culture forms one of the best lines of defence against many cyber-attacks making it an ideal and efficient target to address, in order to better secure organisations. It has its foundations on the information security policies and procedures enforced by its management. It is also dictated and formed by the behaviour, perceptions and attitudes of its employees. These will form the basis of our model which aims to quantify these theoretical constructs in order to analyse them and provide feedback. The close examination of existing security assessment tools and frameworks while identifying the most important security components and sections which need to be addressed and evaluated, resulted in our proposition of a state-of-the-art cyber-security culture tool. The presented approach aims to address existing gaps by adopting a holistic perspective that incorporates both organisational and individual aspects of security culture, including behavioural traits that affect and risk the security level of the company. Our approach and tool will be applied to the EPES sector, where the timely assessment of the security culture is considered essential and of high impact.

KEYWORDS

Cybersecurity Culture, Assessment, Awareness, Security Behaviour

1. INTRODUCTION

Due to the radical technological development of the last decades, cybersecurity has emerged into one of the most demanding and troubling scientific areas absorbing large amount of time, effort, research and funds. Many attempts have been made in the past to define, implement and establish information security frameworks applicable to any kind of organization regardless of structure, size or industry. Although unsuccessful in concluding to a holistic model, they managed to prove the significance of the human element in information security while acknowledging the need for a more sophisticated and generic approach nowadays described under the term "***information security culture***".

Many definitions have been introduced in the past, focusing on various aspects of the information security culture. Although, researchers agree on the levels and the objectives, they tend to differentiate on the domains and components they recognize and try to assess while evaluating the information security culture of an organization.

One of the most important parts of information security is the information security assessment that should be conducted in order to identify possible weaknesses in the organization. This is no different when studying socio-cultural behavior in information security. A complete assessment will provide all the weaknesses that arise in the organization due to either its employees or its policies and procedures that it has established. After identifying them, finding solutions and improving security as a whole becomes much easier and cost efficient.

This paper focuses on finding an appropriate way to conduct an assessment that will provide results that cover every aspect of socio-cultural behaviour in information security. It will also elaborate the most commonly used standards and frameworks on this area while identifying their deficiencies and lacks which, consequently, lead to the need of seeking new methodologies and approaches. A set of concepts and the respective features needed, lead to the design and implementation of a cyber-security culture tool targeting some of the most demanding issues of this field.

2. BACKGROUND

Information security components can be described as the principles that enable the implementation and maintenance of information security while cultivating an appropriate level of information security culture and minimizing risks posed to information assets (Da Veiga & Eloff, 2007). Although their significance is commonly accepted, they have been approached with many ways by the various information security culture frameworks over the last century.

In 1995, BSI Group published BS 7799 as a standard, which consisted of several parts. The first part was revised in 1998 and contained the best practices for information security management. In 2000, it was adopted by ISO as ISO/IEC 17799:2000 "Information technology — Code of practice for information security management". It was then later revised in 2005 as ISO/IEC 17799:2005 and finally incorporated in the ISO 27000 series of standards as ISO/IEC 27002:2007 in July 2007. The later revision of this standard was in 2013.

The second part of BS 7799 was published by BSI in 1999, known as BS 7799 Part 2 and titled "Information Security Management Systems - Specification with guidance for use." BS 7799-2 focused on how to implement an Information security management system (ISMS). In November 2005, this part was adopted by ISO as ISO/IEC 27001:2005 "Information technology — Security techniques — Information security management systems — Requirements". The later revision of this standard was in 2013.

In 2007, the Information Security Governance framework is proposed as a starting point for an organization to govern information security by developing guidelines and implementing controls to address risks identified by the organizations (Da Veiga & Eloff, 2007). It is partitioned into four levels trying to combine the pros of all its predecessors while providing a single point of reference for the governance of information security to inculcate an acceptable level of information security culture.

In 2017, ENISA published the CSC Framework according to which, the concept of Cybersecurity Culture (CSC) refers to the knowledge, beliefs, perceptions, attitudes, assumptions, norms and values of people regarding cybersecurity and how they manifest themselves in people's behaviour with information technologies (ENISA, 2017). Obeying to its principles and guidelines, the Security CLTRe Toolkit breaks CSC into seven dimensions, measured by a staff questionnaire, leading to a graphical representation of the organization's security culture score (Petric & Roer, 2018).

3. METHODOLOGY

3.1 Model Definition

Having glanced into the information security culture background and having identified the most commonly accepted frameworks and tools, we proceeded in conducting a thorough literature review and detailed research on the elements that constitute the critical factors influencing and finally formulating the cyber-security culture.

Much research has been conducted over the years with an apparent trend to move from a technical approach, towards information security, to a socio-cultural approach (Da Veiga, Martins, & Eloff, 2007; ENISA, 2018). In other words, techniques such as technical analyses and testing of information systems, mathematical models or statistical computations of risks and economic analyses of investment justification tend to be substituted by behavioural, organizational and criminological theories (Bernik & Prislan, 2016) as the basis of security assessment. Our tool aims to bridge the apparent gap between these two fundamentally different approaches by combining their methods and enhancing their numerous advantages.

We defined a theoretical model to portray the most important cyber-security domains and sub-domains which need to be evaluated and properly assessed in order to integrate the overall culture at an organizational level. This model aims in depicting the key metrics to be measured along with their dependencies, influences and varieties and focuses on a holistic approach that can be applied to any type of organization. When all those metrics are identified, the model will gather all the results from the assessment conducted and use them to illustrate a uniform representation of the everyday reality of an organization, as well as map the weaknesses identified in the assessment with several known cybersecurity threats. Recommendations for improvement will also be a function that the tool will provide.

Initially, the tool will need to conduct the assessment in order for its other functions to be able to provide accurate outputs. An assessment cannot be conducted before first identifying all the necessary measurements that need to be taken into account. For this purpose, two different kind of measurements will be used. One category will assess the organization's policies and procedures, and the other will assess employees' behavior in relevance with information security. There will be several methods with which the assessments will be conducted, like questionnaires and tests, audits, etc. The assessments will be conducted in various waves, called assessment campaigns, and these will be repeated after a certain period of time.

In the next step, the assessment will provide a score to all the entities in the organization, ranging from each employee separately, to each department and finally the organization as a whole. Each entity will be scored in every relevant domain and sub-domain that describes the organization's information security culture. Various variables will be used to give a more accurate scoring, which will be customizable for each different organization. The results of the assessments will be available to only authorized users and will be protected from unauthorized access.

After the assessment's conclusion, the tool will identify all the known cybersecurity threats that are relevant to the organization. Then, it will map all the weaknesses detected in the assessment with the cybersecurity threats and evaluate which of them have high risk potential.

Finally, it will provide some guidelines, both on personal as well as on organizational level, which, if followed, will improve the organization's information security culture. For this purpose, the tool will create a personal profile for each employee, in which all the areas of information security that need to be improved will be highlighted, and possible actions for this improvement will be provided.

3.2 Metric Quantification & Tool Development

Culture is constituted by collective values, norms, knowledge and behaviour which, as theoretical constructs and mistily notions, are characteristically hard to measure. Consequently, most of the scientific research focuses on its indirect measurement via its artefacts: management, work processes, procedures, policies, etc. (Schlienger & Teufel, 2003). Thus, our challenge is the way of quantifying and measuring all the indicators defined by the previous steps while exploiting other sciences apart from information engineering.

The multidimensional model defined in our study demands an equally multidimensional implementation approach. Therefore, different evaluation and delivery methods, varying from the conventional ones, such as documentation analysis, physical and participative observation, narrative interviews, typical questionnaires (Schein, 1985; Despres, 1995), to the most radical, such as instructor-led, online, game, video and simulation based, shall be used (Abawajy, 2014).

First-level results gathered by these techniques need to be elaborated and finally transformed to value-added knowledge for both individuals and organizations leading to security cultural evolution. Data processing algorithms and advanced analytics shall be the foundations of our cyber-security culture tool. Even among business that are intrinsically interlinked with information systems not all members of the organisations have the same knowledge set and even when dealing with sector experts novel cyber visualisations have been observed to be either too complex or too basic for the intended users (Diane Staheli, 2014). As such it is necessary to ensure that our results are presented with the appropriate complexity and tools corresponding to the knowledge level of each user, from the personal to the organisational level, to achieve the maximum impact.

4. APPLICATION

Having finalized our tool, we shall proceed in applying our research and processes to different organizational types gathering information and calibrating our algorithms based on outputs, findings and user feedback. We will begin with implementing our tool in organizations belonging to the EPES sector, but our ultimate goal is to standardize our techniques and conclude to a cyber-security framework capable of assisting and boosting any type of business while becoming a valuable asset. The tool will be deployed into the servers of each organization, converting it into an internal tool of each organization.

5. CONSTRAINTS AND ISSUES

While improving the cyber-security culture is a task of paramount importance there may be some hurdles that can impede our efforts which must be taken under consideration especially when applying the framework in a real-life environment.

Special attention, procedures and mechanisms need to be applied for the protection of personal data according to both the European Regulations (GDPR) as well as local government laws that apply to the organization using the toolset.

Lastly the main goal of the tool is to assess in a holistic manner the security culture of the organization. In-depth and hands-on technical security testing and vulnerability scanning are outside the scope of the tool and are expected to be used complimentary to our proposed tool.

6. FUTURE WORK

At a later stage, this model shall be enriched, tuned and tailored to the EPES (Electrical Power Energy Systems) value chain (generator, TSO, DSO, consumer) as part of a toolkit combining the latest technologies for vulnerability assessment (automated threat-modelling and security behaviour analysis), monitoring and protection (anomaly detection and DDoS mitigation) and learning and sharing (security information and event management) (Energy Shield, 2019). The toolkit will be validated in large-scale demonstrations by end-users while providing a unique level of security culture visibility.

7. CONCLUSION

In order to achieve an adequate information security level, you need to recognize the importance of the human factor in the security chain (Williams, 2009). Procedures and practices should focus on promoting a cyber-security culture which adapts and evolves as a living mechanism to the continuous demanding technological environment of this century (Wilson & Hash, 2003). Therefore, a promising cyber-security culture tool needs to closely examine and monitor all the domains which formulate, directly or indirectly, the organizational reality while cultivating the employee engagement on a daily basis. Personalized recommendations, training programs, vulnerability identification and proactive initiatives are the ultimate goal of our multidimensional tool. To enhance its validity, after implementation completion, it shall need to be tested and proved against different business types and organizations while identifying possible deficiencies and proceeding in needed adjustments to satisfy all the originally set targets. Additional findings and results are expected during the pilot application of the tool operation.

ACKNOWLEDGEMENT

The cyber-security culture tool described in the previous paragraphs is being developed as part of the H2020 project, "Integrated Cybersecurity Solution for the Vulnerability Assessment, Monitoring and Protection of Critical Energy Infrastructures" (Energy Shield, 2019).

REFERENCES

Abawajy, J. (2014). User preference of cyber security awareness delivery methods. *Behaviour & Information Technology, 33*(3), 237-248. doi:10.1080/0144929X.2012.708787

Bernik, I., & Prislan, K. (2016). Measuring Information Security Performance with 10 by 10 Model for Holistic State Evaluation. (H. Song, Ed.) doi:10.1371/journal.pone.0163050

Business and Advisory Committee to the OECD. (2004). *Securing your business. An companion for small or entrepreneurial companies to the 2002 OECD Guidelines for the security of networks and information systems: Towards a culture of security.* Paris: International Chamber of Commerce.

(n.d.). *Cybersecurity Checklist Series.* JMARK Business Solutions.

Da Veiga, A., & Eloff, J. H. (2007). An Information Security Governance Framework. *Information Systems Management, 24*(4), 361-372. doi:10.1080/10580530701586136

Da Veiga, A., Martins, N., & Eloff, J. H. (2007). Information security culture–validation of an assessment instrument. *11*(1).

Despres, C.-N. (1995). Culture, Surveys, Culture Surveys and Other Obfuscations: A reply to Migliore and Martin. *The Journal of Strategic Change, 4*(2), 65-75.

Diane Staheli, T. Y. (2014). Visualization evaluation for cyber security: trends and future directions. *VizSec '14*, 49-56.

Eloff, J. H., & Eloff, M. (2005). Information Security Architecture. *Computer Fraud & Security*, 10-16. doi:10.1016/S1361-3723(05)70275-X

Energy Shield. (2019, 10 24). Retrieved from Energy Shield: https://energy-shield.eu/

ENISA. (2017). *Cyber Security Culture in Organisations.* European Union Agency For Network and Information Security. doi:10.2824/10543

ENISA. (2018). *Cybersecurity Culture Guidelines: Behavioural Aspects of Cybersecurity.* European Union Agency for Network and Information Security. doi:10.2824/324042

ISO/IEC 17799. (2005). *Information technology - Security techniques - Code of practice for information security management.* International Organization for Standardization.

ISO/IEC 27002. (2013). *Information technology - Security techniques - Code of practice for information security controls.* International Organization for Standardization.

Petric, G., & Roer, K. (2018). *To measure security culture: A scientific approach.* CLTRe North America, Inc.

Schein, E. H. (1985). *Organizational Culture and Lead-ership: A Dynamic View* (1st ed.). San Francisco: Jossey-Bass.

Schlienger, T., & Teufel, S. (2003). Analyzing Information Security Culture: Increasing Trust by an Appropriate Information Security Culture. *14th International Conference on Database and Expert Systems Applications (DEXA 2003).* Prague: IEEE Computer Society.

Shetty N., S. G. (210). Competitive Cyber-Insurance and Internet Security. *Economics of Information Security and Privacy*, 229-247.

Williams, P. A. (2009). What Does Security Culture Look Like For Small Organizations? *7th Australian Information Security Management Conference.* Perth: Edith Cowan University . doi:10.4225/75/57b4029530dea

Wilson, M., & Hash, J. (2003). *Building an Information Technology Security Awareness and Training Program.* U.S. Department of Commerce. Washington: National Institute of Standards and Technology. Retrieved 10 10, 2019, from http://citadel-information.com/wp-content/uploads/2012/08/nist-sp800-50-building-information-security-awareness-program-2003.pdf

Zerlang, J. (2017). GDPR: a milestone in convergence for cyber-security and compliance. *Network Security, Volume 2017, Issue 6*, 8-11.

UNDERSTANDING BLOGGERS AND THEIR IMPACT FROM THE ASPECT OF SOCIAL ATTRACTIVENESS

Zehra Serman and Julian Sims
Birkbeck, University of London
Malet Street
London WC1E 7HX, United Kingdom

ABSTRACT

This paper focuses on the impact of bloggers from the aspect of social attractiveness. It begins by giving an overview about bloggers and how widespread and powerful they have become since the advent of Web2.0. Next, it defines social attractiveness and its relation to bloggers. The paper highlights two important theories, Social Attention Holding Power (SAHP) and Status Derived Fighting Ability (RHS), to understand and analyse the ways consumers are influenced. The paper will define these theories and underline the features from the blogging perspective. Hence, it will define some strategies to gain success, discuss what was applied in psychology over the decades and will explain those strategies from blogging concept. It will give an overview of the looking glass effect and social comparison. Finally, the paper concludes by identifying a literature gap and need for further studies in this area.

KEYWORDS

Bloggers, Social Attractiveness, Social Attention Holding Power (SAHP), Status Derived Fighting Ability (RHP), Looking Glass Effect

1. INTRODUCTION

Bloggers have become a prevalent force in society today due to the emergence and growth of various social media platforms (Suh 2017). The influence of bloggers is increasing. This influence can be explained in various ways. Two step flow theory states that opinion leaders (bloggers) interpret media information they receive and pass it on to others (consumers). This flow mediates and increases the influence. This influence can be analysed by understanding the concept of 'social attractiveness'.

This paper evaluates blogging as digital marketing and bloggers as influencers that influence consumers' decision-making process. It highlights how bloggers are becoming widespread. Next, it gains insight into the question of how consumers are influenced and to understand the influence from the factor of social attractiveness through Social Attention Holding Power (SAHP) and Status Derived Fighting Ability (RHP) strategies (Figure 1).

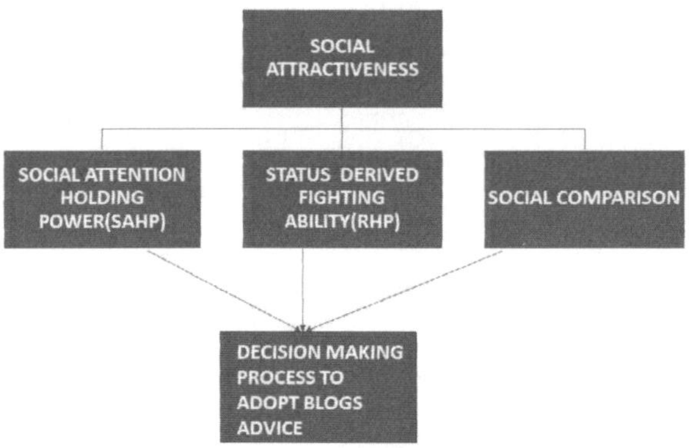

Figure 1. Conceptual Framework

2. BLOGGERS AND ITS IMPORTANCE

The revolution of web based social platforms and rise in Web2.0 technology has led to blogging. Blogs consist of shared experiences, brief texts and posts and writers' recommendations. Writers who share their experiences and recommendations are bloggers. Some studies identify bloggers as opinion leaders because they are present in many sectors: fashion, health, beauty, tourism, food etc (Sokolova 2019). Studies indicate that 900,000 articles are published on blogs every day (Singer 2009); 55 % of people review blogs more than ten times per day (Alsaleh 2017); 81% of consumers read recommendations before purchasing a product (Wegert 2010): this high number was found in 2010, no doubt it has increased. Many readers and reviewers explains the power of bloggers and their influence on consumers. Bloggers who have a reputation are considered most credible and trustworthy. The reasons for this influence and ways of gaining status can be explained by understanding a factor 'social attractiveness', a concept borrowed from psychology.

3. THE EVOLUTION OF SOCIAL ATTRACTIVENESS

The capability of influencing others becomes very important as the number of bloggers and blog readers' dedication increases. Gilbert recognized social attractiveness as the most salient strategy to gain status and maintain success (Gilbert 1989) and argues that humans have innate need to be seen as attractive to others (Gilbert 1970). These needs moderate evaluations of social acceptance, social status and social bonds (Gilbert 1993). The loss of these needs' causes humiliation and shame. Social Attractiveness can be argued as the degree to which a person has ability to influence other people's state of mind and be socially accepted and approved by society. Positive social relationships are crucial for maintaining self and others happiness, therefore, social influence can be gained through cooperation and conformity (Leary 1995). Maintaining social bonds and conformity is not easy, especially when there are millions of bloggers in online platforms. Gilbert highlights the importance of social attractiveness and distinguishes the attracting display from threat of RHP, Gilbert (1989) called it "Social Attention Holding Power". Barkow suggests that status/prestige via attractiveness is an alternative form of status acquisition (Barkow 1980 and Kemper 1990).

4. THE LOOKING GLASS EFFECT

The increase in bloggers and their recommendations becomes very influential as blog readers are influenced in their choices and see them as role models. Gilbert states that many people with a balanced mind scarcely care about what others think of them, including who they are and what they do. In other words, we are image makers (Leary 1989). Pascal highlights that people are not limited with their lives only, but they desire to have an imaginary life in another state of mind, that's why people make an effort to prove themselves (Scheff 1988). Bloggers can be seen as part of this example. Their aim is to influence people and they desire to have an imaginary life in others. Hence, they try to build up reputation and recognition amongst blog readers. Habermas explains this situation as "self is a result of the social process whereby we learn to see ourselves as others see us" (Habermas 1987).

Moreover, Cooley defines the well-developed idea in sociology called looking glass effect, it is one way of understanding the influence of bloggers (Cooley 1902). Cooley argues that people are the result of imagination perceived in another's mind such as appearance, deeds, characters, friends. This imagined judgement forms an emotion Cooley introduces as "self-feeling". These in return influences actions. They are all diversely affected by it. This idea is familiar with the relationship between bloggers and blog readers. Bloggers are influencing consumers' decisions and those decisions cause a domino effect in other factors too. The ability to imagine one's appearance in a mirror can be understand by looking at blogger and blog readers' relationship. The self-reflection of what blog readers' and other bloggers will think about a specific blogger can be seen as a mirror effect. Blog readers have specific expectations or imagined appearances that they want to find or see in bloggers. This could be the way they interact with them or the way they dress or behave. The way they represent themselves. Therefore, Blog readers expectations and their imagined products or services determinates the mirror effect between blog readers' and bloggers. The mirror effect can also be seen between bloggers as they are competitors. Knowing that they are competitors, makes them imagine what others think or expect of themselves or how others judge themselves (Figure 2). This could potentially encourage them to do better or would cause worry, envy and depression leaving them scared of not being able to match the requirements of others' state of mind.

5. SOCIAL ATTENTION HOLDING POWER AND BLOGGERS

Gilbert suggests and that humans are more attracted to people when they feel they are valued by them. That person can be our friend, spouse, colleagues or the most influential blogger, its essential to pass on the positive attention and care in order to influence blog readers. Credibility forms the feeling of cared and valued. Hence Kemper suggests that, to be valued, chosen, admired and accepted, provides high status in others' minds (Kemper 1990). A credible person can be defined as qualified, experienced, trusted and have excellent communication skills. Esteban finds bloggers are more likely to gain status when they are credible and show positive attention communicating with blog readers. Gilbert identified strategies for gaining rank and success called "Social Attention Holding Power" (SHAP). This theory is composed of ability to elicit positive attention and social rewards such as approval, praise, acceptance, showing talent, respect, desire and admiration (Gilbert 1989). Showing talent and inspiring blog readers become challenging as the number of bloggers increases. However, it forms the essential basis of SAHP. Having talent with experience is very important. Blog readers take it seriously when bloggers are talented and experienced or have tried their recommended products. It also shows how much they value their readers. Bloggers who recommend make up products and are also talented in using those products, are considered more attractive than others. SAHP includes affiliative behaviours. An affiliative leader is the type of leader who develops harmony among people upon who they have influence. An affiliative leader tends to be connected to their followers and makes sure they can solve problems if questions or conflict occurs. People more likely to build up trust when there is an affiliation, positive attention from others, and instant communication and appreciation. Alsaleh (2017) studies the crucial importance of trust on consumers finding that trust positively influences blog readers intentions. Trust is vital and consumer behavior will only be influenced by bloggers when there is trust (Hsu et al., 2013).

Gilbert states that a lack of success in encouraging SAHP may result in negative outcomes. One of them is shame. Loss or damage of SAHP may lead to intense anger and fight. SAHP is a strategy to be accepted and gain socially approved from society. It forms social attractiveness. It explains one way of influencing others and how that influence occurs: showing talent, appreciation, positive attention is a way to influence other people's state of mind (Figure 3). Therefore, we can conclude that blog readers are influenced by bloggers who are socially attractive.

6. STATUS DERIVED FIGTING ABILITY (RHP)

Another way of influencing others is through showing fighting ability by undermining other people. This has been used for a very long time to demonstrate power and gain status over others. Many leaders and politicians had adopted this strategy to show overconfidence by fighting ability to influence others to become socially accepted.

Status derived fighting ability (RHP) is opposite to SAHP (Social Attention Holding Power). Signals of RHP are composed of threat, fighting ability, undermining others, showing authority over others. Baumeister (1989) suggests it is unattractive to be seen as weak and overly passive, which might not be an efficient way to influence others. Figure 4 below illustrates strategies for gaining rank and status adapted from Gilbert (1992)

RHP is the strategy whereby individuals evaluate themselves as superior to others (Price 1988). High self-esteem is one way of influencing others: people are more likely to be influenced by bloggers who have high self-esteem. This give them the impression that those bloggers are the experts in their domain. Believing their work and recommendations eventually builds up trust between them. Hence, it positively affects blog readers' intentions to purchase recommended products. Hutton and Baumeister points out that high self-esteem people grab attention by their abilities and talents where low esteem people are shame avoidant.

7. SOCIAL COMPARISON AND ITS IMPACT ON GAINING STATUS

Social comparison is an efficient strategy to maintain or increase status (Gilbert 1992). Gilbert points out that comparing oneself with others enables one to estimate what other people will find attractive in others. This motivates us to perform specific tasks better to obtain favourable attention (Wolfe, Lennox and Cutler 1986). People invite an audience to compare with one or more others in different contexts such as giving musical performance or taking a job interview. In many domains of life, we are faced with situations where social comparisons take place (Gilbert 1992). As this occurs in all domains of life, this scenario must apply in the blogging context as well. The number of bloggers and posts are increasing every day and total numbers of blogs reached 440 million in 2019 (World Press 2019). Social comparison takes place between bloggers and between consumers to bloggers. There are bloggers who perform SAHP and are trying to influence consumers by giving positive attention and there are bloggers who show overconfidence and over self-esteem performing RHP. This paper suggests that the division of strategies becomes a mediating factor of social comparison. Bloggers who compare themselves with other successful bloggers tend to perform better and meet their followers' expectations. Those bloggers who make the comparison and are positively open to change are more likely adopting SAHP. However, there are also bloggers who are using RHP when influencing their blog readers. They are less likely to be involved in any comparison. Thus, they see themselves as best of all. Comparison would cause their self-esteem to break down. Hence, this becomes a mediator between two strategies to gain success and maintain it. Social comparison might occur in two ways. Bloggers to other bloggers might compare each other with their posts, the companies with which they work, the number of followers they have, numbers of comments or dislikes they get. This might encourage them to work harder or might cause jealousy and envy. It can be argued that, another type of social comparison takes place between consumers to bloggers. Blog readers' make comparison between bloggers. Blog readers care about bloggers attitude towards them. Bloggers who frequently post and communicate with them are considered valuable for blog readers. Bloggers who have talent and experience are more likely to persuade blog readers to adopt their recommendations. All these factors form social comparison between blog readers to bloggers. In case of a loss of prestige in any of these factors, it might cause bloggers to lose their followers and be faced with dislikes and unpleasant comments. It is challenging to turn other people's success into one's own opportunity by comparison. However, if that is achieved it could lead to success and social rank.

8. LITERATURE GAP

There have been various studies about bloggers: analysing types of bloggers or understanding how they became a prevalent force in marketing and consumer behaviour. However, very few studies analyse the reasons behind the influence on consumers. This study seeks to understand how status and social rank is gained over a community. Furthermore, existing literature does not shed light onto one of the most important factors: "culture". Culture is very important when analysing consumer attitudes and expectation. Thus, the influence of bloggers on consumers should be studied from a perspective of culture in further studies.

9. CONCLUSION

As bloggers have become popular in marketing products and services, it has created a huge influence over the attitudes and intentions of blog readers (consumers). How they gain success and social rank is discussed in this paper. To understand consumers, psychological theories and strategies have been applied in a blogging context. There are two principal ways to influence others: by passing positive attention to others; and by showing overconfidence and power. Both strategies appear to be practised, but it can be argued that SAHP with social comparison will increase success: it is essential to show confidence without undermining others.

REFERENCES

Alsaleh, D (2017). Understanding the Role of Blogger Recommendations on Consumer Purchasing Behavior. The Journal of Business Inquiry 2017, 17, Issue 1 (Special Issue), 23-40.

Barrett, M., Oborn, E. and Orlikowski, W., 2016. Creating value in online communities: The sociomaterial configuring of strategy, platform, and stakeholder engagement. Information Systems Research, 27(4), pp.704-723.

Baumeister, R. F., Debra G. Hutton (1989, September). Self- Presentational Motivations and Personality Differences in Self-Esteeem. Journal of Personality, 57, pp.547-579.

Cooley, C.H. 1902. Human Nature and the Social Order (Revised edition). New York: Charles Scribner's Sons (1922).

Ebru Uzunoglu, S. M. (2014). Brand communication through digital influencers: Leveraging blogger engagement. Izmir: International Journal of Information Management 34.

Fishbein, M., & Ajzen, I. Belief, attitude, intention and behavior: An introduction to theory and research. Reading, Mass.: Addison-Wesley, 1975.

Gilbert, P. (1997). The evolution of social attractiveness and its role in shame, humiliation,guilt and theraphy. British Journal of Medical Pyschology, 113-147.

Gilbert, P.,Price, J and Allan, S.(1995) Social Comparison, Social Attractiveness and Evolution: How Might They Be Related? New Ideas in Psychology, 13, 149-165.

Habermas, J. (1987) The Theory of Communicative Action, Vol.2, Polity Press, Cambridge.

Hernández-Méndez, J., Muñoz-Leiva, F. and Sánchez-Fernández, J., 2015. The influence of e-word-of-mouth on travel decision-making: consumer profiles. Current issues in tourism, 18(11), pp. 1001-1021.

Ho, C.H., Chiu, K.H., Chen, H. and Papazafeiropoulou, A., 2015. Can internet blogs be used as an effective advertising tool? The role of product blog type and brand awareness. Journal of Enterprise Information Management, 28(3), pp. 346-362.

Hsu, C.L., Chuan-Chuan Lin, J. and Chiang, H.S., 2013. The effects of blogger recommendations on customers' online shopping intentions. Internet Research, 23(1), pp.69-88.

Hwang, Y. and Jeong, S.H., 2016. "This is a sponsored blog post, but all opinions are my own": The effects of sponsorship disclosure on responses to sponsored blog posts. Computers in Human Behavior, 62, pp.528-535.

J.H.Barkow. (1982). A self-presentational view of social phenomena. Psychological Bulletin, 91, 3-312.

Lim, X.J., Cheah, J.H. and Wong, M.W., 2017. The Impact of Social Media Influencers on Purchase Intention and the Mediation Effect of Customer Attitude. Asian Journal of Business Research, 7(2), p. 19.

Lu, L.C., Chang, W.P. and Chang, H.H., 2014. Consumer attitudes toward blogger's sponsored recommendations and purchase intention: The effect of sponsorship type, product type, and brand awareness. Computers in Human Behavior, 34, pp.258-266.

(O'Brien, 5th Edition 2011) Baltes, L.P., 2015. Content marketing-the fundamental tool of digital marketing. Bulletin of the Transilvania University of Brasov. Economic Sciences. Series V, 8(2), p. 111.

Paul Gilbert, J. P. (July 1995). Social Comparison, social attractiveness and evolution: How might they be related? New Ideas in Pyschology, Volume 13, Issue 2, Pages 149-165.

Patrutiu-Baltes, L., 2016. Inbound Marketing-the most important digital marketing strategy. Bulletin of the Transilvania University of Brasov. Economic Sciences. Series V, 9(2), p.61.

Ryan, D., 2016. Understanding digital marketing: marketing strategies for engaging the digital generation. Kogan Page Publishers.

Schafer, J. B. (2001). E- commerce Reccomandation Applications. Data Mining and Knowledge Discovery, 5 115-153.

Scheff, T.J. (1988). Shame and Conformity: The Deference- emotion system. American Sociciological Review, 53(3), 395406

Shrauger, J. S., & Schoeneman, T. J. (1979). Symbolic interactionist view of self-concept: Through the looking glass darkly. Psychological Bulletin, 86(3), 549-573.

Sokolova, K and Kefi, H (2019) Instagram and YouTube bloggers promote it, why should I buy? How credibility and parasocial interaction influence purchase intentions, Journal of Retailing and Consumer Services.

Suh, A. 2017. Self-Branding on Social Media: An Analysis of Style Bloggers on Instagram. Procedia Computer Science, 124, pp12-20

Wegert, T. (2010), Reach your customers while social media peaks. Retrieved January 31, 2014 from www.clickz.com/clickz/column/1699974/reach-your-customers-while-social- media-peaks

Wolfe, Raymond N.,Lennox, Richard D.,Cutler, Brian L.Journal of Personality and Social Psychology, Vol 50(2), Feb 1986.

THE DIGITAL MEDIATION OF MIGRATION: A QUALITATIVE THEMATIC SYNTHESIS

David Pannocchia, Petra Saskia Bayerl and Karen Latricia Hough
CENTRIC, Sheffield Hallam University , 20 Furnival St., Sheffield, UK, S1 2NU

ABSTRACT

The highly complex economic, political, social and cultural processes of migration are increasingly digitally mediated. A rich area of research examining this phenomenon is emerging at the confluence of information and communication technology (ICT) and social sciences. However, little has been done to systematically review this literature. Through a qualitative thematic synthesis (QTS), this paper presents a fusion of recent research to identify: 1) what technologies are being used by migrants to the EU and how and 2) what are the impacts of technology on migrants and migration processes. By bridging the findings of multidisciplinary works, this QTS demonstrates how digital media and technology affect migrant experiences in both positive and negative ways as well as evidence of their impact on migratory trends. It highlights key gaps in the literature and suggests further areas for intervention, identifying the need for a cross-disciplinary research agenda that addresses causal relationships between effects of technology and migration processes.

KEYWORDS

Migration, Social Media, ICT, Literature Review, Qualitative Synthesis

1. INTRODUCTION

Just as digital media and technologies permeate the fabric of daily life, so too have they become an integral part of the migrants' journeys. This reality has received considerable attention in academia and public discourse, particularly within the context of the influx of migratory movements into the EU since 2014. In this debate, migrant uses of technology are often portraited from opposite or at least ambiguous positions – as solutions on the one side (Panagakos & Horst, 2006) or as channel for a 'politics of dehumanisation' on the other (Awad & Tossell, 2019). Studies investigating the phenomenon of 'connected migrants' (Leurs & Pozanesi, 2018) and 'e-diasporas' (Diminescu, 2012) are broad and varied, traversing disciplines from information and communication technology (ICT) studies to sociology and from large-n quantitative studies to in-depth ethnographic work.

The aim of this paper is to synthesise recent research on how digital media and technologies are used by migrants and their impact on migration processes in order to foreground gaps in our understanding of the role of digital mediation in migrant experiences and decision-making. The findings are a subset of data collected for a systematic literature review (SLR) examining narratives of migration to Europe as part of the EU H2020 project PERCEPTIONS. Through a qualitative thematic synthesis (QTS), this paper presents an amalgamation of recent research and highlights the need for a cross-disciplinary research agenda to examine this highly salient phenomenon.

2. METHODOLOGY

Our study is based on a qualitative thematic synthesis (QTS). QTS aims to achieve transparency and rigor in literature reviews by adopting systematic procedures in collecting, selecting and analysing literature while utilising qualitative methods to cross-examine shared or diverging themes (Bearman & Dawson, 2013). This entails that QTS is well situated to examine heterogeneous samples that use diverse methods and hypotheses (Barnett-Page & Thomas, 2009). As such, it is an appropriate method to systematically survey research in multi-disciplinary areas such as migration studies that traverse fields from sociology, political sciences and criminology to psychology and health, amongst others.

The sample for this QTS was drawn from a larger dataset developed as part of PERCEPTIONS. Systematic collection and selection procedures were implemented in five phases. Identification of sources found 856 articles through systematic searches using Boolean search strings containing combinations of keywords such as 'Migration', 'ICT' and 'Social Media'. 225 sources were excluded at this stage due to geographical location, date of publication, language and missing data. During the screening phase, titles and abstracts of the remaining 631 documents were assessed for eligibility leading to 374 exclusions due to duplications, topical irrelevance and lack of access. Further eligibility was determined through a full text review of the remaining 257 sources leading to 36 further exclusions based on their topical relevance and quality. Within this dataset of 221 sources published since 2014 and focused on current migration movements to the EU, 41 sources were identified as relevant for this QTS and were thematically coded using NVivo. The sample was analysed in order to answer the following research questions: What digital media and technologies are used by migrants to the EU and for what purposes? And what are the impacts of these technologies on migrants and migration processes?

3. KEY FINDINGS

There was significant evidence across the sampled literature that digital technologies have become a vital and intrinsic element to migration journeys from departure and transit to settlement in destination countries. Within the dataset, sources explicitly referenced smart and mobile phones (n=28), computers and tablets (n=6), GPS (n=5), digital infrastructures (n=4) as well as e-currency and blockchains (n=1) as being key digital technologies used by migrants. The primary digital media platforms discussed were Facebook and Messenger (n=31), Twitter (n=14), WhatsApp (n=13), Skype (n=10), Instagram (n=4), Google apps like YouTube (n=3), Viber (n=3) and dating apps such as Tinder and Grindr (n=2). The following sections explore the major themes that emerged from the sample of how these technologies are used and their effects on migrants and migratory trends.

3.1 Migrant uses of Digital Media and Technologies

Reported migrant uses of digital media and technology reflect those of the broader population, yet often within the context of migration aspirations and necessities. A key overarching theme was that ICT enables migrants to the EU to gain information about their destinations and provided channels of communication between countries of origin and destination (Bakewell & Jolivet, 2015; Dekker et al., 2016; Dhoest, 2019; Milivojevic, 2018; Fiedler, 2019). Critically, digital media diversifies the means available for migrants to plan their journeys and find modes of entry into the EU (Coskun, 2018; Dekker et al., 2016; Fiedler, 2018; Kutscher & Kreß, 2018; Latenero & Kift, 2018; Mandić, 2017; Milivojevic, 2018). Within the literature, there is considerable agreement that digital media and technology are vital tools to access information and communicate with social networks throughout the journey and are adopted and adapted by individual migrants to their specific needs.

Preferences for certain technologies and specifications were also discussed. For example, computers were most commonly discussed in periods of immobility, e.g. at refugee camps (Twigt, 2018) or while integrating in destination countries (Dekker & Engbersen, 2014). Meanwhile, smartphones were frequently referred to as essential tools at all stages of the journey, but particularly during periods of mobility (Bokert et al., 2018; Chouliaraki, 2017; Dhoest, 2019; Fiedler, 2019; Gillespie et al., 2018; Hunter, 2015; Mandić, 2017; Milivojevic, 2018; Nagy; 2018). Moreover, the literature mentions that a growing proportion of remittances are sent by migrants in Europe to countries of origin via digital transactions (Belloni, 2019 p. 3; Rodima & Grimes, 2019; Hunter, 2015; Fiedler, 2019; Tanzanu, 2018). With access to these technologies, many migrants operate within digitally mediated contexts as archetypal agents of Harvey's (1989) 'time-space compression' with transnational connectivity to social networks and information across the globe.

Although digital technologies are widely used by migrant communities and play a growing role in mediating their experiences, there was also considerable consensus that there are 'digital divides' amongst migrant groups in terms of access to these technologies and ability to use them. These divides are largely due to disparities in digital literacy, gender and age demographics, financial capacity and, critically, ability to access infrastructures such as Wi-Fi at various stages of the journey (Arvanitis & Yelland, 2019; Belloni, 2019;

Dekker & Engbersen, 2014; Dhoest, 2019 p. 3; Gillespie et al., 2018; Leurs, 2016; Kutscher & Kreß, 2018; Maitland, 2018; Ross, 2018; Ruokolainen & Widén, 2019; Whitteborn, 2015). Additionally, while many migrants are highly active online (Chouliaraki, 2017), some irregular migrants are aware that they may be the subject of surveillance by border authorities and prefer applications and platforms with anonymised and encryption features (Dhoest, 2019; Gillespie, et al., 2018; Kutscher & Kreß, 2018; Whitteborn, 2015). Consequently, caution is required not to overstate the dependency of contemporary migrants on technology or generalise preferences for digital media platform, which may be highly variable between cases and at different phases of the journey.

3.2 Impact of Technology on Migrants and Migration Processes

While the types and uses of technology are not a significant point of contention within the sample, their impact on migrants and migration processes are. Several authors argue that digital media and technologies can enable migrants to navigate their journeys to Europe with greater ease and security (Andersson, 2019; Dhoest, 2019; Gillespie et al, 2018; Kutscher & Kreß, 2018; Mandic, 2017; Milivojevic, 2018). The greater connectivity afforded through these mediums facilitates the formation of transnational communities between families, friends and shared sociocultural identities (Alinejad et al., 2019; Almenara-Niebla & Ascanio-Sánchez, 2019; Bayramoğlu & Lünenborg, 2018; Belloni, 2019; Dekker et al., 2016; Dekker & Engbersen, 2014; Dhoest, 2019; Ferra & Nguyen, 2017; Fiedler, 2019; Leurs, 2016; Patterson & Leurs, 2019; Pérez & Salgado, 2018; Tanzanu, 2018; Urchs et al., 2019). As a result, close and long ties can be developed and maintained across territorial boundaries, building transnational networks that are both a product and motor of migration.

Through these networks, crowdsourcing of information on digital platforms may serve as an impetus for departure as well as inform choices on journeys, destinations and shape expectations of the costs and benefits of migrating (Baran, 2018; Bayramoğlu & Lünenborg, 2018; Bokert et al., 2018; Fiedler, 2019). This is argued to increase the dynamism of migration processes. Indeed, multimedia content shared by the diaspora has been argued to increase or decrease motivations for other potential migrants to the EU (Belloni, 2016; Pogliano, 2017; Fiedler, 2019; Mapelli, 2019; Nelimarkka et al., 2018; Twigt, 2018). Additionally, information gained through interpersonal communication and with greater accessibility to information online before, during and after journeys to Europe may lead to changes in travel trajectories and choices of destination (Bakewell & Jolivet, 2015; Belloni, 2016; Borkert et al., 2018; Crawley & Hagen, 2018; Dekker et al., 2016; Dekker & Engbersen, 2014; Fiedler, 2019). Other authors also contend that digital platforms may facilitate integration into host states by providing opportunities for social contact with hosts and increasing access to employment and services (Bayramoğlu & Lünenborg, 2018; Dhoest, 2019).

Next to positive aspects, there are ways in which technologies may negatively impact migrants. With greater access to information and communication there are higher possibilities of encountering untrustworthy information or connecting to criminal entities such as human smugglers and traffickers via digital channels (Bokert et al., 2018; Dekker & Engbersen, 2014). The impact of social media on migrants may also include increased anxiety and social pressures along social, cultural, economic and political dimensions (Hunter, 2015; Almenara-Niebla & Ascanio-Sánchez, 2019; Belloni, 2019; Dhoest, 2019; Hunter, 2015; Leurs, 2016; Talhouk et al., 2019; Tanzanu, 2018). This may in fact lead to counterintuitive outcomes. For example, some authors have observed that sociocultural pressures resulting from greater transnational connectivity leads to some migrants distancing from social ties with friends and families in countries of origin (Hunter, 2015; Witteborn, 2015). Therefore, technology plays an ambivalent role that may help or hinder migrant users travelling to and integrating in Europe. What is currently lacking is an integrated view that helps to explain the mechanisms and conditions of digitalization's ambiguous role in migrants' experiences and decisions – also in their combination with non-mediated settings.

The literature also indicates reasons to be reserved about the extent to which technology impacts migration trends. While this sample points towards the digitalisation of migrant journeys, there is a considerable degree of caution in attributing a causal role to technology effects on migration trajectory. For example, Fiedler (2019) finds that close, interpersonal social networks have a stronger effect on migrant aspirations and decisions than long ties, whether online or offline. This indicates that interpersonal connections rather than the effects of digital technologies or media themselves impact migration decisions. As Dekker et al. (2016) and Maitland (2018) suggest, technology may act to mediate migration processes rather than catalyse them. The status of ICTs thus requires further investigation.

4. CONCLUSION

The highly complex economic, political, social and cultural processes of migration are increasingly digitally mediated. This QTS has demonstrated key areas where research is being undertaken to examine this phenomenon. Significant strides are being made to understand which technologies and channels are used and how. Preferences for certain technologies and platforms often mirror uses of non-migrant users yet may be adapted to the context-specific requirements of migrants. Also, as is the case with virtually all uses of technology, our review outlines the potential for positive and negative impacts on migrant users as a result.

A further result of our synthesis are topics and areas that have not yet been addressed or received only passing attention. Most prominent is the lack of an integral view of digitalisation along the migration trajectory. We therefore advocate more longitudinal investigations into the shifting choices, meanings and consequences of ICTs throughout migrant journeys. Such work should also consider the parallel importance of digital and non-digital means. There is further a significant gap in research exploring causal relationships between migration and technology with regards to fundamental dynamics such as push and pull factors as well as networked nonlinear feedback mechanisms. While past studies relied largely on qualitative enquiries, issues of causality, especially in terms of long-term impacts and migration trends, require attention. Addressing this gap would help to better understand the mechanisms and conditions underlying migration trends and trajectories. In addition, digitalisation is often conceptualised as either individual or collective phenomenon, calling for greater attention to the intersections between personal and collective choices and experiences. At the same time, migrants are a highly heterogeneous group in terms of demographics, aspiration and experiences. Our review highlights a lack of systematic – and particularly comparative – investigations into specific migrant groups. For instance, we found relatively few studies investigating media choices by vulnerable groups such as unaccompanied minors, pregnant women or members of the LGBTQ+ community.

Methodologically, using QTS to explore digitalisation in the migration literature proved an effective means of surveying a highly heterogenous research landscape while maintaining a systematic approach to the collection, selection and analysis of sources. A potential limitation of our approach may be the lack of quantifiable or longitudinal analyses of this body of research to identify larger-scale trends. However, this approach may be challenged by the largely qualitative nature of studies in this area. Also, our search focused specifically on migration to the EU, limiting the scope of our review.

Ultimately, this QTS aimed to provide a survey of contemporary research and an agenda for further investigations into this rich area of research situated at the confluence of ICT and social science disciplines. Migration is a topic of tremendous societal, political and humanitarian importance. Better understanding migrants' experiences and choices is thus not only a rewarding research exercise but can support ICT developments and policies that address migration realistically and in its full complexity.

ACKNOWLEDGEMENT

This project has received funding from the European Union's Horizon 2020 Research and Innovation Programme under Grant Agreement No 833870. We would like to thank the PERCEPTIONS Consortium for their contributions to the dataset that forms the basis of this paper.

REFERENCES

Alinejad, D., Candidatu, L., Mevsimler, M., Minchilli, C., Ponzanesi, S. and Van Der Vlist, F.N. (2019), Diaspora and mapping methodologies: tracing transnational digital connections with 'mattering maps'. *Global Networks*, 19: 21-43.

Almenara-Niebla, S., & Ascanio-Sánchez, C. (2019). Connected Sahrawi refugee diaspora in Spain: Gender, social media and digital transnational gossip. *European Journal of Cultural Studies*. 1-16.

Andersson, K.B. (2019). Digital Diasporas: An Overview of the Research Areas of Migration and New Media through a Narrative Literature Review. *Human Technology*, 15(2), 142–180.

Arvanitis, E. & Yelland, N. (2019). Home Means Everything to Me ...': A Study of Young Syrian Refugees' Narratives Constructing Home in Greece. *Journal of Refugee Studies.*

Awad, I. & Tossell, J. (2019). Is the smartphone always a smart choice? Against the utilitarian view of the 'connected migrant'. *Information, Communication & Society*.

Bakewell, O., & Jolivet, J. (2015). *Broadcast feedback as causal mechanisms for migration*. (International Migration Institute working papers, Oxford university, paper 113), retrieved from Migration Institute website: https://www.migrationinstitute.org/publications/wp-113-15.

Baran, D.M. (2018). Narratives of migration on Facebook: Belonging and identity among former fellow refugees. *Language in Society*, 47, 245–268.

Barnett-Page, E., Thomas, J. (2009). Methods for the synthesis of qualitative research: a critical review. *BMC Med Res Methodol* 9, 59.

Bayramoğlu, Y., & Lünenborg, M. (2018). Queer Migration and Digital Affects: Refugees Navigating from the Middle East via Turkey to Germany. *Sexuality & Culture*, 22 1019–1036.

Bearman, M. & Dawson, P. (2013). Qualitative synthesis and systematic review in health professions education. *Medical Education*. 47, 252-260.

Belloni, M. (2016). Refugees as Gamblers: Eritreans Seeking to Migrate Through Italy. *Journal of Immigrant & Refugee Studies*, 14(1), 104-119.

Belloni, M. (2019). When the phone stops ringing: on the meanings and causes of disruptions in communication between Eritrean refugees and their families back home. *Global Networks, a journal of transnational affairs*. 1-18.

Borkert, M., Fisher, K.E. & Yafi, E. (2018). The Best, the Worst, and the Hardest to Find: How People, Mobiles, and Social Media Connect Migrants In(to) Europe. *Social Media + Society*.

Chouliaraki, L. (2017). Symbolic bordering: The self-representation of migrants and refugees in digital news. *Popular Communication*, 15 (2), 78-94.

Coskun, E. (2018). Criminalisation and prostitution of migrant women in Turkey: A case study of Ugandan women. *Women's Studies International Forum*, 68, 85-93.

Crawley, H., & Hagen-Zanker, J. (2018). Deciding Where to go: Policies, People and Perceptions Shaping Destination Preferences. International Migration Vol. 57 (1) 20-35.

Dekker, R. & Engbersen, G. (2014). How social media transform migrant networks and facilitate migration, *Global Networks, a journal of transnational affairs*, Vol 14 (4) 401-408.

Dekker, R., Engbersen, G., & Faber, M. (2016). The use of online media in migration networks. *Population, Place and Space*, 22, 539–551.

Dhoest, A. (2019). Digital (dis)connectivity in fraught contexts: The case of gay refugees in Belgium. *European Journal of Cultural Studies* 1 –17.

Diminescu, D. (2012). Introduction: Digital methods for the exploration, analysis and mapping of e-diasporas. *Social Science Information*, 51(4), 451–458

Ferra, I., & Nguyen, D. (2017). "#Migrantcrisis: "tagging" the European migration crisis on Twitter". *Journal of Communication Management*. 21 (4) 411-426.

Fiedler, A. (2019). The gap between here and there: Communication and information processes in the migration context of Syrian and Iraqi refugees on their way to Germany. *The International Communication Gazette*, 81(4), 327–345.

Gillespie, M., Osseiran, S., & Cheesman, M. (2018). Syrian Refugees and the Digital Passage to Europe: Smartphone Infrastructures and Affordances. *Social Media + Society*.

Hardy, D. (1989). *The condition of Modernity: An Enquiry into the Origins of Cultural Change*. Oxford: Blackwell

Hunter, A. (2015). Empowering or impeding return migration? ICT, mobile phones, and older migrants' communications with home. *Global networks, a journal of transnational affairs*, Vol 15 (4) 485-502.

Jones, K. (2004). Mission Drift in Qualitative Research, or Moving Toward a Systematic Review of Qualitative Studies, Moving Back to a More Systematic Narrative Review. *The Qualitative Report*, 9(1): 95-112.

Kutscher, N. & Kreß, L.-M. (2018). The Ambivalent Potentials of Social Media Use by Unaccompanied Minor Refugees. *Social Media + Society*.

Latenero, M., & Kift, P (2018). On Digital Passages and Borders: Refugees and the New Infrastructure for Movement and Control. Social Media + Society, 1 –11

Leurs, K. & Ponzanesi, S. (2018) Connected migrants: Encapsulation and cosmopolitanization. *Popular Communication*, 16:1, 4-20.

Leurs, K. (2016) Young connected migrants and non-normative European family life: exploring affective human right claims of young e-diasporas. *International Journal of EPolitics*, 7(3), 15-34.

Maitland, C (ed.) (2018). *Digital Lifeline? ICTs for Refugees and Displaced Persons*. Cambridge: MIT Press.

Mandić, D. (2017). Trafficking and Syrian Refugee Smuggling: Evidence from the Balkan Route. *Social Inclusion*, 5(2), 28-38.

Mappelli, G. (2019). The Identity Construction of Migrants on Facebook. *Languages*, 4, (52).

Mendoza Pérez, K., Morgade Salgado, M. (2019). Unaccompanied' Minors? Accompanied Foreign Minors, Families and New Technologies. *Int. Migration & Integration* 20, 121–136.

Milivojevic, S. (2019). 'Stealing the fire', 2.0 style? Technology, the pursuit of mobility, social memory and de-securitization of migration. *Theoretical Criminology*, 23(2), 211–227.

Nagy, V. (2018). Roma Networks: Ethnic Solidarity in an Internet Age? *Intersections. EEJSP*, 4(3), 158-179.

Nelimarkka, M. Laaksonen, S-M. & Semaan, B. (2018). Social Media Is Polarized, Social Media Is Polarized: Towards a New Design Agenda for Mitigating Polarization. In *Proceedings of the 2018 Designing Interactive Systems Conference (DIS '18). Association for Computing Machinery*, New York, NY, USA, 957–970

Panagakos, A.N. and Horst, H.A. (2006). Return to Cyberia: technology and the social worlds of transnational migrants. *Global Networks*, 6: 109-124.

Patterson, J. and Leurs, K. (2019). 'We Live Here, and We Are Queer!' Young Adult Gay Connected Migrants' Transnational Ties and Integration in the Netherlands. *Media and Communication*, 7(1), 90-101.

Pogliano, A. (2017). Media, Migration, and Sociology. A Critical Review. *Sociologica*, 1.

Rodima-Taylor, D. & Grimes, W.W. (2019). Virtualizing diaspora: new digital technologies in the emerging transnational space. *Global Networks*, 19(3), 349–370.

Ross, A. (2018). Young Europeans: A New Political Generation? *Societies*, 8, 70

Ruokolainen, G., & Widén, H. (2019). Conceptualising misinformation in the context of asylum seekers. *Information Processing and Management*, 102127, 1-6.

Talhouk, R., M. Balaam, A. L. Toombs, A. Garbett, C. Akik, H. Ghattas, V. Araujo-Soares, B. Ahmad, & K. Montague (2019). Involving Syrian Refugees in Design Research: Lessons Learnt from the Field. In *Proceedings of the 2019 on Designing Interactive Systems Conference*, 1583–1594. New York, NY: ACM.

Tazanu. P.M. (2018). Communication technologies and legitimate consumption: making sense of healthcare remittances in Cameroonian transnational relationships. *Africa,* 88(2), 385–403.

Twigt, M. A. (2018). The Mediation of Hope: Digital Technologies and Affective Affordances Within Iraqi Refugee Households in Jordan. *Social Media + Society.*

Urchs, S., Wendlinger, L.. Mitrović, J. & Granitzer, M. (2019). MMoveT15: A Twitter Dataset for Extracting and Analysing Migration-Movement Data of the European Migration Crisis 2015. In *IEEE 28th International Conference on Enabling Technologies: Infrastructure for Collaborative Enterprises* (WETICE). Napoli, Italy, 146-149.

Witteborn, S. (2015). Becoming (Im)Perceptible: Forced Migrants and Virtual Practice. *Journal of Refugee Studies*, 28(3), 350-367.

ASSESSMENT PLATFORM OF WATER AND ENERGY EFFICIENCY IN COLLECTIVE IRRIGATION SYSTEMS

André Antunes, Diogo Felicíssimo, Bruno Ferreira and Nelson Carriço
Instituto Politécnico de Setúbal, Campus do IPS – Estefanilha, 2910-761 Setúbal, Portugal

ABSTRACT

Southern European countries do not have regular precipitation to assure the agricultural water needs, since precipitation occurs scarcely from April to October. As such, irrigation is essential for agriculture and is only possible with the existence of hydraulic infrastructures for storage and water conveyance. In Portugal, these hydraulic infrastructures are mostly public, forming collective irrigation systems, and managed by Irrigation Associations.
The efficiency of irrigation should be assured through a set of guidelines and procedures promoting a more efficient use of water and energy. Furthermore, in Portugal there are currently no performance assessment system developed to evaluate the water and energy efficiency in CIS. The current practice for the assessment of water and energy efficiency is a set of reactive and unintegrated actions. As such, the gathered information is not usually organized and does not follow systematic procedures. Additionally, appropriate indicators for water and energy loss diagnostic are not defined, thus making it impossible to compare efficiencies between CIS.
In this context, the AGIR R&D project aiming the establishment of a performance assessment system for water and energy efficiency assessment in CIS was developed. One of the outcomes of the project was the development of a user-friendly platform for the CIS management utilities to assess its water and energy efficiencies.
This paper presents the platform AGIR, its functionalities and main components. The platform was designed allowing systematic and uniform data introduction, for usage by various decision support modules.

KEYWORDS

Water Efficiency, Energy Efficiency, Collective Irrigation Systems, Assessment Tool, Information System

1. INTRODUCTION

In Portugal, water usage and energy efficiency are some of the main concerns of Irrigation Associations (IA) managing collective irrigation systems (CIS) (Carriço, N. et al., 2018; DGADR, 2017), and is a priority of recent public policies, mostly due to increasing regulatory pressure from Common Agricultural Policy (CAP), and achieved through the promotion of economic and environmental efficiency.

Currently, however, there is no objective-oriented assessment system nor a set of appropriate performance indicators allowing IAs to quantify water and energy efficiencies in their conveyance and distribution networks, as well as to support the decision-making process.

The AGiR project

The AGIR research project is born in this context. Named "AGIR - Water Use and Energy Efficiencies' Assessment in Collective Irrigation Systems", is coordinated by the Portuguese National Irrigators Federation (FENAREG) and funded by PDR2020 in Operation 1.0.1 - Operational Groups.

This project has as its main objectives the establishment of a performance indicators system for water and energy efficiency assessment in CIS and the development of a set of usable and user friendly tools to be used by CIS management utilities. These developments should provide ways for assessment and identification of the inefficiencies within the systems, as well as to support the selection of interventions for improving the water use and energy efficiency' and energy recollection. One of AGIR research project outputs is a software platform for water and energy balance calculation and a performance assessment system, allowing CIS and agricultures to evaluate the efficiency of water use and energy consumption.

The software platform

The software development project uses an agile methodology. The project has the support of the research team and end-user partners, following the development process through work meetings for discussion and evaluation. As such, the requirement analysis has been an iterative process. System design has been updated as needed to reflect the needs presented by the research team and end-user partners. The methodology used in the development of the project allows easier change management and adaptation for change integration, since project changes can be rather frequent and relevant during the development process. As such, the process of analysis and design for the current stage of the platform was an iterative process, where an initial requirement analysis allowed the establishment of some fundamental actions for the platform.

IA and other water resources managing utilities need a tool for water and energy efficiency assessment of CIS. This tool must be generic enough to accommodate the distinct system infrastructures and measurements needed for the several expected calculations.

As described above, the assessment of water use and energy consumption efficiency is not a common practice among CIS and irrigators. As such, the software platform development faced some challenges, namely, data insertion (i.e., considering that most CIS don't currently use geographical information systems) and visualization (i.e., requirements for simple and intuitive dashboards and menus).

This paper focus on the development of the modules and tools, as well as the implementation of functionalities in the software platform. This platform allows the uniform and systematic data insertion by the IA, for later use by the several integrated decision-making support modules. These modules include the water and energy balance' calculations, allowing hydric efficiency assessment (Loureiro, D. et al, 2019; Cunha, H. et al, 2019), and energy efficiency assessment (Cunha, H., 2018), as well as a performance assessment system.

In addition, a farmer login functionality is provided, allowing the qualitative hydric efficiency evaluation of the irrigation network, obtained through terrain analysis, irrigation mechanics and meteorological conditions (regarding the farmer context) in a simple and intuitive way. So, the platform is designed for two distinct users, IA and farmers. The user type is defined during the registration process and determines the available platform areas and functionalities.

The platform developed during the AGIR project presents itself as a novel alternative for the system performance assessment, allowing IA to perform organized and dynamic calculation of the diverse system profile components, from network total length to more complex calculations (i.e. minimum operation volume in canals), that were previously done using spreadsheets.

The platform uses a logical hierarchy, imposing dependencies between system components (e.g. the infrastructure component is inaccessible before the selection of a given CIS). In this way, the user is lead in providing the needed data for the water and energy balance's and performance assessment system. In the end, performance indicators are produced, thus allowing the IA to assess the CIS performance during a time period.

2. SYSTEM DESIGN

The process of system analysis and design for the current stage of the platform was an iterative process. An initial analysis, based on the research project requirements, allowed definition of the fundamental components and modules for the platform. System design has been updated as needed to reflect the needs presented by the research team and end-user partners.

2.1 Platform Architecture

Platform deployment is based on Docker. Docker technology is used in system deployment allowing greater development and maintenance flexibility. Two distinct Docker images are used. A first Docker image contains the MySQL Database Management System (DBMS) and system database. The second Docker image contains the environment and platform application. Communication between the two Docker images is established. The server was implemented using Node.js technology employing the JavaScript language. A set of web services and a frontend web application are provided. The client-server system architecture can be visualized in Figure 1.

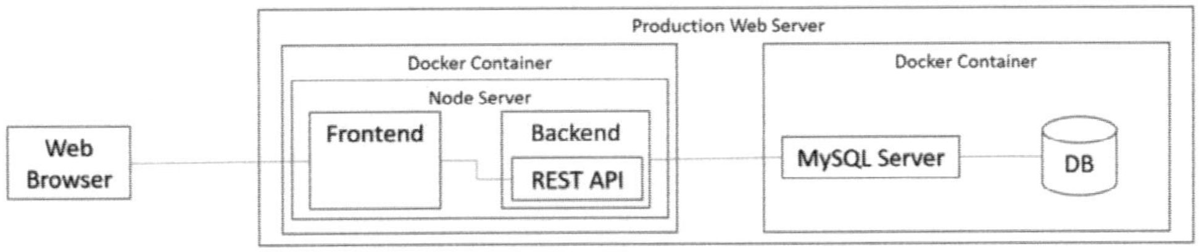

Figure 1. System Architecture

Users access the system with a session login, using the internet and a browser. In order to be able to initiate a session, users must first register in the platform. The application starting page provides users with registration and login functionalities. The platform has been designed for two distinct actors, IA and farmers. The user type is defined during the registration process and determines the accessible application areas and available system functionalities.

Each IA can manage one or more CIS. Each CIS has its own infrastructure, consisting in catchments, canals and canal elements, pipes and pipe elements, stations and reservoirs. Each CIS managed by the IA can have years of analysis set up. For each year of analysis, the IA can add irrigation seasons. The irrigation season allows the IA to associate measurements to the CIS infrastructural elements. These measurements are afterwards used in the calculation of water and energy balances and assessment system.

Farmers are independent from any IA and can use the system for the evaluation of the water use efficiency of their irrigation systems. However, they can associate their applications to a certain IA, allowing the later access to the farmer's water use efficiency data. That allows the IA to query those efficiency evaluations through the web application.

Figure 2 shows the diagram of the logical hierarchy described.

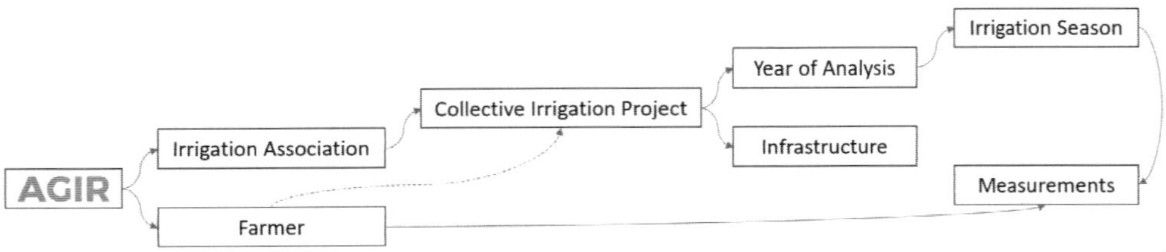

Figure 2. Logical hierarchy

2.2 Data Model

For the development of this platform, a data model was designed from scratch (Figure 3), reflecting the data needs for the end-user partners when modelling their systems. The DBMS used is MySQL.

Since the water and energy balances and the performance assessment system have distinct data calculation requirements, the platform has 4 main sections, namely: authentication, farmer efficiency, infrastructure and measurements. Infrastructural data refer to structural elements, relatively stable in time, such as intakes, canals, canal elements, pipes and pipe elements, pumps and pumping stations and intermediate reservoirs. Measurements refer to data measured through time during a specific Irrigation Season, from a distinct Year of Analysis. These measurements are used afterwards for water and energy balance' and the performance evaluation system.

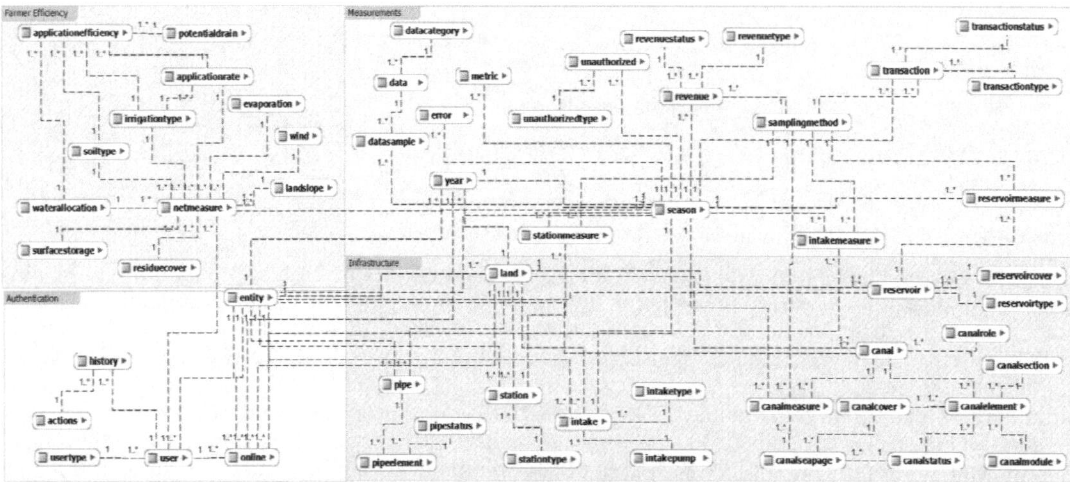

Figure 3. AGIR Data Model

2.3 Modules

The system follows a modular approach and is composed by a set of four main modules: authentication, infrastructure, water balance and farmer's irrigation network modules. Modules for energy balance and the performance assessment system are under research and will be implemented and integrated in the platform. The following section present the infrastructure module and the novel water balance and farmer's irrigation network modules.

2.3.1 Infrastructure Module

The infrastructure module allows the introduction of infrastructural elements. Each CIS has a specific infrastructure that needs to be inserted. Infrastructural elements include intakes, canal and canal element, pipe and pipe element, pumping stations and reservoir.

An infrastructure full report is available, listing all CIS infrastructural elements.

2.3.2 Water Balance Module

The water balance module allows the calculation of water balance (H. Cunha et al, 2019), for an irrigation season (in a specific year of analysis), of a specific CIS.

Measurements associated with infrastructural elements such as intakes, canals and reservoirs are used in the calculation of water balance (e.g., canal cross-section). Other considered measurements are authorized and unauthorized consumption, as well as metering inaccuracies.

Several complex calculations are carried for the different infrastructures. As an example, for each reservoir a water balance is carried and for each canal section the surface subject to evaporation is calculated. Due to the complexity involved in the calculation of water balance, the developed module is novel a valuable tool the efficient management of water use in CIS.

2.3.3 Farmer's Irrigation Network Module

The farmer's irrigation network module allows the assessment of the water usage efficiency of their water applications. The calculation has several interdependent variables the user can set up with the resulting efficiency calculated and displayed in real time (Figure 4).

Variables used to obtain a final efficiency for the water usage include soil type, regarding hydraulic conductivity (light, medium, heavy or crust) and irrigation mechanism (sprinkler, center pivot or drip). Each irrigation mechanism has its own intrinsic property values such as wet area and flow. The calculation of the water application rate is based on the entered values.

Land slope (<2%, 2 to 5%, >5%) and green cover (low, medium, high) values determine the surface storage quantity and potential runoff. The average wind intensity (low, medium, high) and evaporation (low, medium, high) are meteorological factors to taken into consideration directly into the water use efficiency. The irrigation rate (low, medium, high) is also required for the application efficiency calculation.

Application efficiency and apparent losses percentages are displayed as final calculation result. A chart with the applicable ranges for the resulting efficiency is displayed. The range associated to the resulting efficiency is highlighted, when applicable. Chart ranges vary according to soil type and irrigation mechanism' used. (Luz, P. B., 2002; Luz, P. B. & Silva, L. L., 2004).

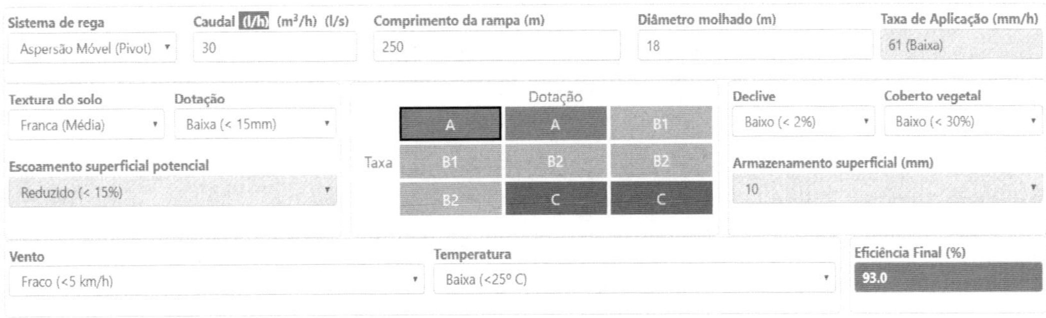

Figure 4. Farmer's Irrigation Network module

3. CONCLUSION

This paper presented an innovative software-platform to the data integration and assessment of water use in Collective Irrigation Systems. This platform presents itself as the first step in the development of a reference tool to support decision-making in Collective Irrigation Systems, enabling the improvement of the water usage and energy efficiencies. Future work includes the implementation of the remaining modules, such as, energy balance and performance evaluation system.

ACKNOWLEDGEMENT

The authors gratefully acknowledge all project AGIR partners that directly or indirectly contributed to the presented paper. This research was funded by PDR2020 grant number PDR2020-101-031878.

REFERENCES

Carriço , N. et al., 2018, Eficiência hídrica e energética em aproveitamentos hidroagrícolas. *14º Congresso da Água.*

Cunha, H., 2018. *Balanços Hídrico e Energético em Aproveitamentos Hidroagrícolas - Uma nova abordagem para sistemas mistos*. Instituto Superior Técnico - Universidade de Lisboa.

Cunha, H. et al, 2019. A comprehensive water balance methodology for collective irrigation systems. *Agric. Water Manag.*, vol. 223, no. May, p. 105660.

DGADR, 2017. *Sistema de Informação do Regadio*. Autoridade Nacional do Regadio. [Online]. Available: http://sir.dgadr.gov.pt/stat. [Accessed: 21-Jan-2020].

Loureiro, D. et al, 2018, Proposta de balanços hídrico e energético para diagnóstico de perdas de água e de ineficiências energéticas em aproveitamentos hidroagrícolas. *VII Congresso Nacional de Rega e Drenagem.*

Luz, P. B., 2002, Sistematização da informação para apoio ao regadio no âmbito agro-ambiental. Avaliação do risco de escoamento superficial em rampas rotativas. *Actas do 6º Congresso da Água*. APRH. Porto.

Luz, P. B. & Silva, L. L., 2004, Avaliação de objectivos ambientais na rega por rampa rotativa. Aplicação de metodologias em solo mediterrâneo. *Actas do 7º Congresso da Água*. APRH. Lisboa.

CHALLENGES IN BUILDING ONTOLOGY FOR SHARING ECONOMY DOMAIN

Ummul H. Mohamad[1a], Ahmad Mujahid Ubaidillah Zakaria[2,1], Mohammad Nazir Ahmad[1] and Nor Hazila Mohd Zain[3]

[1]*Institute of Visual Informatics, Universiti Kebangsaan Malaysia, 43600 Bangi, Selangor*

[2]*Faculty of Business, Finance and Information Technology, MAHSA University, Jalan SP2, Bandar Saujana Putra, 42610 Jenjarom, Selangor*

[3]*Faculty of Business, Information and Human Sciences, Infrastructure University Kuala Lumpur, 43000 Kajang, Selangor*

ABSTRACT

The sharing economy (SE) is one of the emerging domains in this digital era. Yet, little is known on how far or how well the ontology development has been executed for this domain. Ontology development in the SE domain is important, especially to manage the interoperability of heterogeneous systems. This paper presents the challenges in building the ontology for the SE domain. Among them are collaborative platform management issues, tackling information overload, the sustainability of the SE domain and the preference to build application ontology in SE. By understanding all these challenges, the ontology development in the SE domain can be refined to a more systematic structure.

KEYWORDS

Collaborative Consumption, Domain Ontology, Knowledge Management, Ontological Issues, Peer-To-Peer Sharing

1. INTRODUCTION

In contrast to the traditional business, the sharing economy (SE) can be defined through these characteristics (Matzner, Chasin, von Hoffen, Plenter, & Becker, 2016): (i) existence of economic transactions between individuals or stakeholders, (ii) absence of any permanent ownership transfer, (iii) the interaction manner falls between sharing and trade, (iv) it involves IT-based technology and, e) it allows sharing of physical objects that are owned or accessible by one of the parties involved.

SE involves communication across multiple players such as people (users, merchants) and machines (software, program, algorithm and many more). Therefore, it can be difficult for the players to understand the meaning of concepts and terms without the presence of a common language which is understandable to players of the SE domain. This is one of the reasons why ontology is needed for the SE domain; i.e. to serve as a standard to manage commonalities. For example, having a common framework for the SE domain will help capture the heterogeneous SE data, manage the information (Khantong & Ahmad, 2019) and allow knowledge sharing (Ahmad, Zakaria, & Sedera, 2013) across multiple players of the SE domain.

Moreover, the SE domain mainly involves the integration of various digital platforms (e.g. IT systems). If each of the digital platforms uses different terminologies to describe the same thing, this will affect the interoperability of the supposedly integrated systems. Ontology bridges the terminology gap by providing a common knowledge for smoother integration. Additionally, the development of digital platforms in the SE domain will refer to this common knowledge.

Since everything in the SE domain happens in digital or virtual form, the information will accumulate faster and expand larger, to become more complex within a short time span. Being heavily reliant on digital mediation, SE needs optimization in terms of convenience, speed, and seamlessness of digital interactions (Sutherland & Jarrahi, 2018). Ontology is deemed as the way to unveil the complexity of the SE domain in a more understandable manner. These reasons justify the need to have an ontology for the SE domain, simply to make the domain knowledge become more explicit. Ontology enhances the flexibility and agility of the SE domain by helping the involved players to speak and understand the same language.

[a] Corresponding author: ummulhanan@ukm.edu.my

Gruber (1993) defined ontology as "an explicit specification of a conceptualization". In other words, ontology is a study on making information understandable in a machine-readable format within a domain of interest (Musen, 2002). Ontologies can be categorized as upper ontology, domain ontology, task ontology and application ontology. The upper ontology describes the general-purpose or flexible concepts that can be applied universally, common across all domains. Domain ontology describes the controlled vocabulary related to a specific domain specialized in the terms introduced in the upper ontology. Task ontology, on the other hand, corresponds to specialized concepts that are activity-related to carry out a particular task. Finally, application ontology is defined as the ontological concepts that depend on specific applications.

Hashemi, Khadivar, & Shamizanjani (2018) claimed that many organizations viewed ontology-driven knowledge management as a competitive advantage or their economic survival key. Since there is yet to be any common domain ontology for SE that can systematically describe the domain knowledge for sharing economy, this research is of importance.

2. A REVIEW OF ONTOLOGY DEVELOPMENT IN SHARING ECONOMY DOMAIN

Initially, a total of 225 papers were identified from several major publishers such as Web of Science (apps.webofknowledge.com), Emerald Insight (https://www.emerald.com/insight/), Springer (www.springerlink.com) and IEEE (http://ieeexplore.ieee.org/Xplore). The papers included were the papers with full-text articles published after 2014. Then, papers with relevant abstracts that discussed ontology in the SE domain were selected, to obtain a manageable number of papers for narrative review. Table 1 shows the findings based on the 10 finally selected papers.

Table 1. Ontology development in SE domain

No.	Ontology classification	Challenges	References
1	Application ontology (*sedl*)	Difficulty to find the right platform due to the availability of multiple platforms in a similar domain	(von Hoffen, 2017)
2	Application ontology (*discover2share*)	Current ontology exists for platforms on sharing physical resources only	(von Hoffen, Matzner, & Chasin, 2015)
3	Domain ontology (designer-user interaction)	No formalized ontology on designer-user interaction, leading to missing knowledge on understanding customers and their behaviors	(Park & Ramaprasad, 2018)
4	Application ontology (*CrowdStrom*)	Sharing of non-physical resources is neglected due to much focus on ontological development for sharing of physical resources	(Matzner et al., 2016)
5	Domain ontology	No formal ontology for knowledge management techs	(Hashemi et al., 2018)
6	Domain ontology (maritime product/ service-systems)	Lack of a systematic knowledge gathering to effectively evaluate the existing service solutions	(Pagoropoulos, Andersen, Kjær, Maier, & McAloone, 2014)
7	Domain ontology	A rising need to integrate heterogeneous systems for inter-agency collaboration as it is becoming more widespread and requires lots of information systems for support.	(Lv, Ni, Zhou, & Chen, 2016)
8	Upper ontology	Complicated document management to automate data exchange from one domain to another domain	(Cverdelj-Fogaraši, Sladić, Gostojić, Segedinac, & Milosavljević, 2017)
9	Application ontology (CIK-Net)	Inadequate management of intra-organizational knowledge due to ontological designs based on own business environment	(Leung, Lau, & Tsang, 2013)
10	Domain ontology (business model canvas for P2PSCC)	Existence of different customer roles in peer-to-peer sharing collaborative consumption (P2PSCC) is not addressed; too much heterogeneity of P2PSCC services lead to a quick exit from the market	(Plenter, Fielt, Hoffen, Chasin, & Rosemann, 2017)

3. CHALLENGES IN ONTOLOGY DESIGN IN SHARING ECONOMY DOMAIN

Based on the review shown in Table 1, the common ontology design challenges in the sharing economy relate to these: (i) collaborative platform management issues, (ii) tackling information overload, (iii) sustainability of the SE domain, and (iv) preference to build application ontology in SE.

3.1 Collaborative Platform Management Issues

The issues involving the escalating IT-enabled marketplace platforms include isolated platforms, redundancy of platform data and the short platform viability period. This creates a hassle for both merchants (providers) and users (buyers) when selecting the right platform for their needs. For example, browsing through many different platforms to compare the offers and conditions is not only time-consuming but is impractical in the long run (von Hoffen, 2017). Additionally, the redundancy of platform data often arises due to the existence of different data structures (von Hoffen et al., 2015). Plenter et al. (2017) claimed that the inability of many digital platforms to integrate efficiently cause the peer-to-peer sharing services to quickly enter and leave the digital marketplace. Hence, this suggested that ontology development in the SE domain is crucial to allow easier integration of various digital platforms (Lv et al., 2016).

3.2 Tackling Information Overload

In the SE domain, we have to deal with the abundance, diversity and complexity of the data derived from the knowledge of multiple agencies that are interconnected with each other (He et al., 2015). Without ontology, this condition would continue to result in losses of knowledge and information (Park & Ramaprasad, 2018), and complexities in document management (Cverdelj-Fogaraši et al., 2017). However, designing ontology that is based on one's own business environment may also be insufficient, as it leads to inadequate management of inter-agency knowledge (Hashemi et al., 2018). Therefore, this highlighted not only the importance of having an ontology for a domain but also the need to carefully design the ontology based on a common framework.

3.3 Sustainability of SE Domain

In a widespread domain such as the SE, the interaction between the data often involves multiple systems (Valaski, Malucelli, & Reinehr, 2012). Despite the versatility of ontology, the existence of multiple ontologies in a domain may lead to heterogeneity systems (Visser & Cui, 1998). When multiple ontologies exist, the domain common language and their interactions lack consistency, resulting in difficulties for any one system to understand, share and reuse these ontologies. In addition, heterogeneity requires massive information systems support and higher resources demand, to build and maintain the ontology. Cverdelj-Fogaraši et al., (2017) also highlighted the need to govern the domain ontology so that an effortless exchange of data can be sustained.

3.4 Preference to Build Application Ontology in SE

Despite the adoption of ontology in the SE domain, Table 1 showed that the ontology development is very much centered to the application ontology for specific applications. Some papers discussed the domain ontology, but it is dedicated to other related domains such as knowledge management, user-design and business. Hence, this demonstrated that no common framework to assist the ontology development in the SE domain exists so far (Pagoropoulos et al., 2014). One of the possible reasons could be that the SE domain is currently at an infancy stage and is progressing. However, ontology development from a top-down approach should be considered as it is much easier and time-efficient. In addition, integrating a few applications with their own ontologies may still be doable, but integrating hundreds of applications at an application ontology level will be disastrous due to the non-existence of common knowledge. This depicted the need to opt for domain ontology development to make the knowledge in the SE domain more explicit and structured.

4. DISCUSSION

This study digs deeper to further understand the behavior, characteristics and challenges in the SE domain with regards to ontology development. As every different domain faces a different set of challenges, we need to consider all the contributing factors and understand the challenges for the right ontology to be designed and developed. To further explain, we are using the "Trivago" analogy as an example. "Trivago" provides the solution to cater to the needs of hotel industries that involve inter-agency interactions (merchants who provide the hotel accommodation services and users who need the hotel accommodations, mediated by digital platforms). The existence of various digital platforms for this service is unfeasible since each platform is often standalone, making it difficult and tedious for the user to compare and get the best offers. "Trivago" understand that a common language is needed to serve as a standard that will allow integration of the various platforms and ensure systems interoperability. In short, ontology acts like the "Trivago" of the SE domain, rebuilding knowledge of systems to provide a solution to the challenges mentioned earlier. The best practice for SE ontology development is to firstly aim for simplicity through a fixed ontology during the initial phase. Then, the process may be extended to develop a more dynamic ontology for flexibility and agility, to ensure that the knowledge of this domain can be structured properly, systematically and explicitly.

5. CONCLUSION

The sharing economy is an emerging domain that is very knowledge-intensive and involves complex, inter-agency interactions. This paper has twofold contributions. Firstly, this paper has reviewed the state of ontology development in the SE domain and secondly, it has identified the challenges with regards to ontology design and development. There were four major challenges in building an ontology for the sharing economy, which include, collaborative platform management issues, tackling information overload, the sustainability of the SE domain and preference to build application ontology in SE. Hence, ontology development in the SE domain is important to provide a common language to allow communication between multiple players in the SE domain. Ontology is also important to manage knowledge sharing and to allow integration of various digital platforms. In SE, the development of domain ontology needs to be highly considered and focused on, rather than application ontology. This is because application ontology is mostly developed in an *ad hoc* or *in-silo* manner, suitable to fulfill the needs for a specific application. However, when integrating many existing application ontologies, issues such as heterogeneity in systems may arise. The future works of this study are to come up with the right ontology development for the SE domain through a common ontological framework.

ACKNOWLEDGMENT

This research is supported by Research University Grant (GUP), Universiti Kebangsaan Malaysia (UKM), Vot. No: GUP-2018-125. High appreciation goes to the above sponsors.

REFERENCES

Ahmad, M. N., Zakaria, N. H., & Sedera, D. (2013). Ontology-based knowledge management for enterprise systems. In *Competition, Strategy, and Modern Enterprise Information Systems* (pp. 184–212). IGI Global.

Cverdelj-Fogaraši, I., Sladić, G., Gostojić, S., Segedinac, M., & Milosavljević, B. (2017). Semantic integration of enterprise information systems using meta-metadata ontology. *Information Systems and E-Business Management*, *15*(2), 257–304.

Gruber, T. R. (1993). A translation approach to portable ontology specifications. *Knowledge Acquisition*, *5*(2), 199–221.

Hashemi, P., Khadivar, A., & Shamizanjani, M. (2018). Developing a domain ontology for knowledge management technologies. *Online Information Review*, *42*(1), 28–44.

He, L., Ming, X., Ni, Y., Li, M., Zheng, M., & Xu, Z. (2015). Ontology-based information integration and sharing for collaborative part and tooling development. *Concurrent Engineering*, *23*(3), 199–212.

Holsapple, C. W., & Joshi, K. D. (2004). A knowledge management ontology. In *Handbook on Knowledge Management 1* (pp. 89–124). Springer.

Khantong, S., & Ahmad, M. N. (2019). An Ontology for Sharing and Managing Information in Disaster Response: In Flood Response Usage Scenarios. *Journal on Data Semantics*, 1–14.

Leung, N. K. Y., Lau, S. K., & Tsang, N. (2013). An ontology-based collaborative inter-organisational knowledge management network (CIK-NET). *Journal of Information & Knowledge Management*, *12*(01), 1350005.

Lv, Y., Ni, Y., Zhou, H., & Chen, L. (2016). Multi-level ontology integration model for business collaboration. *The International Journal of Advanced Manufacturing Technology*, *84*(1–4), 445–451.

Matzner, M., Chasin, F., von Hoffen, M., Plenter, F., & Becker, J. (2016). Designing a peer-to-peer sharing service as fuel for the development of the electric vehicle charging infrastructure. In *2016 49th Hawaii International Conference on System Sciences (HICSS)* (pp. 1587–1595). IEEE.

Musen, M. A. (2002). Medical informatics: searching for underlying components. *Methods of Information in Medicine*, *41*(01), 12–19.

Pagoropoulos, A., Andersen, J. A. B., Kjær, L. L., Maier, A., & McAloone, T. C. (2014). Building an ontology of Product/Service-Systems: Using a maritime case study to elicit classifications and characteristics. In *Working Conference on Virtual Enterprises* (pp. 119–126). Springer.

Park, J., & Ramaprasad, A. (2018). Toward ontology of designer-user interaction in the design process: a knowledge management foundation. *Journal of Knowledge Management*, *22*(1), 201–218.

Plenter, F., Fielt, E., Hoffen, M., Chasin, F., & Rosemann, M. (2017). Repainting the business model canvas for peer-to-peer sharing and collaborative consumption.

Sutherland, W., & Jarrahi, M. H. (2018). The sharing economy and digital platforms: A review and research agenda. *International Journal of Information Management*, *43*, 328–341.

Valaski, J., Malucelli, A., & Reinehr, S. (2012). Ontologies application in organizational learning: A literature review. *Expert Systems with Applications*, *39*(8), 7555–7561.

Visser, P. R. S., & Cui, Z. (1998). On accepting heterogeneous ontologies in distributed architectures. In *Proceedings of the ECAI98 workshop on applications of ontologies and problem-solving methods*.

von Hoffen, M. (2017). The Sharing Economy Meets the Semantic Web: An Ontology for the Matchmaking of Peers. In *2017 IEEE 11th International Conference on Semantic Computing (ICSC)* (pp. 212–219). IEEE.

von Hoffen, M., Matzner, M., & Chasin, F. (2015). Designing an Ontology-based Web Directory for the Discovery of Sharing and Collaborative Consumption Platforms. In *2015 IEEE 17th Conference on Business Informatics* (Vol. 1, pp. 108–115). IEEE.

QUALITY ASSESSMENT IN SCRUM SOFTWARE DEVELOPMENT THROUGH METRICS: A CONCEPTUALIZATION USING CONCEPT MAPS

Sirine Zaouali[1] and Sonia Ayachi Ghannouchi[2]
[1]Higher Institute of Computer Science and Communication Techniques, University of Sousse
12 Beach Route, Sousse, Tunisia
[2]High Institute on Management of Soussse, University of Sousse
Road of Abdlaaziz il Behi. Bp 763. 4000, Sousse, Tunisia

ABSTRACT

In Scrum software development projects, plenty of quality metrics may be measured and used for quality assessment. Selecting the required metrics thus becomes a critical step. Scrum projects are fundamentally conducted around three elements: team, artifacts and events. These elements can be helpful for guiding the involved stakeholders in selecting the most pertinent ones. Hence, in this paper we propose concept maps that promote quality assessment through a classification of Scrum quality metrics based on the three aforementioned elements. These Concept Maps will guarantee that all considered elements would be controlled and thus facilitate the improvement of the quality process. Their adoption in the quality assurance approach will certainly be advantageous.

KEYWORDS

Quality Assessment, Agile Software Development, Scrum Metrics, Concept Map

1. INTRODUCTION

IT organizations aim to implement practices and processes in order to increase their product quality. Consequently, using metrics is so important to assess the quality within Agile Software Development (ASD). So, measuring quality through metrics guides managers and agile team to make decisions about projects in their organizations (Agarwal et al., 2014). To implement measurement culture in ASD, it is recommended not to collect several metrics, but only to keep the most pertinent ones. But, Scrum still now the most useful in software development organizations thanks to its fast response to change demands and also its short development cycle. It guarantees in short time to deliver a higher Business Value. In addition, Scrum is still used even for perform complex software development projects (Mishra and Abdalhamid, 2018).

Therefore, different approaches may be used in Scrum to select the appropriate metrics for quality measurement most of them are goal based approaches. As for example Goal Question Metric (GQM) which is a top-down approach that permits the identification of a desired goal, then a set of questions helps to achieve it and metrics helping to answer each question. Other approaches are based on stakeholders' goals (IT management, team members, Scrum Master and customers). But in spite of that, applying GQM is difficult in case of lacking stakeholders' vision of project goals since metrics selection is mostly conducted in a subjective way (Karklina and Pitra, 2018).On the other hand, Scrum is a framework process conducted and managed fundamentally around three components: Team, Artifacts and Events. We consider that this can be a perfect solution to categorize and select the appropriate Scrum metrics. In addition, Concept Mappings are graphical representations widely used to organize, understanding and share knowledge. They were originally developed by Novak for representing knowledge (Mejri et al., 2016). Inspired by this work, we decided adopting a concept map which conceptualizing metrics in Scrum process under its fundamental components. Metrics described by these concept maps were selected from literature. Moreover, according to the systematic mapping study conducted by (dos Santos et al., 2017); concept mapping was applied as an educational tool in multiple domains such as Computer Science. One from the main purposes of implementing CMs is knowledge organization.

More precisely, via this work we proposed a solution to determine How to assess quality in Scrum process through metrics?

The remainder of the paper is structured as follows: in section 2, we introduce the background to discuss for Scrum method, Scrum metrics and concept map; in section 3, we describe; in section 3 we present the research works that have treated the similar questions; in section 4 we describe our proposed Concept map; finally, in section 5 we present conclusions and future works.

2. BACKGROUND

2.1 Scrum

Scrum is a framework performed on a sequence of Sprints (iterations). So, every Sprint is a time-box of one month or less which ends by creating a potentially releasable product Increment (Scrum Guides, 2017). Requirements are expressed in form of a simple description named "User Stories" (US) (Vannieuwenhuyze, 2013). The three fundamental Scrum' components are cited below.

Artifacts are the Product Backlog (PB) regroups all the US prioritized based on their Business Value by the Product Owner. The PB is dynamic; it is continually adapted in order to deliver a useful product satisfied client needs. Second, the Sprint Backlog regroups US selected from the PB with higher value of priority selected for the Sprint by the development team. It includes needing tasks to deliver it into "Done" Increment (Scrum Guides, 2017) (Vannieuwenhuyze, 2013).

Scrum team consists of three roles; a Scrum Master, a Product Owner and the development team described below (Scrum Guides, 2017) (Vannieuwenhuyze, 2013). They have all the necessary competences to accomplish the work. Scrum Master (SM) is responsible for promoting Scrum as defined in the Scrum guide. SM helps every member to understand Scrum theory, values, practices and rules. Product Owner (PO) is the unique responsible for managing the PB, including its content, availability and order. He/she is also the spokesperson of future users and all stakeholders. Development Team is a group of professionals who develop US in the SB to deliver a potentially releasable increment at the end of each Sprint. The optimal development team size is between 3 to 9 persons, SM and PO aren't taken into account. Development team is self-organizing. Self-organizing means that only its members choose how to accomplish its work.

The Scrum events are Sprint planning Meeting, Daily Scrum, Sprint Review and Sprint Retrospective (Scrum Guides, 2017) (Vannieuwenhuyze, 2013). During the Sprint Planning Meeting, all Scrum team collaborates to select US from PB that will be developed in next Sprint. Selected US are estimate by development team through effort point. Once the Sprint begins, Daily Scrum is held every day and it lasts 15 minutes. During this meeting, development team updates columns of Sprint Backlog Board (to do, in progress, done, impediment). Once the Sprint ends, Sprint Review is held to inspect the increment and adapt the PB if required. Scrum team and key Stakeholders collaborate on work done in the Sprint and validate it. Then, the Sprint Retrospective is held. During this meeting, Scrum team inspects its work and constructs a plan of improvements which will be implemented in the next Sprint.

2.2 Scrum Metrics

As mentioned by Lord Kervin about the usage of metrics that it cannot be improved without measure it. Also Pfleeger affirms that metrics help to understand, monitor and improve done work and how it was done. In addition, Jones affirms that the most performant IT organizations such as Microsoft and IBM widely use metrics in their activities. (Kupiainen et al., 2015) proved that agile teams use it for many purposes focusing on different areas as for example sprint planning, detecting software process problems, tracking progress, etc. In ASD, the whole process and also Sprints must be planned and monitored.

So, measuring quality through metrics helps to identify and fixe process problems. In the case of Scrum plenty of metrics are adopted a base for quality assessment and improvement such as story point determined, % of automated test, test coverage, % of US done in a sprint, etc. (dos Santos et al., 2017).

2.3 Concept Map

Concept maps originally were developed in the courses of Novak's research program in 1972 at Cornell University as a result of following and understanding changes in children's knowledge of science (Novak and Canas, 2007). In fact, a concept map is a top-down diagram underlying relationships between concepts. It permits to show the systematic relationships between sub-concepts relating to a main concept (Eppler, 2006). Concept Maps represent organized knowledge which are needed to answer a focus question(s) (context dependent).

Thus, organized knowledge is composed of concepts and propositions. Concepts are perceived regularities or patterns, labelled with words and symbols and connected using linking words used to form propositions. Propositions are units of meaning and may be crosslinks showing interrelationships between map segments (Novak and Canas, 2006). Graphically, concepts are represented as boxes or bubbles connected with labelled connector arrows. The characteristic of concept maps is that concepts are hierarchically structured with the most inclusive concepts at the top of the map and the most specific concepts positioned at the bottom (Novak and Canas, 2006).

3. STATE OF THE ART

In literature, authors proposed different solutions in different manners to choose quality metrics in agile or Scrum software development process as stated below.

(Mahnic and Zabkar, 2008) proposed a Scrum measurement repository in order to collect project data and store measurement results. It results from a Scrum meta-model using entity-Relationship notation extended by adding appropriate metrics. These measures have been chosen referring to Scrum and Measurement Analysis Process Area of CMMI practices. So, proposed measures aim to monitor satisfaction of Scrum stakeholders which refers to process performance. (Mahnic and Vrana, 2007) presented a metrics plan which monitors and improves continuously the software development process performance in Scrum method. This plan consists of a set of indicators and corresponding metrics that measure the performance based on stakeholders' goals (IT management, Team members, and customers). In addition, each indicator can be evaluated using direct metrics which are calculated by an appropriate project management tool. So their proposed stakeholder-driven Scrum process performance measurement provides a guarantee for process and software quality. An agile metric mind-map has been mentioned by (Oza and Korkala, 2012) which regroups the most useful agile metrics. This mind-map classifies agile metrics measuring quality into seven categories: engineer, strategic, economic, test, iteration, code, automation and project management.

(Downey and Sutherland, 2013) proposed a set of nine fundamental Scrum metrics measure and monitor team performance if problems arise; Velocity, Work Capacity, Focus Factor, Percentage of Adopted Work, Percentage of Found Work, Accuracy of Estimation, Accuracy of Forecast, Targeted Value Increase, Success at Scale, and the Win/Loss Record of the Team. By this way, Scrum team maintains a high energy state that generates a hyper-productivity. We consider that collecting these quality data on team performance is one of the powerful information allowing to deliver a software of high quality. (Karklina and Pitra, 2018) proposed an approach to identify quality metrics and retrieve data from project management systems. This approach was represented as a process workflow. It permits defining the appropriate metrics for the proposed goals using GQM approach and choosing a project management tool (JIRA, Redmine, etc.) according to required features. As a result, authors proved that this approach can be used successfully for quality control in agile projects and helps stakeholders in their decision making. (Boerman et al., 2015) presented a measuring and reporting model for quality, progress and predictions in agile projects. To design this model, metrics have been derived using GQM approach. As a result, the measurement model can be considered as a way which describes these metrics. We conclude that indicators proposed at this work on quality are helpful especially for project owners (external stakeholders) by monitoring quality and controlling project status only via PB. Another solution was also intended to deal with quality requirements. (Guzmán et al, 2017) proposed Q-Rapids methodology to manage quality and functional requirements concurrently in Rapid Software Development. Software quality is then based on quality-related metrics by adopting Quamoco approach to define quality model. Q-Rapids helps decision makers to identify and monitor quality problems continuously throughout the development process.

All these work have used metrics in order to measure, monitor and improve software/process quality. These metrics are selected based on different approaches. In contrast, our contribution in this work is based on a concept map as a different approach for choosing appropriate metrics for Scrum development process.

4. PROPOSED CONCEPT MAPS

As specified by (Novak and Canas, 2006) and (Novak and Canas, 2007), to construct a good concept map, we followed the following steps: First, define the domain of knowledge by setting an appropriate focus question which will be answered by the mapped knowledge. In our case, the focus question is "How to assess quality in Scrum process through metrics?". Second, identify key concepts: concepts defined in our map are presented in next sub-sections. Scrum components are all represented (PB, SB, Sprint Review, etc.) as concepts and their corresponding metrics too. Third, construct a preliminary concept map: accordingly, we used CmapTools as software tool. Forth and finally, revise the concept map: readjusting our preliminary concept map based on experts opinion. For a more comprehensive and readable concept map, we proceeded from general to more specific concepts. Thus, at the first stage, we constructed a "macro concept map" classifying metrics in Scrum process according to belongs to its 3 principal aspects which are team, events (ceremonies) and artifacts. Then, "micro concept maps" are constructed to show metrics related to each specific concept of this macro map. So, these maps are described below.

4.1 Macro Concept Map

As illustrated in figure 1, Scrum process metrics can be categorized according to Events, Team and Artifacts. Events derived metrics correspond to metrics measured during a given event. They include Sprint Planning meeting derived metrics, Daily Scrum derived metrics, Sprint Review derived metrics and Sprint Retrospective derived metrics. Therefore, this map describes when metrics can be derived. Team related metrics include Team Performance.

Moreover, Size of team and Percentage of team member's engagement are metrics that refer to teams and calculated during the Sprint Planning Meeting. Other metrics are related to artifacts which include PB and SB. They are consequently composed of PB's User Story and SB's User Story related metrics.

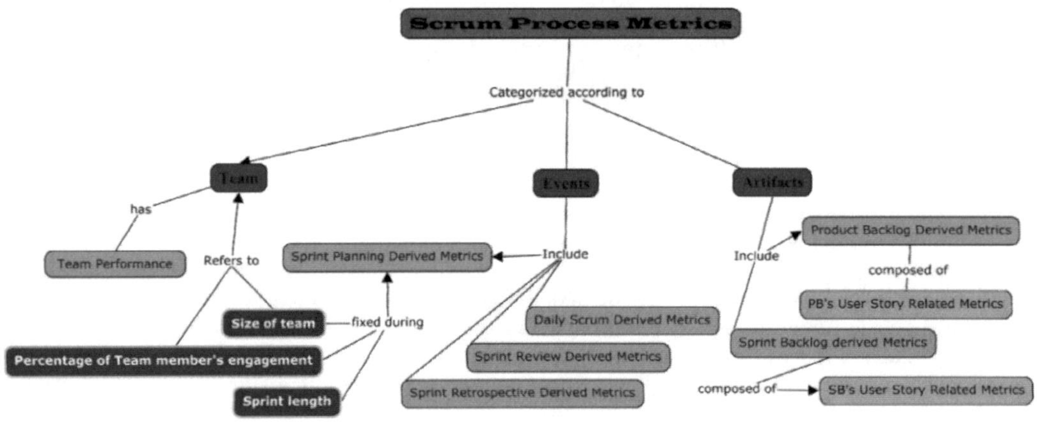

Figure 1. Macro map for Scrum process metrics

4.2 Micro Concept Maps

Figure 2 shows a micro map for Team Performance which is measured through a set of metrics as for example Velocity and work capacity.

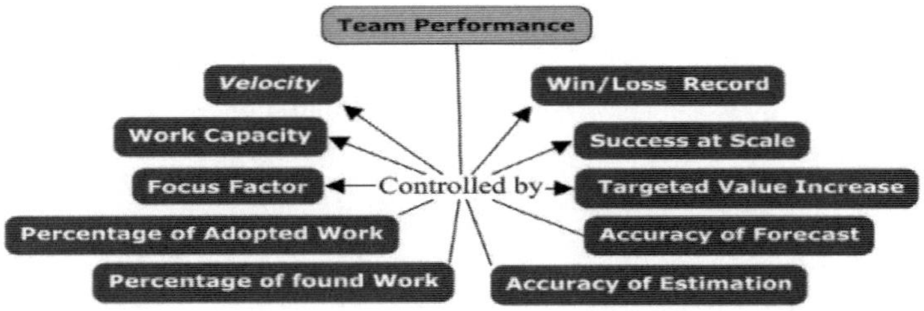

Figure 1. Micro map for team performance

Figure 3 shows a micro map for expanding more details about the following concepts: Daily Scrum, Sprint Review and Sprint Retrospective related metrics. Metrics determined during Daily Scrum are number of impediments for a given task, number of tasks in progress, number of tasks realized/done and number of tasks to do. Metrics determined during Sprint Review are total number of errors, total number of accepted US and total number of rejected US. Metrics determined during Sprint Retrospective and calculated for a given Sprint are total number of tasks in Sprint, number of tasks completed in Sprint, etc.

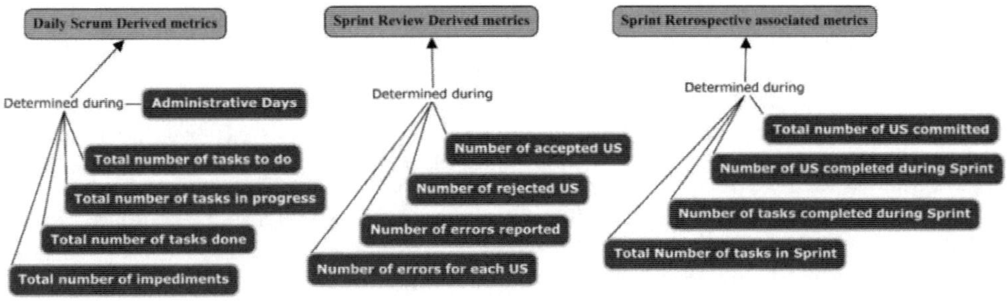

Figure 2. Micro map for metrics determined during events

In addition, Figure 4 shows a micro map for expanding more details about the following concepts: SB's User Story and PB's User Story. The corresponding metrics are determined for each of these concepts. SB's User Story related metrics are number of unit tests, number of Acceptance tests, number of functional tests, etc. These metrics are themselves categorized into two main classes: test related metrics and task related metrics. PB's User Story related metrics are total number of US, total number of deleted US, etc.

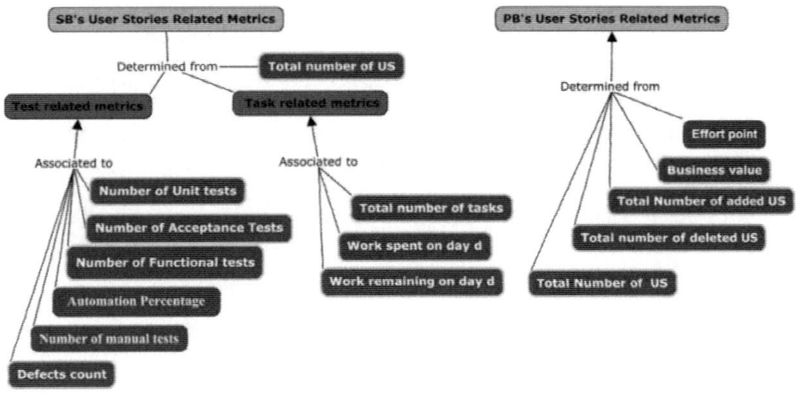

Figure 3. Micro map for metrics determined from Sprint Backlog and Product Backlog

5. CONCLUSION AND FUTURE WORK

In this work, we proposed a conceptualization of Scrum software process metrics using concept maps. As a result, these concept maps classify Scrum metrics firstly according to Scrum fundamental elements of (team, events and artifacts) as concepts in a macro map. Then, each of these concepts is more detailed (presenting appropriate metrics) in micro maps. To conclude, our contribution is a new means to select appropriate metrics based on this classification that promotes quality assessment to improve the quality process and consequently quality product. These concept maps are a graphical representation dedicated to Scrum metrics and their classifications according to the three fundamental elements of Scrum. They offer a means for deeper understanding knowledge related to their usefulness and a guarantee that the basic elements are controlled.

In terms of future work, it would be interesting to accomplish the fourth step of the construction of the concept map (mentioned in section 4) to validate incorporated metrics from practitioners and Scrum experts. Additionally, we aim to implement, in an agile way, these concept maps in Scum process in order to facilitate Scrum Master' decision-making through the visualization of their metrics measurement results in a dashboard. Besides, determining when and how to collect data for measuring these metrics without distracting Scrum teams would also be a challenge.

REFERENCES

Agarwal, A., Garg, N.K and Jain, A., 2014. Quality Assurance for Product Development using Agile. *International Conference on Reliability, Optimization and Information Technology.* Faridabad, India, pp. 44-47.

Boerman, MP. et al, 2015. Measuring and Monitoring Agile Development Status. *Proceedings of the Sixth International Workshop on Emerging Trends in Software Metric.* Florence, Italy, pp. 54-62.

dos Santos, V. et al., 2017. Analyzing the Use of Concept Maps in Computer Science: A Systematic Mapping Study. *In Informatics in Education,* Vol. 16, No. 2, pp. 257–288.

Downey, S. and Sutherland, J., 2013. Scrum Metrics for Hyperproductive Teams: How They Fly like Fighter Aircraft. *46th Hawaii International Conference on System Sciences.* Wailea, Maui, HI, USA.

Eppler, M., 2006. A comparison between concept maps, mind maps, conceptual diagrams, and visual metaphors as complementary tools for knowledge construction and sharing. *In Information Visualization,* Vol. 5, No. 3, pp. 202-210.

Guzmán, L. et al, 2017. How Can Quality Awareness Support Rapid Software Development?. *23d International Conference on Requirements Engineering: Foundation for Software Quality.* Essen, Germany, pp 167-173.

Karklina, K. and Pitra, R., 2018. Quality Metrics in Agile Software Development Projects. *In Information Technology and Management Science,* vol. 21, pp. 54–59.

Kupiainen, E., Mäntylä, M.V., Itkonen, J., 2015. Using metrics in Agile and Lean Software Development – A systematic literature review of industrial studies. *In Information and Software Technology,* Vol. 62, pp. 143-163.

Mahnic, V. and Vrana, I., 2007. Using stakeholder-driven process performance measurement for monitoring the performance of a Scrum-based software development process. *In Electrotechnical Review: Ljubljana, Slovenija,* Vol. 75, No. 5, pp. 241-247.

Mahnic V. and Zabkar, N., 2008. Measurement repository for Scrum-based software development process. *CEA'08 Proceedings of the 2nd WSEAS International Conference on Computer Engineering and Applications.* Acapulco, Mexico, pp. 23-28.

Mejri, A. et al., 2016. Representing Business Process Flexibility using Concept Maps. *Conference on ENTERprise Information Systems / International Conference on Project MANagement / Conference on Health and Social Care Information Systems and Technologies.* Porto, Portugal.

Mishra, D. and Abdalhamid, S., 2018. Software Quality Issues in SCRUM: A Systematic Mapping. In Journal of Universal Computer Science, vol. 24, no. 12, pp. 1690-1616.

Novak, JD. and Canas, AJ., 2007. Theoretical origins of concept maps, how to construct them, and uses in education. *In Reflecting Education,* Vol. 3, No. 1, pp. 29-42.

Novak, JD. and Gowin, DB., 1982. Learning how to learn. *In Cambridge University Press.*

Oza, N. and Korkala, M., 2012. Lessons Learned In Implementing Agile Software Development Metrics. *UK Academy for Information Systems Conference Proceedings 2012.* UK, United Kingdom, pp 38-50.

Scrum Guides: The Definitive Guide to Scrum: The Rules of the Game (2017), available at https://www.scrumguides.org/docs/scrumguide/v2017/2017-Scrum-Guide-US.pdf

THE IMPLEMENTATION OF TOOL FOR THE FACILITATION OF ELECTORAL PROCESSES IN NIGERIA: A CASE STUDY OF THE INDEPENDENT NATIONAL ELECTORAL COMMISSION

Aishatu Shuaibu, Muhammadou M. O. Kah and Olumide B. Longe
American University of Nigeria
Department of Information Information Systems, School of IT and computing, Nigeria

ABSTRACT

In the last decade, the electoral processes were purely manual where the verification process is limited to physical checking from voters list to confirm the genuineness of the voters' card. The process of verification was lengthy and cumbersome during the election, in most cases; there were problems of multiple registrations. The remarkable growth in Information and Communication Technology (ICT) to electoral processes created new voters verification opportunities for the electorates. This opportunity was known as Smart Card Reader (SCR). This research aims to investigate the implementation of Smart Card Reader (SCR) and its challenges during the verification process of election. Through Actor-network Theory the theoretical lens, the study will present the processes of the implementation looking at the challenges. This will include the Problems in Problematisation that started the implementation challenges, imperfect interessement that led way to more challenges and incompetence in the enrollment. This study proposes a case study methodology to understand the phenomenon under investigation. Multiple data collection methods; observation, interview, focus groups will be used to collect data. The research is expected to contribute to the IS research adding to the literature on ICT to electoral processes.

KEYWORDS

Actor-network Theory, Smart Card Reader, Independent National Electoral Commission, Implementation Challenges, Nigeria

1. INTRODUCTION

Information and Communication Technology (ICT) is believed to play a vital role in improving electoral processes (Debrah, Effah, & Owusu-Mensah, 2019; Avgerou, Masiero, & Poulymenakou, 2019). This is due to its role in ensuring transparency by providing free and fair elections (Effah & Debrah, 2018). The electronic electoral process (e-electoral) refers to the use of ICT for improving the electoral process, increasing trust and efficiency in its management (Wolf et al., 2011). It is a techno-organizational disposition which is embedded in the processes of an election with different socio-economic context around the globe (Avgerou et al., 2019). Thus, it aims at improving the processes of election to overcome historical forms of electoral fraud (McGrath and Maiye, 2010).

The implementation of e-electoral processes has become popular around the world in representing present democracy (e.g., Avgerou, 2013). It provides an opportunity to improve both the governmental agency and the public in general by enhancing efficiency, transparency, and effectiveness for politicians, citizens, and civil servants (Twum-Darko, Noruwana, & Sewchurran, 2015) However, when real implementation materializes, the intended end result does not occur (Gunawong & Gao, 2017) The unpleasant part is that the implementation is bedeviled with challenges (Ashaye & Irani, 2019). Some of these challenges include; lack of proper internet connectivity and properly skilled training (eg., Sambo & Alexander, 2018; Ramli, 2017).

In the developing countries, discourse around the implementation of e-electoral processes are dominated with failure, such studies have been carried out; In Nepal (Sharma, 2014), Uganda (Asiimwe, 2013), Sri Lanka (Heeks and Stanforth, 2014) and Ghana (Effah and Debrah, 2018). In some cases, about 80% of the projects in developing nations have failed and abandoned (Gunawong and Gao, 2017). Despite studies on the implementation of Smart cards, there is little understanding of the implementation of ICT to electoral processes (Adeshina and Ojo, 2017). Heeks & Stanforth, (2014) argued that implementation practice is under-researched. Thus, Walsham (2017) emphasized on the need for more research reflecting on technology intervention to political discourse. In terms of studies associated with Smart card for verification during an election, most of the studies tend to investigate the causes of failure of Smart Card for multiple purposes or other purposes in e-government research, and suggestions were given based on the multifunction of the smart card instead of strictly for verification during an election (Gunawong & Gao, 2017: McGrath, 2016). Although, the study by Effah & Debrah (2018) investigated biometric technology for voter verification and identification, the study adopted activity theory as a lens to guide the research. It is argued that the verification process by the use of Smart Card guarantee (SCR) a credible, free and fair and transparent election (Alebiosu, 2016), which is the main process of election. The verification by the use of SCR increased public trust and confidence in the electoral process (Alebiosu, 2016). This reality encouraged this research to focus on the implementation of smart card for verification and its challenges during elections in Nigeria.

Globally, democracy has been widely accepted as the best means of electing leaders for good governance (Abdulhamid et al., 2013). However, the election process has always been questioned and in some instances results in creating social, political and economic instability (Abdulhamid et al., 2013). Similarly, the electronic voting system (e-Voting) has also been widely accepted as an alternative to the manual paper voting method (Nkohkwo and Islam, 2013). In addition, the use of card readers in the 2015 and 2019 elections restored confidence in the electorates. Consolidating the gains and improving the electoral process is therefore imperative to sustainable democracy and good governance in Nigeria. Theoretically, the implementation process that is categorized with human and non-human actors have not been ignored; rather, the majority of the research on the implementation of ICT to electoral processes reported cases of failure at the initial stage of problematisation (Gonawong & Gao, 2017) This could be achieved by integrating all the actors in the electoral process through in-depth analysis.

Thus, the purpose of this study is to investigate the implementation of Smart Card Reader (SCR) in the Nigerian electoral processes, and to understand its challenges using ANT as a lens to view the processes and explore the relationship between human and non-human actors. This research will build on the concept of generalized symmetry by maintaining the interaction between human and ICT in terms of implementation.

1.1 Aim and Objectives

The aim of the research is to understand the implementation of Smart Card Reader, the relationship among heterogeneous actors on Nigeria's electoral process and challenges to implementation.

Thus, the specific objectives of the research are:

- To investigate the process of implementation of SCR to the Nigerian electoral process as the phenomenon of this research under investigation
- To use ANT, human and non-human actors as the theoretical lens for building new findings into the electoral processes in Nigeria
- To further understand the causes of the challenges of SCR used in the Nigerian electoral processes

1.1.1 Research Questions

Based on the underlying problems and the stated objectives, the study intends to pose the research question thus:

- How does the implementation of SCR impact on the electoral processes in Nigeria emerged?
- What are the causes of challenges to SCR in the Nigerian electoral processes?
- How do the relationships between heterogeneous actors in the translation model influence the implementation of ICT for the Nigerian electoral processes?

2. RESEARCH DESIGN

To address the research aim, an inductive research approach will be adopted. The research will be empirical in nature and investigation will be conducted to understand the actors involved both non-human and human for the implementation SCR during the verification process in the Nigerian election. Interpretive approach will be adopted for the research (Walsham, 2006). This is because meanings will be derived from the motivation of individual interpretation. Interpretivist believes that meanings are understood through social context that is social constructivist (Adom et al., 2016). The interpretivist approach aimed at understanding the cultural and social life of people's characters and rules out the natural science method (Walsham, 1995; Chowdhury, 2014). This will enable the researcher to understand the reality of the phenomenon under investigation.

The research will be carried out at the Independent National Electoral Commission (INEC), and the general public (electorate). The research will be exploratory in nature (Rahi, 2017) with the aim of understanding how the implementation of ICT on the verification process of election in Nigeria emerged. The qualitative data will be identified and analyzed through thematic analysis (Maguire and Delahunt, 2017).

2.1 Research Procedures

The research will adopt an interpretivist case study approach (Klein and Myers, 1999) due to its ability to explain the complex socio-technical interaction process using interviews, case descriptions, and empirical observations (Thapa, 2011). Qualitative data will be collected from Independent National Electoral Commission (INEC) staff and the electorates.

2.2 Data and Collection Procedure

Interviews, participants Observations and organizational documents will be applied as techniques for data collection (Walsham, 2006). The interviews will be conducted with participants. The design of the interview questions will be guided by the translation models of ANT (Nurdin et al., 2014). The participants will be INEC officials both lower and upper bureaucrats and the electorates. The interview questions will be semi-structured that will involve both open and closed-ended questions. This will allow interviewees to be flexible while answering the questions. The use of interviews will allow the researcher to absorb into the project's social, cultural, contextual, and organizational reality of the various actors (Klein and Myers, 1999).

Participant observation and document analysis will be carryout. Participant observation will assist in carrying out a database on day-to-day activities happening at the INEC. Feelings, ideas, and reactions of the participants will be observed and noted for the study. Additionally, how systems works and support given to the systems will be observed.

Besides, documents will be analyzed as other sources of data collection. Document analysis will give more details of things that were not clear during observations and interviews. INEC project documents and Nigeria ICT tools for election policy documents will be collected and analyzed. The aim was to understand the relationship and influence of other non-human actors within the project network (Fenwick and Edwards, 2011). The use of various qualitative methods to collect data will help in ensuring triangulation and a rich data set to illustrate the various networks of actors involved in the implementation and use of ICT-enabled interventions aimed at improving the electoral process.

2.3 Data Analysis

Qualitative data analyses will be carried out to analyze all the data that will be collected. Interviewed data will be transcribed through examining, pinpointing and recording patterns into themes following the teachings of thematic analysis (Braun and Clarke, 2013). An iterative process will be used for reading the transcript samples that will lead to the creation of a codebook. All related obscurity will be clarified after the coding of the transcripts samples and codebook will be filtered. The themes will be categorized reflecting respondents' feedback relating to the implementation of ICT and challenges. The transcripts will be coded and merged into larger themes. Different themes relating to the relationship of actors on issues of the implementation and challenges will be contained in the codebook. The coding will follow the movement of heterogeneous actors as it relates to the case study (Wright, 2015). The main themes will be obtained through playing and re-playing of recorded interviews. Also, reading and re-reading the interviewed transcript as discussed by the participants will be analyzed. Secondly, the themes will be grouped in relation to the translation models of Actor-Network Theory (Bengtsson & LundstrÃ, 2013). These will be done with careful consideration for the implementation of ICT tools to electoral processes as a phenomenon for the research. Field note taken during observations will be analyzed using codes that will be used for the interviews.

2.4 Theoretical Approach

The research is theoretically based on the sociology of translation upon human and non-human actors of Callon, Latour and Law translation model of Actor-Network Theory (ANT) (Callon, 1986; Latour, 1996; Law, 1992a). ANT will explain interacting actors towards achieving goals or objectives of the verification process of Nigerian election. ANT serves as a theoretical lens through which the underpinning reality of the implementation phenomenon under investigation will be viewed. It is of the view that knowledge is the end product of a heterogeneous network of aligned interests. The ANT considered the process of a heterogeneous network as pieces from technical, textual, social and conceptual which are put together and translated to produce an end product (Law, 1992). It is concerned with the link between human and non-human (institutions, organization, society, machines and, agents). It is regarded as the "*sociology of translation*" and it is worried about the "*Mechanics of Power*" (Law, 1992). The *"Mechanics of Power"* and its relationship to organization believes that there is a Macrosocial or Macroactor and Microsocial or Microactor in translation (Law, 1992). The Macro and Micro actors are referring to human and non-human actors involved in ANT translation. Both non-human and human actors are not separated from each other in the translation process (Callon, 1986).

3. CONCLUSION

In conclusion, the study will make three broad contribution; First, the study will contribute to; the literature of IS research on the analysis of ICT on electoral processes using ANT, it will increase the deliberation on the implementation of ICT and theorization for developing countries, and depicting the intervention of ICT for electoral processes and exposing more of the loopholes for deploying ICT to the electoral process. Secondly, it will contribute to the theory where the study is first of its kind to look into the ANT and the verification process of an election using SCR in developing countries. Thirdly, the study will contribute to practice where findings from the study will help in curbing e-electoral processes fraud. The research will be limited only to the phases of implementation of the Smart Card Reader focusing on its challenges during the verification process of an election. The expected recommendation is that findings from this research will proffer solution to overcoming the challenges associated with SCR.

REFERENCES

Abdulhamid, S.M., Adebayo, O.S., Ugiomoh, D.O., AbdulMalik, M.D., 2013. The Design and Development of Real-Time E-Voting System in Nigeria with Emphasis on Security and Result Veracity. *International Journal of Computer Network and Information Security* ,5, 9–18. https://doi.org/10.5815/ijcnis.2013.05.02

Adeshina, S.A., Ojo, A., 2017. Factors for e-voting adoption - analysis of general elections in Nigeria. Government Information Quarterly. https://doi.org/10.1016/j.giq.2017.09.006

Adom, Yeboah, (second), Ankrah, (third), 2016. Constructivism Philosophical Paradigm: Implication for Research, Teaching and Learning 4, 9.

Alebiosu, E., 2016. Smart Card Reader and the 2015 General Elections in Nigeria. JAE 15, 69–89. https://doi.org/10.20940/JAE/2016/v15i2a4

Ashaye, O.R., Irani, Z., 2019. The role of stakeholders in the effective use of e-government resources in public services. *International Journal of Information Management* 49, 253–270. https://doi.org/10.1016/j.ijinfomgt.2019.05.016

Avgerou, C., 2013. Explaining Trust in IT-Mediated Elections: A Case Study of E-Voting in Brazil. *Journal of the Association for Information Systems,* 14, 420–451. https://doi.org/10.17705/1jais.00340

Avgerou, C., Masiero, S., Poulymenakou, A., 2019. Trusting e-voting amid experiences of electoral malpractice: The case of Indian elections. *Journal of Information Technology,* 34, 263–289. https://doi.org/10.1177/0268396218816199

Bengtsson, F., LundstrÃ, J.E., 2013. ANT-Maps: Visualising Perspectives of Business and Information Systems. Thirty Fourth International Conference on Information Systems, Milan 17.

Braun, V., Clarke, V., 2013. Successful qualitative research: a practical guide for beginners. SAGE, Los Angeles.

Callon, M., 1984. Some Elements of a Sociology of Translation: Domestication of the Scallops and the Fishermen of St Brieuc Bay. The Sociological Review 32, 196–233. https://doi.org/10.1111/j.1467-954X.1984.tb00113.x

Chowdhury, M.F., 2014. Interpretivism in Aiding Our Understanding of the Contemporary Social World. OJPP 04, 432–438. https://doi.org/10.4236/ojpp.2014.43047

Debrah, E., Effah, J., Owusu-Mensah, I., 2019. Does the use of a biometric system guarantee an acceptable election's outcome? Evidence from Ghana's 2012 election. African Studies 78, 347–369. https://doi.org/10.1080/00020184.2018.1519335

Effah, J., Debrah, E., 2018. Biometric technology for voter identification: The experience in Ghana. The Information Society 34, 104–113. https://doi.org/10.1080/01972243.2017.1414720

Fenwick, T., Edwards, R., 2011. Introduction: Reclaiming and Renewing Actor Network Theory for Educational Research. Educational Philosophy and Theory 43, 1–14. https://doi.org/10.1111/j.1469-5812.2010.00667.x

Gunawong, P., Gao, P., 2017. Understanding e-government failure in the developing country context: a process-oriented study. Information Technology for Development 23, 153–178. https://doi.org/10.1080/02681102.2016.1269713

Heeks, R., Stanforth, C., 2014. Understanding Development Project Implementation: An Actor-Network Perspective: Development Project Implementation: An Actor-Network Perspective. Public Admin. Dev. 34, 14–31. https://doi.org/10.1002/pad.1671

Klein, H.K., Myers, M.D., 1999. A Set of Principles for Conducting and Evaluating Interpretive Field Studies in Information Systems. MIS Quarterly 23, 67. https://doi.org/10.2307/249410

Latour, B., 1996. On actor-network theory: A few clarifications 369–381.

Law, J., 1992. Notes on the theory of the actor-network: Ordering, strategy, and heterogeneity. Systems Practice 5, 379–393. https://doi.org/10.1007/BF01059830

Maguire, M., Delahunt, B., 2017. Doing a Thematic Analysis: A Practical, Step-by-Step Guide for Learning and Teaching Scholars. 8, 14.

McGrath, K., 2016. Identity Verification and Societal Challenges: Explaining the Gap Between Service Provision and Development Outcomes. MISQ 40, 485–500. https://doi.org/10.25300/MISQ/2016/40.2.12

McGrath, K., Maiye, A., 2010. The role of institutions in ICT innovation: learning from interventions in a Nigerian e-government initiative. Information Technology for Development 16, 260–278. https://doi.org/10.1080/02681102.2010.498408

Nkohkwo, Q.N., Islam, M.S., 2013. Challenges to the Successful Implementation of e-Government Initiatives in Sub-Saharan Africa: A Literature Review 11, 15.

Nurdin, N., Stockdale, R., Scheepers, H., 2014. Coordination and Cooperation in E-Government: An Indonesian Local E-Government Case. *The Electronic Journal of Information Systems in Developing Countries*, 61, 1–21. https://doi.org/10.1002/j.1681-4835.2014.tb00432.x

Rahi, S., 2017. Research Design and Methods: A Systematic Review of Research Paradigms, Sampling Issues and Instruments Development. *International Journal of Economics & Management Sciences,* 06. https://doi.org/10.4172/2162-6359.1000403

Ramli, R.M., 2017. e-Government Implementation Challenges in Malaysia and South Korea: A Comparative Study. The Electronic Journal of Information Systems in Developing Countries 80, 1–26. https://doi.org/10.1002/j.1681-4835.2017.tb00591.x

Sambo, P., Alexander, P., 2018. A scheme of analysis for eVoting as a technological innovation system. E J Info Sys Dev Countries 84, e12020. https://doi.org/10.1002/isd2.12020

Thapa, D., 2011. The Role of ICT Actors and Networks in Development: The Case Study of a Wireless Project in Nepal. The Electronic Journal of Information Systems in Developing Countries 49, 1–16. https://doi.org/10.1002/j.1681-4835.2011.tb00345.x

Twum-Darko, M., Noruwana, N., Sewchurran, K., 2015. Theoretical Interpretation of E-Government Implementation Challenges in South Africa: A Case Study of a Selected Provincial Government. *Journal of Governance and Regulation* 4. https://doi.org/10.22495/jgr_v4_i1_c2_p2

Walsham, G., 2017. ICT4D research: reflections on history and future agenda. Information Technology for Development 23, 18–41. https://doi.org/10.1080/02681102.2016.1246406

Walsham, G., 2006. Doing interpretive research. European Journal of Information Systems 15, 320–330. https://doi.org/10.1057/palgrave.ejis.3000589

Walsham, G., 1995. The Emergence of Interpretivism in IS Research. *Information Systems Research* 6, 376–394. https://doi.org/10.1287/isre.6.4.376

Wolf, P., Nackerdien, R., Tuccinardi, D., 2011. Introducing electronic voting: essential considerations, Policy paper. International Institute for Democracy and Electoral Assistance, Stockholm.

Wright, S., 2015. Exploring actor-network theory and CAQDAS : Provisional principles and practices for coding, connecting and describing data using ATLAS.ti. institutional Repository of Technische Universität Berlin 31. https://doi.org/DOI 10.14279/depositonce51

REFLECTION PAPERS

TOWARDS CENTRAL REPOSITORY DESIGN FOR DOMAIN INTERLOCKING INSTITUTIONAL WORLDS

Mohd Ismawira Mohd Ismail[1], Nor Hidayati Zakaria[2], Mohammad Nazir Ahmad[3] and Ali Mehimed Ahmad Ireda[4]

[1]*Universiti Teknologi Malaysia, Skudai, Johor, Malaysia*
[2]*Universiti Teknologi Malaysia, Kuala Lumpur, Malaysia*
[3]*Universiti Kebangsaan Malaysia, Bangi, Selangor, Malaysia*
[4]*Infrastructure University Kuala Lumpur, Kajang, Selangor, Malaysia*

ABSTRACT

Interlocking Institutional Worlds (IWs) is a concept explaining the needs to interoperate between institutions to solve common interest in a given domain. Managing knowledge in IWs domain is complex, but promoting knowledge sharing based on standards and common terms agreeable to all is essential and must be established. To support this purpose, establishing a Central Repository (CR) is crucial. Unfortunately, there is a clear gap in designing CR for supporting IWsdomain. The current CR available lacks the capability to support interoperating at domain level. Therefore, this paper attempts to present the gaps that must be addressed to answer why a new CR design is needed to support IWs domain.

KEYWORDS

Central Repository, Inter-agencies, InterlockingInstitutional Worlds, Database, Knowledge Sharing

1. INTRODUCTION

The government agencies and the academics have long agreed the importance of inter-agencies collaboration. The rich potential of inter-agencies collaboration has resulted it as strategic imperative for governments to urgently solved pressing issues requiring inter-agencies collaboration. Some of the benefits include (i) reduction in duplication and overlap in programs, (ii) improving and streamlining services to citizens, (iii) potential cost savings and (iv) leveraging digital technologies capabilities. But sustainable and effective collaboration in inter-agencies are very challenging as it involved formal agreements, defined roles and responsibilities, pooled resources, knowledge sharing and shared goals. Studies shown persistent problem such as poor coordination, lack of coordinative decision-making agreement, distributed resources and technology limitation to support knowledge sharing are the things that must be addressed. We focus on central repository (CR) as a platform to store and manage data to support inter-agencies knowledge sharing needs. The question remains if the current CR designs can support inter-agencies requirements.

In discussing Flood Management (FM) domain in relation to inter agency collaboration, we borrowed the concept of Interlocking Institutional Worlds (IWs) as introduced in (Colomb & Ahmad, 2007; Colomb & Ahmad, 2010). The theoretical foundation of the IWs concepts are strongly grounded by the prominent philosophical studies from general theory of Institutional Facts (Searle, 1995) and the Speech Act Theory (Austin, 1962). IWs are collection of organizations interacting together and exchanging information through technologies to achieve common goals in a domain. Among domain cases of IWs include the semantic web, the Olympics, Postal codes, Map preparation and Geographical information governance (Colomb & Ahmad, 2007; Colomb, 2013), flood management (Khantong, 2018; Khantong& Ahmad, 2019) and Lesson learned management (Badr, 2016). In IWs, when organizations start to cooperate, a standard and common terminology must be established to enable smooth communication to avoid misunderstanding.

However, there are differences that must be addressed in designing CR for supporting domain like IWs. Most of the CR designs reported in literatures have been designed for a single enterprise and not in the sense of domain IWs characteristics or behavior. Furthermore, most designs were influenced by database (Db) model focusing on data rather than business needs and this introduces heterogeneity issues and the need to establish standards to govern the users' participation.

2. CONSTRAINTS IN INTER-AGENCY COLLABORATION INFLUENCING CR DESIGN

Evidence shows many governments in the world today are moving toward improvements of public sector performance. Government leaders are tasked to find new and innovative ways to tackle long-standing public management challenges. In Malaysia, the government is exploring the possibility to induce collaboration among ministries, departments and agencies to break silos in order to be more efficient and effective (Ramadass, Sambasivan, & Anton, 2018). Studies have addressed why coordination matters and why it is difficult to deliver. Even though there are striking similarities between managing across boundaries and managing within agency, however, working across agencies requires extra persuasion, strict regularized workflow, establish and maintain communication in a network (Roberts, 2011). Studies have drawn similar conclusion that information sharing, and coordination remains at the top of research agenda, despite the progress made over the years. Below we discuss key findings related to this study and how these influence the CR design needs.

2.1 Growing Population that Demands More and Better Services

The responsibilities of government have grown in volume and complexity in tandem with growing population. This has also increased greater separation between the citizens and those who are supposed to serve them. Information and knowledge sharing are important contributions to overcome growing feeling of alienation from the government. With technologies, these demands can be better managed. Therefore, a CR platform design needs to address two main things, that were not considered much in database modelling in (i) people collaboration and (ii) process collaboration.

People collaboration is to allow people across work jurisdiction to use the CR and promote knowledge sharing based on their professional experience around the problem. It could be the single source of truth for collective decision based on lesson learned and to innovate new ideas based on shared knowledges (Fountain, 2001). Process collaboration looks at how the collaboration are effectively managed through operations, strategy and systems where the CR platform design must fulfil those requirements. The CR design must emphasize on clarity of the CR functionality, attract usage and encourage new resource contribution (Fountain, 2001).

2.2 The Problem of Inter-Agency Co-Ordination in Disaster Management

A list of inter-agency coordination issues in disaster management can be compiled but some of the common issues include lack of coordination between various agencies involved (Bealt, Barrera, &Mansou, 2016). This can be seen in the UK King's Cross underground incident in 1987 where it is said that each agency diligently pursued its own duty but there had been breakdown in communication at command level (Fennell, 1989). Disorganized multi-agency response to the 9/11 attacks were as a result of agencies were unable to share information (Jacobson, Ernie, & Lee, 2006). In Malaysia, it has been confirmed on the lack of coordination in disaster management cycle, lack of planning process, imbalanced decision between top-down and bottom-up approaches resulted to low resilience to disasters (Chong & Kamarudin, 2018).

2.3 Evolution of Database - Why do we need Ontology to support IWs at domain level CR design?

Data modelling and Db evolved together dating back in the 1960's. It can be said the Db evolution happened in four waves. Starting with the hierarchical, moving to relational. Next the Online Analytical Processing (OLAP) wave was introduced and the latest was the NOSQL wave for big data and graphs. Each wave comes with its own limitation. The relational Db modelling had struggled with normalization and performance issues. It is reported the modern Db uses schema free approach thus has poor consistency (Phiri &Kunda, 2017).

The Db modelling contributes towards our CR design. However, most Db modelling are meant for single institution approach. Hence, we look at Ontology to fill in the gaps to address inter-agency requirements. Ontology is a formal description of knowledge as a set of concepts and relationship that hold between them. It overcomes Db schemas limitation by being flexible to link multiple concepts to other concepts in a variety of ways.

The benefit of ontology for CR design in IWs includes the main features to address essential relationship between concepts. This is important in addressing domain like IWs to capture the domain knowledge and embrace changes where possible dynamically. Ontology acts like a brain working with reasons the way human perceive interlinked concepts. It provides easy navigation concept through the ontology structure. And in IWs domain it controls standardization and common terminologies to provide understanding between stakeholders. As a result, the model can grow without the constraint of data issue. Ontology can represent any data format including unstructured, semi structured and allows easy data integration, concept, mining, reporting and analytics capabilities.

3. DISCUSSION

Integrating and sharing knowledge is important as it accelerates learning process, improve decision making capabilities, and learn from the past and many more. One of the best options to capture, preserve and distribute knowledge is through a CR. While acknowledging a lot of work has been done in CR design, we believe that some issues are still open in addressing IWs domain like FM and detailed as following:

3.1 Lack of Standards

The purpose of having standard is to establish enterprise-wide standards and guidance for CR usage. These standards must be established and a vital requirement in our CR design as guideline for agencies in participating in the FM repository as to create mutual understanding.

It has been documented that Malaysia faces lack of coordination and duplicating relief efforts issues in current FM system (Centre for Public Policy Studies, 2017). Thus standards must be established and a vital requirement in our CR design as guideline for agencies in participating in the FM repository as to create mutual understanding between the participating agencies.

3.2 Semantic Heterogeneities

Heterogeneities had also been a vital issue in inter-agencies collaboration. Amongst the heterogeneities discussed includes (i) technology difference including hardware and operating system, (ii) difference in data model including structural, constraints and query language and (iii) Semantic heterogeneities (Abdullah, Ibrahim, &Zulkifli, 2017).These challenges must be addressed in order to integrate these agencies in a centralized platform or the issues such as overlap amongst applications, storing of duplication data and misunderstanding in responsibilities will keep on occurring (Tekiner& Keane, 2013).

3.3 Repository for Domain like IWs

Most repositories are tailored towards one organization or institution. Most repository were used to answer one corporation needs. Furthermore, in FM like domain, very little effort can be seen regarding usage of CR to be the integral component. Authorities are still struggling to produce integrated information to meet the domain needs. To the best of our knowledge there is no repository for FM like domain in Malaysia that is available. Most repositories are still silos towards agency's needs. The CR would enable the stakeholders to understand and predict what kind of threat coming their way as agencies can share the platform thus giving a broader perspective

3.4 Available CR are Data Oriented

Today, the demand for organizations to react to business changes to be more competitive and flexible is highly desired thus has called for a platform that able to support business point of view rather than technical perspective (Gao &Krogstie, 2010). We believe the CR design for domains that involves many agencies must be done on domain level and flexible to meet business requirement that is ever changing.

3.5 Loosely Coupled Stakeholders

In an integrated project such as FM, one of the most basic questions is how to get data from the source system. Common practices are using a push or pull method. Data can be pull from the source or the source can push the data to the landing zone. Tightly coupled consists of components that require detailed knowledge between the components be it within the same application or collaborating components. While loosely coupled offers more flexibility as components can stand independently and be more resilient to changes.

4. CONCLUSION

To design CR which tends to be reusable for similar domain is relatively new. This paper inspires to define the gaps in order to propose a new way of CR design for supporting domain of IWs. Designing CR that work at domain level requires a new thinking. In a given domain IWs (such as FM), there is a need to bridge disparate sources of information that exist within the domain. Future studies must be able to define the essential requirements in the design of CR for this kind of domain (IWs).

REFERENCES

Abdullah, M. F. et al, 2017. Big Data Analytics Framework for Natural Disaster Management in Malaysia. In *International Conference on Internet of Things, Big Data and Security,* Vol. 2, pp. 406-411.

Austin, J.L., 1962. *How to do things with words*. Oxford University Press.

Badr, K. B, 2016, An Ontological Approach to Conceptual Modeling Lessons Learned Management. *Faculty of Computing, Universiti Teknologi Malaysia.* Johor Bahru, Malaysia.

Bealt, J. et al, 2016. Collaborative relationships between logistics service providers and humanitarian organizations during disaster relief operations. In *Journal of Humanitarian Logistics and Supply Chain Management*, pp. 118-144.

Centre for Public Policy Studies. (10, 2017). *CPPS Policy Fact Sheet: Malaysia Flood Management.* Retrieved from Standards in Malaysia Flood Management Interoperation Strategy: http://cpps.org.my/wp-content/uploads/2017/10/Malaysias-Flood-Management-Mechanism-Factsheet.pdf

Chong, N. O., & Kamarudin, K., 2018. Disaster Risk Management In Malaysia: Issues And Challengges From Perspective Of Agencies. In *Journal of the Malaysian Institute of Planners*, pp. 105-117.

Colomb, R.M. and Ahmad, M.N., 2007. Merging ontologies requires interlocking institutional worlds. In *Applied Ontology*, Vol. 2, No. 1, pp. 1-12.

Colomb, R.M. and Ahmad, M.N., 2010. A perdurant ontology for interoperating information systems based on interlocking institutional worlds. In *Applied Ontology*, Vol. 5, No. 1, pp. 47-77.

Colomb, R.M., 2013. Representation of Action is a Primary Requirement in Ontologies for Interoperating Information Systems. In *Ontology-Based Applications for Enterprise Systems and Knowledge Management*, IGI Global, pp. 68-76.

Fennell, D., 1989. King's Cross Fire. *Fennell Report. UK Parliament.*United Kingdom.

Fountain, J.E., 2004. *Building the virtual state: Information technology and institutional change*. Brookings Institution Press, Washington D.C., USA.

Gao, S. and Krogstie, J., 2010. A repository architecture for business process characterizing models. In *IFIP Working Conference on The Practice of Enterprise Modeling*. Springer, Berlin, Heidelberg, pp. 162-176.

Jacobson, S. et al, 2006. *The 9/11 report: A graphic adaptation.* Macmillan.

Khantong, S., & Ahmad, M. (2019). An Ontology for Sharing and Managing Information in Disaster Response: In Flood Response Usage Scenarios. *Journal on Data Semantics*, 1-14.

Khantong, S., 2018. A Design of Domain Ontology to Support Flood Response Management and Sharing. *Faculty of Computing, Universiti Teknologi Malaysia*. Johor Bahru, Malaysia.

Kunda, D. and Phiri, H., 2017. A comparative study of nosql and relational database. *Zambia ICT Journal*, Vol. 1, No. 1, pp. 1-4.

Ramadass, S.D. et al, 2018. Collaboration outcomes in a public sector: impact of governance, leadership, interdependence and relational capital. In *Journal of Management and Governance*, Vol. 22, No. 3, pp. 749-771.

Roberts, N.C., 2011. Beyond smokestacks and silos: Open-source, Web-enabled coordination in organizations and networks. *Public Administration Review*, Vol. 71, No. 5, pp. 677-693.

Searle, J. R., 1995. *The Construction of Social Reality*. The Free Press, New York.

Tekiner, F. and Keane, J.A., 2013, Big data framework. In *2013 IEEE International Conference on Systems, Man, and Cybernetics*. pp. 1494-1499.

WECHAT VS. WHATSAPP: WHY CHINA IS NOT A NATION OF COPYCATS

Ghosia Ahmed and Miguel Baptista Nunes
School of Information Management, Sun Yat-Sen University, Guangzhou, China

ABSTRACT

Whilst the preconception of China in the West is often that of a "copycat nation" or "the world's factory", the reality of China, however, is very different to how it had been portrayed to us. Coming to China from the West, it has become clear to us that China is establishing itself as a global leader in technology and innovation, far beyond Western nations. As a fast-paced and ever-evolving innovative nation, China already appears to be a leader in service innovation, cashless mobile payments, e-commerce and artificial intelligence. In particular, WeChat - the hi-tech social media platform that integrates functions for almost everything from messaging and calling services, cashless mobile payments, social media and e-commerce, to name a few - and the likes of which is difficult to find anywhere else in the world. WeChat is China's "app for everything"; it is the first app you will discover when you come to China.

In this paper, we compare WhatsApp and WeChat; two messenger apps, one from the East and the other from the West, that seemingly started with similar aims – to connect people through instant messaging and calling functions – yet the evolution of both has been so significantly different that it can be compared to the *East–West* dichotomy. Through this comparison and paper, we aim to draw attention to and provide a glimpse into the enormous realm of innovation and technological advancement in the world's most populous country.

KEYWORDS

Innovation, WhatsApp, WeChat, China, Social Media, Messenger Applications

1. INTRODUCTION

Growing up in the West, like most Westerners, we had various preconceptions about China derived from society, the media, the internet and stories from various people. Some of those preconceptions are misconceptions, particularly when it comes to the subject of originality and authenticity in technological advancement; our experience of living and working in China has taught us that China is no longer a "copycat nation" or "the world's factory", but instead it is becoming a global leader in technological and service innovation.

In this paper, we explore two of the leading and competing messenger applications, WhatsApp and WeChat, how their journeys started and how they have evolved respectively, followed by a comparison of their evolution and through which we draw attention to the huge contrast in that evolution. Through this comparison, we aim to not only show the contrast between two comparable applications – one, a global giant, and the other, a goliath in China, but also draw attention to the gap in understanding and reality of technological advancement between the West and China.

2. BACKGROUND

On 3rd December 1992, Neil Papworth, an engineer at Vodafone, sent a message that changed the world: "Merry Christmas"; text messaging is now such an integral part of daily life for most people and often a preferred method of communication (McSweeney, 2018). Although text messaging initiated 27 years ago, in the past decade in particular, there has been a "massive adoption of a raft of mobile instant messenger applications and services on smartphones", often referred to as Over The Top (OTT) applications as they are independent of the mobile network (O'Hara et al, 2014: 1131). These include applications such as WhatsApp, WeChat, Facebook Messenger, iMessage, Viber, Skype, etc.

Digital technology revolution and the enormous growth in smart phone usage has led to over 66% of the world's population now using mobile phones and more than half are using social media, making mobile social networking (MSN) a key communication tool and a necessity in people's lifestyles (Wan et al, 2019). Further, the adoption of social media and messenger applications on smartphones is now in its billions, according to MessengerPeople (2019). O'Hara et al (2014: 1131) argue that whilst these applications are free or relatively cheap to use and they offer capabilities for communicating and sharing media, "What is curious about these applications is that, prima facie, they seem to offer little in the way of conceptual novelty; their cheapness eliding the fact that much of this functionality has been present on communication tools provided on PCs and Laptops for some time – in Gmail, Outlook, Skype.". The success of such applications may be attributed to not only the ubiquity of multiple communication methods and media, integration of various functions but to such applications being used as a key component of 'connection' in daily lives and situated "within the ebb and flow of lives lived together, within the web of other connections, both real and virtual" (O'Hara et al, 2014: 1143).

Whilst a wide range of messenger applications are available on the market, two of the leading, WhatsApp and its counterpart, WeChat – are smartphone messenger applications that were launched within two years of each other with the aim to provide reliable and free messaging and calling functionality to its users, both currently lead by comparison and have over 1 billion active monthly users each (MessengerPeople, 2019). Whilst the two applications initially started alike and with similar functionality and aims, the evolution and direction both have taken since has been extraordinarily different.

In the following sections we firstly explore the evolution and features of WhatsApp, followed by the evolution and features of WeChat and then make a comparison and discuss the similarities and differences between the two messenger applications to highlight their remarkably varying journeys.

3. WHATSAPP EVOLUTION AND FEATURES

WhatsApp was created in 2009 by Jan Koum and Brian Acton as an alternative to SMS messaging. Later, it was purchased by Facebook in 2014, although it is claimed that WhatsApp continues to operate as a separate application that focuses entirely on building a fast and reliable global messaging service (WhatsApp, 2020). The messenger application "is the pioneer and most popular leading messenger worldwide" with significant market penetration (Wan et al, 2019: 1094-1095). Further, the current 1.6 billion active monthly users in over 180 countries (WhatsApp, 2020; Statista, 2019), makes WhatsApp the leading messaging application globally in 169 countries (MessengerPeople, 2019).

WhatsApp is available on multiple platforms including Android, iPhone, Mac, Windows PC and Windows Phone. The application has evolved over the years with the primary focus still being on the messaging functionality but also incorporating calling functions. The application now supports the exchange of multimedia including text, photos, videos, documents, voice notes, voice and video calls, location sharing and 24-hour media status updates where users can share photos, text and videos with their chosen contacts. The application is still free to download and use. According to WhatsApp (2020), the application has been designed with user security and privacy at its core and claims to offer secure messaging with end-to-end encryption i.e. "Our messages and calls are secured with end-to-end encryption, meaning that no third-party including WhatsApp can read or listen to them."

In January 2018, WhatsApp launched its 'WhatsApp Business App' (Sulleyman, 2018). The application is separate from the main WhatsApp messenger application and like the messenger application, it is also free to download and use. The WhatsApp business application has been developed with the small business owner in mind where businesses can create catalogs for showcasing products and services, connecting with customers by using the inbuilt tools to automate, sort and quickly respond to messages (WhatsApp, 2020). In addition, the application also allows medium and large businesses to offer customer support and deliver notifications to their customers (WhatsApp, 2020).

4. WECHAT EVOLUTION AND FEATURES

"Today, people can do almost everything with one device. But in China, you can do everything you want with one single app" (Charlotte et al, 2018: 1). WeChat, the first application one will most probably discover when arriving in China, also often referred to as China's "app for everything". WeChat, originally named and still referred to by most Chinese people as 'Weixin', was founded by the Chinese company Tencent in 2011 and is the main communication, social media networking, cashless payment and service application in the country. WeChat is available to users on multiple platforms including Android, iPhone, Mac, Windows PC and Windows Phone.

Although originally a messaging and calling application, WeChat has evolved in various ways since its launch. Wan et al (2019: 1094) describe the current version of WeChat as "A Way of Life", to emphasise the extent to which the application has evolved into an enormous multi-purpose platform targeted at consumers who seek daily life conveniences. The current platform of WeChat can be described as a multi-faceted portal where it offers services starting from messenger, communication and social media, to mini-programs and e-commerce to cashless mobile payment and business services – also known as WeChat Pay.

4.1 WeChat Messenger

The messenger side of WeChat offers text and voice messaging, group chats, audio calls and individual and group video calls, entertainment, social media and gaming (Wan et al, 2019). WeChat has also developed a feature called 'Moments' which allows users to share their experiences or news with WeChat friends who they have selected and granted permission to through photos, videos and web links, and receive 'likes' and comments as feedback on the posted content (Vodanovich et al, 2017). In addition, WeChat has also introduced novel features within a messenger application such as subscriptions, 'Split Bill', 'Red Packet' for sending money as a gift to family and friends, 'People Nearby' and 'Shake' which allow users to chat with other random users globally who are also shaking their phone simultaneously (Vodanovich et al, 2017).

4.2 WeChat Pay

By far the most notable part of WeChat and its evolution is called WeChat Pay (see Figure 1). "WeChat Pay empowers merchants to connect with consumers before, during, and after sales through innovative marketing platforms in the WeChat ecosystem" and is a leading payment platform used by Chinese consumers within and outside China and it is claimed to be used by over 800 million monthly active users (WeChat, 2020). In addition, licensed financial institutions are able to provide acquiring services to merchants as the partners of WeChat Pay, and merchants or store owners, whether online or offline, can sell products or services through WeChat Pay after integrating it and comprehensive support is offered to merchants to help grow their businesses and improve customer experience, utilise marketing resources and increase traffic (WeChat, 2020). WeChat Pay offers services including the following:

- **Quick Pay** –WeChat Pay payment code presented by user and scanned by merchant
- **QR Code Payment** – Users scan code, confirm the amount, and make the payment
- **Mini Program Payment** – Users make payments in Mini Programs inside WeChat
- **Official Account Payment** – Users pay inside a merchant's Official Account
- **In-App Payment** – Users make purchases in merchants' applications using WeChat Pay
- **Web Payment** – Users use WeChat to scan a payment code on a webpage to pay (WeChat, 2020)

Figure 1. WeChat Pay

4.3 Mini Programs

In 2017, WeChat released a significant new feature called 'mini programs' (see Figure 2); "WeChat mini program is an application embedded in WeChat that users can use without downloading and installing" and thus does not require additional storage space on the smartphone (Chenga et al, 2019: 490). Further, for convenience and ease of use, the mini programs not only incorporate WeChat's default functions, but also additional functions including authentication, payment, sharing and communication (Chenga et al, 2019). Mini programs allow users to engage in various online services, including "paying bills, shopping, finding new friends, getting information, finding stores, reserving taxis, booking appointments, etc" (Wan et al, 2019: 1099).

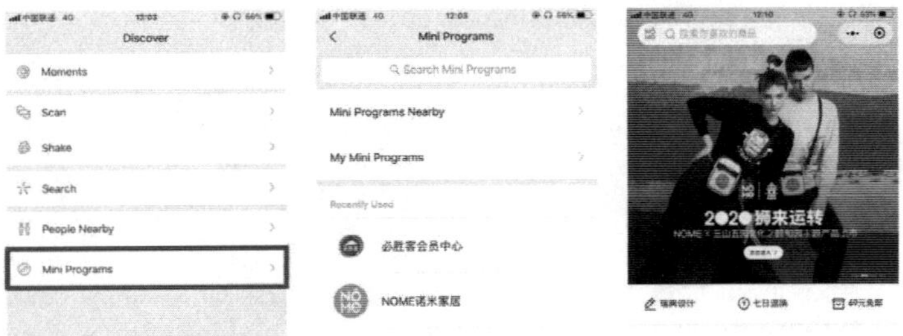

Figure 2. WeChat Mini Programs

5. COMPARATIVE DISCUSSION

5.1 Users

When beginning to compare WhatsApp and its counterpart WeChat, both applications that started within a period of two years and with similar initial aims and features to provide messaging and calling functionality to users, the first and most noticeable similarity that becomes apparent is their users and popularity. Both applications have gained vast success in terms of their user reach and are the first and third most popular global messenger applications respectively. Moreover, Figure 3 shows the most popular global mobile messenger applications as of October 2019, based on number of monthly active users; the two globally leading applications are WhatsApp with 1.6 billion and Facebook Messenger with 1.3 billion monthly active users. Based on these statistics, WeChat is behind WhatsApp and Facebook Messenger with 1.1 billion.

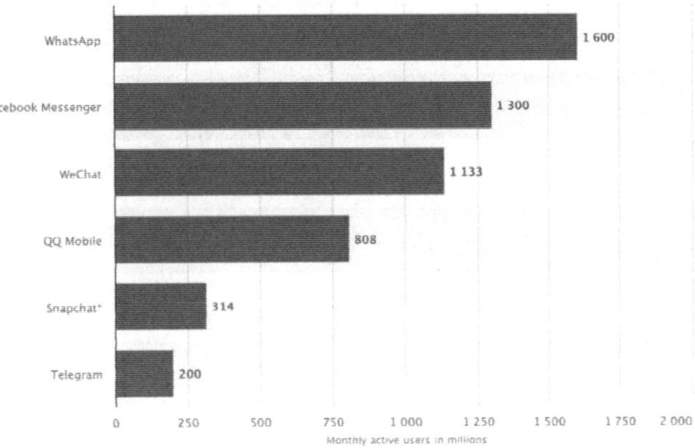

Figure 3. Most popular global mobile messaging apps 2019 (Statista, 2019)

5.2 Global Reach

Whilst in terms of uptake, both applications boast over 1 billion active monthly users, as per Figure 4 that shows the top messaging applications dominating each country, it is clear that WhatsApp has conquered the international market by reaching 180 countries, and in 169 of which it has gained dominance over other messenger applications, whereas WeChat is the leader in China alone (WhatsApp, 2020; MessengerPeople, 2019). Wan et al (2019: 1097) compare the global reach of WhatsApp and WeChat and argue that "WhatsApp succeeded in rapid global expansion through fulfilling consumers' needs for simple, reliable and no- frills functionalities". However, it is important to note that whilst WhatsApp has a wider reach, i.e. its users spread across 180 countries where it is the leading application in 169 of those countries, WeChat has gained its 1.1 billion user-base within a single and more concentrated market.

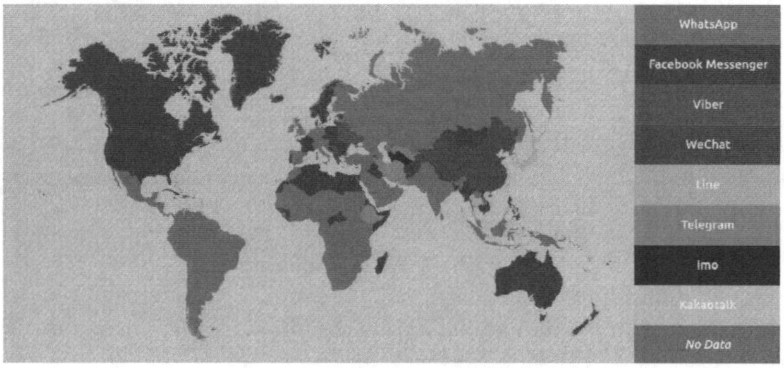

Figure 4. Top messaging apps by country (MessengerPeople, 2019)

5.3 Functionality

Table 1. Brief comparison of features between WhatsApp and WeChat

Functionality/Feature	WhatsApp	WeChat
Cost	Free	Free
Founded	2009	2011
Multi-platform	Yes	Yes
Security/encryption	End-to-end encryption	Not known
Monthly users	1.6 billion	1.1 billion
Leading in countries	169	1
Text and voice messaging	Yes	Yes
Voice and video calling	Yes	Yes
Document sharing	Yes	Yes
Group chats and calls	Yes	Yes
Voice to text	No	Yes
Status updates	Yes – 24 hours	Yes – 3 days – permanent
Read receipts	Yes	No
Online status	Yes	No
Scanning QR codes	No	Yes
Mini programs	No	Yes
Cashless payment	No	Yes
Taxi service	No	Yes

When comparing the consumer value proposition (CVP) for WhatsApp and WeChat, Wan et al (2019) state that the biggest differences between the two applications are customers' perceived ease-of-use, perceived usefulness, perceived risk and perceived enjoyment. Furthermore, whilst WeChat's functionality and innovation in its services proceeds WhatsApp in various ways, WhatsApp has succeeded internationally due to its continuous focus on the mass market through its simple yet user-friendly and reliable functionalities; the "benefits that WeChat offers may not necessarily be required/accepted by international consumers due to differences in culture settings and security/privacy risk exposure. WeChat target market is not as universal as WhatsApp" (Wan et al, 2019: 1097). Thus, Montag et al (2018) argue that despite its huge number of users in Asia, WeChat is still not very well-known in Western countries.

Within China, WhatsApp is entirely dependent upon and can only be accessed through the use of a VPN and thus its uptake is limited and restricted, whereas "WeChat is getting more consumers in the West than WhatsApp is in China" (Charlotte et al, 2018: 3). Charlotte et al (2018) also argue that WeChat is not a contestable market due to the security barriers between China and the outside world which are reflected in the permissions and access to technological applications. Also, for many people outside China to communicate with individuals inside China, results in the download of and uptake of WeChat usage. However, WeChat's success is evidently due to deeper reasons than merely the accessibility issues. Whilst one reason for the dominance and prevailing success of WeChat in China could be due to the fact that "social media such as Facebook, YouTube, and Twitter are blocked in the country, WeChat has been specifically created deep-rooted in and based on important Chinese cultural elements" such as collectivism; as culture, cultural values and core beliefs influence our communication patterns, they subsequently play a significant role in the creation of social media platforms (Vodanovich et al, 2017: 618).

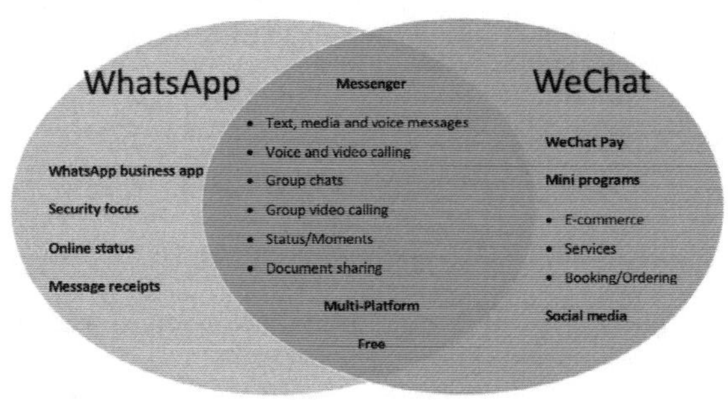

Figure 5. High-level comparison of WhatsApp and WeChat features

5.4 Security and privacy

In terms of security, in comparison to WeChat, WhatsApp places a great deal of emphasis on its security features – "Our messages and calls are secured with end-to-end encryption, meaning that no third-party including WhatsApp can read or listen to them. Behind every product decision is our desire to let people communicate anywhere in the world without barriers" (WhatsApp, 2020). Whereas, Wan et al (2019: 1096-1097) claim that "WeChat has a reputation of being heavily monitored" and there are concerns relating to surveillance and privacy. Although such claims are not verified, despite such claims, the success of the application within China has not been hindered but may be a cause behind the lack of international uptake.

From a privacy perspective, WhatsApp shows a user's online activity such as their online status or whether a message has been received and read, which WeChat conceals and thus offers greater user privacy. In addition, for individual users, WeChat only allows communication between contacts, thus in order to communicate with another individual, a contact request must first be sent and accepted by the other user. WhatsApp allows a user to send a message to another WhatsApp user using their telephone number, however, this can be accepted or rejected by the recipient.

6. CONCLUSION

To conclude, despite the setback from the international audiences where WeChat failed to compete with the leading messenger apps such as WhatsApp and take a notable slice of the international market, it has concentrated its primary focus within China. Since its launch, WeChat has become an entire Chinese social media platform that has innovated underpinned by Chinese cultural values (Vodanovich et al, 2017) and demonstrated its success through this dominance; "research has only recently begun to examine the impact of this development on the societal and individual levels" (Montag et al, 2018: 1). On the other hand, whilst WhatsApp's reach is global, its scope and evolution have not changed significantly in the decade since its launch.

WeChat has not only become an integral part of our lives in China and integrated and replaced various other applications and methods for doing things, but has also changed many of our preconceptions about China and its originality, and given an insight and subsequent research focus into the fascinating technological and service innovation within the rich context of the world's most populous country. Thus, the key question we now ask is, can WeChat - that is built on Chinese cultural values - innovate in ways through which it can create a significant influence in the West and succeed globally?

REFERENCES

Charlotte, H., Solène, R., Coste-Manière, I., Laura, F. and Emmanuelle, M. (2018) WeChat®: The Present and the Future. *In IEEE Proceedings of International Conference on Intelligent and Innovative Computing Applications (ICONIC) 2018*. Plaine Magnien, Mauritius, 6-7 December, pp. 1-4.

Chenga, A., Renb, G., Hongc, T. and Kood, C. (2019) The WeChat Mini Program for Smart Tourism. *Asia Pacific Journal of Information Systems*, 29(3), pp. 489-502.

McSweeney, M.A. (2018) *The Pragmatics of Text Messaging: Making Meaning in Messages*. New York: Routledge.

MessengerPeople (2019) *WhatsApp, WeChat and Facebook Messenger Apps – Global Messenger Usage, Penetration and Statistics*. [online] Available at: https://www.messengerpeople.com/global-messenger-usage-statistics/ [Accessed 29 December 2019].

Montag, C., Becker, B. and Gan, C. (2018) The Multipurpose Application WeChat: A Review on Recent Research. *Frontiers in Psychology*, [e-journal] *9(1)*, p.2247. Available at: https://www.ncbi.nlm.nih.gov/pmc/articles/PMC6297283/ [Accessed 03 January 2020].

O'Hara, K.P., Massimi, M., Harper, R., Rubens, S. and Morris, J. (2014) Everyday Dwelling with WhatsApp. *In Proceedings of the 17th ACM Conference on Computer Supported Cooperative Work & Social Computing*. Baltimore, Maryland, USA, 15-18 February, pp. 1131-1143.

Statista (2019) *Most Popular Global Mobile Messenger Apps as of October 2019, based on Number of Monthly Active Users*. Available at: https://www.statista.com/statistics/258749/most-popular-global-mobile-messenger-apps/ [Accessed 29 December 2019].

Sulleyman, A. (2018) '*There's a new version of WhatsApp', The Independent,* January 19, 2018. Available at: https://www.independent.co.uk/life-style/gadgets-and-tech/news/whatsapp-business-app-download-android-google-play-iphone-features-a8167631.html/ [Accessed January 2, 2020].

Vodanovich, S., McKenna, B. and Cai, W. (2017) Cultural Values Inherent in the Design of Social Media Platforms: A Case Study of WeChat. . *In Proceedings of the 30th Bled eConference*. Bled, Slovenia, 18-21 June, pp. 617-628.

Wan, W.S., Dastane, O., Satar, M., Safie, N. and Ma'Arif, M.Y. (2019) What WeChat Can Learn From WhatsApp? Customer Value Proposition Development for Mobile Social Networking (MSN) Apps: A Case Study Approach. *Journal of Theoretical and Applied Information Technology*, *97(4)*, pp. 1091-1117.

WeChat (2020) Weixin. [online] Available at: https://weixin.qq.com/ [Accessed 04 January 2020].

WhatsApp (2020) WhatsApp.com. [online] Available at: https://www.whatsapp.com/ [Accessed 05 January 2020].

EVALUATING INFORMATION SECURITY AWARENESS AND COMPLIANCE IN SUB-SAHARAN AFRICA: AN INTERPRETIVIST PERSPECTIVE

Sadiq Nasir and Narasimha Rao Vajjhala
American University of Nigeria
Yola, Nigeria

ABSTRACT

Information security awareness and compliance are at low levels in Sub-Saharan African countries. The low level of awareness is partly because of several factors, including low Internet penetration rates, lack of adequate technological infrastructure, low levels of literacy, and high costs of acquiring new technology. However, there are other issues, including behavioral, social, cultural, and organizational issues that are often ignored. Most of the current literature on information security awareness and compliance is centered in developed countries and, to some extent, developing countries in Asia and the Middle East. There is limited literature on information security awareness and compliance, especially in Small and Medium-Sized Enterprises (SMEs) in Africa, and in particular in Sub-Saharan African countries. The purpose of this interpretivist study is to identify the significant challenges that SMEs in Nigeria, the most populous Sub-Saharan African country face concerning information security awareness and compliance. The purpose of this qualitative, multisite, exploratory case study will be to identify and explore the various social, cultural, organizational, and behavioral factors that influence the adoption and compliance with the information security policies in Nigerian SMEs. Results of this study could assist organizational leaders with maintaining higher levels of information security in their organizations and avoiding loss of brand equity and revenue because of information security breaches. Observations from audio recorded, in-depth personal interviews with 50 managers working in different departments in 20 different medium-sized companies in Nigeria will be used in this case study. The 20 medium-sized companies included two companies each from the ten key economic sectors forming the core of Nigerian economy.

KEYWORDS

Information Security, Awareness, Africa, Interpretivist, Compliance

1. INTRODUCTION

Technological innovations in the last decade have increased significantly bring several new challenges and opportunities. SMEs are critical for the development of developing countries (Vajjhala & Vucetic, 2013), especially countries in Sub-Saharan Africa, such as Nigeria, because of the role played by these companies on employment generation, technological innovation, and sustainable development (Vajjhala & Vucetic, 2013). SMEs also represent a significant portion of the national GDP and employ the most workers, especially in Sub-Saharan African countries (Abubakar, 2016), including Nigeria. One of the main challenges facing companies, especially, SMEs is information security awareness and compliance. Cyber threats at national and international levels have forced large companies as well as SMEs to examine and evaluate their current information security awareness and readiness in the context of compliance with national and international standards. Most of the existing research on information security awareness and compliance is focused on developed countries, as well as developing countries in Asia and Africa. The current studies have identified several factors, including low Internet penetration rates, lack of adequate technological infrastructure, low levels of literacy, and high costs of acquiring new technology. There is limited literature on information security awareness and compliance, especially in SMEs in Sub-Saharan African countries. Also, most of the current research on information security is focused on the technical aspects, including the hardware and software issues, with limited literature focusing on adoption and awareness. There is a growing need for studies that are carried out in these various Sub-Saharan African countries by indigenous researchers (Abubakar, 2016). As the term Sub-Saharan Africa is used to representing a vast geographical region, including several countries and areas under the Saharan belt, this study focuses mainly on SMEs in Nigeria, the most populous country in Sub-Saharan Africa. The purpose of this interpretivist study is to identify the significant challenges that SMEs in Sub-Saharan African countries face concerning information security awareness and compliance.

2. LITERATURE REVIEW

Information security as a phrase can be traced back to 1980s, and only in early-2000 did the technical professionals in the domain of information security started to identify the term. Information security as a domain of research study is still an emerging field of study (Korovessis, Furnell, Papadaki, & Haskell-Dowland, 2017). Information security compliance assures protection of vital information systems assets. The challenge of regulating the complex domain is met with a lack of diversity in the theory and the methods used to understand this domain (Chatterjee, Sarker, & Valacich, 2015). The severity of information security threats and the importance of information security awareness and compliance in organizations has significantly increased over the last decade (Haeussinger & Kranz, 2017; Maynard, Tan, Ahmad, & Ruighaver, 2018; Safa et al., 2015; Willison, Lowry, & Paternoster, 2018). The human aspect of organizational resources is considered as the weakest link in the information security domain (Chatterjee et al., 2015). Information security awareness and compliance can help organizations address the issue around information and cybersecurity threats (Moody, Siponen, & Pahnila, 2018).

A large number of organizations face challenges in assuring compliance with information security policies (Gaia et al., 2020). User non-compliance with security policies was identified as a significant barrier in organizational information assurance (Feng, Zhu, Wang, & Liang, 2019). Over half of the security breaches are caused by a low level of compliance by the system users (Feng et al., 2019). There is a need for understanding the factors that can help organizations in assuring higher levels of information security awareness and compliance. Countries in Sub-Saharan Africa are characterized by different social, cultural, and economic dimensions as compared to countries in the Americas, Asia, and Europe. Hence, even though findings from studies on information security compliance carried out in other countries may help understand some of the challenges, there is a definite need for studies to be carried out in the Sub-Saharan African countries to help understand and validate these findings as well as explore any additional factors.

Bulgurcu, Cavusoglu, and Benbasat (2010) suggested that the attitude of an employee determines their level of compliance with information security policies. Bulgurcu et al. (2010) suggested that the theory of planned behavior underpins the attitude of the employees and also identified a direct connection between the attitude of the employees and the cost of compliance, the benefit accrued from compliance, cost of non-compliance, and belief over general compliance and non-compliance. Haeussinger and Kranz (2017) define security awareness as a state of knowledge and consciousness about issues around security. Hence, information security awareness should self-promote security compliance behavior. There is a need to fill in the knowledge void by examining the factors that influence compliance with information security policies. Haeussinger and Kranz (2017) established a connection between information security awareness and behavioral intention.

Training and educating employees is essential to achieve higher levels of compliance with information security. Eminağaoğlu, Uçar, and Eren (2009) proposed that the success of compliance of personnel is attained through multiple means, mainly training and education. However, several researchers have suggested that poorly structured and planned information security training programs can adversely influence the effectiveness of training and education programs. Some of the studies have indicated that most of these information security awareness programs lacked a theoretical grounding and empirical evidence of practical applicability (Kirova & Baumöl, 2018).

3. RESEARCH APPROACH

The interpretivist paradigm in research provides the theoretical lens that would provide the direction for the research. The use of positivism in this research is not ideal because positivism uses hypotheses, while an interpretivist approach would use propositions. The assumption of positivism limits its exploration potential, and exploring the social context in which a phenomenon is occurring is not possible. Hence, in this study, an interpretivist approach would be adopted. The purpose of adopting the interpretivist approach is to obtain meaning from the social process by which societal constructs are formulated. The adoption of an inductive approach as a strategy will allow the research to gather knowledge from experience. The interpretivist approach enables the researchers to start by interfacing with observations and theories to drill down for answers. This approach will also allow the researcher to conduct observations and to come up with an explanation for the research phenomenon.

In this qualitative, multisite, exploratory case study the influence of various social, cultural, organizational, and behavioral factors on compliance with information security policies in medium-sized enterprises in Nigeria will be examined. Case studies provide an opportunity to combine several data collection techniques, including interviews, questionnaires, archived documents, and observations (Vajjhala & Baghurst, 2014). The study is driven by the central research question: How do various social, organizational, cultural, and behavioral factors influence employees' perceptions about compliance with information security policies? Qualitative in-depth interviews will be conducted with 50 managers working in 20 medium-sized enterprises in Nigeria. Open-ended interview questions will be used as the data collection instrument for this qualitative, multisite, exploratory case study. The interview questions will be formulated in a manner to obtain descriptive data from the participants that would address the central research question. The criteria set forth by the African Union and Nigerian governments would be considered and used for establishing whether a firm was an SME. The qualitative data collected in this study will be analyzed using qualitative techniques, including assigning codes to the phrases, and then analyzing the keywords in context using visual pattern comparisons to identify and group similar words together with the help of NVivo or similar content analysis software.

4. CONCLUSION

The findings from this study could assist organizational leaders with maintaining higher levels of information security in their organizations and avoiding loss of brand equity and revenue because of information security breaches. The findings from this study should also add value to the existing literature on the factors contributing to higher levels of information security compliance in Nigerian SMEs as well as other countries in the Sub-Saharan African region. The limitations of this study are generalizability and applicability of the findings to other countries in the Sub-Saharan African region. The Sub-Saharan African region is quite large and has a number of countries and regions with diverse set of economic, political, and cultural differences. Hence, the findings of this study need to be replicated and validated across the region to explore the applicability as well as identify any additional factors that were not identified in this study. Future research could help address the issue of generalizability by replicating this study across the regions and demographics.

REFERENCES

Abubakar, D. A. (2016). *Cloud computing adoption by SMEs in Sub-Saharan Africa.* (Ph.D. Doctoral), Robert Gordon University, Aberdeen, Ireland.

Bulgurcu, B., Cavusoglu, H., & Benbasat, I. (2010). Information security policy compliance: An empirical study of rationality-based beliefs and information security awareness. *Management Information Systems Quarterly, 34*(3), 523-548.

Chatterjee, S., Sarker, S., & Valacich, J. S. (2015). The behavioral roots of information systems security: Exploring key factors related to unethical IT use. *Journal of Management Information Systems, 31*(4), 49-87.

Eminağaoğlu, M., Uçar, E., & Eren, Ş. (2009). The positive outcomes of information security awareness training in companies - A case study. *Information Security Techology Report, 14*(4), 195-201.

Feng, G., Zhu, J., Wang, N., & Liang, H. (2019). How Paternalistic Leadership Influences IT Security Policy Compliance: The Mediating Role of the Social Bond. *Journal of the Association for Information Systems, 20*(11), 1650-1691.

Gaia , J., Ramamurthy, B., Sanders, G., Sanders, S., Upadhyaya , S., Wang, X., & Yoo, C. (2020). *Psychological profiling of hacking potential.* Paper presented at the Hawaii International Conference on System Sciences, Hawaii, USA.

Haeussinger, F., & Kranz, J. (2017). *Antecedents of employees' information security awareness -Review, synthesis, and directions for future research.* Paper presented at the European Conference on Information Systems, Guimarães, Portugal.

Kirova, D., & Baumöl, U. (2018). Factors affecting the success of security education, training and awareness programs – A literature review. *Journal of Information Technology Theory and Application, 19*(2), 24-38.

Korovessis, P., Furnell, S., Papadaki, M., & Haskell-Dowland, P. (2017). A toolkit approach to information security awareness and education. *Journal of Cybersecurity Education, Research and Practice, 2*(5), 1-32.

Maynard, S. B., Tan, T., Ahmad, A., & Ruighaver, T. (2018). Towards a framework for strategic security context in information security governance. *Pacific Asia Journal of the Association for Information Systems, 10*(4), 65-88.

Moody, G. D., Siponen, M., & Pahnila, S. (2018). Toward a Unified Model of Information Security Policy Compliance. *MIS Quarterly, 42*(1), 285-311.

Safa, N. S., Sookhak, M., Von Solms, R., Furnell, S., Ghani, N. A., & Herawan, T. (2015). Information security conscious care behaviour formation in organizations. *Computers & Security, 53*(1), 65-78.

Vajjhala, N. R., & Baghurst, T. (2014). Influence of cultural factors on knowledge sharing in medium-sized enterprises within transition economies. *International Journal of Knowledge Management Studies, 6*(4), 304-321.

Vajjhala, N. R., & Vucetic, J. (2013). Key barriers to knowledge sharing in medium-sized enterprises in transition economies. *International Journal of Business and Social Sciences, 14*(4), 90-98.

Willison, R., Lowry, P. B., & Paternoster, R. (2018). A tale of two deterrents: Considering the role of absolute and restrictive deterrence to inspire new directions in behavioral and organizational security research. *Journal of the Association for Information Systems, 19*(12), 1187-1216.

DOCTORAL CONSORTIUM

IT CONTINUOUS USE IN MOBILE RIDESHARING APPLICATIONS: DRIVER PERSPECTIVE

Reem Alsaedi[1], Thomas Chesney[2] and Robert Pasely[3]
Business School, University of Nottingham, Nottingham, UK
[1]PhD candidate
[2]Prof
[3]Dr

ABSTRACT

Information and communication technologies have boosted a new culture of consumption, the so-called sharing economy. Sharing economy (SE) can be defined as a peer-to-peer (P2P) online marketplace where individuals (a peer-provider) connect with other individuals (a peer-consumer) through online platform for sharing, swapping, or lending resources. As an off shoot of SE, ridesharing mobile apps (RMA) such as Uber and Lyft have been introduced. RMA have achieved incredible growth and success in the taxi business. However, it is noticed that there are many campaigns against RMA that are organized by peer-drivers. This can mean that while peer-drivers' satisfaction is low with RMA, they still continue use these apps. This is inconsistent with predictions from the extant theories in information systems (IS).

The reason behind this inexplicable behaviour might be that, in RMA, how user attitudes formed and value experienced is fundamentally changed as more entities are involved. Ridesharing apps are experienced within the triple-interaction; peer-peer interaction, and peer-app interaction rather than double-interaction; user-app interaction as in the conventional IT in previous research. This new innovative context of IT has been neglected in current IT use research and IT theories. To address these gaps, this research plans to understand this phenomenon through incorporating not only past-and current-related factors (as in previous studies) but also future-related factors into the prediction of IT continuance models. This is because these IT are rapidly growing and individual expectations about future are changing fast. Based on the expectation-confirmation theory, the unified theory of acceptance and use of technology, and some constructs of psychological literatures, this study will focus on the effect of integrating future-related factors into IT continuance model on the interpretation of continuance intention in RMA. This aim will be achieved through conducting several quantitative studies (i.e. questionnaire and experiment) on the Uber app as a case study. The first study will develop a research framework and test it through collecting data from Uber drivers through questionnaires. Based on the results of the first study, other studies will be designed. It is hoped that this research will extend IS continuance models to include future aspects of user experience rather than only past and present experiences. In addition, the findings of investigating continuous use behaviour will add more understanding for user needs in the disruptive phenomenon of SE.

KEYWORDS

Sharing Economy, Ridesharing Apps, Usage Behavior

1. INTRODUCTION

1.1 Background

Sharing economy is variously called a collaborative consumption (Malhotra and van Alstyne, 2014), a peer economy (Bellotti et al., 2015), and access-based consumption (Bardhi and Eckhardt, 2012). These overlapping terms characterize by: 1) they are operationalized by the Internet capabilities and mobile technologies where value is co-created between users; 2) they are distinguished by efficient use of underutilizing resources such as labour, cars, and skills (Bellotti et al., 2015).

As an off shoot of SE, RMA have been introduced. The innovative idea of RMA is to create a platform of peer-drivers with their own cars who offer transportation services to peer-passengers and charge a service fee via apps. The sustained success of RMA is primarily based on understanding the participation behaviour of potential drivers who own cars and supply transportation services and the passengers who need these services.

While RMA have achieved incredible growth and success in the taxi business, they have raised significant debate worldwide, as well as concerns regarding drivers' rights and their well-being (Laufer, 2019). For example, Uber drivers have conducted several campaigns against Uber with the aim of improving several features of apps such as adding tipping, displaying the fare price, and increasing security (Bhuiyan, 2018). At the same time, Uber is still considered one of the most dynamically growing startups in the world (Hall and Krueger 2018). This leads to the puzzling phenomenon where drivers might continue to use RMA even though their satisfaction is low. This is inconsistent with predictions from the extant theories in IS as the main assumption of information technology (IT) continuance theories posits that users' continuous intention is determined by satisfaction, and in turn, satisfaction is determined by perceived usefulness with the past IS use (Bhattacherjee, 2001a). In addition, this issue might lead to consideration the role of non-monetary factors in shaping the user satisfactions in RMA.

Based on the above discussion, it can be postulated that continuance theories and IT might be one of the areas influenced by disruptive innovation of SE technologies. SE disrupted a broad variety of conventional business models, spurred by proliferation of mobile apps and ubiquitous internet access that allow individuals to trust each other's, share underutilized assets and trade with low transaction costs (Guttentag 2015). It has disrupted the most existing traditional models of the different sectors such as the business, low, policies, and IT (Guttentag, 2015; Cramer and Krueger, 2016). Moreover, through P2P apps, how user attitudes formed and value experienced is fundamentally changed as more entities are involved. P2P apps are experienced within the triadic interaction; peer-peer interaction, and peer-app interaction rather than dyadic interaction user-app interaction as in the conventional IT. For example, from peer-provider perspective, the experience is evaluated based on the relationships between peer-provider and peer-customer from one side and between peer-provider and an app from the other side. This new form of IT experience has been overlooked in current IT use research.

With focusing on new IT aspects in ridesharing, there are other disruptive aspects. Whiles RMA is characterized that have two-side end users with two different interfaces and two-side rating systems, driver-peer acts as a user of apps and as an employee in the same time (Baron, 2018). In addition, as users communicate face-to-face with strangers with different backgrounds and situations, RMA have generated a need to the emotional users to deal with problematic psychological events, such as unpleasant thoughts and feelings which might happen when dealing with difficult peer-customers (Biron and van Veldhoven, 2012; Berger *et al.*, 2018; Glöss et al., 2016). Regard to the positive side of the disruption, flexibility of apps usage appears clearly in this new generation of utilitarian IT (Baron, 2018). Users can access apps and gain the benefits at any time and in any place as these apps are a place-based presence through utilizing GPS. In addition, real images of users and their possessions (i.e. cars) is a requirement to take the full benefits of RMA.

In addition to the new IT aspects, determining the usage context of RMA is a new challenge of disruption. The usage context of RMA can be considered as a combination of different contexts. To demonstrate that, and based on extant literature in IT, the usage context taxonomy (Figure.1) is developed in order to facilitate where RMA can be classified as a context usage. The first dimension is the IT usage area, technology can either be used for work purposes or for private purposes. The second dimension is the extent of voluntariness as a technology usage can be mandatory or voluntary. After investigating literature in ridesharing (e.g. Baj-Rogowska, 2018; Hall and Krueger, 2018; Cramer and Krueger, 2016; Berger, Chen and Frey, 2018), RMA can be placed on the middle of this taxonomy as they have aspects of all these classifications. This is considered a new context in IT usage as the most investigated IT in literature tend to be more mandatory for work purposes such as document management systems (Bhattacherjee & Lin 2015) or voluntary for private purpose such as social apps (Hsiao et al., 2016).

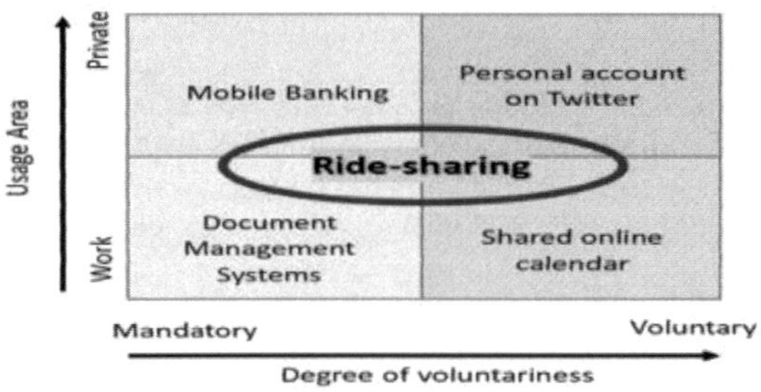

Figure 1. IT usage context taxonomy

Hence, it appears that the concurrence of advanced internet technologies raised a SE disruption, and in turn, this disruption has promoted IT with new capabilities and challenges. Therefore, the focus of this research is to understand peer-drivers' continuance behaviour in the disruptive phenomenon of SE.

1.2 Knowledge Gap

Based on the above discussion, it can be demonstrated that there are a new context of IT (i.e. ridesharing), a new IT experience (triadic interaction and shared experience), a new usage context (i.e. mixed) and new abilities of IT. IT usage research postulates that the new innovative technologies and IT context usage are important as they determine individual behaviour and its antecedents (Brown and Venkatesh, 2005; Venkatesh and Brown, 2001). This might partly explain the occurrence of the puzzling phenomenon and imply that there are other influencing factors should be investigated in this new phenomenon.

Although there is little research on the information systems facet of the ridesharing phenomenon, there is no research on the continuing use of RMA based on the best of our knowledge. Therefore, to address these gaps, this research plans to understand this phenomenon by incorporating not only previous experience but also current and anticipated future user experiences into the prediction of IT continuance models. By considering the anticipated future consequences, this research addresses another gap founded in IT continuance models. In existing IT continuance model, user behaviour has been studied based on prior and present-moment experience without considering the impact of the anticipated future experience. However, the evidence from psychology and service literature posits that consumer behaviour is constructed based on previous, current, and imaginary future experiences (Strathman et al, 1994; Helkkula et al. 2012a). This postulate may apply to IT users as the IT research considers the users as consumers of IT (Bhattacherjee, 2001b).

In addition, affective factors such as unfairness, and emotional personality traits such as the emotional flexibility, and self-disclosure will be integrated with the cognitive factors of continuous use theories in order to try explain why ridesharing app users (i.e. drivers) continue using apps even if their satisfaction is low. This can be justified that as this new innovative IT (i.e. SE apps) generated emotional users, it is important to incorporate appropriate emotional factors with continuous use theories. Especially, if we know that the extant IT continuance models tend to be more cognitive.

The trend of using only one service of apps is also one of the behaviour that is noticed in ridesharing. For example, most of Uber drivers are used only UberX service (Cramer & Krueger 2016; Hall & Krueger 2018) although there are more than six services of Uber app provide the same benefits. Therefore, this postadoption behaviour also will be investigated in this research as to date there have been no research studies undertaken to explain this behaviour based on the best of our knowledge.

Therefore, based on the expectation-confirmation model, unified theory of acceptance and use of technology, and some psychological theories, this study will focus on the effect of integrating emotions and future expectations into ECM on the interpretation of post-adoption behaviour in SE apps.

1.3 Research Aim and Objectives

The main aim of this research is to investigate the influencing factors on drivers' postadoption behaviour. To achieve this goal, the research objectives are developed as the following:

1. To clarify the SE phenomenon within IT context.
2. To identify and evaluate theories for assessing the adoption and postadoption of IT with the current generation of technology.
3. To establish research framework for explaining the factors that influence RMA driver' continuance intention with particular focus on the role of 'consideration of future expectations'.
4. To understand the main factors influencing the drivers' satisfaction.
5. To conduct an empirical test of the research framework.
6. To evaluate and provide the implications of the empirical results for interested stakeholders and future studies.

These aims will be achieved through conducting several quantitative studies. The first study was developed a research framework and tested it through collecting data from RMA drivers through questionnaires. Based on the results of the first study, other studies have been designed. It is hoped that this research will extend IS continuance models to include future aspects of user experience rather than only past and present experiences. In addition, the findings of investigating continuous use behaviour will add more understanding for user needs in the disruptive phenomenon of SE.

REFERENCES

Anderson, M., Alstyne M.V., Avital M., Nickerson, J., Sundararajan, A., and Verhoeven D. (2014) 'The Collaborative Economy: A Disruptive Innovation or Much Ado about Nothing?', 35th International Conference on Information Systems, pp. 1–7. Available at: http://aisel.aisnet.org/icis2014/proceedings/Panels/5/.

Baj-Rogowska, A. (2018) 'Sentiment analysis of Facebook posts: The Uber case', 2017 IEEE 8th International Conference on Intelligent Computing and Information Systems, ICICIS 2017, 2018–Janua(Icicis), pp. 391–395. doi: 10.1109/INTELCIS.2017.8260068.

Bardhi, F. and Eckhardt, G.M. (2012). Access-based consumption: The case of car sharing. Journal of consumer research, 39(4), pp.881-898.

Baron, D. P. (2018) 'Disruptive Entrepreneurship and Dual Purpose Strategies: The Case of Uber', Strategy Science, 3(2), pp. 439–462. doi: 10.1287/stsc.2018.0059.

Bellotti, V., Ambard, A., Turner, D., Gossmann, C., Demkova, K. and Carroll, J.M., (2015). A muddle of models of motivation for using peer-to-peer economy systems. In Proceedings of the 33rd Annual ACM Conference on Human Factors in Computing Systems (CHI'15), New York: ACM, pp.1085-1094.

Berger, T., Chen, C. and Frey, C. B. (2018) 'Drivers of disruption? Estimating the Uber effect', European Economic Review. Elsevier B.V., 110, pp. 197–210. doi: 10.1016/j.euroecorev.2018.05.006.

Berger, T., Frey, C., Benedikt L., Guy D., and Santosh R. (2018) 'Uber Happy? Work and Well-being in the "Gig Economy"', in 68th Panel Meeting of Economic Policy in October 2018, pp. 5, 16–19. Available at: https://www.oxfordmartin.ox.ac.uk/downloads/academic/201809_Frey_Berger_UBER.pdf.

Bhattacherjee, A. (2001b) 'Understanding Information Systems Continuance: An Expectation-Confirmation Model', MIS Quarterly, 25(3), p. 351. doi: 10.2307/3250921.

Bhattacherjee, A. and Lin, C. P. (2015) 'A unified model of IT continuance: Three complementary perspectives and crossover effects', European Journal of Information Systems, 24(4), pp. 364–373. doi: 10.1057/ejis.2013.36.

Bhattacherjee, A., and Premkumar, G. (2004). Understanding changes in belief and attitude toward information technology usage: A theoretical model and longitudinal test. Management Information Systems Quarterly, 28(2), 229–254.

Bhattacherjee, A., Perols, J. and Sanford, C. (2008) 'Information Technology Continuance : A Theoretical Extension and Empirical Test', Journal of Computer Information Systems, 49(1), pp. 17–26.

Bhuiyan, J. (2018). Drivers don't trust Uber. This is how it's trying to win them back.. [online] Recode. Available at: https://www.recode.net/2018/2/5/16777536/uber-travis-kalanick-recruit- drivers-tipping [Accessed 15 Feb. 2019].

Biron, M. and van Veldhoven, M. (2012) 'Emotional labour in service work: Psychological flexibility and emotion regulation', Human Relations, 65(10), pp. 1259–1282. doi: 10.1177/0018726712447832.

Brown and Venkatesh (2005) 'Model of Adoption of Technology in Households: A Baseline Model Test and Extension Incorporating Household Life Cycle', MIS Quarterly, 29(3), p. 399. doi: 10.2307/25148690.

Cramer, J. and Krueger, A. B. (2016) 'Disruptive Change in the Taxi Business: The Case of Uber', American Economic Review, 106(5), pp. 177–182. doi: 10.1257/aer.p20161002.

Glöss, M., McGregor, M. and Brown, B. (2016) 'Designing for Labour: Uber and the On-Demand Mobile Workforce', Proceedings of the 2016 CHI Conference on Human Factors in Computing Systems - CHI '16, pp. 1632–1643. doi: 10.1145/2858036.2858476.

Guttentag, D. (2015) 'Airbnb: disruptive innovation and the rise of an informal tourism accommodation sector', Current Issues in Tourism, 18(12), pp. 1192–1217. doi: 10.1080/13683500.2013.827159.

Hall, J. V and Krueger, A. B. (2018) 'An Analysis of the Labor Market for Uber's Driver-Partners in the United States', Review, 71(3), pp. 705–732. doi: 10.1177/0019793917717222.

Helkkula, A., Kelleher, C. and Pihlström, M. (2012a) 'Characterizing Value as an Experience: Implications for Service Researchers and Managers', Journal of Service Research, 15(1), pp. 59–75. doi: 10.1177/1094670511426897.

Hsiao, C. H., Chang, J. J. and Tang, K. Y. (2016) 'Exploring the influential factors in continuance usage of mobile social Apps: Satisfaction, habit, and customer value perspectives', Telematics and Informatics. Elsevier Ltd, 33(2), pp. 342–355. doi: 10.1016/j.tele.2015.08.014.

Laufer, D. (2019). Uber: A Great Service, Less Great for Drivers. Wall Street. [online] Available at: https://www.wsj.com/articles/uber-a-great-service-less-great-for-drivers-11556480665 [Accessed 3 May 2019].

Malhotra, A. and Van Alstyne, M. (2014). The dark side of the sharing economy... and how to lighten it. Communications of the ACM, 57(11), pp.24-27.

Strathman, A., Gleicher, F., Boninger, D., and Edwards, C. (1994) 'The consideration of future consequences: Weighing immediate and distant outcomes of behavior', Journal of Personality and Social Psychology, 66(4), pp. 742–752.

Venkatesh, V. and Brown, S. (2001). A Longitudinal Investigation of Personal Computers in Homes: Adoption Determinants and Emerging Challenges. MIS Quarterly, 25(1), p.71.

International Association for Development of the Information Society (IADIS)
Rua Sao Sebastiao Da Pedreira
No. 100, 30, 1050-209
Lisbon, Portugal

ISBN 978-1-7138-1011-7

CURRAN ASSOCIATES INC.
proceedings.com